SEAHORSE SOLDIERING

MacArthur's Amphibian Engineers From New Guinea to Nagoya

Robert Meredith Watson, Jr.

To order additional copies of this book, contact:
Xlibris Corporation
1-888-795-4274
www.Xlibris.com
Orders@Xlibris.com
19367

CONTENTS

PREFACE

The generation of Americans who fought in World War II is rapidly fading from the scene, and while there has been an enormous outpouring of literature devoted to that conflict on the European continent, considerably less attention has been focussed upon its course in other parts of the globe, most notably in Gen. Douglas MacArthur's Southwest Pacific theatre. There has been an even more remarkable void in works recognizing the unique contribution of the U.S. Army's amphibian engineers, who were employed for the most part in that arena, and with whom I served as a young enlisted man. Their story deserves fuller treatment than military historians have thus far accorded it. The following account centers upon my personal memoirs as recorded in a fairly voluminous wartime correspondence with my parents, which they carefully preserved. The thread of my individual story is herein interwoven with a narrative of my regiment and the brigade to which it was organic, the 4th Engineer Special Brigade (of which to my knowledge little or nothing has been published), with added reference to the two other Army amphibian brigades operant within MacArthur's domain. The resultant fabric has been set within the larger tactical and strategic framework of the campaigning in which the amphibs were engaged.

This work is intended for the edification of a general readership interested in the Pacific war, and aspires to be a forthright portrayal from one who, coming of military age in 1943, halfway through the conflict, was eyewitness to some of the crucial struggles antecedent to what would have been an horrific invasion of the Japanese home islands but for America's resort to the atom bomb. The experience was a crash course in maturation, both pyschological and spiritual, not only for the author, but for a host of other youths who were similarly products of relatively-protected middle-class environments. As such, it was the most valuable learning experience of my life. My saga may afford reassurance for subsequent generations confronting abruptly altered circumstances; that, at least, is my hope. It is also offered as a well-earned tribute to my comrades-in-arms.

An enormous debt of gratitude is owed to those whose support has enabled the undertaking—my family of origin whose love and affirmation kept me afloat during the trauma of war, my wife and four children who patiently and loyally encouraged my investigations and literary efforts, the friends whose unflagging interest in the project kept me focussed, and certain other caring individuals without whose substantial contributions it could not have been brought to fruition, most prominently Mr. and Mrs. O. Mason Hawkins, Dr. Major L. Wilson, and Messrs. Frank A. Jones and William L. Oates III, each of Memphis, Tennessee. To others who have generously given of their time to read and critique the manuscript, and proffered constructive advice and nurture during its gestation, I tender my heartiest appreciation.

R.M.W., Jr., January 15, 2002.

I

PROLEGOMENA

In the year of our Lord 1925, humankind being one-quarter of the way along its troubled trek through the twentieth century, I was introduced to its ranks bewildered and bawling. To be precise, my transition from womb to world, climaxed by a slap on my rump, occurred at 2:30 A.M. on a chill Saturday, the 21st of November, at my parents' domicile on Hamilton Street in the dusty little textile-mill town of Leakesville in North Carolina's Rockingham County. Merged in 1967 with two adjoining hamlets, Spray and Draper, the municipality now bears the more idyllic name of Eden. Hence, I am one of a select company of earthlings who, like our primeval progenitors, Adam and Eve, can rightly claim to have begun life in Eden.

A few hours later that same day, 500 miles to the northeast, another newcomer was being heralded, though in rather more regal fashion. On the railway tracks beneath Manhattan's Pennsylvania Station, a luxurious, state-of-the-art, all-Pullman passenger train, the Seaboard Air Line Railway's *Orange Blossom Special,* was christened by the breaking of a bottle of champagne across its rear before gliding off southward on its maiden run to West Palm Beach, Florida, the winter playground of the rich and famous.[1] (Perhaps there was some mystical linkage here, for I have always had an inordinate fondness for trains.; they were the media whereby I gained my first awareness of our nation's geographical immensity, climatic variations, and cultural diversity.) The *Special*'s debut was a more accurate paradigm than my own of the flush times in which America was then revelling—it was also portentious, for eighteen

years hence, not only would it be the SAL Ry. that would carry me
to the obscure Army installation at which I would receive my basic
military training, but find myself assigned to a very unconventional
type of unit, called, of all things, an Engineer *Special* Brigade,
with dramatic and far-reaching consequences. Although Henry
Ford's automobiles were becoming ubiquitous, trains were still by
all odds the nation's dominant mode of land transportation, and
steam engines their primary motive power. With only 6% of the
world's population, the United States embraced 37% of its total
railway mileage, and our rail passenger service set a universal
standard for reliability, speed, and comfort.

At about the time of my conception, the nation's incumbent
Republican President, Calvin Coolidge, having scored a stunning
electoral victory over Democratic challenger John W. Davis and
the Progressive Party candidate, Robert M. LaFollette, had taken
office as 30th President of the United States. "Silent Cal" had already
been occupying the chief executive's chair for more than two years,
thanks to the untimely death of his predecessor, Warren G. Harding.
"The business of America is business," pronounced Coolidge,
sounding the theme of the so-called "Marvelous Prosperity Era"
which would play out its flamboyant course during my first four
years of existence. Tantalized by the mirage of quick riches, hordes
of the citizenry-at-large were absorbed in frenzied stock-market
speculation. Though the wartime legacy of Prohibition had seriously
reduced their customary consumption of spirituous beverages,
Americans were puffing cigarettes in ever more prodigious
quantities, to the palpable benefit of my tobacco-growing native
state. So lucrative, in fact, had the manufacturing and marketing
of cigarettes become that in the year of my birth tobacco magnate
James B. Duke bestowed $40 million upon Durham's Trinity
College, whose name its handlickingly-grateful trustees promptly
changed to Duke University, and there, thirty-nine years down
the road, I would earn a master's degree in History.[2]

Regrettably, the year 1925 was also something of a high-
watermark for bigotry and racism, most blatantly, though far from
exclusively, south of the Mason-Dixon line, where the Ku Klux

Klan ran amok with impunity, and a Tennessee court tried and convicted public school educator John T. Scopes for teaching Darwin's theory of Evolution. Dixieland, "the Sahara of the Bozarts," in the caustic judgment of journalist H. L. Mencken, had not yet fully recuperated from the trauma of military defeat six decades in its past. A few hoary veterans of the bitter "War between the States," as the natives of our region chose to call it, were still ambulatory, though my own Confederate great-grandfather, Robert Meredith Price (1828-1901), one-time cavalryman in the 6th Virginia regiment of Lee's Army of Northern Virginia, had long since passed to his eternal reward. Oppressed by the persistant poverty of their homeland, Southerners of Caucasian ethnicity sustained their battered morale by endlessly adorning and fine-tuning the myth of their forebears' heroic struggle against overwhelming odds in behalf of the noble but Lost Cause of States' Rights, the preservation of Cavalier gentility, and Biblical orthodoxy.

The year 1925 was notable for other reasons as well; not only did the worst tornado ever to ravage this continent to date cut a wide, straight swath of destruction and death across southern Illinois, Indiana, and Ohio, but several exceptionally high-grade literary works rolled off the presses, among them, F. Scott Fitzgerald's *The Great Gatsby*, Theodore Dreiser's *An American Tragedy*, Sinclair Lewis's *Arrowsmith*, and John Dos Passos's *Manhattan Transfer*, along with the first issue of *The New Yorker* magazine. A lesser-known work of fiction also appeared in London, authored by Hector C. Bywater, naval correspondent of the *Daily Telegraph*, and entitled *The Great Pacific War*, an eerily accurate prophesy of what lay in store for America sixteen years later. Bywater wrote of a "tremendous conflict" triggered by Japan's seizure of strategic points in Manchuria, Formosa, and Korea. Driven by her need for raw materials to support her expanding industry, this rampant territorial aggression, issuing in the virtual enslavement of China, incurs the opprobrium of the Western Powers. During an exchange of diplomatic notes with a United States determined to avoid the catastrophe of war, Japan mounts a surprise attack by carrier-based aircraft, pouncing upon the American Asiatic Squadron as it is cruising off Manila Bay, and completely destroying its combat capabilities. Bywater also envisioned a Japanese aerial assault on Guam by planes "evidently from Saipan" aiming at its vital radio tower, followed within a few days by a massive naval bombardment and landings on that island's eastern and western shores by troops borne in from their transports on specially-designed landing craft, or "motor-barges," thereby forcing the surrender of its outnumbered Marine defenders. Simultaneously, the Philippines are assailed by Japanese invaders, who, avoiding the fortified bases at Corregidor and Olongapo (Subic Bay) on Luzon, go ashore at Lingayen Gulf and Lamon Bay to converge on Manila. Mindanao, second largest island in the Archipelago, is also overrun. America retaliates by island-hopping across the Pacific (along pretty much the same lines later chosen by Douglas MacArthur and Chester Nimitz), sparking a stupendous naval engagement, the "Battle of Yap," the equivalent, in effect, of the actual 1942 Coral Sea and Midway clashes. Aside from a few particulars, Bywater's predictions were amazingly accurate, for example, that Japan would employ Kamikazes, that American torpedo-armed carrier planes would account for the majority of the enemy's capital ship losses, and that bombing of the Japanese home islands would finally compel her to surrender and accede to a treaty of peace. Although Bywater's book would be resurrected from obscurity and perused avidly in the months following Pearl Harbor, how much better-prepared our nation might have been in 1941-42 had our military leadership not ignored it at the time of its publication![3]

In the America of 1925, science and technology, jump-started by the voracious demands of World War I and lavishly subsidized by corporate profits, were breaking new ground on all fronts. Scotsman John Baird demonstrated the world's first televised transmission of a moving image, while in industry the steadily accelerating pace of mass production, spurred on by Frederick W. Taylor's seminal treatise, *Principles of Scientific Management*, was lowering the price of automobiles and electrical appliances to within range of the average citizen's pocket-book. Urbanites flocked to the cinemas to view Charlie Chaplin's antics in *The Gold Rush*, a singularly apt metaphor for the times.

The global conflict into which Woodrow Wilson had reluctantly led the nation was then seven years past, and his protracted disability and demise in 1924 added a melancholy footnote to the fate of his emasculated League of Nations. A bled-white Europe had been left to its own devices as Americans withdrew into their congenital isolationism. Adolph Hitler, newly freed from imprisonment, published *Mein Kampf* and resumed his subversion of the fragile German Republic, whose moderate president, Friedrich Ebert, dying in February 1925, was replaced by ultraconservative Field Marshal Paul von Hindenburg. In remote Russia, behind the Kremlin walls, Joseph Stalin was stealthily outmaneuvering all rivals for the seat of the late "Red Czar," Vladimir Lenin. Little did the most prescient among my elders suspect that within a mere fourteen years, the smouldering embers of unresolved national resentments would be fanned into a second and even more horrendous worldwide conflagration.[4]

Meanwhile, a more imminent catastrophe was poised to descend upon our land, an economic breakdown bred by the maldistribution of wealth in our domestic economy. Throughout the "roarin' twenties" of my early childhood, agricultural prices remained stagnant, while in the hyperactive industrial and commercial sectors, real wages failed to keep pace with profits, and as inventories grew, consumption would soon begin to lag. Within a few years it had become dismally apparent that one-third of the personal income generated by our booming free-enterprise establishment was being garnered by a mere 5% of the population. The inevitable collapse of this house of cards came in 1929, as the stock market crashed, ushering in the most paralyzing depression in our national experience, and dragging down my own family's material fortunes. Just on the eve of the crash, my paternal grandparents saw their assets evaporate with the failure of the once-thriving Morotock Manufacturing Company, a Danville, Virginia, producer of bib-overalls, of which my grandfather, James Carson

Watson, Jr. (1867-1952), was a part-owner and executive. With the onset of the Great Depression, he was reduced to earning his livelihood as a bookkeeper and account-collector for a Danville pharmaceutical house.

Born in Amelia, Virginia, 60 miles east of Appomattox Courthouse, two years after Lee's surrender, and reared in Onancock on Virginia's Eastern Shore, he was the sixth child and youngest son (by first marriage) of a Methodist clergyman of lower Shenandoah Valley (Winchester) origins, the Rev. James Carson Watson. My Grandpa was only nine when his mother died, whereupon his father remarried, sired three more sons, and in 1895 relocated to Danville (in Virginia's Piedmont just above the North Carolina state line) for the remainder of his life and ministry. Grandfather Watson, or "Carson" (as J.C., Jr., was generally referenced), was of spare build, emotionally-reserved, and rather humorless—a stern, abstemious, morally-and-physically-upright pillar of Danville's Main Street Methodist Church, of which he was a lay official and Sunday School superintendant. I admired and respected him deeply.

His devoted wife, my grandmother, Margaret ("Maggie") Harrison Price Watson (1866-1946), was the third of five off-spring of aforementioned Confederate veteran Robert Meredith Price, a planter of FFV lineage from the Danville vicinity, and wife Louisa Knight Price. (A 17th century progenitor of this branch of the Price family tree was the Rev. Thomas Price, rector of St. Chad's Anglican Church in Shrewsbury, Shropshire, England, the same locale from which my mother's paternal forebears had emanated.) "Mammy," as I affectionately addressed my Grandma Watson, was a warm-hearted, generous, and selfless lady par excellence, beloved by all who knew her, most assuredly by my parents, my sisters, and me, as well as by everyone else in our wider family circle. My Danville grandparents bore their financial reverses stoically and with admirable grace; they were scarcely strangers to adversity, for my father, Robert Meredith Watson (1901-1959), was the only one of their six children—all males—to survive childhood, the others succumbing to such then-commonplace maladies as diptheria, typhoid, and scarlet fever.

I revered my dad, popularly known as "Bob," a scrupulously honest, compassionate, and reflective individual, yet gregarious, good-humored, and sweet-natured. An amateur philosopher, literateur, and poet, he related affirmingly and affectionately to us children, and was, by my lights, an exemplary model of emotional maturity and Christian character. He embodied the enduring moral integrity and earnest spirituality of his progenitors, and I was always proud to bear his name.

My equally-estimable mother, Ruth Adelaide Cadman Watson (1902-1992), born in Glassport, Pennsylvania, was the oldest of three children of a then-Methodist clergyman, the Rev. William Lester Cadman (1873-1943) and his first wife, Georgie Stokem Cadman (1881-1921). Mother was a pretty, vivacious homemaker, warmly-nurturing, orderly, neat, and personable, with a flair for interior decorating. My Cadman grandmother died of a brain tumor at age 40 (four years before my birth), leaving to her grief-shattered mate the rearing of their two minor children, Dorothy Marie, then seventeen, and William Lester, Jr., eleven, with the help of Ruth, who was nineteen at the time. Within two years of Georgie's death, my mom's sister, Marie, a popular beauty just out of high school, was also fatally stricken (with a ruptured appendix.)

My grandfather, "Will" Cadman, was a stocky, thrifty, and stolid Englishman who loved gardening. An inveterate pipe-smoker and mimic, he could not desist from parodying our languid Southern speech and mannerisms. A native of Ketley Bank (Wellington), Shropshire, he was one of ten offspring of Samuel Cadman (1828-1906), a coal-mining entrepreneur and Primitive Methodist lay minister. In 1890, Will, at age 17, and his 13-year-old brother, Maurice Danks Cadman, had followed the lead of an older sibling, Samuel Parkes Cadman (1864-1936), in migrating to the United States. "Sam" (or S. Parkes, as he preferred to be formally addressed}, one-time "pony-boy" in the family mines, had won a scholarship to Richmond College, University of London, at which he completed his undergraduate education prior to entering the Methodist ministry. Returning to Shropshire and appointed to a Wesleyan Methodist charge at Lawley Bank, he met and married Lilian Esther Wooding. The couple determined to try their fortunes in America, where Esther had relatives. Sam came over first, settling in Dutchess County, N.Y., and pastoring Methodist Episcopal congregations in Millbrook and Verbank, where he was soon joined by Esther and his younger brothers Will and Maurice. Within three years, the highly-gifted young cleric was called to lead the Central M.E. Church in Yonkers, and by 1895 had advanced to the pastorate of New York City's large Metropolitan Temple M.E. Church (whose membership had once included ex-President U. S. Grant and family.) In 1901, S. Parkes Cadman was offered and accepted the pastorate of Brooklyn's prestigious Central Congregational Church, whose pulpit he would occupy for the rest of his busy life (aside from a brief interlude in 1916 when, as a chaplain in the New York National Guard, he accompanied its 23d Infantry Regiment to the Mexican border in pursuit of Pancho Villa.)

My great-uncle Sam's outstanding homiletical eloquence and erudition catapulted him into national prominence. A man of prodigious energy and author of some fourteen widely-read books, he became extremely influential in Protestant circles, held multiple university lectureships, and was the recipient of numerous honorary degrees. Best known for his pioneering radio ministry under the auspices of the National Broadcasting Corporation, he served as president (1924-28) of the Federal Council of Churches of Christ in America (forerunner of today's National Council of Churches), and as Moderator of the National Council of Congregational and Christian Churches.[5] Under Sam's wing, Will, also aspiring to the ministry, completed his higher education on these shores, and upon graduation from a New Jersey seminary, was ordained to the Methodist clergy in 1906, while their younger brother Maurice, at the conclusion of his collegiate studies, entered the pharmaceutical profession.

My grandfather met his wife-to-be, Georgie, a native of Newark, N.J., at New York's Metropolitan Temple, where she was a chorister during my great-uncle Sam's tenure. Following their espousal, the newly-minted Rev. William Cadman held Methodist charges, initially in the western Pennsylvania town of Glassport (birthplace of my mother, Ruth), and subsequently in the Dutchess County, N. Y., hamlets of Elizaville, Poquag, and Millbrook, where Georgie bore him two additional children, Marie and William L., Jr. At length (1912) my Cadman grandparents converted to the Episcopal Church, and Will, electing to enter its ministry, was duly ordained as priest in 1916 in the Diocese of New York, thereafter serving as Rector of St. Andrew's Church, Arlington, a suburb of Poughkeepsie. Here Will and his family were to reside for the ensuing seven years, until the tragic losses of his wife and younger daughter and the transplantation to Danville of newly-married Ruth prompted him to accept the post of Assistant Rector at Manhattan's Holy Trinity Parish. He and his youngest child, William Lester, Jr., dwelt in New York City for five years before relocating to Midland Park, N.J., for the final phase of his ministry, at the Church of the Good Shepherd, from which he retired in 1941. At age 56, just prior to the 1929 crash, he became espoused to Emily Rhoades, a 37-year-old teacher in the Hackensack, N.J., public schools.

These, then, were the genetic determinants of my existence—there were no professional men-of-war among my almost-exclusively Anglo-Saxon forebears, but plenty of religionists, suggesting that my own scholarly and theological proclivities were both a paternal and a maternal heritage. As for the more environmental factors, my east-coast acculturation, Southern yet with strong Northern and English leavening, accounts, no doubt, for whatever philosophical tendencies or social prejudices may surface in the ensuing account of my wartime adventures. An objective survey of my rearing must begin, as Sigmund Freud would have it, with my Dad, for whom I was named. Born and bred in Danville, he attended that city's public schools (except for a brief interim at Randolph-Macon Military Academy in Front Royal, Va., which he heartily disliked and from which he begged off at his earliest opportunity, returning home for the remainder of his secondary education.) Envisioning a career in textiles, he enrolled in the Georgia Institute of Technology, joining the Sigma Phi Epsilon fraternity. After a year or so of somewhat casual scholarly endeavor amid the heady social atmosphere of Atlanta, he transferred at his father's insistence to Eastman College in Poughkeepsie to prepare himself more single-mindedly for the world of business. Here, he and Ruth Cadman, who had been awarded a scholarship to Vassar College, met and became enamored, their formal engagement ensuing after the requisite visit to his hometown for the approbation of the senior Watsons. True love having supplanted Ruth's aspirations for a college education, and with the blessings of both families, immediately upon Bob's graduation from Eastman, the two were united in wedlock in Poughkeepsie by the Rev. Mr. Cadman in his Worrall Avenue rectory (May 1922.) Settling in Danville, the newlyweds resided for a year with Dad's parents until they could afford separate lodging.

My father's first employment was in the payroll department of Dan River Mills, the community's major industry, whose chief executive, Harry Fitzgerald, was an old family friend and fellow member of Mount Vernon Methodist Church, with which the Watsons had long been affiliated. Once the young couple had become established in their own domicile, my mother brought forth their first child, Margaret Harrison ("Peggy") Watson (1923-1996.)

Persuaded after two years at Dan River Mills that he should seek greener pastures, my father elected to move his dependents to nearby Leakesville/Eden, just south of the Virginia-North Carolina border, where he had been hired as an accountant for a lumber firm. Thus it came about a few months later that my eyes first beheld the light of day in that setting. I suspect that Dad was always a journalist at heart, for he soon became no less restive in the lumber trade than at Dan River Mills, resulting in his resignation after a similarly-brief tenure and our return to Danville so that he could join the staff of its daily newspaper, the *REGISTER*. (Perhaps his affinity for the fourth estate was innate, for my great-grandfather, J. C. Watson, Sr., had been proprietor of a Winchester, Va., journal before the Civil War and his entry into the Methodist pastorate.) Journalism must have proven insufficiently lucrative, however, for not long after our resettlement in his place of origin, Dad accepted a local sales position with a national advertising firm specializing in street-car placards, Barron G. Collier, Inc., headquartered in New York City. By that juncture, alas, the national economy was beginning to unravel, and in 1928, the Morotock Company, Grandfather Watson's textile enterprise, foundered. In the wake of the following year's stock-market crash, Barron Collier went under as well, and by 1930, my dad found himself jobless. This calamity prompted our second move to North Carolina in hopes of repairing our fortunes, this time to Winston-Salem.[6]

Nestled in the foothills of the Blue Ridge mountains, Winston-Salem was currently the world's foremost manufacturer of tobacco products—the home of R. J. Reynolds Tobacco Company, makers of "Camel" cigarettes and "Prince Albert" pipe tobacco. It also harbored extensive woolen-goods, underwear, and hosiery industries (dominated for the most part by the local Hanes family.) A tidy little metropolis of about 110,000, mostly Protestants of Scotch-Irish, Scottish, and German extraction, Winston-Salem was, as its hyphenated name suggests, a merger of the bourgeoning industrial community of Winston and the sedate little pre-Revolutionary settlement of Salem, founded by a colony of Moravian pietists in the eighteenth century. The populace of the so-called "Twin City" included a sizeable minority of rigidly segregated African-Americans, for whose uplift Winston-Salem Teachers College, one of the community's only two institutions of higher learning, had been founded. The other, Salem College, a small female liberal arts institution spawned by the Moravians, was nationally famed for its excellent School of Music.

Producing two-thirds of the nation's total cigarette output, Winston-Salem was not impacted quite as severely by the Great Depression as most Dixie municipalities because millions of anxiety-ridden Americans consumed tobacco products in ever-growing quantities during those stressful years, and females had taken up the habit with no less avidity than males during the Jazz Age.[7] Although my parents were never to have an easy time of it there financially, they managed to make ends meet—though sometimes only by the barest—and we never lacked for any of the more basic necessities. Luxuries, however, were few and far between.

During our first three years on that scene, Dad worked in the advertising department of the daily *JOURNAL AND SENTINEL*, and did parttime news-reporting. In 1933, that grim year when the nation's business activity bottomed out and Franklin D. Roosevelt took the helm in Washington, while Adolf Hitler came to power in Germany, my father felt compelled to switch careers a final time, hiring on as salesman and accountant with a small insurance agency, Brown-Ruffin Company, representing automobile, fire, and casualty underwriters. (Two decades later, following the end of World War II, he would become third partner in the firm with the title of Secretary.) Dad had little to loose by leaving the newspaper—it had fallen on such hard times that its employees were being compensated in scrip redeemable only at stores and businesses with accounts owable to the paper. He was to remain with Brown-Ruffin until his death in 1959 at age fifty-seven from pulmonary thrombosis.

Throughout my childhood in Winston, we inhabited a succession of rental houses in middle-class neighborhoods, all in relatively close proximity to the two public schools Peggy and I attended, Calvin H. Wiley Grammar School and Richard J. Reynolds High School, ensuring continuity of academic environment and peer—group stability. Due to heavy medical expenses incurred when Dad suffered a near-fatal attack of appendicitis in the early 1930's, my folks remained hard-pressed by debt even after a decade of FDR's New Deal and the general upsurge in employment and corporate profits generated by rearmament. With the onset of World War II, Winston-Salem's business climate was reinvigorated not only by a burgeoning demand for tobacco and textile products, but by the opening of a large Western Electric Corporation defense plant.

Though in Danville my parents had attended the same Methodist congregation with which my paternal forebears had been long associated, upon our Winston resettlement, my Dad adopted Mother's Anglicanism. Upon his confirmation by the Rt. Rev. Edwin A. Penick, Episcopal Bishop of North Carolina, they became active communicants of the city's oldest parish, St. Paul's, and there my sister and I received our spiritual nurturance. Though we could not contribute much in the way of alms, Dad gladly assumed various ecclesiastical responsibilities, ushering at worship services, teaching Sunday School classes, and writing a weekly precis of the rector's sermons for the newspaper. The Episcopal Church would forever after occupy an important niche in our family's routines, and on at least one of my grandfather Cadman's visits with us, in July 1932, he was guest preacher at St. Paul's. I followed in my parents' footsteps as a steadfast worshipper, and have found the Episcopal Church's stately liturgy and "via media" theological blend of Protestant evangelicalism and Catholic sacramentalism not only congenial, but an indispensable source of strength and comfort throughout my days. I also came to appreciate and share my father's love of literature and philosophy. I do not think it wide of the mark to state that both my parents were hard-working, literate, devout, and honorable individuals. Financial strictures notwithstanding, we children enjoyed the inestimable advantages of a stable home environment, virtually free of conflict, surrounded by books and stimulating conversation, and gently disciplined by parents who displayed a lifelong mutual affection and who allowed us an appropriate degree of autonomy.

I look back upon my grammar schooling wistfully, and spent many blissful summer days with kids in our neighborhood playing at baseball or football, raising pets, damming up a nearby creek to create swimming holes, building tree houses in the woods or shacks on vacant lots, making toys "from scratch," and hammering out "soapbox cars" or "pushmobiles" for downhill racing, in brief, doing all the things by which boys fraternize and learn basic manual and social skills. The routines of our pre-war domestic life were puncuated by episodic Sunday round trips to Danville, 65 miles to the northeast, to visit my grandparents and extended family members, among them Granddad's amiable half-brothers, Charles B. and J. Marvin Watson, and spouses. Driving over in our secondhand Essex 4-door sedan (which not infrequently developed a flat tire or an overheated radiator enroute, mandating hasty repairs at the nearest crossroads hamlet), we would usually arrive in time to dine with the elders. After the meals, I would tag along with the men on their walkabouts through the town. During summer breaks, I would occasionally stay on for a week or so, running errands, going to Church with my relatives, and viewing baseball games at the ballpark of the Danville "Bees" with Grandpa and my great-uncles. My favorite Danville resort, however, was Green Hill Cemetary, several blocks east of my grandparents' roominghouse, where the remains of so many Watsons and Prices were interred. The graveyard overlooked the Southern Railway's double-track mainline with its endless procession of trains. One of my most enduring recollections is of the passing freights festooned with penniless hoboes and itinerant job-seekers. A similarly-ineradicable impression is of the meticulous state of maintenance of the railroad properties then prevalent, doubtless due to the ready availability of cheap labor. Railroads at that time were very labor-intensive industries, and each section of their rights-of-way had a resident maintenance crew to keep the tracks properly aligned, crossties replaced, ballast neatly trimmed and free of vegetation and debris, and drainage ditches cleared. Locomotives, cars, and stations were clean, brightly-polished, and frequently-painted—in poignant contrast to the rundown, weedgrown, rust-streaked, generally-unkempt properties of so many carriers in the aftermath of World War II.

While I thoroughly relished these Danville sorties, I was most enthralled by our infrequent long-distance excursions to my mother's native region. Because of Dad's vocational demands and our sparse financial resources, he took few vacations aside from a brief journey in 1934 (a year of record-breaking heat and drought in the midwest) to the Chicago World's Fair as the guest of my great-uncle Sterling H. Price, Grandmother Watson's younger brother, a prospering fruit-and-produce wholesaler in Mount Vernon, Illinois. Usually, Mother alone shepherded my sister and me to reunions with her family-of-origin. I have vague memories from age four, as the economy was turning sour, of the three of us sharing an upper berth on an overnight sleeper from Danville to New Jersey to attend her Poppa's second wedding. Sometime during the mid-thirties, my Dad, borrowing a more reliable auto from one of his bosses, drove us up from Winston via Roanoke and U.S. Route 11 through the scenic Shenandoah Valley and lush Pennsylvania Dutch farm country for a brief visit with the Cadmans at their summer retreat in Dutchess County, New York. (He unwittingly made a wrong turn somewhere north of Harrisburg, taking us through Pennsylvania's blighted anthracite coal region, thereby adding to our itinerary a good many fatiguing miles on bad roads.) With this sole exception, however, our long-distance journeying was by rail.

A round-trip coach ticket at that time cost a mere 1-&-1/2 cents per mile, considerably less than Pullman accomodations, but offering few amenities. While Southern Ry. operated numerous mainline passenger trains, its more up-scale limiteds were scheduled for the convenience of businessmen travelling straight through from one to the other of its principal terminals, Atlanta and Washington, and passed through North Carolina and Virginia during nocturnal hours. At Washington, New York-bound Pullman sleeping cars from a variety of Southeastern points (including Winston-Salem) were attached to Pennsylvania Railroad expresses, allowing their occupants uninterrupted slumber, while coach patrons had to detrain and reboard there. Moreover, Winston-Salem was served only by secondary lines or branches of the Southern, Norfolk & Western, and Winston-Salem Southbound railroads, and in order to access Southern's mainliners, coach passengers originating there had to take a local to Greensboro, 29 miles to the east, and transfer. This created a problem for those who preferred to travel north in the daytime. Of the three daily northbound trains stopping at Greensboro during morning hours, only one, No. 30, meshed with a Pennsylvania R.R. express affording arrival in the New York vicinity before dark. The trouble was that none of the four locals from Winston were scheduled to connect with No. 30, which departed Greensboro at the ungodly hour of 4:12 A.M. On the other hand, with its 11:20 A.M. arrival in Washington, No. 30 enabled convenient transfer to PRR's *Senator* reaching Newark, N.J., at 3:48 P.M., a place and time at which my elderly grandpa Cadman could meet us without undue inconvenience. Hence, for us, No. 30 was it, providing my Dad could drive us to Greensboro, or as a last resort, send us over on a crowded bus. (New York to Winston itineraries presented no such difficulties.)[8]

Our most memorable northerly peregrination occurred in July 1936, prompted by the sudden death of my Great-uncle Sam (from a ruptured appendix, the same disability that had smitten my father and caused Aunt Marie's early demise.) With tickets purchased in advance, Dad drove us over in a friend's car in the dead of night to the Greensboro depot to catch No. 30. We mounted the stairs to the trackside platform just as the long train, headed by one of Southern's singularly handsome green-and-gold-liveried heavy-Pacific-type locomotives, rolled in right on time from High Point, the next station to the south. We trailed Dad aboard one of its non-air-conditioned steel coaches with their straight-backed brown-plush double seats. He selected a spot for us toward the middle of the half-empty car, reversing the back of the seat ahead so that we could ride facing one another, stowed our luggage in the rack overhead, hugged us goodbye, and strode off to the platform outside. As soon as the last of the checked baggage, mail-sacks, and express packages had been hoisted aboard the head-end cars, the engine's melodious deep-throated whistle sounded and we blasted off toward Virginia. An hour later, as the sky began to lighten, we shuddered to a ten-minute stop at the Danville depot. Then, laboring upgrade out of the Dan River Valley, we struck a leisurely 50 m.p.h. pace across the undulating profile of upcountry Virginia, halting only at Lynchburg, Monroe, Charlottesville, Culpepper, Manassas, and a few intervening flag-stations. The sun mounted higher in a cloudless sky and the atmosphere in our coach grew steamier as No. 30 loped along through the torrid forenoon. Foregoing an expensive breakfast in the diner, we snacked on sandwiches and drinks purchased from the Union News Company huckster who passed through the train at intervals. Dampened with perspiration and dusted with the soft-coal smoke and cinders wafting through the open windows—a sore trial for my fastidious mother—we rolled across land once savagely contested between my rebel ancestors and their blue-clad foes.

After an 11:30 A.M. stop at Alexandria, just down the Potomac River from the nation's capital, we steamed alongside the Richmond, Fredericksburg, and Potomac Railway's Potomac Freight Yard, one of the nation's largest, past endless strings of yellow refrigerator cars awaiting servicing or re-icing at the Fruit Growers Express Company's sprawling maintenance facility. All the fruit and perishables shipped to the Northeast from South-Atlantic states funnelled through this yard, and it was a sight to see! Soon, while rolling across the Potomac River bridge, we could glimpse above the treetops and intervening structures the obelisk of the Washington monument, the Jefferson memorial, and the pristine dome of the Capitol. In a few minutes all was eclipsed by darkness as No. 30 penetrated the tunnel under Capitol Hill, and, upon emerging from its gloom, slowed gradually and almost imperceptably to a halt on a lower-level platform of Washington's immense Union Station. When the perspiring trainman announced our destination and opened the trapdoor to the vestibule steps, we gathered ourselves together and descended for what seemed a long hike to the cavernous station concourse. Following a light repast at Savarin's lunch-counter, my mother anxiously sought out the gate to the upper-level platform from whence PRR's *Senator* was to depart.

The Pennsy's Washington-New York trunk line was newly-electrified, thanks to a Federal Government Reconstruction Finance Corporation loan (one of the few emergency relief measures initiated by the Hoover administration), and it bore the heaviest volume of traffic of any in the nation, and maybe the world. We located and boarded our express just in the nick of time, and found its tuscan-red coaches with their immaculate air-conditioned interiors and individual reclining-back seats a welcome change from the Southern's more spartan conveyances.[9]

Precisely at 12:05 P.M., the streamlined glossy-black GG1-class electric locomotive up ahead eased our long string of cars forward gently and quietly, and once clear of Washington terminal's maze of trackage, swiftly accelerated to a sustained speed of 70 m.p.h.

down the high-rail corridor to Manhattan. I kept my nose glued to the windowpane as we sped smoothly across Maryland and over the sun-speckled Susquehanna River on a long, lofty span at Havre de Grace, then through upper Delaware into Pennsylvania, our progress arrested only briefly at Baltimore, Chester, and Wilmington. The hands of Mother's watch had scarcely reached the 2:00 P.M. mark before we were hurtling past a dizzying array of suburban housing developments, tank farms, and chemical plants strung along the west bank of the Delaware River, and into South Philadelphia with its squalid factories and monotonous red-brick tenements. At length we ground to an abrupt stop beneath the brand-new, elegant 30th Street Station on the west bank of the Schuylkill River across from the city center. The instant a mob of fresh passengers had boarded our *Senator*, she glided off again into the smoggy sunlight and up a stiff gently-curving grade, past the pristine Municipal Art Gallery on the river's opposite side, to weave through a tangled web of trackage where PRR's fabled main line from Harrisburg, Pittsburgh, and Chicago merged with the Washington-New York trunk. Hurdling the tree-lined Schuylkill high above Fairmont Park, we paused at North Philadelphia's venerable station to take on additional New York-bound commuters. Once our motion resumed, there was no deceleration until the motorman reined in for the Delaware River bridge crossing into New Jersey's capital city of Trenton in midafternoon. A succession of huge letters adorning the girders of an adjacent span spelled out the slogan "What Trenton Makes The World Takes." The profusion of industrial properties lining PRR's four-track right-of-way through this region like beads on a string was almost more than I could mentally register, with scores of freight and passenger trains thundering past. Three-quarters of an hour beyond Trenton, the train's brakes began clamping on for Newark, where we were to alight. Since detraining passengers had to step lively in this milieu of split-second timing, we had gathered up our belongings and toted them to the end of the coach well in advance, and the moment the wheels stopped turning, right on the money at 3:48 P.M., we emerged onto the car-floor-level platform of another of

PRR's gleaming new stations, suffused in the blue haze and acrid odor of scorched brake shoes.

Grandpa Cadman, spotting us from afar, rushed up, and, after warm embraces, guided us through the station to his waiting auto, at whose wheel sat my step-grandmother, Emily, who would be chauffeuring, she averred, because Will's driving had become so incurably erratic. Once our luggage was deposited in the boot and we were ensconced in the rear seat, she drove us northward for twenty miles or so to their Midland Park rectory.

After a good night's rest, the five of us motored east on U.S. Route 202 to the near shore of the sparkling Hudson River, and over Bear Mountain Bridge to Peekskill, then up U.S. 9 along the river's eastern flank through Rip Van Wynkle "Sleepy Hollow" country into Dutchess County. Picturesque highlands cradling the West Point Military Academy campus towered over the opposite riverbank, while Hudson River Dayline excursion boats and ferries churned across the waterway's broad surface. Beyond Poughkeepsie and the Roosevelt family estate at Hyde Park, near the hamlet of Pleasant Plains, lay the weathered nineteenth-century farmhouse and bit of acreage which Grandpa and Emily had recently purchased for their summering. In this rustic setting, we enjoyed several weeks of relaxation, picnicking, swimming, playing crocquet and parlor games, reading, and sightseeing. One afternoon, as we were driving down a rural lane, we overtook two mounted equestrians cantering along on the roadside, who turned out to be First Lady Eleanor Roosevelt and a uniformed escort.

My step-grandmother, having scant tolerance for much aimless lazing about, assigned me such chores as picking vegetables, weeding the garden, or white-washing the fences and outhouse. In due course, we drove up to Lakeville, in Connecticut's northeastern corner, where my late great-uncle Sam and family had their vacation abode, to call on his widow and two spinster daughters (We were unable to link up with his son, Frederick L. Cadman, a married attorney who lived and practiced in New York City.) As the end of our summer idyl drew nigh, we motored down to Briarcliff Manor in Westchester County, N.Y., for a brief visit with mother's Uncle

Maurice (proprietor of nearby Pleasantville's sole drugstore) and wife, Estelle, who accorded us a warm reception. Before seeing us off on the train at Newark, Grandpa and Emily took us over to the Jersey shore at Asbury Park for a refreshing romp on the beach.

The citizenry-at-large whom I had encountered in those parts, whose crisp enunciation and proper grammar reflected a superior and well-funded educational system, seemed to me a race apart from the provincials back home—more energetic, articulate, well-informed. Not surprisingly, given the naivete of a ten-year-old, I quite overlooked the fact that most of them represented a relatively-privileged minority. Totally entranced by the industrialized upper east coast with its teeming megacities, manicured suburbs, and cultural eclecticism, I was crestfallen when it was time to return south. Insulated as I had been from the grime and crime, deprivation and depravity, on the underside of this exotic cosmos, I concluded that the quality of life in the North was immeasureably superior to that in my langorous homeland, with its red-clay hills, piney forests, muddy streams, and hick towns. In my newly-acquired sophistication, I confess to my shame, the forlorn face of Carolina's rural Piedmont—its sagging tobacco barns, weathered tenant shacks, and muledrawn wagons, its rutted dirt roads, faded general stores, and two-pump gas stations—had suddenly become an almost-unbearable affront. Although these absurdly undiscerning sentiments were soon to undergo radical revision, my dual regional rootage has inculcated a life-long ambivalence in self-identity and sectional loyalty. In straddling the Yankee-Rebel fence, my feet have hung over on the Dixie side, however, for there, except for a few intervals, I have continued to dwell—though, perhaps in unconscious emulation of my father, I would one day chose to mate with a Northern girl (from Elizabeth, N.J., and Baltimore, Md.) The over-crowded, relentlessly-competitive Northeast no longer holds much appeal for me.

Toward the end of my primary schooling, I also developed an infatuation with the American Civil War, largely from sky-larking about with an ex-Fredericksburg, Va., classmate who was steeped in Confederate lore; we spent countless hours playing war games, poring over military texts, and debating the relative merits of the Blue and the Gray; military history has remained one of my abiding predelictions. One sun-drenched afternoon, after reading about Zeppelins in World War I, as we were lolling around on the school playground during our lunchhour, my buddies and I were transfixed by the passage overhead of a huge dirigible—the *Hindenberg*, or maybe it was the *Macon*—floating majestically and serenely on its way to the upper east coast.

From age twelve on, I earned "spending money" by delivering newspapers, stocking shelves and sweeping floors at the corner grocery store, jerking sodas in an ice-cream parlor, mowing grass and raking leaves, and other low-skill endeavors, as my physical stature grew, voice deepened, facial hair sprouted, and interest in females surged. By all odds, the crucial year of my adolescence was 1939, in November of which I turned fourteen. I had been confirmed at St. Paul's Church in April, and, as a full-fledged communicant, assumed the duties of an altar boy. My mother had become pregnant and that May delivered her third and last child, a female given the name Ruth Cadman. At first I harbored some negative feelings about Ruthie's advent, for it complicated my life to a degree. She quickly evolved into a cute, winsome, blonde tot, however, and although her care preempted most of Mother's time and energies, I quickly became resigned to the new dispensation. (Tragically, Ruthie, was fated to develop leukemia just as she was on the verge of becoming a tennis star, and died in her fourteenth year.)

I had become deeply involved in Boy Scouting as a member of Troop 49 sponsored by our parish, and was currently preoccupied with earning my first-class badge. That mid-summer our troop chartered a bus to the New York World's Fair at Flushing Meadows, Long Island—it was my first long-range foray sans parents. We "forty-niners" had a glorious time sampling the wonders of "The World of Tomorrow," as the exposition was billed. Centering upon its trademark "Trylon" and "Perisphere" physical structures, the fair was designed to showcase American ingenuity and productivity and to upstage the displays mounted by the other developed nations (with the exception of Nazi Germany, whose Fuehrer disdained to participate.) An inordinate amount of my time was spent gaping at two exhibitions in particular: the "RAILROADS ON PARADE" extravaganza with its display of "ultra-modern" stream-lined motive power and rolling stock, and General Motor's FUTURAMA, modelling the utopian world envisioned by the automobile and highway technocrats and urban planners. We strove tirelessly to see and sample everything the fair had to offer until, with time and pocketbooks exhausted, and laden with brochures, souvenirs, and handouts, we had to head home.

That autumn I entered upon my freshman year at Reynolds High. Named in honor of the city's preeminent industrialist, it was considered academically and socially superior to the city's other two secondary schools for whites, and the majority of its scholars were college-bound. There was a more pervasive class-consciousness among the student-body here than in grammar school. Being gangly and relatively unathletic, a lousy dancer, and usually short of cash, I was viewed, I suspect, as only marginally-acceptable by the insiders and trend-setters, and had little confidence in my abilities to impress the opposite sex—or anyone else, for that matter. (The fact that among the earlier celebrity lecturers imported by RJR's Fine Arts Foundation had been my great-uncle Sam added little, if any, luster to my public image; I never mentioned it, and it probably would not have mattered anyway). Among the classmates with whom I most enjoyed associating were a set of identical twins, sons of a Southern Ry. trainman. Exceptionally good-looking and outgoing, they were much sought-after, and almost indistinguishable, except that one limped slightly from a congenital foot abnormality. He was later to serve in Korea, while the other died in the European conflict.

The semester was barely underway when Hitler launched his blitzkreig against Poland, precipitating World War II. Our circumscribed and stratified juvenile world was as rudely shaken as though long-quiescent subterranean tectonic plates had collided and overridden one another, and the tremors were to intensify throughout the remainder of my adolescence. RJR's red-brick classroom building and auditorium were located atop a steep hill at the fringe of the town's higher-toned western precincts, Buena Vista and Reynolda. The school plant overlooked a little valley running northeast-southwest through which coursed Peters Creek, a minor tributary of the Yadkin River bounding Forsyth County on the west. Upon this verdant swath of bottomland, known as Hanes Park, was sited our gymnasium and athletic playing fields. As one looked eastward from the elevated schoolhouse/auditorium across the valley toward downtown Winston, the paralleling ridge on the far side was crowned by older, tree-shaded homes lining Summit Street and the squat stone gothic bell tower of St. Paul's Church. Angling up the lower flank of the western height whereon the high school reposed, the Southern Railway's single-track Greensboro-Winston-Salem-Asheville/Charlotte secondary line divided the city's southwestern suburbs into middle-class and upper-class ghettos. A broad window covered the entire east wall of the room in which my first-period class met, revealing a sweeping panorama of the railway track just below, the valley beyond, and the far hillside, profiled by the tower of my church and the more distant downtown high-rise office buildings, hotels, and factory smokestacks. At 8:59 A.M., the first of six daily trains, a two-car local passenger run, chuffed noisily up the grade beneath the school, triggering in our sophomoric psyches—or mine, at least—fantasies of a larger world of adventure and romance. Its successors were no less distracting, momentarily erasing the nagging anxieties of unfinished homework and looming tests. Most of us were so destabilized by newly-emergent sexual appetites and inflamatory news reports from the war's far-flung battlefronts that we could hardly contain the urge to break free from the confines of academia.

I eventually switched from the Boy Scouts to a newly-introduced Sea Scout program. Though it is doubtful that my seafaring competencies advanced much beyond the ability to tie a few nautical knots and master a bit of shipboard terminology like "port" and "starboard," "jib" and "mainsail," or "bow" and "stern,"

I did fancy that my outward appearance was enchanced by the uniform bell-bottomed trousers, jumper, and jaunty white cap, and hugely enjoyed sailboating on the nearby lakes and streams.

Although the pace of my physical maturation had lagged behind that of a number of my contemporaries, and being myopic, had to wear relatively-strong eyeglasses, by my sixteenth year, I was a six-footer, though too slight of build to compete effectively in most body-contact sports. By nature cautious and not particularly self-assertive, I, like most teenagers, was forced at times to do battle with persecuting bullies, from which I usually emerged, if seldom victorious, at least with slight damage other than a bloodied nose or blackened eye now and then. My sports potential appeared so unpromising to our Physical Education instructor, a bull-necked boor with the physique (and the demeanor) of a professional wrestler, that he dubbed me "Olive Oyle" (the willowy paramour of cartoon character "Popeye"), an indignity which stung me to the quick, but, having no other recourse, I endured with mute stoicism. I compensated for my presumed anatomical inadequacy by applying myself ever more assiduously to my studies, from which I drew increasing satisfaction, not only in the subject of history, but in mathematics and foreign languages, thanks to some exceptionally dedicated and able teachers.

As an upperclassman, I befriended another train afficionado whose father was an engineman on the Winston-Salem Southbound Ry., and together we took every opportunity to explore on our bicycles the railyards and lines radiating from the city. Through his dad's connections, we were invited one day by the superintendant of the High Point, Thomasville and Denton Ry. to ride in the engine cab on an overnight freight run from High Point to High Rock and return. Other railwaymen were similarly supportive; the pilot of Southern's switching engine #776 at the Union Station frequently took us aboard while shunting cars about, and Mr. Baine Gabriel, one of my favorite Sunday School teachers, a conductor on the daily Winston-North Wilkesboro passenger run, patiently explained many of railroading's technical mysteries.

Halfway through my Junior year, the United States was sucked into the maelstrom of global war by the bombing of Pearl Harbor. Our school principal assembled the entire student body in the auditorium on December 8th to hear President Roosevelt's radio announcement of the declaration of war against Japan. Throughout my final three semesters, everyone was increasingly caught up in the crisis of national defense. Not until the spring of 1943, as my secondary schooling drew to a close, did the tide of war begin to turn in favor of the Allies, and the long and dismaying succession of disasters that had been bedevilling the Western democracies recede into memory. In January, after a titanic struggle raging across the plains of Russia, Stalin's troops had forced the surrender of the German Sixth Army at Stalingrad, the 900-day seige of Leningrad had been lifted, and the Soviets were everywhere on the offensive. In North Africa, Erwin Rommel's Afrika Korps, blocked at El Alamein and rolled back by the British Eighth Army, was heavily embattled on its opposite flank by a joint Anglo-American force which had gone ashore the previous November in French Morocco and Algeria, and would soon be ground up inexorably between these two mighty pincers. Far across the Pacific, the Aussies and Yanks had expelled the Japanese from Papua in New Guinea, and before long would be overmatching them in the skies as well. The previous summer's victories by the U.S. Navy in the Coral Sea and off Midway Island had so severely crippled Nippon's Naval air arm that any further threats to the Australian continent or strikes toward Hawaii had been forestalled. The stalemate on Guadalcanal had been broken to our advantage, and up in the Aleutians, Attu had been recovered and the enemy occupants of Kiska ordered withdrawn by Tokyo.

The staggering toll in Allied tonnage exacted by German U-boats in the North Atlantic was being dramatically reduced by novel anti-submarine tactics, and in Central Europe, Royal Air Force and U.S.A.A.F. bombers were smashing Germany's industries and incinerating her cities. At Casablanca in January, Roosevelt and Churchill had agreed that the next Allied initiative would be an invasion of Sicily. Four months later, at the TRIDENT conference in Washington, a tentative date of 1 May 1944 had been set for the cross-channel invasion of France, and plans formulated to knock Italy out of the war once Sicily was retrieved, launch an accelerated island-hopping campaign across the Central Pacific against Japan, and provide additional aid to China. The prodigious industrial infrastructure of the United States was now at full throttle, and scores of thousands of ships, planes, tanks, and guns were pouring forth from our factories and shipyards, while Axis productivity was faltering. In short, the odds had dramatically reversed; just as in the American Civil War following the July 1863 Federal victories at Gettysburg and Vicksburg, the outcome appeared less and less dubious, though the most bitter and costly struggles were yet to come. Both Germany and Japan had overreached themselves and were now on the defensive.[10]

II

EAGER EPHEBE

Scrubbed, starched, and sweating in the moist heat of a Carolina June night, the three hundred and ten of us in the graduating senior class of 1943 were seated front and center in the Kate Bitting Reynolds Auditorium. The proceedings got underway at 8:00 P.M. with a lack-luster performance by the school band and an impassioned invocation by a Baptist pastor whose son was among the graduates. Following the "Annual Literary Address," delivered by the editor of the *JOURNAL AND SENTINEL*, Principal Claude R. Joyner, father of another of my classmates, dispensed awards for outstanding achievement in scholarship, athletics, and extra-curricular activities. Though I was a member of the National Honor Society, and had earned one of the highest grade-point averages in the class, I was surprised to find myself the recipient of the History award endowed by the local chapter of the Daughters of the American Revolution. Joyner then relinquished the podium to a member of the School Board, who led us in a recitation of the "Athenian Oath," more traditionally known as the "Ephebic Oath." This rite was a legacy of ancient Athens, where it was required of adolescent males of the upper class, or "Ephebi," upon reaching the age of seventeen, before training for the responsibilities of patrolling the frontiers and policing the highways. It had been resurrected by American educators during the war years to imprint upon their departing charges a selfless devotion to the service of the homeland. Already thoroughly brain-washed by months of relentless hot-war propaganda, we dutifully mumbled in unison,

"We will never bring disgrace to this, our city, by any act of dishonesty or cowardice, nor ever desert our suffering comrades in the ranks. We will fight for the ideals and sacred things of the city, both alone and with many; we will revere and obey the city's laws and do our best to incite a like respect and reverence in those above us who are prone to annul or set them at naught; we will strive unceasingly to quicken the public's sense of civic duty. Thus in all these ways we will transmit this city not only not less, but greater than it was transmitted to us."

We were then handed our diplomas, and with the conclusion of the ceremonies, exited to fulfill, presumably, the obligations to which we had just committed ourselves. Imitating our British co-belligerents, most of us had already undertaken some form of voluntary civil defense duty, along with American city-dwellers all across the land, where air-raid sirens had been installed, bomb shelters constructed, and auxiliary fire-fighting brigades and ambulance squads organized. My father had volunteered as an auxiliary fireman, and I as a junior air raid warden. Along with most of the other 139 males in our class, I had enviously chafed at the bit as we had seen our forerunners over the previous year-and-a-half flocking into the uniformed services, and we could scarcely wait to enter the fray. At least 54 of us were signed up rather promptly—23 in the Navy or Coast Guard, 20 in the Army, and 3 in the Marines, with 8 more opting for some ancillary service such as the Merchant Marine. Most of the remainder, unless physically incapacitated or taking civilian jobs critical to the war effort, would eventually be drawn into the military before the war's end.

In anticipation of the Allied offensives soon to be unleashed in Europe and the Pacific, the armed services and defense industries were now fiercely competing for manpower. In November of the previous year, Congress had lowered the age for military induction from twenty to eighteen. In addition to the extant Army, Navy, and Marine Corps pre-enlistment programs designed to lure the more physically-fit and intellectually-endowed high school seniors into officer-candidate, pre-flight, and technical-specialist tracks, a couple of new college cadet categories, the V-l2 (Navy) and A-12 (Army), had recently been inaugurated. The latter, or "Army Specialized Training Program" [ASTP], introduced in December l942, was designed to channel some l50,000 of the more scholarly potential recruits or draftees into colleges and universities at government expense to alleviate an acute shortage of active-duty personnel with competencies in engineering, medicine, mathematics, and foreign languages. The V-12/A-12 programs would also help resuscitate the nation's higher education establishment which was finding itself in dire straits as student enrollments plummeted.[1] Before my graduation, I had taken the qualifying exam for A-12, the physical prerequisites for which were somewhat less stringent than those of the standard Officer Candidate programs or the V-12, both of which barred anyone who was very myopic (even though my vision was correctible with glasses to 20/20.) Having demonstrated an aptitude for mathematics and languages, I assumed that my chances for acceptance into the ASTP were not unfavorable, and was enormously gratified a few weeks later upon receiving notification of an A-12 appointment.

With my secondary schooling now behind me, and my eighteenth birthday less than six months off, I was determined to get a head start by enrolling for two sequential abbreviated summer terms at nearby Guilford College (which my sister Peggy had attended before moving to Maryland's Eastern Shore to work in an Easton restaurant owned and operated by my grandfather Watson's widowed sister, Ida Watson Riley, and her daughter Cora.) A small and inexpensive, but academically-reputable, four-year residential liberal arts institution founded by Quakers on the western outskirts of Greensboro, Guilford granted me a partial scholarship. This, together with a National Youth Administration government loan and a part-time campus job, would just about cover my expenses.

Accordingly, early in June, with $25 in my pocket, I caught the early morning train to Guilford Station, from which, suitcase in hand, I trudged the two miles to the tree-shaded campus.

There I passed a busy summer, absorbing some excellent instruction in English and American Literature, Integral Calculus, and Spherical Trigonometry. There were only two other students in my math courses, a girl of Japanese ethnicity, and my roommate, a somewhat indolent but good-natured jock, son of an affluent High Point banker. My parttime campus employment, it developed, was that of library janitor, a not-very-demanding responsibility for which I was paid the munificent stipend of 20 cents an hour.

Our recreational pursuits there were considerably hobbled by the tight rationing of gasoline, tires, shoes, clothing, meat, sugar, and the host of other items on which the military had first call, as well as by the financial austerity binding most of us. We spent a good many of our leisure hours in front of radios or phonographs mesmerized by the silky rythms and syruppy lyrics of vocalists Frank Sinatra, Helen O'Connell, Helen Forrest, or "Gorgeous Georgia" Carroll, gracing the big bands of the Dorseys, Glenn Miller, Harry James, or "Carolina's own" Kay Kyser. We envisioned ourselves surfing and sunning on some golden beach surrounded by shapely females, or strolling down Broadway, where Rogers and Hammerstein's *Oklahoma* was currently shattering all attendance records. Most of us, though, had to settle for a weekly ten-cent movie matinee featuring such idols as Bogart and Bergman in *Casablanca* (the preeminent exemplars of "coolness") or Greer Garson with her masterful portrayal of *Mrs. Minniver*. If one could possibly afford it, he sported a "zoot suit", or at least had a tailor restyle a pair of baggy pants into something appropriately modish by pegging them at the cuffs. The summer's choice for leisure-time reading was Betty Smith's immensely popular *A Tree Grows In Brooklyn*, while the more serious among us tackled Wendell Wilkie's *One World*.

While I dutifully swept floors, stoked the water-heating furnace, dusted books, shelves, and furniture, and struggled with trigonometric functions and the satires of John Dryden, momentous events were breaking abroad. German propaganda Minister Joseph Goebbels brayed that Berlin was now "free of Jews," and history's mightiest tank battle was raging at Kursk, where the Nazi invaders had attempted to pinch off a Russian salient. Their efforts unavailing, the Teutons were soon pushed back well beyond their jumping-off point, never again to regain the initiative on the Eastern front. All across Russia, in fact, Stalin's re-equipped armies began inflicting heavier and heavier blows upon Hitler's punch-drunk legions. In Germany itself, during July and August, the city of Hamburg was blanketted with British incendiary bombs and consumed by firestorms, leaving the charred remains of 20,000 citizens. Twelve American and British divisions under Mark Clark and Bernard Montgomery landed on Sicily and sliced across to its north coast, and by mid-August had completely expelled their opponents from the island. On the Italian mainland, Mussolini was overthrown and forced into exile, and a newly-installed successor government opened peace negotiations with the Allies. In early September, as Italy abrogated her Axis ties, German troops were rushed in to repel the impending Allied invasion. To borrow the words of Winston Churchill's unforgettable rallying-cry, in regard to the European Theatre of War, it was the beginning of the end, though in the Asiatic-Pacific, it was merely the end of the beginning. Nonetheless, in both hemispheres, the enemy's expansion had been arrested, and though the Allied counteroffensives were yet in their infancy, with each fresh gain, the resistance would become more obdurate.[2]

There seemed little point in re-enrolling at Guilford for the upcoming fall semester, since I would turn eighteen before the term should end, and at any time thereafter become subject to the Army's call-up. I was in such a fervor for my ASTP activation that I petitioned the draft board to send me off as soon as possible. Upon the conclusion of my last summer classes on August 2d, I bought a round-trip ticket to New Jersey and boarded a train with the aim of bidding farewell to my now seriously-ailing Grandfather Cadman and other relatives in that vicinity, and on the way back stopped off in Philadelphia for a final tete-a-tete with my uncle Bill Cadman and wife. The trip was by no means a joy ride; the railway coaches were so overcrowded in both directions south of Washington that I had to stand up or sit on my suitcase in the aisles. Once back in Winston-Salem, I took temporary employment as an elevator operator and clerk at the Anchor Company, a downtown dry-goods store, pending my call-up. During the first week in December, we received word of my grandfather's death (from coronary disease), but none of us Watsons were able to attend his funeral. Simultaneously, a letter arrived from the Draft Board directing me to present myself early Tuesday morning, 9 December, at Winston's Union Bus Depot for transportation to the Camp Croft, South Carolina, Induction Center.

On the day appointed, in company with a motley assortment of other draftees—callow youths, distinctly unenthusiastic older bachelors, and even glummer married men—I boarded a chartered Greyhound bus for the 250-mile round trip to the camp, a temporary cantonement on the southern edge of Spartanburg. Here the personal data forwarded by our draft board was reviewed, and we were herded through a sequence of physical, mental, and psychological examinations and interviews by medical officers and technicians. Most of us (including the bus driver himself) were pronounced acceptable and "sworn in" by taking the following Oath of Allegiance: "I do solemnly swear (or affirm) that I will bear true faith and allegiance to the United States of America, and that I will serve them honestly and faithfully against all their enemies whomsoever, and that I will obey the orders of the President of the United States and the orders of the officers appointed over me, according to the rules and articles for the government of the Army." Thus I became one of 13,333 Forsyth Countians to serve in the Second World War.

Pending our summons to active duty, we were each placed on "enlisted reserve" status—presumably, I had been pre-assigned to the ASTP Corps for Basic Military Training and subsequent posting to some college campus. Reboarding our bus that same day, we were hauled back to the Twin City to await the final determination of our respective military destinies. Shortly before the upcoming Christmas holiday—the last that I would celebrate at my family hearth until the world should be at peace again—my long-anticipated active-duty orders came in the mail, directing me to check in once more at the bus station early on Wednesday, 29

December 1943, for delivery to the Fort Bragg, N.C., Reception Center. On that fateful day, my parents saw me off reluctantly on a Greyhound in the frigid dawn's wan light. Somberly waving farewell to loved ones, our contingent of inductees lumbered off for Fort Bragg.

One of the nation's foremost permanent military posts, located in the pine-forested sandhills between the towns of Fayetteville and Southern Pines, the Bragg facility was a field-artillery and paratrooper training center, housing some 80,000 troops, including the 82d Airborne Division. Just to its south, at Hoffman, N.C., lay Camp Mackall, an adjunct paratrooper-training establishment.[3] We stepped off the bus and into a maelstrom. Bemused by endless blocks of identical two-story white frame barracks, mess-halls, warehouses, headquarters buildings, recreation halls, drill-fields, and motor pools, and distracted by the demented yells of non-coms herding troop formations, we spent the next couple of weeks stumbling awkwardly through the alien "hurry-up-and-wait" routines so characteristic of military life. The intrusive notes of bugle calls roused us before daybreak, heralded each scheduled activity, prefaced all meals, and closed out every evening. Badgered mercilessly by even the lowest-ranking and least-intellectually-endowed of the longer termers, we eventually became inured to profane screams of "Move it, goddamit, move it" or "consign your soul to God, fresh meat, 'cause your ass belongs to Uncle Sam now." We were henceforth formally addressed only by rank, namely, "Private" (or more often, by less tasteful appellations, not infrequently of an obscene character), the rationale for which I was never able to discern, since we enjoyed no privacy whatsoever. We quickly adjusted to having our given and surnames transposed and linked irrevocably to an 8-digit serial number (indelibly imprinted upon my memory is my own: 34896630.) Although I was not to take up the tobacco habit until the closing days of the war, the smokers among us were made to "field-strip" their cigarette butts, and we were relentlessly enjoined to "police the area" (i.e., pick up off the ground "everything that don't grow—I don't wanna see nothin' but asses and elbows!"} Everyone soon became desensitized to the initially-embarrassing "short-arm inspections" (episodic examinations of one's genitalia for symptoms of venereal disease— "skin it back and milk it down"), conducted en masse by medical personnel. My most ineradicable memory of Ft. Bragg, oddly, is of the pungeant aroma of the bituminous coal smoke which belched from every chimney that frigid winter.

The arrival of the new year 1944 passed almost unnoticed, assailed as we were by a plethora of training films pitched at the lowest level of mentality, or hustled through such time-honored rituals as "white-sidewall" hair trims and immunizations against typhoid and tetanus (by injections in both arms simultaneously.) We were shown how to make up our bunks with sheets and blankets so taut that a quarter tossed upon their surfaces would bounce in the air, and brow-beaten until we learned to hand-salute all commissioned officers in a rigidly-prescribed fashion and preface each communication directed at their august personnages with "sir." Since the army is a pyramid of "units" governed by a "chain of command," a relational terminology as fundamental as the multiplication table had to be mastered, as follows:

Formation	Approximate Strength	Rank of Commander
Squad	8 to 12 men	Sergeant
Platoon	2 or more squads	Lieutenant
Company (Battery)	2 or more platoons	Captain (Troop, Flight)
Batallion	2 or more companies	Lt. Colonel or Major
Regiment	2 or more battalions	Colonel
Brigade	2 or more regiments	Brigadier General
Division	2 or more brigades	Major General
Corps	2 or more divisions	Lt. General
Army	2 or more corps	General

The "Articles of War," specifying penalties for willful violations of army regulations or lawful orders, were solemnly read to us, and we were required to memorize and repeat the "General Orders" (only one of which can I recall at present: "I will walk my post in a military manner . . .") How one should distinguish between lawful and unlawful orders was never made clear; I concluded that the only prudent course was to keep my mouth shut and do what I was told with a poker face. Everyone was given a pair of "dog-tags" engraved with his name, rank, serial number, blood type, and religious preference—"P" for Protestant, "C" for Catholic, or "J" for Jewish (posing somewhat of a dilemma for us Episcopalians, who considered ourselves both Protestant and Catholic)—to be worn at all times on a chain around our necks for ready identification in case of disability or death.

We were issued two pairs of sturdy brown high-top brogans and an assortment of uniform dress and fatigue clothing and personal equippage, including a woolen olive-drab blouse and matching shirts, trousers, and overseas cap, for winter wear, a set of cotton khakis for summer, and green "fatigues" and billed cap or floppy hat for work details and field duty, plus puttees (leggings), overcoat, field jacket, raincoat, gloves, plastic helmet liner, handkerchiefs, underwear, belt, socks, toilet articles, and a pair of blankets, along with two canvas barracks bags (marked "A" or "B") in which to stow it all. Clad in our new winter garb, we were easily identifiable as rookies, since, unassigned as yet to permanent units, we wore no divisional shoulder patches, brass collar insignia, or piping around our overseas caps (indicating arm of service, i.e., light blue for infantry, scarlet for artillery, yellow for cavalry, scarlet-and-white for engineers, etc.), and our uniforms were typically ill-fitting and wrinkled.

Personnel specialists interrogated each of us, and we were given a series of objective tests measuring intelligence and aptitude, among them the A.G.C.T. [Army General Classification Test] and the R.O.A.T. [Radio Operation Aptitude Test.] Each recruit was then placed in one of five categories according to his AGCT scoring and assigned an M.O.S. [Military Occupation Specialty] code number, specifying the "job slot" for which he was judged best qualified in the T.O. [Table of Organization] of the unit to which he would be permanently assigned. Insofar as most of us could discern, one's MOS bore little, if any, relationship to his actual talents, preferences, or civilian calling. I have long forgotten my initial MOS code number, and in any case, a momentous redirection in my designated form of servitude had already been determined—though typically no one had bothered to inform me.

Back in early November, one month before I had been sworn in, the powers-that-be in the Pentagon had decided to abort the entire ASTP project for which I had been earmarked. The ground-combat arms, it seems, were becoming critically short of higher-quality manpower just at the point where heavy casualties were anticipated in the pending cross-channel invasion of Europe and the roll-back of the Japanese, to say nothing of a pressing need to find replacements for the significant losses already incurred in North Africa, Italy, and the South Pacific. Too many of the brighter and more robust young selectees had been siphoned off by the Navy, Marines, Air Corps, and Army Officer Candidate Schools, or for the more desireable and cushy technical specialties, leaving only culls and second-raters to fill out the ranks of the ground-combat units, most notably the "Queen of Battles," the Infantry. Consequently, in a momentous change of policy, the War Department had summarily ordered a wholesale diversion of personnel from the ASTP, as well as from surplus or lower-priority units such as tank-destroyer, anti-aircraft, and coast-artillery, into the infantry. The strength of the ASTP was peremptorily slashed from 150,000 to 30,000, and further eviscerated one month later, in effect closing out the program except for a handful of medical students. Virtually all ASTP trainees or inductees were to be promptly reassigned to combat units as "fillers" or replacements.[4]

As soon as a recruit's processing had been completed at a Reception Center, which usually took about two weeks, he and others consigned to the same category of service were dispatched to a basic training facility. My turn came in the third week of January 1944, when the one hundred or so with whom I was lumped was bussed to the Fort Bragg railhead and hustled onto a waiting troop train. Any movement by rail of military personnel in sufficient numbers as to require several cars or an entire train was called a "main," and tightly regulated. As a temporary military entity, each main was assigned a number and had an on-board commander and a staff of assistants including a transportation officer to handle ticketing and related paper work, a medical officer to treat health problems, a quartermaster officer to supervise loading and unloading of whatever equipment or supplies accompanied the troops, a mess officer to oversee preparation and service of meals enroute, and, if necessary, a baggage officer. Each car in the train had its own designated commander as well. The troops were not permitted to ride on car platforms or vestibules, to move unnecessarily to other cars, nor to leave the train without specific authority. A civilian railroad official known as an "escort" accompanied each main as liaison, along with the usual complement of railway operating personnel—conductor, trainmen, and enginemen.

For all journeys lasting more than twelve hours and ending after midnight, Pullman sleepers were authorized, each tended by a porter under the supervision of the train's Pullman conductor. For shorter trips, day-coaches sufficed. Buses were not utilized for long-distance troop movements because of their limited baggage capacity, lack of sleeping and mess facilities, and the need to conserve fuel. Except for movements of less than 500 miles, the Army preferred not to use its own motor vehicles. During peak years of the war, when more than a million military personnel required railway transportation each month (to say nothing of the enormously increased patronage on regularly-scheduled trains), the carriers could not always assemble the requisite sleeping cars at the specified times and places, so that troops on long-distance movements were not infrequently hauled in day-coaches. For the most part, however, the Pullman Company managed to accomodate this unprecedented volume of passengers, principally because at the war's outbreak it had on hand some 2,000 surplus cars, mostly obsolete "tourist sleepers" which had been sidelined during the lean Depression years and scheduled for eventual scrapping.

Aboard troop-main Pullmans, officers and higher-ranking non-coms were customarily allotted space in drawing rooms or compartments, while lesser ranks occupied "sections." The pair of opposing seats comprising a section were made up at night into a lower and an upper berth, with two soldiers occupying the lower and one the upper. (The Navy, however, required that each individual have a berth to himself.) During daytime, when the berths were folded up, three individuals thus occupied the section's two facing double seats, with their baggage stowed in the unoccupied seat space or the women's lavatory at the end of the car. Since a standard sleeper had twelve sections and one drawing room, it could accomodate 36 enlisted men and 3 officers. Day-coaches had a considerably larger capacity—older cars with reversible seat-backs, like those of the Southern Ry. on which I had so often ridden, seated about 54.

For meal service, kitchen cars were included on all movements of 200 or more troops if the journey were to exceed 24 hours. Empty baggage cars, in which stoves, refrigerators, and kitchen equipment were temporarily installed, normally served this function, one to every four or five coaches, or every six to eight sleepers. A typical on-board meal consisted of two weiners with ketchup, one slice of bread, one pat of butter, a ladlefull of peas, one boiled potato, a fruit cup, and iced tea. The food-service procedure was rigidly prescribed: the passengers in a given car (and sequentially in each of the other cars fore or aft of the kitchen car) would walk single-file through and beyond the kitchen car, gathering paper plates, cups, and utensils in passing, then do an about-face and retrace their steps, with food and beverages dispensed on the return through the galley car. Meals were eaten at one's seat, with the detritus collected in garbage cans carried through the train by "K.P.'s" [Kitchen Police], and stored in the kitchen car for disposal at the final destination or dropped off at intervening stations. On the shorter hauls when kitchen cars were omitted from the train's consist, cellophane-wrapped beef, ham, or cheese sandwiches were usually dispensed to the troops at their seats. If possible, station stops were made at six-hour intervals or so to allow the troops to detrain briefly for physical exercise.[5]

Upon boarding our main at Fort Bragg, our contingent was told that our destination was some obscure post named Camp Gordon Johnston at Carrabelle, south of Tallahassee, Florida, on the Gulf of Mexico, some 670 miles distant, or 18 hours travel-time. [Map M1] Although this was to be an overnight trek, we were loaded aboard a couple of day-coaches rather than sleepers. As I remember it, the main to which our cars were coupled operated as the second section of regularly-scheduled Seaboard Air Line train #107, the *Sun Queen,* (a Washington, D.C., to Miami-Tampa/ St.Petersburg express) as far as Jacksonville, where the Camp Gordon Johnston cars were to be switched onto the rear of another SAL train from Jacksonville to Tallahassee. Since only a couple of meals would be required enroute, no kitchen car was included in our main, to my knowledge. In fact, we didn't even rate sandwiches, but were simply handed two or three "K" rations to hold us until arrival. Designed for the nurturance of troops in combat, K-rations were packed in small containers about the size and shape of a crackerjack box, and were of three varieties, breakfast, dinner, and supper. The breakfast packet contained compressed cereal, cracker-like biscuits, a small can of egg-and-meat mixture, a fruit bar, chewing gum, a few water-purification tablets, and some small sheets of toilet paper. The dinner box included a tin of spam or some other compressed meat or fish, a packet of crackers, a melt-resistant chocolate bar, an envelope of powdered coffee, a packet of sugar, and four cigarettes. For supper, there was the same minsicule can of meat, sometimes mixed with apples or carrots, plus packets of biscuits and of cheese, a candy bar, lemon or grape powder, sugar, cigarettes, matches, salt tablets, and a wooden spoon. None of this was especially appetizing, but it was energy-restorative.

Darkness had descended upon Fort Bragg before the last "casuals," as we were called (not to be confused with "casualties," meaning killed, wounded, or missing in action), had finished boarding at the railhead, whereupon our troop special was towed to the Seaboard's mainline, which ran alongside the western boundary of the immense 130,000-acre military reservation, over a bucolic little "streak of rust" known as the Aberdeen and Rockfish Railroad. The A&R line described a flattened "V," looping around the eastern and southern borders of the base to connect with the Seaboard mainline at Aberdeen.

A bustling little community with several small industries, Aberdeen was located immediately south of two more imposing municipalities, Southern Pines and Pinehurst, world-renowned golf resorts and in pre-war times a mecca for the affluent. Our train rocked and rolled at a leisurely pace over some forty miles of the A&R's light rails and thin ballast before coming to rest at its stately two-story depot/headquarters in Aberdeen, alongside the Seaboard's heavy-duty tracks and station.[6] Being a total stranger to this region of my home state—never, in fact, having ventured farther south or east than Charlotte or Raleigh before my recent jaunt to Camp Croft, courtesy of Uncle Sam—I zealously scanned the darkened landscape outside my coach window. Our A&R motive power was exchanged for one of Seaboard's more modern, high-wheeled passenger engines as we waited on the interchange track. About 11:00 P.M., the distant glow of a headlight from the direction of Southern Pines heralded the *Sun Queen's* approach, and moments after she had roared past and the red marker lights on her rear had receded into the blackness of the southern horizon, our new iron horse jerked us into motion and propelled us down a 25-mile stretch of double track to Hamlet in her wake. Hamlet, site of the railway's largest freight yard, was the hub of five SAL lines, the one traversed by all Florida-bound through passenger trains cutting across the hilly up-country via Columbia. Our main drew to a halt behind #107 at Hamlet's large frame depot, a beehive of activity— 22 daily passenger trains halted there to change crews and transfer passengers, mail, and express.[7] Though most of my companions were already slumbering soundly, sleep was the last thing on my mind as I surveyed the surroundings. Within twenty-five minutes or so, we were in motion again, slamming around the serpentine curves and over the undulating profile of the Columbia line. I remember little of our passage through South Carolina's capital city except for a fleeting vision of the lighted dome of the capitol building near the tracks.

Still trailing the *Sun Queen* (which had made a scheduled stop at Columbia), we sprinted up and over successive ridges of the Sand Mountains at a brisk speed, and as the railway levelled out across what natives of the Palmetto State call the "low country", our pace quickened. We slid into Savannah about 5:30 A.M. by which time my eyelids had long since grown heavy, and I drowsed intermittently as we hammered across the intersecting tracks leading eastward to that picturesque old seaport's two stub-end terminals in the historic downtown district laid out by General Oglethorpe in the 1730's. While #107, like Seaboard's other regular passenger trains, had been switched onto the track leading eastward into Savannah's Union Station, our troop special was detained on the main line. Though I desperately tried to will myself to stay alert to developments, the strain of the preceding weeks had wearied me more than I realized, and Morpheus prevailed. Slumbering too deeply to register the resumption of our passage out of the city, I did not regain consciousness until sunup, as we were rocketing down long, flat tangents across soggy pinelands and tidal swamps on trestlework and earthen fills carrying the tracks twelve to fifteen feet above water level. Spanish moss festooned the branches of live oak and cypress trees, its gray hue and gossamer texture suggesting decayed burial shrouds, tingeing my spirits with an indefineable melancholy despite the now cloudless sky and the sun's warming rays.[8]

By the time we had crossed the meandering St. Mary's River marking the Georgia-Florida boundary just south of Kingsland, and were racing alongside U.S. Route 17, the coastal highway, the sunlight was dazzling and the temperature bland and soothing. Six miles into Florida, at Gross, the railway divided, the mainline bearing southeast into Jacksonville itself, while a bypass angled off southwest to Baldwin enabling through freight trains to circumvent the city's congested terminal complex. All SAL limiteds, together with those of the other carriers serving the Florida peninsula, halted at that city's huge Union Station for locomotive changes, car-swapping, and servicing, before continuing on to their ultimate destinations. Sprawled along both banks of the St. John's River, Jacksonville (which liked to refer to itself as "the working son in the Florida family of playboys"), the largest seaport in the Southeast, was booming. The tourist gateway to the Sunshine State in normal times, its imposing passenger terminal handled well over 100 trains every 24 hours. Our main, alas, was diverted onto the bypass, leaving me grievously disappointed at being in close proximity to such a railfan's paradise yet denied even a glimpse of it.

At Baldwin, eighteen miles west of Jacksonville, the Seaboard's mainline rejoined the bypass over which we had been routed, to continue on down the peninsula. From the Baldwin junction, another important Seaboard line led almost due west across north Florida into the state's panhandle through Tallahassee linking up at Chattahoochee with the Louisville & Nashville Railroad to New Orleans and the Southern Pacific Railway's "Sunset Route" connection to southern California. Our coaches, dropped off at Baldwin, were attached to the rear of No. 37, a Jacksonville-New Orleans accomodation, pausing there about 10:00 A.M., to be hauled westward across the top of Florida, more or less alongside Route 90, throughout the remainder of that morning and half the afternoon.[9]

This section of the state was distinctively Old South in ethos and outlook, a world apart from the Yankee-infested peninsula. Seemingly endless stretches of pine barrens interspersed with farms and cattle ranches unrolled outside our car windows. It was a langorous region bisected by a succession of dark and sluggish rivers flowing southward into the Gulf, among them the fabled Suwanee, draining Georgia's Okeefenokee Swamp. We chuffed through a succession of run-down marketing communities with such prosaic names as Lake City, Live Oak, and Monticello, whose railway sidings held countless cars loaded with pulpwood, bright-leaf tobacco, cotton, corn, pecans, and peanuts. As we neared Tallahassee, the terrain grew more undulating, dotted with numerous spring-fed lakes, and by mid-afternoon we eased to a stop in Florida's capital city, some 165 monotonous miles from Jacksonville.

Tallahassee was surprisingly hilly and laced with broad avenues shaded by stately oaks, magnolias, and dogwood trees. Its citizens, in common with the other Floridians of the state's northern counties, known as "porkchoppers," bore a hearty disdain for the more prosperous and urbane Yankee emigres, or "lambchoppers," who had taken up residence in the middle and lower peninsula. In state politics, the porkchoppers exerted leverage out of all proportion to their numbers, and Tallahassee, the seat of government since 1824, enjoyed a cultural preeminence quite surprising in view of its modest population of 38,000. Despite its relaxed ambience, it was an oasis of economic vigor in a sparsely-populated region of few natural resources other than the almost-boundless pulpwood forests. In addition to the state government facilities, Tallahassee boasted two college campusses, Florida State College for Women (present-day coeducational Florida State University) and Florida Agricultural and Mechanical College (for Negroes), along with a recently-developed Army Air Corps base, Dale Mabry Field. [10]

From Tallahassee, a couple of Seaboard branchlines led down to the Gulf shore, a more easterly one terminating at the old settlement of St. Mark's, in Wakulla County, the other stretching fifty miles southwest to the fishing village of Carrabelle in Franklin County. The Carrabelle branch, the southernmost segment of a once-independent carrier known as the Georgia, Florida, and Alabama Railway, had been slated for abandonment until the advent of hostilities brought a sudden surge in military traffic and rendered it essential to the war effort. (With the return of peacetime, it would be promptly scrapped.) In pre-Depression days, a single daily passenger train had operated between Tallahassee and Carrabelle, but had eventually proved so unprofitable that it had been discontinued, and busses now provided the only public transportation between the two.[11]

At the Tallahassee depot, our cars were dropped from No. 37 and coupled to a light-weight "teakettle" (to use railwayman slang) for the final leg of our trek to Camp Gordon Johnston. With bell clanging and smoke trailing, our truncated conveyance rattled through the capital's less affluent southern suburbs and soon the last vestiges of civilization vanished as we penetrated the eastern fringes of Appalachicola National Forest. Noting my mood of mounting anxiety and despondency, one of the more mature among my new recruit friends, Pvt. Lonnie Squires of Washington, N.C.,

an ex-real-estate-dealer in his thirties, a well-bred gentleman of
benign countenance and tranquil disposition, sought to reassure
me. "Keep an open mind," he counselled; "it probably won't be
half as bad as you think." Lurching over the flimsy weed-grown
trackage down a corridor walled by impenetrable thickets and
subtropical jungle, we whistled grandly past a few rustic hamlets
that seemed forlorn ghosts of a far more prosperous past—Arran,
Ashmore, Sopchoppy—and at length rumbled over a watercourse
known as the Ochlockonee River and tidal swamps at the head of
Ochlockonee Bay. As the sun sank to the horizon, the sparkling
waters of the Gulf itself came into view until obscured by blocks of
green tar-paper-sheathed single-story barracks resembling poultry
barns or the shacks of the compounds housing road-gang felons
back home in North Carolina. We shuddered to a stop at Lanark,
a village of some 250 souls (in peacetime), now the nucleus of one
of several sprawling military cantonements strung along U.S.
Highway 98 which linked Tallahassee with the port of Carrabelle
just to our west and the coastal towns of Appalachicola, Panama
City, and Pensacola beyond.[12] As we gathered up our gear
preparatory to detraining, the car commander bellowed, "Welcome
to Camp Gordon Johnston, boys! Anyone who goes overseas from
here is a coward." With Lonnie's admonition echoing in my brain
(and calling to mind Mark Twain's pithy assessment of Richard
Wagner's music, "It's not as bad as it sounds"), I resolutely
shouldered my barracks bags and stepped warily onto this strange
soil.

III

THE MISBEGOTTEN SEAHORSE SOLDIERS

Camp Gordon Johnston had been conceived in haste, controversy, and confusion. Its raison d'etre was the urgent imperative to gear up for a style of warfare with which America's military establishment was painfully unfamiliar. It was, in fact, a visual testimony to a tangle of short-lived compromises at the highest command levels to resolve the thorny issue of how amphibious operations—or, to use British terminology, Combined Operations—were to be conducted, whether the Army or the Navy should control them, and exactly where in the process lines should be drawn to safeguard the respective provinces of the two main branches of the Armed Services.

Amphibious assaults have figured in military campaigning for thousands of years. Always complicated and risky, they have become more hazard-prone with every advance in weapons technology. The ill-fated British invasion of Gallipoli in 1915-16, aborted after heavy losses, affords a classic example of the catastrophic consequences of undertaking amphibious expeditions without painstaking preparation, systematic prosecution, and appropriate equipment.

Prior to World War II, the U.S. Army and Navy had overlapping responsibilities in the transoceanic movement of expeditionary forces and their landing on enemy-held shores. Traditionally, both services had scrupulously conformed to a general policy that neither would "attempt to restrict in any way the means and weapons used by the other service in carrying out its own functions." The Army would furnish all vessels necessary for its own transport and sustenance ashore, "except when naval opposition by the enemy is to be expected, in which case they are to be provided and operated by the Navy."[1] Accordingly, when the U.S. declared war on Japan, the Army's Transportation Corps owned (or leased) and worked a fleet of troop transports and cargo ships substantially larger than that of the Navy, whose modest flotilla of vessels dedicated to amphibious operations sufficed only for the accomodation of its own small Corps of Marines (limited by law to 20% of the Navy's total personnel complement and numbering in 1940 a mere 65,000 officers and men.) It was presumed that in any future landings by Army formations on enemy-held shores, naval personnel would man whatever shallow-draft boats, or "lighters," were to be employed in lifting the troops, equipment, and supplies from ocean-going vessels to the edge of the beach. After the collapse of France, when the whole continent of Europe had fallen under Axis domination, it was self-evident that its reconquest would involve ferrying vast numbers of troops across the English Channel or the Mediterranean Sea and putting them ashore in the face of a thoroughly-fortified, battle-hardened, and expectant enemy.

On our Pacific Ocean flank, the Navy had for decades anticipated that Japan's defeat would require a progressive seizure of her island holdings in the Central Pacific to secure advanced bases before a knockout blow upon her homeland could be inflicted. A plan known as *ORANGE* had been devised with this eventuality in mind, and as early as 1933 a Fleet Marine Force instituted; soon thereafter, the Marine Corps had published a ground-breaking tactical manual of landing operation, followed by a formal *Landing Operations Doctrine* in 1938. As relations between the U.S. and Nippon deteriorated with each fresh act of Japanese aggression in China, the Marines began to practice amphibious warfare in earnest, while new prototypes of landing barges and amphibious vehicles were evolved in concert with the ship-building and automotive industries.

Despite these proactive efforts, however, in the hectic aftermath of Japan's attack on Pearl Harbor, the Navy found itself distressingly undermanned and underequipped to initiate amphibious or "joint" operations [the terminology preferred by the American military] on the scale which would be demanded the moment the Allies went over to the offensive. Island-hopping across the Pacific would not only entail a succession of long-range expeditions, but innumerable movements of lesser scope over shorter distances and shallower waters. In light of these considerations, American tactical planners began to draw a distinction between landings that would be "ship-to-shore" and those that would be "shore-to-shore." In the latter mode, troops would embark in the same small shallow-draft boats or "lighters" from which they would be disgorged onto the hostile beaches. But for either modality, an acute shortage of specialized landing craft and of experienced seamen to crew them had to be addressed without delay.[2]

Outfitting new attack transports with adequate quantities of on-board beaching lighters for ship-to-shore assaults while simultaneously equipping independent amphibious units for the extensive shore-to-shore campaigning contemplated, to say nothing of finding or training the legions of small-boat specialists to operate and maintain them, was simply beyond the capability of the hard-pressed Navy in the first half of 1942. Not only did the naval arm have its hands full fending off the Nazi submarines rampaging all across the Atlantic, but it was struggling to rebuild the capital ship fleet so badly crippled at Pearl Harbor.

Army planners, for their part, had little, if any, experience in amphibious warfare to draw on, aside from a few relatively minor operations such as the seaborne assaults by Federal forces on Confederate Fort Fisher, guarding Wilmington, North Carolina, in December 1864-January 1865, or the landings near Santiago, Cuba, during the Spanish-American War. In the first World War, Gen. John J. Pershing's AEF had disembarked on friendly shores at established ports, encountering enemy opposition only when it was well into the interior.

The British, haunted by the memory of Gallipoli and reeling from their recent humiliating setbacks in Southeast Asia at the hands of Japanese invaders employing imaginative amphibious tactics and innovative beaching craft, were particularly sensitized to the need for more specialized landing vessels and procedures. As a result, their preparation for joint operations was considerably more advanced than ours, though they were severely constrained by the limited capabilities of their domestic industrial infrastructure.

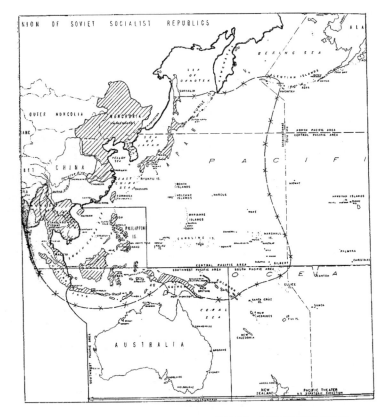

MAP 1. MAXIMUM EXTENT OF JAPANESE HOLDINGS, 6 AUGUST 1942 (CROSS-HATCHED LINE) AND ALLIED AREA BOUNDARIES IN THE ASIATIC-PACIFIC.

While Roosevelt and Churchill had already agreed that an offensive in Europe would take precedence over any major move against Japan, infighting between the War and Navy departments immediately erupted over the fundamental priorities which should govern strategic moves in the Pacific. The controversy centered around the allocation of the sparse resources available for that theatre and the sequence of objectives. In late March 1942, the Joint Chiefs-of-Staff reached a momentous decision to separate the Asiatic-Pacific Theatre into a Southwest Pacific Area/Command under Gen. Douglas MacArthur and a Pacific Ocean Areas/Command under Adm. Chester Nimitz. MacArthur's army and its adjunctive naval arm, the Seventh Fleet, were to battle northward from Australia, while the naval and ground forces under Nimitz would thrust westward from Hawaii.[3] The Navy's top brass, especially Adm. Ernest J. King, Chief of Naval Operations as of March 1942, were by no means resigned to yielding their service's time-honored prerogative of exclusive control over the waterborne phase of all amphibious assaults (i.e., to the edge of dry land), but reluctantly conceded that for the time being they had no recourse other than to hand over to the Army the responsibility for a crash program of training crews for short-distance shore-to-shore operations. This was emphatically a temporary retreat on the Navy's part to buy time for American ship-builders to step up production and for Congress to rescind the legislation restricting Navy recruitment to voluntary enlistments rather than draftees. Pursuant to this concession, the Joint Chiefs of Staff, in the early spring of 1942, relegated the responsibility for an expedited and expanded shore-to-shore amphibious-training enterprise to the Army, specifically, to the Corps of Engineers, on the theory that moving troops across short stretches of salt water was more or less the same as ferrying them across rivers, a chore in which Army engineers were well-practiced. In fact, a couple of imaginative engineer officers, Colonels Daniel Noce and Arthur Trudeau, were seeking authorization to form special units of amphibian engineers for that task.[4]

Having made a careful study of the pre-war landing maneuvers conducted by the Marines, Noce and Trudeau noted that not only had there been persistent foul-ups in small-boat handling, but malfunctioning of beachhead complexes once the "invaders" and their equipment and supplies had been put ashore. They attributed the latter to a lack of properly trained "shore parties," i.e., teams skilled in the techniques of unloading the landing vessels and getting troops and supplies across the beaches. The engineer analysts also stressed that efficient insertion of men and materiel on the "far" or hostile shore was predicated upon carefully-planned-and-executed stowage on the "near" or friendly shore, i.e., at the point of embarkation. The novel amphibian engineer units Noce and Trudeau conceptualized should include, then, not only seasoned small-boatmen, but expert shore-party specialists as well. The mission of the shore-party teams would be a critically important one, especially during those harrowing early hours of an invasion when the assailants would have only a precarious lodgement on a thin strip of bare sand, exposed to heavy fire from defenders holding all the advantages. A recent series of joint landing exercises held in late 1941 at New River, North Carolina, by the 1st Marine Division and the 1st Army Division, had been executed sloppily, demonstrating continuing inadequacies and underscoring the conclusions registered by Noce and Trudeau. The High Command was now convinced that no further time should be lost in taking remedial measures.[5]

Like Caesar's Gaul, the administrative structure of the Army at that juncture was divided into three parts: The Army Ground Forces [AGF], embracing all combat troops; the Services of Supply [SOS]—soon to be renamed the Army Service Forces [ASF]—comprising all support troops or rear-area service personnel; and the Army Air Forces [AAF], including all airmen and their ground support auxiliaries. The Corps of Engineers had traditionally been subsumed under SOS/ASF. But under which of the first two agencies should the proposed amphibious engineer formations be placed? As combat specialists, were they to be classified as combat troops or as support troops? Once again, there was resort to a temporizing compromise. The ASF's Corps of Engineers was directed to create a new entity, the Engineer Amphibian Command [EAC], to organize, equip, and train the amphibian units, while AGF would inaugurate a parallel mechanism, the Amphibious Training Command/Center [ATC], to conduct the Joint Operations training program. This arrangement still provided no clearly defined niche for the amphibian engineers, who eventually were simply declared "combat support" troops, to be armed and trained to fight as infantry and attached to an AGF formation for designated combat operations, but as technical specialists to remain administratively accountable to ASF. Thus, from their inception, the Army amphibs were condemned to occupy an ambiguous niche, evoking universal unease, like illegitimate children at a family reunion.[6]

Pursuant to this not-very-artful dodge, the Army Ground Forces were ordered to pick a suitable site somewhere along the nation's southern coast for a year-round amphibious training base. Pending that decision, a hasty survey was made of every extant ocean-front Army installation which might temporarily accomodate the start-up of the program. A vacant antiaircraft artillery post, Camp Edwards, at Falmouth, Massachusetts, on Cape Cod, seemed the most readily adaptible for that purpose, and was quickly preempted. There the Engineer Amphibian Command, with Noce, former head of the Corps' Memphis District (1937-40), in command and Trudeau as Chief-of-Staff, was activated on 10 June 1942, two months after Maj. Gen. Jonathan Wainwright's surrender of the American and Filipino forces at Corregidor in the Philippines. A sector of Cape Cod's south shore east of Buzzard's Bay afforded a prime locale for amphibious exercises with its convenient beaches, ample docking and boat-maintenance facilities, and proximity to Camp Edwards. Washburn Island in Wacquoit Bay was leased for landing practice, augmented by a stretch of beach along Cotuit Bay. The Falmouth Marine Railway and other boat-maintenance installations at Osterville were requisitioned, along with the Tower Hotel at Falmouth Heights and the Wacquoit Yacht Club. As soon as some new channels were dredged, camp sites levelled, and additional roads, piers, and structures built, the AGF's Amphibious Training Center, under Brig. Gen. Frank A. Keating, got underway (15 June 1942.)[7]

Noce and Keating had been handed truly formidable assignments, since the EAC and ATC were compelled to function within an extremely compressed time-frame. The InterAllied

European Theatre planners in London, under intense pressure from the desperately-embattled Russians to open a second front quickly and draw off as many of Hitler's hordes as possible from their beleaguered homeland, were contemplating an invasion of France at the earliest practicable moment, perhaps even in 1942, but certainly in 1943, lest the Soviet Union collapse. Consequently, the ATC was mandated to provide amphibious training for twelve infantry divisions in succession, beginning no later than 15 July 1942 and concluding by 1 February 1943. This meant that the EAC would have only five weeks to assemble and whip into shape the first of the projected amphibian engineer formations charged with supporting the infantry divisions which were to rotate sequentially through the ATC course. Concurrently, EAC was charged with assisting and stimulating research-and-development efforts already underway to design and produce improved types of landing craft and equipment, and to devise techniques for loading and landing troops, equipment, and supplies efficiently, and moving them swiftly across the beaches.[8]

It seems to have been taken for granted at the supreme command levels that the looming cross-Channel invasion, involving a relatively short hop from Britain, would be a shore-to-shore enterprise, involving small landing craft, since so many of the British Expeditionary Force troops hastily evacuated from Dunkirk in 1940 had been sea-lifted home on small vessels of all types. On the other hand, American naval and Marine Corps tacticians, addressing themselves to the future offensive operations in the Pacific Theatre, under the assumption that these would be the exclusive prerogative of the Navy, based their plans on a ship-to-shore modality. Given these disparate expectations of the role of amphibian specialists, the Army amphibs were presumably to be employed in Europe for the most part, leaving the heavy work against the Japanese exclusively to the Navy and Marines of Admiral Chester W. Nimitz's Pacific Fleet. Whatever amphibious endeavors Gen. MacArthur might choose to pursue in his Southwest Pacific sideshow, in the Navy's assessment, was an altogether secondary consideration, involving only the Seventh Fleet. Fate would soon turn these assumptions topsy turvy.

At Camp Edwards, the Engineer Amphibian Command attacked its daunting task with prodigious energy. As its basic troop instrumentality it opted for a brigade-sized unit to be known as an Engineer Amphibian Brigade [EAB], numbering 7,282 officers and men, with the capability of landing and supporting one infantry division. Each EAB would contain two large regiments, one of small-boat operators and one of shore-party specialists, together with a boat-maintenance battalion and other ancillary units of medical, ordnance, signal, and quartermaster troops. Twelve such brigades were projected, one for each of the infantry divisions tentatively slated for the cross-Channel invasion.[9] To fill the ranks of these brigades, EAC scanned the personnel records of hundreds of thousands of soldiers to identify those with small-boat-navigating, marine-engine-maintenance, or cargo-handling experience, and have them transferred, if possible, to Camp Edwards. Advertisements were circulated to lure civilian harbor-craft watermen, yachtsmen, fishermen, stevedores, and small-boat-repairmen into the amphibs. British officers with Combined Operations expertise were seconded to the EAC, along with U.S. Navy and Coast Guard officers, to serve as instructors. Newly-commissioned graduates of Officer Candidate Schools and ROTC programs were brought in to fill the remaining comissioned officer slots. In short order, a colorful assortment of "web-foot" soldiery was assembled and oriented, and from their ranks emerged the First Engineer Amphibian Brigade, formally activated on 15 June 1942, followed five days later by a second. Both were immediately subjected to a gruelling regimen of on-the-job training.[10]

For identifying insignia, the amphibs were issued shoulder patches duplicating those worn by British Combined Operations personnel—including the intrepid Commandos—though of a different color scheme. Designed by Lord Louis Montbatten, the patch depicted a spread-winged eagle and a tommy gun atop an anchor whose shape suggested the triple-towered castle emblematic of the Corps of Engineers. The U.S. Amphibian device was executed in gold thread upon a deep-blue backing. Not to be outdone, the Navy's amphibs soon adopted the same insignia, but in gold upon scarlet. To further distinguish its troops, EAC also distributed a patch of its own design, featuring a red seahorse on a white oval bordered in blue, to be worn on the breast pocket of their tunics. Included in each amphibian soldier's clothing issue were two pairs of brown leather paratroop boots for surer footing and added protection in surf and sand, together with a set of water-repellant outerwear—pants and hooded parka—to shield the wearer from wind and spray while afloat.[11]

In addition to the soldiering basics, the men in the boat regiments of the two initial brigades had to hastily learn the duties of coxswains, enginemen, signallers, and deckmen, such as steering their craft in simple formation in daylight and darkness, maintaining position in landing waves, grounding their boats and holding them in place at the water's edge, and retracting. Simultaneously, their shore-party counterparts were introduced to the techniques of demolition, rigging, road-building, bridging, and general construction, along with cargo-loading-and-discharge, and beachead operation. The 1st EAB had a scant four weeks to get its act together before the 45th Infantry Division was to descend upon the Cape to be trained for amphibious operations. Scarcity of watercraft quickly proved such an intractible problem that the Army General Staff was compelled to slash summarily the number of divisions targetted for joint training from twelve to eight.

Day and night, the hard-pressed seahorsemen drove their boats through the waters off Cape Cod, hitting the sands repetitively on the nearby islands of Nantucket and Martha's Vineyard as well as on the Cape itself.[12] At the outset they had to employ whatever watercraft were available, including three less-than-satisfactory types designed by the Navy's Bureau of Ships: the LCP(L) [Landing Craft, Personnel, Large], which had no ramp, compelling its passengers to jump down into the surf from its bow and sides; the smaller LCP(R) [Landing Craft, Personnel, Ramped], whose ramp was too narrow for rapid exit; and the broader-ramped LCV [Landing Craft, Vehicle], designed to carry only one light truck or bulk cargo. These were eventually displaced by two superior models of invasion lighter, both developed in consultation with the ingenious New Orleans boat-designer and manufacturer Andrew J. Higgins, who had created a prototype as early as l939. The first of the two pioneered by Higgins was the LCVP [Landing Craft, Vehicle/Personnel], combining the best features of the LCP(R) and the LCV. It was a light-weight wooden 36-ft. barge with a full-width bow ramp, a beam of l0'6", and a single drive-shaft and screw, powered by a 250-hp. gasoline engine. Reaching a top speed of 11 knots, the LCVP, or "Higgins Boat," as it was popularly called, was steered by a small horizontally-mounted wheel, and could transport either 36 fully-laden soldiers, 4 tons of cargo, a light truck, or a couple of jeeps. LCVP's were eventually repowered with 225-hp. marine diesels to reduce the risk of explosions under shell-fire, and retrofitted with a thin layer of 1/4-in. armor plate on the bows and sides. Higgins' second innovation, the LCM [Landing Craft, Mechanized], followed soon thereafter. A more versatile and seaworthy steel-hulled lighter, larger and hardier than the LCVP, it was 50 ft. long and l4 ft. wide. Propelled by twin diesel engines and screws, the LCM could attain l0 knots, and haul either 60 men, l8 tons of cargo, a tank, a couple of trucks, or several jeeps. Its distinguishing visual characteristics were a wide, flaring, grilled bow ramp and, at its stern, a square wheelhouse for the coxswain's protection. (After EAC's researchers found that the addition of a mere six feet to the length of the original-model LCM would increase its cargo capacity by 25%, a newer 56-ft. version eventually became normative.) The LCVP's and LCM's, normally crewed by three men, a coxswain, an engineman, and a deckman/bow-hookman, soon displaced their inefficient predecessors as the basic watercraft utilized by EAB's. The wooden LCVP's were the first to be produced en masse, but at the time of activation of the first two EAB's, neither type could be supplied in the vast numbers needed. Once the heftier and hardier LCM's were forthcoming in sufficient volume, they would become the mainstay of the Army amphibs in the Southwest Pacific.

Emerging from the assembly lines of auto manufacturers at

the same time were three novel amphibious vehicles: DUKW's, Amphibious Jeeps, and LVT's. The DUKW, or "Duck," was a scow-shaped bouyant 2.5-ton 6 X 6 truck, with a small propellor and rudder at the stern, which could be driven with equal ease across land or water. Capable of a road speed of 50 mph, it was superbly adapted to hauling troops and materiel from deep-draft ships across relatively calm waters to nearby inland destinations, eliminating the necessity for unloading and reloading at the shoreline. The DUKW had a 5,000-lb. payload and enough space for 25 men and their gear. The Duck and its little brother, a 1/4-ton floating jeep resembling a bathtub on four wheels, jocularly called a "Peep," proved to be wondrously versatile harborcraft, and were extensively utilized by the amphibs. A third equally-handy seagoing motor vehicle was the LVT [Landing Vehicle, Tracked], developed by the Marine Corps. Dubbed "Amphtracs" [or Amtracs], "Buffaloes," or "Alligators," these were essentially bouyant open-top tanks. About 26 ft. in length, they could not only churn across water, but climb over rocks, reefs, and dunes, or plow through swamps. Ubiquitously employed by the Marines, no LVT's were initially allocated to the Army amphibs, though some would be acquired later in the war.[13]

A fully-equipped Engineer Amphibian Brigade was authorized 270 LCVP's and a like number of LCM's, 36 DUKW's, 21 utility power boats, 32 command boats, and 51 patrol and fire-and-salvage boats. Until American boat builders could be tooled up to supply such staggering requisitions, the EAB's had to make do with whatever watercraft could be diverted from the Navy or Coast Guard. Once full levels of production had been achieved, however, entire trainloads of LCVP's, propped sideways on flatcars, were consigned to Falmouth's railway station, from which they were trucked to the inner harbor. The wooden Higgins Boats arrived for weeks in a steady stream, at a rate of 32 a day, six days a week, while the larger LCM's, in their turn, were usually delivered to the Cape by water.[14]

Concurrently, under naval auspices, an assortment of commodious transoceanic amphibious vessels, designed in concert with the British, were being fabricated in the U.S., and would eventually play a major role in joint warfare in all theatres of war. Among these, in descending order of magnitude, was the LSD [Landing Ship, Dock], a stern-gated 5,000-ton behemoth, 458 ft. in length with a beam of 72 ft., and a speed of 15 knots. Essentially a powered floating dry-dock, it had berthing and mess accomodations for hundreds of troops, was armed with 5-inch guns, and could tote scores of LCVP's, LCM's, or LVT's in its belly for off-shore launching.

A more universally-employed long-range vessel, smaller than the LSD and designed for beaching, was the LST [Landing Ship, Tank], 50 ft. in width and varying from 328 to 336 ft. from bow to stern. Approximately the size of a destroyer, and displacing some 1,600 tons, the LST had a hinged ramp together with a pair of huge doors or gates at its bow. Its bridge/superstructure, engines, crew quarters, and troop accomodations were located aft. Often carrying a half-dozen LCVP's or LCM's suspended from its davits, the LST was equipped with enough folding bunks and sanitary and galley facilities to transport substantial numbers of soldiers and their equipment over long distances. Thirteen medium tanks, 20 light tanks, or dozens of jeeps, trucks, and artillery pieces could fit into its cavernous tank deck and on its open top deck (with an elevator connecting the two), from which they could be driven directly onto the beach. An LST could even carry railway locomotives and rolling stock on portable tracks secured to the floor of its tank deck. Powered by twin engines and cruising at 10 knots, with a flat bottom and a draft of some 14 feet fully loaded, an LST could beach itself at low tide and float off, or retract, at high tide. It soon acquired the nicknames "Large Slow Target" or "Long Slow Trip." American shipyards at inland river ports such as Pittsburgh, Pa., Seneca, Ill., and Evansville and Jeffersonville, Indiana, would eventually be turning them out by the thousands, and I myself was to make a couple of lengthy voyages aboard them.[15]

Of smaller dimensions and lighter draft, but no less capable of cross-seas voyaging, were the LCI's [Landing Craft, Infantry], dubbed "Elsieitems" by their passengers and crewmen. These exceptionally narrow ships, 157 ft. by 24 ft., had messing and toilet facilities and sleeping accomodations for 183 soldiers in addition to quarters for their 25-man crews. From a distance, the profile of an LCI, with its prominent cylindrical midship conning-tower and cutaway stern, resembled that of a surfaced submarine. A pair of gangways carried on each side of its bow section were shoved forward and dropped when its flat-bottomed hull grounded on the beach. (At a later stage, some Elsieitems were stripped of their gangway-fittings and equipped with rocket-launchers for close-in fire-support on landings.)

A final exemplar of the more capacious vessels designed for amphibious warfare (and by all odds the ugliest duckling of the lot), was the LCT [Landing Craft, Tank.] Grotesquely wide and flat, and normally transported over long stretches of ocean in an LSD's well deck or on the weather deck of an LST, it was the smallest of the beaching craft—or the largest of the open-deck, bow-ramp landing barges, as you will—ll4 ft. in length and 32 ft. in width. An LCT could hold a dozen or so tanks or wheeled vehicles, and reach a speed of l0 knots. Its crew of 2 officers and l0 men sheltered in a boxy superstructure at the stern or along the flanks of its afterdeck. Army amphibs had hoped to get their hands on some LCT's for shore-to-shore work, but were rebuffed by the Navy, who laid exclusive claim to all the bigger beaching vessels.[16]

As the seahorse novitiates on Cape Cod resolutely set about learning their trade with their sparse stock of lighters, there was inevitably a high incidence of mechanical breakdowns resulting from constant use and unavoidably-deferred maintenance. A modicum of order was beginning to emerge from the early chaos when, only one month into the forced-draft training regimen, word came down from higher echelons that Fleet Admiral Ernest J. King had announced that it was the Navy's intention to take over the entire amphibious enterprise, lock, stock, and barrel, the moment it was in a position to do so. (Gen. Dwight Eisenhower, now heading the American Forces in the European theatre, had already yielded to Navy pressure by ruling that the Navy alone would thereafter man all watercraft in any joint operations undertaken within his domain.) Brig. Gen. Clarence

L. Sturdevant, Assistant Chief of the Corps of Engineers, promptly sought a clarification of EAC's future status from the Army's High Command, and was informed in mid-July that only four rather than the previously-authorized eight Engineer Amphibian brigades would henceforth be needed. In other words, only two additional brigades were to be activated.

At the same time, and just as it was commencing its joint exercizes with the 45th Infantry Division, Col. Henry C. Wolfe's 1st EAB was alerted for movement overseas to Britain "on an emergency basis." After a rather frantic embarkation from Boston in early August, and while still at sea bound for a Scottish port, the brigade learned that InterAllied headquarters in London had decided to abort any attempts to mount a cross-Channel invasion in 1942. Instead, a ship-to-shore invasion of North Africa was to be mounted, with the Navy providing all landing craft and crews. Since this revision in strategy precluded any need for 1st EAB's boat elements, soon after its disembarkation in Britain, the boat regiment was disbanded and its hapless personnel reassigned to other organizations in that theatre. The mission of Wolfe's remaining units would be confined solely to shore-party or general engineer functions in the projected campaigning in North Africa, Sicily, and Italy (and, eventually, Normandy.)[17]

In Massachusetts, meanwhile, Col. William F. Heavey's 2d EAB, still understrength and with a scant four weeks of training under its belt, assumed the responsibilities of Wolfe's brigade in joint exercises with the 45th Infantry Division. On 8 August 1942, shortly after 1st EAB's precipitate exit to Britain, a third EAB had been activated at Camp Edwards, its command vested in Col. David A. D. Ogden. Ogden's webfeet managed to squeeze in three months' training before taking on scheduled maneuvers with an infantry division.

As if the bewildering revisions in European theatre requirements were not sufficiently disruptive to the planning and functioning of the harrassed Engineer Amphibian Command, it was dealt a further one-two punch in the form of orders transferring a large contingent of 2d EAB's shore personnel to Britain to beef up the forces being assembled for the North African invasion. This obliged Ogden's 3d EAB, in turn, to detach many of its shoremen to replenish Heavey's depleted ranks. These abrupt dislocations inevitably compromised the efficiency and morale of all the seahorse units. Not unpredictably, the final 2d EAB/45th Inf. Div. joint exercise miscarried when several waves of boats lost their bearings in the pre-dawn darkness and failed to land at the prescribed place and time. The boatmen of the 2d learned from their mistakes, however, and in September, on their concluding maneuver with the next infantry cohorts rotating through the Amphibious Training Center (36th Division and a battalion of Rangers), Heavey's boys performed flawlessly.[18]

After some four months' trial, EAC concluded that the basic two-regiment configuration of the amphibian brigades was too cumbersome and that they should be reshaped, not only for greater flexibility, but to conform to the recently-introduced "triangular" format of the standard infantry division (now having three regiments, each with three 900-man battalions, or 8,100 combat troops, plus 6,000 support personnel, for a total divisional strength of 14,100.) Congruently, the restructured amphibian brigade would henceforth comprise, in addition to its headquarters and headquarters company and companies of quartermaster, ordnance, and signal troops, three so-called "boat-and-shore regiments" (each having one boat battalion and a matching shore battalion), along with a boat-maintenance battalion and a medical battalion. Under the new dispensation, an EAB's authorized complement (with some slight subsequent revisions) would henceforth number 7,340 officers and men, or 2,023 in each of its three regiments. A regimental boat battalion would embrace 1,079, and its shore battalion, 704, each including a headquarters company and three line companies (designated A, B, and C if a boat battalion, and D, E, and F if a shore battalion.)

From the outset of the whole EAC/ATC project, it had been recognized that the Cape Cod sites would no longer be viable for amphibious maneuvers after November, given the severity of the winter weather and resultant high seas at that latitude. Accordingly, the Corps of Engineers, having considered several alternative locations farther south on the East Coast for year-round amphibious training, had selected an area adjoining the Gulf Coast town of Carrabelle in Franklin County, Florida, as the most feasible permanent home for the ATC, and was proceeding at top speed with its development.

On the other side of the globe, in Brisbane, Australia, Gen. Douglas MacArthur, contemplating his strategic options for rolling back the Japanese, and harboring no great love for the Navy, had discerned the potential value of the Army amphibian brigades in moving his forces and supplies through the uncharted, shallow, reef-choked waterways fringing New Guinea and its adjacent islands. In September he requested that an EAB be assigned to his command. There was one overriding obstacle to its deployment, however. The modest fleet of freighters available for trans-Pacific carriage at that juncture had no deck space to spare for the hundreds of LCVP's and LCM's requisite for EAB operations. Every square foot of deck capacity was preempted by the aircraft so desperately needed to neutralize Japanese air superiority in the Southwest Pacific. Grappling with this dilemma, the indefatigable Colonel Trudeau and his civilian colleagues at the Higgins plant in New Orleans put their heads together and devised a clever solution. Why not ship the wooden LCVP's in prefabricated sections, "knocked-down," as it were, in the cargo holds of the freighters, thus preserving the deck space for planes? Several hundred barges could be transported on a single Liberty ship in this manner. Similarly, the larger steel-hulled LCM's could be cut into sections for convenient transoceanic shipment. Upon delivery overseas, both types could be reassembled at a local boat plant. (Actually, the Navy had fleetingly entertained the same notion, but had discarded the idea in light of Australia's deplorably primitive boat-building facilities, which were altogether inadequate for a reassembly enterprise on such a massive scale.)

The EAC brass thoroughly fine-tuned the concept, calculating that its own highly-experienced boat-maintenance specialists could manage the reassembly chore, if only authorization were forthcoming. Having secured the blessing of the Pentagon, an EAC envoy headed by Trudeau flew out in early November 1942 to SWPA Headquarters in Brisbane to present the project to MacArthur. Trudeau had no trouble winning the Area Commander's acquiescence, and promptly set about finding a feasible location along the northern stretch of Australia's east coast for a barge assembly plant. Although a site was procured for the project at Cairns, on the Coral Sea, he was unable to obtain a convenient bivouac area for an EAB, and was forced to settle for a reservation at Rockhampton, 600 miles south of Cairns. All in all, however, Trudeau's mission had been a resounding success, and he and his associates returned home triumphantly. Thanks to their resourcefulness and persuasiveness, the War Department was prevailed upon by SWPA Headquarters not only to forward an EAB forthwith, but to commit another two in the bargain, thereby rescuing the EAC and its creations from further emasculation, if not oblivion, at the jealous hands of the Navy.[19]

Paradoxically, the hastily-contrived Army amphibian formations (with the sole exception of the mutilated 1st EAB), originally intended for mounting shore-to-shore assaults on the European continent, were now to fight their war exclusively in the Southwest Pacific, while the Navy's newly-emergent 'phibs, with their ever-growing ship-to-shore capabilities, would handle all European Theatre joint operations, as well as those in Nimitz's pending westward offensive across the Central Pacific.[20]

IV

ALCATRAZ-BY-THE-SEA

The County of Franklin was one of Florida's poorest and least-developed, having less than 6,000 inhabitants in 1940. Its 545 square miles of tangled forests and tidal swamps offered plenty of empty real estate for the EAC/ATC's purposes. The region's economic fortunes had peaked in the 1920's with the flourishing of its timber industry, only to suffer a precipitous decline in the following decade. Franklin's largest town and seat of government, Apalachicola, home to about half the county's populace, was a mouldering relic of what had a century before been one of the Gulf Coast's busiest cotton-shipping ports, rivalling New Orleans and Mobile. Apalachicola Bay, however, was one of the nation's richest repositories of shellfish, though its yields were becoming endangered by pollutants from nearby pulpwood mills. The only other settlement of note within the county was Carrabelle, a ramshackle little fishing village of some 970 souls, most of whom eked out a marginal living by net-fishing and marketing the mullet and other seafood with which the adjoining waterways abounded, or by catering to deep-sea sports fishermen. A couple of narrow, uninhabited barrier islands, St. George's and Dog Islands, lay two or three miles offshore, affording long stretches of undeveloped beachfront whereon the seahorse soldiers could practice their landings with little or no civilian surveillance or interference. Similarly, the empty wilderness in the interior of the mainland lent itself readily to tactical maneuvering and jungle warfare exercises.

The War Department negotiated a lease on a 165,000-acre tract in the southern half of the county, owned principally by the

St. Joe Paper Company, part of the empire of canny Edward Ball of Jacksonville, the economic and political czar of North Florida. Brother to Jessie Ball DuPont, widow of Alfred Irenee DuPont of the Delaware gunpowder/chemical dynasty, Ball, as the trustee of DuPont's enormous estate, controlled hundreds of thousands of acres in Florida's panhandle, along with the Florida East Coast Railway and scores of banks, sugar refineries, and pulp mills.[1]

The mainland portion of the future military reservation was actually an island itself, known as St. James's, shaped rather like a flattened obtuse triangle. With Carrabelle at its southwestern tip, the base of the triangle extended eastward for twenty-one miles along the Gulf shore, with its northwestern and northeastern boundaries defined respectively by the aptly-named Crooked River and the Ochlockonee River and estuary into which the latter drained. The reservation's sole link with the outside world, aside from the SAL branchline from Tallahassee, was U.S. Highway 319, which ran along a portion of the shoreline, connecting Tallahassee with Panama City and Pensacola to the west through the Franklin County settlements of Lanark, Carrabelle, and Apalachicola. Florida Rte. 110 (present-day U.S. Highway 98) diverged from U.S. 319 at the hamlet of Medart, made a 17-mile southerly loop, crossed Ochlockonee Bay, and rejoined the federal highway about five miles east of Lanark. The only clusters of habitation, by and large, were to be found along these arteries. The lesser of the two offshore barrier islands, Dog Island, lay opposite Carrabelle and the hamlet of Lanark to its east, while the more extensive St. George's Island shielded Apalachicola and enclosed its bay at the mouth of the Apalachicola River. A channel known as East Pass separated the two islands, giving Carrabelle access to the open Gulf. The shallow body of water separating the mainland from the barrier islands was called St. George Sound.

If not employed as watermen, Carrabelleans provided guide services, dogs, and outfitting for game hunters venturing into a forbidding wilderness a few miles northwest of the town limits known as Tate's Hell Swamp, where wild deer, turkeys, wildcats, black bears, and razor-back hogs freely foraged. Alligators infested

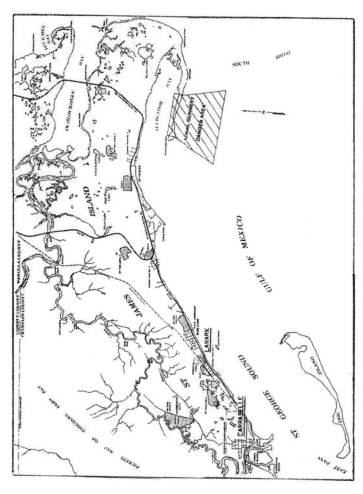

MAP 2. CAMP GORDON JOHNSTON, FRANKLIN COUNTY, FLORIDA, 1943–44.

the swamplands, and the area abounded with reptiles, including venemous cottonmouth moccasins, rattlers, and deadly little coral snakes. Inland from the narrow fringe of human habitation along the shore, Franklin County's acreage was blanketted by long-leaf and slash pines, cypress, and gum trees, with a ground cover of titi and saw palmettos. The terrain was low-lying and virtually flat, sloping almost imperceptably up from the edge of the shoreline.[2]

Surveyors employed by the Corps of Engineers staked out the military reservation in a record-setting twenty-one days, and on 8 July 1942, teams of laborers began slashing away at the jungle with machetes and bush axes to clear five tracts designated as "special training areas," one of which surrounded an abandoned lumber camp called Harbeson City, three miles north of Carrabelle. The Harbeson ruins were to be resurrected as a mock enemy village for simulated door-to-door combat. Most of the interior wilds were left undisturbed except for an occasional track cut through the bush for training hikes and field maneuvers. The two offshore islands were kept in their natural state for landing exercises. Troop cantonements were erected at three widely separated locations along Highway 31, dubbed "combat team sites" 1, 2, and 3 (one for each of an amphibian brigade's boat-and-shore regiments and the corresponding regiment of whatever infantry division with which the brigade happened to be training at the moment.)

The base camp itself, consisting of the post headquarters, hospital, chapel, service club, and an assortment of administrative, storage, and maintenance buildings, was constructed just to the east of Lanark village. Three long parallel piers were erected at right angles from the Lanark waterfront for landing-craft moorage, and boat-fuelling facilities installed. Marine repairs were handled at Carrabelle, four miles to the west of Lanark. All of the cantonement buildings were "of light wood construction, with prefabrication used to a maximum," and painted dark green. The troop quarters were single-story and uninsulated, sheathed in tarpaper and, except for those at the Main Post, devoid of flooring other than duckboards running down the aisles, with double-deck bunks resting atop the sandy soil. No inside latrines were provided, nor seating in the mess-halls—meals were consumed out of the diners' own messkits while standing at waist-high trestle tables. Messkits and utensils were cleansed by immersion—and scrubbing with a long-handled brush—in a garbage-can of sudsy water atop a portable stove, then rinsed successively in two cans of clear boiling water. In short, the facilities were about as primitive as could be devised, the rationale being that such a crude habitation would replicate the conditions to be encountered in the war zone, and the sooner the troops became inured to it, the better.[3]

The builders were still hammering and sawing away at the summer's end of 1942 when the initial cadres of headquarters, military police, and medical personnel from Ft. Rucker, Alabama, rolled in, appropriating the Lanark Hotel for a temporary post headquarters. On 10 September, the "Camp Carrabelle Amphibious Training Command Military Reservation" officially opened. A tidal wave of soldiery soon engulfed Franklin County's drab little communities as the ATC staff and units of the 2d EAB began relocating from Cape Cod to their new posting. At any given time thereafter, as many as 30,000 troops would be stationed in the vicinity.[4]

In early October, the first of several 2EAB echelons clambered off their trains and trucks, and within thirty days, all the brigade's components except for 542d EB&SR had completed the change of station. Some of the landing barges were brought under their own power down the Atlantic coast to Franklin County via the Inland Waterway, but the rest were hauled overland on four special railway trains. Routeing the boat trains to Carrabelle, especially those with cars bearing the 14-ft.-wide LCM's, proved something of a nightmare for the railroaders. Restricted tunnel and bridge clearances and limited tonnage allowances along many of the older northeastern railways precluded the quickest and most direct haulage from Cape Cod. The only solution was to navigate the LCM's down to Weehauken, N. J., where their fuel tanks were drained, engines and hulls blocked, and widths trimmed by a foot-and-a-half, before being propped on their sides atop 52-ft. gondola cars or flatcars. Even so, the trains had to be forwarded over an exceptionally circuitous route through Elmira, Cape Charles, Norfolk, Augusta, Willacoochee, and Dothan.[5]

Heavey's seahorsemen found their new Gulf Coast domicile, with its relative isolation, exotic flora and fauna, and lack of urban amenities, distinctly less palatable than their former Bay State habitat. Not only did the shoremen have to pitch in to complete unfinished roads, buildings, and facilities at the hastily knocked-together installation, but the climate in Florida's panhandle fell appallingly short of the salubrious paradise touted in tourist brochures. The winds in November, December, and January blew predominantly from the frigid mid-continent, and though there were considerably more sunny days than on the New England coast, when rains came, they were typically torrential, and the spells of below-freezing temperature were genuinely bone-chilling due to the high humidity. And there were other vexations; so gradual were the slopes of the beaches and so shallow and strewn with sandbars the camp's environing waters that the boatmen found that their barge propellors abraded rapidly and drive-shafts bent readily, inundating the boat-maintenance crews with extra work.[6]

A revised joint training program was laid out predicated upon the assumption that 2EAB would be stationed at Carrabelle until April 1943. Accordingly, everything was made ready for the arrival from Camp Shelby, Mississippi, of the 38th Infantry Division, a federalized National Guard outfit hailing from Kentucky, Indiana, and West Virginia, booked in from 23 November 1942 until early January 1943.[7] The ATC staff had scarcely completed the paperwork for these exercises when 2EAB was abruptly alerted for shipment to Ft. Ord, California, with an ultimate destination of Australia, as the first of the three brigades to be assigned to MacArthur's Sixth Army, currently positioning itself for a westward offensive up the New Guinea coast. Heavey's seahorsemen were to be preceded overseas by the 411th Base Shop Battalion (still at Cape Cod), charged with getting the projected LCVP-assembly plant at Cairns up and running. The two 2EAB regiments at Carrabelle and the third which had not yet vacated Cape Cod were hastily packed aboard nine troop trains and dispatched to the West Coast, leaving their boats and training plans behind for use by their successors in the ATC enterprise.

As soon as Heavey's rear elements had cleared Camp Carrabelle, Colonel Ogden's 3d Brigade was brought south from Camp Edwards to take up where 2EAB had left off. As had their predecessors, some of Ogden's boatmen brought their organic watercraft southward via the Intracoastal Waterway down the East Coast and around the Florida peninsula, while the remainder of the brigade came by overland transport. All in all, 3EAB's transfer of stations was completed with remarkable celerity, and its only-partially-trained personnel slid as gracefully as they could manage into the shoes—or boots—of their departed colleagues in maneuvers with the shivering infantrymen of the 38th. Upon the conclusion of this round of joint exercises in January 1943, and after a few days' respite, Ogden's amphibs girded up their loins for a reprise with the 28th Division, federalized National Guardsmen from Pennsylvania, led by one of the Army's rapidly-ascending stars, Maj. Gen. Omar Bradley. Upon arrival in Franklin County, Bradley and his wife were appalled to discover that the only suitable lodging to be had anywhere around was a hotel in Wakulla Springs, fifty miles northeast of the base camp! (So closely did the Wakulla Springs boondocks replicate Africa's primeval jungle that Hollywood film makers in the 1930's had shot the scenes for their Johnny Weismuller "Tarzan" movies there.)[8]

With the dawning of the New Year of 1943 had came an announcement from the War Department that the Carrabelle Training Center was to be renamed in honor of a much-decorated old-Army cavalryman, Col. Gordon Johnston (1875-1934). Son of a Confederate general and a native of Charlotte, North Carolina, Johnston, a pioneer footballer during his undergraduate years at Yale, had coached the University of North Carolina team prior to his Army enlistment during the Spanish-American War. The highlights of his military career had included leading troops against Aguinaldo in the course of the 1899 Philippine Insurrection, combat duty in France in World War I, and a stint as special assistant to the Governor-General of the Philippines. Johnston had been serving as Chief-of-Staff of the 2d Infantry Division at Ft. Sam Houston, Texas, when he was fatally injured in a polo match. Though it seems somehow fitting that the home of the seahorse soldiers should bear the name of a veteran horse soldier, one cannot help but wonder how enthusiastically the redoubtable colonel would have welcomed immortalization in such fashion had he himself been posted to Carrabelle.[9] Virtually everyone who ever served there registered a hearty distaste for the place, not least among them Omar Bradley, who remarked in his memoirs,

> Camp Gordon Johnston was the most miserable army installation I had seen since my days in Yuma, Arizona, ages past. It had been hacked out of palmetto scrub along a bleak stretch of beach. We were forced to scatter our three infantry regiments miles apart and thus could never train as a complete division. Every training exercise was a numbing experience. The man who selected that site should have been court-martialed for stupidity.[10]

The popular newspaper columnist Walter Winchell once defamed Camp Gordon Johnston as "the Alcatraz of the Army, the only post where the chaplains went A.W.O.L. [Absent Without Official Leave.]" One disgruntled trainee stationed there habitually wrote as his return address on mailings to his wife, "Carrabelle, Hell-by-the-Sea, Florida."[11]

Bradley's Division, slated for service in the European theatre, was condemned to pass the entire spring of 1943 at GJ, though their commander precipitately—and no doubt thankfully—bade adieu to the place on 17 February upon receipt of unanticipated orders to join Eisenhower's staff (and thereafter assume command of II Corps in the North African operations.) Not until early June would the 28th itself jubilantly move on to its final stateside posting, Camp Pickett, Virginia, preparatory to embarking for England and, eventually, landing at Normandy. In fact, they outlasted their 3d Brigade affiliates at Hell-by-the-Sea by more than a month, for in the latter part of April, Colonel Ogden's units were pulled away to Ft. Ord, California, for ultimate deployment under MacArthur, leaving all of their watercraft behind for the use of their successors.[12]

Meanwhile, the fourth—and last—seahorse brigade had been birthed at Fort Devens, Massachusetts. (While two provisional amphib brigades, the 5th and 6th, would one day be cobbled together in the European Theatre for shore party labors in the future Normandy landings and reconstituted later for the anticipated landings on the Japanese home islands, these were only temporary aggregations, atypical in composition.) Five weeks after 4EAB's activation, the long simmering dispute between the Army and the Navy over the locus of responsibility for Joint Operations training was resolved once and for all by the Joint Chiefs of Staff. A "Memorandum of Agreement" was signed by Chief of Naval Operations Admiral King and Lt. Gen. Joseph T. McNarney (acting for Chief of Staff Gen. George C. Marshall), on 8 March 1943, specifying that

> a. The Army will discontinue all amphibious training activities except as noted in (c) below. The Army will retain responsibility for all training, other than amphibious, of Army units designated to receive training under the Navy.
> b. The Navy will continue amphibious training of boat operating and maintenance personnel to meet future Army requirements of this nature, and also will train at a later date Army replacements for existing amphibian units if this should become necessary. c. The 3d and 4th Engineer Amphibian Brigades (Army), which have been especially organized for shore-to-shore operations in the Southwest Pacific, will be retained under Army control and their training completed by the Army pending their movement to that theatre. d. The control and assignment of amphibian units and amphibious training activities in overseas theatres will be as determined by the theatre commander concerned. e. Upon completion of the training of the 3d and 4th Engineer Amphibian Brigades, the boats, shops, spares, tools, and

other facilities, not part of the organizational equipment of these units, shall be transferred to the Navy when and if required by that Service and the Amphibian Training installations and facilities at Camp Edwards, Massachusetts, and Camp Gordon Johnston, Florida (Carrabelle), will be made available to the Navy for its use. The actual transfer of land is not contemplated.[13]

This document sealed the fates of both the EAC and the ATC. In the interests of interservice harmony, even the nomenclature of the four extant seahorse brigades was altered {at General MacArthur's suggestion} to avoid offending the prickly Navy. An Engineer Amphibian Brigade [EAB] was henceforth to be designated an Engineer Special Brigade [ESB].[14]

Although this sovereign pact sounded the death knell of the Engineer Amphibian Command, and its days were now numbered {its mission would officially be declared fulfilled in December 1943}, one of its last accomplishments proved of signal worth: this was its publication of the only complete set of training manuals for the guidance of amphibian troops to be issued during World War II. These training aids, distilled from EAC's own painfully-acquired empiricism, were of such manifest quality and utility that they were swiftly adopted by the sister Services as well as by other Allied military establishments. Their publication measureably enhanced the quality of training afforded the new 4EAB.[15]

This, the last brigade to be generated by the EAC, was activated at Ft. Devens on 1 February 1943 (and redesignated the 4th Engineer Special Brigade three-and-a-half months later.) Its three constituent boat-and-shore regiments were the 534th (Col. Robert H. Naylor), 544th (Col. John R. Crume, Jr.), and 594th (Col. Francis H. Falkner), rounded out by the 564th Boat Maintenance Battalion, 264th Medical Battalion, and the requisite signal, ordnance, and quartermaster companies. [The final digit in the enumeration of amphibian regiments and auxiliary units indicated the brigade to which they were organic.] The Fourth Brigade's basic cadre was drawn from Ogden's 3EAB at Carrabelle, supplemented by detachments from the EAC's own personnel complement. (The truncated EAC, though at the time officially stationed at Camp Edwards, was about to decamp for Florida.) The brigade's command was temporarily assumed by the newly-minted General Noce himself, and delegated to his Chief-of-Staff, Colonel Trudeau, pending appointment of a permanent C.O. Several factors in addition to the newly-published training aids enabled them to do a more thorough job in shaping this brigade than circumstances had permitted with regard to the other three. For one thing, the chronic shortage of boats had eased. For another, greater care could be invested in the selection of its cadremen. Moreover, 4EAB's rank and file were of generally higher calibre, in terms of age, physical condition, and AGCT scores, than those in the earlier brigades. The majority of its initial "fillers" (recruits filling out its ranks) had been drawn from the 1st, 2d, and 6th Service Commands, emcompassing the geographical regions centering on Boston, New York, and Chicago, and therefore presumed to be healthier, better educated, and possessed of more savvy in general than yokels from the nation's less cosmopolitan hinterlands (including "rebel hicks" like those of us from Dixieland's 4th Service Command headquartered in Atlanta.) Most of the Fourth's original levy were between ages 18 and 22, and came to Ft. Devens directly from reception centers. On the other hand, three-quarters of its commissioned officers were recent OCS graduates with no prior amphibious or maritime experience whatsoever, so everyone had much to learn.[16]

Within a month of 4EAB's activation, General Noce was ordered to Britain on a special mission to European Theatre Headquarters, whereupon its command, together with that of the almost-defunct EAC, temporarily devolved upon Col. Henry Hutchings, Jr., a 51-year-old Texan and West Pointer (class of 1917.) Favored with an accelerated rise to the rank of Major in Pershing's AEF during WWI, and having earned an Engineering degree from Massachusetts Institute of Technology in the interwar years, Hutchings was a full colonel at the outbreak of World War II.[17] Noce's formal appointment to a staff post at SHAEF [Supreme

Headquarters, Allied Expeditionary Forces] in London assured confirmation of Hutchings as 4EAB's permanent CO on 19 May 1943. By that juncture, his fledgling seahorsemen had become adept at the basic soldiering skills, and at their first brigade review, performed their drill with a precision that impressed all observers.[18] In the aftermath of Noce's departure, the EAC which he had so ably shepherded from its inception continued to undergird the seahorse units it had spawned until the end of 1943, when it was ordered south to Gordon Johnston preparatory to its dissolution.[19]

Meanwhile, upon completion of the initial phase of its training at Fort Devens, 4EAB moved over to Camp Edwards for its technical education under EAC's direct supervision, and in April its formations were parcelled out to Washburn Island, Cotuit, and Falmouth. Here Hutchings' tyros were schooled in a wide-range of specialties, beginning at the individual level and then in incrementally larger configurations, company, battalion, and regimental. Selected apprentices were sent off to civilian schools across the nation, such as those operated by the Higgins Industries in New Orleans or by General Motors Corporation at its marine diesel engine plant in Detroit, to acquire specific expertisse, while others underwent instruction at various Army specialist-training institutions or locally at EAC's own facilities. Upon attaining the requisite standards of proficiency, 4EAB's elements were reasssembled to tackle their first brigade-sized test problem (28-30 June 1943.) Having jumped this hurdle (in a manner of speaking), they spent July and August in simulated combat and general engineer practicum, culminating in a grand maneuver on the open waters of Nantucket Sound. One shore company from each regiment was then assigned to temporary duty at the Boston Port of Embarkation to become familiarized with port operations and cargo stowage and discharge.

All brigade personnel received individual instruction at the hands of Red Cross experts in swimming, diving, and life-saving.[20] One prim and proper female citizen of Davisville on Cape Cod recalled her discomfiture at the sight of a large formation of amphibs at the village beach dropping their trousers upon command preparatory to swimming drill. To her relief (or so she averred), all were wearing swim trunks underneath, and, at a second stentorous order, plunged in unison into the Sound to perform their aquacade.[21]

With the completion of their technical schooling, the personnel of 4ESB (as it was now known) were deemed ready to undergo the final, or tactical, phase of their preparation for amphibious warfare. While those in the three regimental boat battalions were given four weeks of instruction in the navigation of watercraft in formations, and three weeks of special-weapons training, and then sent out on repetitive night problems to enhance their nautical skills, the shore battalion units performed multiple team tasks such as road-building, bridging, boat-loading-and-unloading, beach organization, and general engineering and construction. At the conclusion of these exercises, the brigade was considered sufficiently conditioned to take on joint maneuvers with the infantry. In September 1943, it was shipped south to the purgatory of Camp Gordon Johnston, where it employed the hard-used watercraft of the departing 3ESB to train with Maj. Gen. Raymond O. Barton's 4th Infantry Division of seasoned regulars (activated in June 1940.) More tautly-disciplined ground-pounders than those with whom the other ESB's had been teamed, Barton's troops no doubt set a high standard of efficiency and soldierly conduct for Hutchings' seahorsemen.

With the EAC's demise, all joint training, including that at Camp Gordon Johnston, was now being conducted under the aegis of the Navy's Amphibious Training Command, Atlantic Fleet. The Navy had established a base of its own for that purpose at Little Creek, Virginia (on Chesapeake Bay), soon augmented by others on the East Coast and in Florida. October and November of 1943 passed swiftly as the boys of Hutchings' Fourth were introduced to the rigors of web-foot soldiering on the Gulf shores in tandem with the GI's of Barton's Fourth.

Like their predecessors, the 4ESB boatmen had to familiarize themselves quickly and thoroughly with the waters off Franklin County. Carrabelle's harbor was not only miniscule, but the channel linking the port with the open sea through the East Pass was so narrow that it could be negotiated by nothing larger than an LCM, forcing deeper-draft vessels to anchor out in the Gulf. Moreover, the seas lapping the exterior or southside beaches of the barrier islands all too often were disconcertingly placid, generating such moderate surf that opportunities to practice landings in rough waters were infrequent, but when storms did occur, they could be perilous.[22]

Whether ship-to-shore or shore-to-shore, assaulting beaches and organizing beachheads in any geographic or topographic setting was a very complex business. For a typical practicum, the boat crewmen donned their waterproof outerwear and life jackets, while the shoremen were burdened with steel helments, combat packs and web equipment, gas mask containers, bayonets, entrenching tools, and firearms. Landings were usually scheduled at daybreak (and occasionally at night) to catch the "enemy" by surprise. "Beach parties" went ashore surreptitiously in advance to mark landing lanes for the guidance of incoming water-craft, using red, green, or blue signal lamps in darkness (or flags and panels of various colors if in daylight.) Then the landing itself would commence. Forming up in successive waves of 8 to 12 boats, the loaded barges were driven as far up on the sands as possible—though not so far as to prevent retraction, and with due regard for tidal variations—so that ideally the invaders could alight on dry ground, and vehicles driven ashore without drowning out or bogging down. When emptied, the boats had to be retracted by reversing engines and reeling in their stern anchors which had been dropped overboard on the run in at precisely the right moment. The greatest fear of all boat crews was that their craft might broach in the surf, that is, by running in at the wrong angle or speed, end up broadside on the sands, held fast by wind, waves, or current, or even capsize in the shallows. This would not only endanger the occupants and cargo, but expose the boat to destruction by enemy gunfire, or by obstructing the beach, block others coming in astern.

The shore battalion troops (nicknamed "shovels" in contradistinction to the "boats" crewing the landing craft) faced a no-less-intricate and demanding challenge. The most dangerous and delicate chore of all was clearing the landing area of underwater obstacles or mines and booby traps, and blasting paths with bangalore torpedoes or fixed charges through barbed-wire entanglements and concrete, steel, or wooden barriers. In actual combat landings, shore parties would be mercilessly exposed to air attacks and hostile fire, with no time to dig themselves in or seek cover as the assaulting infantry could. They would be totally committed to getting vehicles and cargoes ashore with all possible speed, ensuring that the equipment and supplies needed first were deposited at optimal locations on the beachhead. Since the "shovels" went ashore in the initial assault waves, their own bulldozers, tractors, DUKW's, trucks, jeeps, and ambulances, along with the 30-cal. and 50-cal. machine-guns, 60-mm. mortars, and towed 37-mm. light artillery pieces with which each company was equipped for defense against counterattacks, had to be quickly offloaded, in addition to such other priority machinery as self-propelled cranes, drag-lines, and road-graders. They had to be prepared to lay cyclone-fence matting if necessary for vehicles to gain traction on loose sand, and assist in debarking the infantry's tanks, vehicles, and ordnance. If the offshore waters were shallow, the shore battalion's mission also might involve the construction of earthen jetties or roadways out to the prows of beached LCT's and LST's, so that wheeled and tracked vehicles and artillery pieces could be driven off. These jetties were usually shaped by throwing up parallel banks of sandbags (emplaced by files of amphibs standing in the water), while bulldozers shoved sand or dirt into the aperture. Beachhead defenses had to be installed, exit roads from the beach carved out, supply dumps established, communications posts installed, telephone wires strung, medical aid stations set up, prisoner-of-war compounds erected, and a thousand other tasks rendered to sustain the invasion's momentum. Once the combat moved inland, the beachhead had to be cleared of accumulated wreckage and debris and reorganized. An avalanche of supplies to sustain the operation, including food, ammunition, fuel, stores and equippage of all types, arriving in succeeding echelons, had to be sorted out and dispatched as needed. Channelling the hosts of reinforcements and their vehicles pouring ashore, and evacuating the wounded and prisoners-of-war to outbound vessels brought added complications.

No matter how well-rehearsed landing scenarios might be, serious accidents were bound to occur from time to time. In the course of a March 1943 night exercise near St. Mark's, as several hundred of 3ESB's landing craft were bringing in troops of the 28th Division, fourteen infantrymen were accidentally drowned. The boat formations had been sixty-some miles offshore when a storm suddenly formed out in the Gulf with winds gusting over forty-five miles per hour and generating waves of twelve to fifteen feet. They proceeded to their destination without foundering, but while steering into the inlet in the darkness, the bow of one of the Navy-designed LCP(R}'s struck a hard sandbar and stuck fast. Its coxswain, thinking his craft had beached, lowered the ramp. As the trainees, trussed in their heavy gear, rushed off the barge, all but three sank helplessly to the bottom in a deep trench between the bar and the strand. (Andrew J. Higgins, who had refused to build LCP(R)'s for the Navy, judging them underpowered and bow-heavy, charged that the accident stemmed from their faulty design, and asserted that he had received numerous testimonials of similar mishaps from troops attempting North African landings from the same class of boat. Higgins' considerable political influence soon led to the Navy's acceptance of his own more reliable and seaworthy LCM.)[23]

Eight months later, in November of the same year, on the final joint maneuver with the 4th Infantry Division and some III Corps troops, 594th EB&SR's boat battalion was also caught by a storm blowing up from the tropics. Despite the 10-ft. waves buffeting their heavily-laden barges, Colonel Faulkner's crews adroitly brought all but five safely to shore at the planned landing sites. The luckless five, however, foundered and sank, casting over one hundred men into the sea. Happily, all were saved, thanks to the water-rescue and life-saving instruction his seahorsemen had received at Cape Cod.[24]

With the culmination of their training that month, all of Barton's 4th Division units were transferred to Fort Jackson, S.C., before deployment to Britain. This division was fated to play a leading role in the assault on Normandy's Utah Beach and the ensuing crusade across Western Europe. In the aftermath of their departure, there was a fundamental change in the status of Camp Gordon Johnston.[25] Since no more amphibian brigades were scheduled for activation, and the EAC itself would be completely dissolved by 1 April 1944, the Pentagon had decreed that the reservation should be converted into the Army Service Forces Training Center [ASFTC], effective 1 January. Its oversight was temporarily vested in Colonel Hutchings, who was promoted to Brigadier General. Gordon Johnston would henceforth be given over to the technical training of Transportation Corps amphibian truck and harborcraft units. A sizeable contingent of 4ESB's personnel, mostly from the boat battalions, were detached to serve as cadre and instructors for this enterprise. A melange of marine-engine maintenance, ship-repair, stevedoring, and port-construction units would also be learning their trades at Gordon Johnston. Since the camp's run-down physical plant required renovation and alteration in view of its amended role, 4ESB's shore units were temporarily employed in the rehabilitation. Companies of the 594th, for example, built a 300-ft. pile bent bridge over the Crooked River and corduroyed approach roads through the surrounding marsh, as well as constructing two large school buildings at the main post, rebuilding rifle ranges, and improving sanitary facilities.

Early in January, 1944, while I was still enmeshed in the Fort Bragg Reception Center processing, the brigade was alerted for its move to the Southwest Pacific. Its men had been the beneficiaries of far more intensive and extensive training than those in the preceding brigades, and though now undeniably ready for overseas service, it had to be kept on hold until sufficient ships were available on the West Coast for its trans-Pacific haulage, and "fillers" could be added to satisfy overstrength requirements. (Some anonymous wag proposed that the E.B.& S.R. suffix in regimental nomenclature actually meant "eager, but still resting.") Final leaves and furloughs were granted, and in early February, to mark 4ESB's first anniversary, a parade/review was staged at which Hutchings briefed everyone on the latest developments (without, however, disclosing their overseas destination.) Given this state of suspension, it is little cause for wonder that the rank-and-file were somewhat on edge when a levy of greenhorns fresh from basic training were introduced on the weekend of January 22-23, 1944.[26]

V

THE SHAPING OF A SEAHORSE SOLDIER

Ranged along the trackside at Lanark awaiting our arrival from Ft. Bragg was a convoy of amphibious trucks, or "Ducks" [DUKW's], which taxied us five miles eastward along the shoreline on U.S. 319 to the Area 2 cantonement at the junction with Fla. 110. Here we joined company with other recruits just in from Camp Shelby, Mississippi in what was called the Replacement Training Group. There were about 150 of us, as I recall, divided into three platoons by alphabetical order, each assigned to a barrack crammed with closely-spaced double-deck bunks and dimly lit by low-wattage bulbs suspended from the rafters. I selected the lower tier of a bunk, stowed my gear, made my bed, climbed into it, and passed a restless night. We were awakened well before daylight by the sounding of reveille, and after breakfast were divided into platoons and addressed by our new officers.

The officer in charge of my platoon, a 1st Lieutenant Monteleoni with Chemical Corps insignia on his collar, was a noticeably tense chap bearing an uncanny resemblance to a portrait of Napoleon Bonaparte in one of my old history textbooks. He was to prove a decent, hard-working, straight-forward superior. Our non-coms, a staff sergeant who was assistant platoon leader, and my squad leader, a buck sergeant, neither of whose names come to mind, also turned out to be reasonable and sane individuals, as drill instructors go.

The training regimen for inductees in the Corps of Engineers was a somewhat truncated version of that mandated for the ground combat arms. It entailed a process of physical and mental hardening to prepare recruits for the rigors of soldiering in the field, and to instill the military fundamentals. Teamwork in various configurations (squads, platoons, companies) was integral to the program. The initial, or basic, phase was of 6-weeks' duration, normally succeeded by 8 weeks of individual technical, or specialist, training, and concluding with 3 weeks of field, or tactical, training. Thus, at the end of 17 weeks, the fledgling soldier was considered ready for a permanent duty assignment.[1]

The initial 6-week, or basic, phase was the most demanding, involving intensive instruction and practice in such subjects as Military Courtesy and Discipline; Weaponry; Field Sanitation, First Aid, and Hygiene; Defense Against Chemical Attack; Marches, Bivouacs, and Shelter-tent Pitching; Close-Order Drill; Equipment and Clothing Maintenance; Interior Guard Duty; Hasty Field Fortifications; Elementary Map Reading; Physical Training; Inspections; Protection of Military Information; and Organization of the Army.[2]

The first order of business was the issuance of our "field equipment," including a steel helmet, canvass cartridge belt and suspenders, first-aid pouch, field blanket, carrier pack, haversack, leggings, gas mask, canteen and cup, mess kit and eating utensils, shelter-half, pup-tent pole, rope, and pegs, entrenching tool (small folding shovel), bayonet, and, most important of all, a rifle, and rifle-cleaning kit. The rifles were World-War-I-era bolt-action 30-calibre Springfields, simple, reliable old pieces slathered with cosmolene, a thick grease which required considerable effort to remove. Top priority, insisted the non-coms, must always be given to keeping one's firearm in perfect condition—we were taught a little ditty to help us remember the proper nomenclature: "This is my rifle" [pointing to one's firearm]; "this is my gun" [pointing to one's crotch]; "The first one is for fighting; the second one is for fun." The dismounting [disassembly] of the rifle and the cleaning and oiling of all its parts—barrel, bore, sights, bolt, trigger mechanism, magazine, sling, and stock—and their reassembly became a daily routine. Next came the mastery of the "manual of arms"—gripping the firearm in various prescribed positions and manipulating it ceremonially "by the numbers" in unison with the group—in response to such commands as "Order Arms," "Present Arms," "Right (or Left) Shoulder Arms," "Port Arms," "Parade Rest," etc. All the other items of field and personal equipment and clothing had to be kept spotlessly clean and polished as well. On Saturday mornings, the commissioned officers made formal barracks inspections at which our quarters, our gear, and our persons were subjected to minute scrutiny as we stood at attention in dress uniform at the foot of our tautly-made-up bunk beds, atop which everything had to be displayed in precise order.

Each day we were roused from slumber well before dawn— Reveille sounded at 5:00 A.M. (0500 military time), as I remember it—and after making our ablutions and donning fatigue uniforms, we "fell in" (assembled in ranks) in the company street for roll call and calisthenics such as bending and stretching, "side straddle hops," push-ups, running in place, and other mild tortures. After repairing to the mess hall for breakfast, we returned to barracks to make our beds, "neaten up" our quarters, and "police the grounds" (pick up and dispose of all trash and cigarette butts—"everything that don't grow"), then reassembled in formation to hear the orders of the day. From that point on, we were marched from one activity to another. Other than ten-minute breaks on the hour, there was no time out until long after dark except for meals or to relieve one's bladder or bowels. "Taps" sounded in the evening about 10:00 P.M. (2200), after which lights were extinguished. From this invariable routine we were liberated only on Saturday afternoons (usually) and Sundays, unless one's name appeared on the rosters for extra duty such as K.P. (kitchen police), latrine or barracks orderly, or guard mount. Discipline, defined as prompt, willing, and cheerful obedience to orders, compliance with regulations, and team loyalty, was constantly emphasized, and the drill was unrelenting. Most of one's limited down time had to be devoted to "spit-and-polish."

Among the more memorable exercises was the chemical warfare training; it was a gas—literally—involving repetitive "dry runs" (military slang for replicating a given procedure.) When the sergeant yelled "Gas!" headgear and eyeglasses were instantly doffed, the gas mask was extracted from its carrier (a shoulder-suspended canvass bag, worn on one side of the chest and strapped around the body, containing an air-purification cannister to which the mask was attached by a flexible hose), and the mask pulled over one's head and positioned on the face while tightening its head straps securely to ensure that no gas could leak in around the edges. The idea was to do this until it could be executed with no lost motion and almost without thinking. At length we were taken into an airtight tent where poison gasses, namely, chlorine and phosgene (or so we were told), were released. We were instructed to take a sniff, exhale strongly, and, while holding one's breath, don the mask and breathe the filtered air through it for a few minutes before exiting the tent and removing the mask in the open air. (Happily, this was one procedure that we never had to employ during the entire war, since neither side resorted to gas. In fact, the gas mask was the first piece of equipment that most of us jettisoned as superfluous as soon as we got overseas, salvaging only a couple of rubber rings from the flexible tubing with which to encase our metal dog tags to prevent their clinking when we were in close proximity to the enemy and needed to move silently.)

We also had a lot of practice in pitching pup tents. The shelter-half which I had been issued was an obsolete model with a triangular flap on one end only. Each soldier's shelter-half was designed to be buttoned to that of a buddy to make a pup tent with space for both inside. The up-to-date models which everyone else had been issued had triangular panels sewn on both ends so that the heads and feet of even the tallest occupants would be shielded from the elements. Mine, however, with its single end-panel, stuck out like a sore thumb when we pitched camp with all of the pup tents perfectly aligned. I was repeatedly railed at for messing up the esthetic symmetry of the platoon's encampment, but my entreaties to the supply sergeant for a replacement were ignored.

On the first weekend, we were released from duty at noon Saturday and allowed to go to the Main Post, where Lonnie Squires and I repaired to the Service Club for a leisurely and sumptuous dinner (costing the grand sum of 55 cents), followed by a movie—

Alfred Hitchcock's *Lifeboat*. In late afternoon, after nosing about a bit, we hitched a ride in a jeep back to Area 2. Sunday morning was occupied in washing clothes, shining shoes, and scrubbing leggings and other canvass gear. At midday the mess hall served an unusually ample dinner, featuring turkey (too cold and inadequately seasoned for my taste, regrettably) with dressing and lemonade. Afterward, some of us rode down to the Main Post again in a "deuce-and-a-half" (the standard ten-wheel, canvass-topped, 2-&-1/2-ton Army truck), shopped at the drug store, quaffed a milkshake, toured the big PX (Post Exchange store), and caught another flick, *A Guy Named Joe,* topped off by a very satisfying supper at the Club. Having thus exhausted all the apparent sources of recreation, we thumbed a ride back to the barracks, and found that there had been a mail delivery in our absence. Letters from loved ones are the greatest of treats to servicemen, aside from furloughs and week-end passes, and I found several letters from home on my bunk. A rumor was floating about that upon the completion of our seventeen-week ordeal, we were going to be parcelled out among 4ESB's boat or shore battalions or sent to DUKW companies or Harbor Craft outfits. Some non-com was reported to have disclosed that at least one of 4ESB's regiments would be in the Southwest Pacific by April, a sobering prospect indeed, but I was still clinging naively to the illusion that as an ASTP designate, I could count on being transferred to a college campus after Basic Training, and passed it all off as a mere "latrinogram" of no concern to me. In a letter to my parents that night, I wrote of mourning the loss of my recently-deceased Grandfather Cadman, especially upon waking in pre-dawn darkness and gazing up at "the black sky and the beautiful stars shining in the stillness, broken only by the sounds of an army waking from slumber," and vowing to be "a good soldier" to keep faith with him (I had the instincts of a poet, if not the talent.)[3] I wrote them again toward the end of the following week with little more to report than that the G.I. laundry to which I had experimentally entrusted my soiled socks, handkerchiefs, towels, and underwear had failed to return the socks and handkerchiefs, and had given me someone else's towels—a costly lesson which persuaded me to do my own laundering thereafter. I commented that when standing on the scales at the PX, my weight had registered 134 lbs. fully clothed, indicating a modest fleshing-out of my spare frame, and that my appetite had become so voracious that I was beginning to suspect that I harbored a tapeworm.[4]

I took every opportunity to visit the Main Post on subsequent weekends to escape the unsavory atmosphere of the barracks, with its raucous poker and blackjack games, stupid horseplay, foul language, and scatalogical jokes. The prevalence of such behavior came as a rude shock to me, given the relatively-protected circumstances of my middle-class Protestant rearing. I was dismayed when a fellow inductee from Fort Bragg, having had all he could take of army life, went "over the hill" one day, and to my knowledge was never apprehended. Another older draftee in my squad, father of six children (one a newborn), whose wife was suffering from a serious post-partum illness with no one to help her, requested an emergency furlough. His request was denied, which I thought unduly harsh on the part of the authorities.

At about this juncture I made a new friend, Pvt. Benjamin R. Weaver, from Williamston, N.C., an extroverted, high-spirited lad of my own age, with a winsome personality and lively sense of humor. "Bennie," as we called him, was a farmer's son, and a loyal Baptist of high principle. He would become my closest and most trusted companion throughout the war. Bennie could mimic the sounds and verbal expressions of Walt Disney cartoon character Donald Duck to perfection, and could always be counted upon in tense situations to levitate our sagging spirits by quacking a la Donald. He and I visited the Service Club the following Sunday for a meal of baked ham and candied yams, and viewed the film, *Standing Room Only*, starring Paulette Goddard and Fred MacMurray. There we ran into a couple of other RTG companions who passed on a hot rumor that we were all to get furloughs as soon as the first phase of our training ended.[5]

When all of us had the Manual of Arms routine down pat and had acquired some expertisse in handling and firing our bolt-action

Springfields, they were replaced by more state-of-the-art gas-operated semi-automatic 30-cal. M1 Garand rifles with insertable 8-round magazines and short trench-knife bayonets. Weighing 9.5 lbs., the M1's were heavier and more troublesome to take apart and reassemble, and took some getting used to. At rifle inspections, the automatic bolt had to be smartly opened with the heel of the right hand, presented to the inspecting officer, and when thrust back, closed by pressing the right thumb down on the ammo clip in the aperture, thereby releasing the bolt. It slammed shut with a vengeance, so that if one's thumb were not extricated pronto, it could be severely mashed. This happened to a few of my buddies, though not to me. During the week of 7-13 February, one of the more formidable tests required of us was to dismantle and reassemble our Garands while blind-folded, which, by the mercy of God, I passed. That Saturday we endured a gruelling march of six miles into the wilderness and back through loose sand with slung rifles and full-field packs—some eighty pounds of gear. This marked the half-way point in the basic training phase, at which we were officially informed of our permanent unit assignments—dashing once and for all any lingering prospects of an ASTP continuum. Rather than furthering my formal education and attaining some significant level of military employment, I, along with everyone else in the RTG, were to serve as fillers in 4ESB units, in my case, the Shore Battalion of the 534th EB&SR. This, we were told, would occur upon completion of our technical-specialist training, which for me and a few others was to be in Radio Operation and Maintenance.[6]

By the end of the ensuing, or fourth, week, of basic, I had contracted a sore throat and high fever, and that Friday I went on sick call. The medical officer at the dispensary prescribed sulfathiazole tablets, of which a side effect was mild nausea, so I was allowed to take the rest of the day off. I spent most of it sewing amphib and seahorse insignia on my blouse and shirts, with results, I'm afraid, that looked rather amateurish. The following week's pace was exhausting, and since I was still battling a raw throat, when Sunday rolled around, I slept late, attended Church services in the forenoon, and loafed about afterwards, putting off until evening the inescapable tasks of washing clothes, polishing shoes, and writing letters. Everyone else in the platoon was industriously spit-shining the two pairs of highly-prized paratrooper boots they had just been issued; as luck would have it, the supply room had none in my size (9-&-1/2-C), so I had to wait several more days for mine. That same weekend, a contingent of fresh inductees from West Virginia, Ohio, and Pennsylvania showed up at the Replacement Training Center. After one look at Alcatraz-By-The-Sea, they were even more deflated than we had been upon our arrival there. Though I was profoundly empathetic, the weekend had been a downer for some of us more seasoned heads as well; one of our platoon-mates from Dillard, S.C., whom we all had esteemed for his gentility and congeniality, had been battling severe abdominal pains for a couple of days for which he had received only cursory medical attention; on Friday night he had died, much to our regret and consternation.[7]

Our concluding week of basic was climaxed by a day on the firing range. I had some difficulty manipulating the complicated leather sling on my rifle, with its buckles and keepers, to form the requisite tight loop around the upper left arm, designed to steady the heavy M1 until its sights were perfectly centered on the bullseye before the trigger was squeezed. I much preferred using a simpler technique known as the "hasty sling" to help my aim, but there was no way to get by with it on this occasion. Although the M1's recoil was gentler than that of the '03 Springfield, my hearing was deadened and my shoulders ached for hours after repetitive shooting from the standing, sitting, kneeling, and prone positions. To my immense relief, my performance was ruled satisfactory, so I didn't have to repeat it. We also had a go at bayonet practice, for which we were marched to a clearing where several poles topped with straw-filled burlap bags about the size and shape of a human torso were emplaced vertically in the ground. Lining up in front of the dummies, on the order to "Fix Bayonets!" on the end of our rifle barrels, we took turns assailing them as though they were live adversaries, using the prescribed close-combat procedures—

"Thrust," or "Parry," or "Butt Stroke"—jabbing them in the throat, chest, or abdomen, or smashing them full in the face or up under the chin with the butt of the rifle, or whatever. We were goaded into displays of savage aggression and exhorted to scream maniacally and lunge ferociously at the dummies. The instructors advised that in case the bayonet were to become lodged tightly in a real enemy's tissues, we should simply pull the rifle trigger and shoot it free rather than waste time trying to pull it out. I had not minded firing on the rifle range, but this kind of mayhem did not come easily to me, though in the attempt to ratchet up my level of aggression, I found it distinctly helpful to envision the dummy as my high-school PT coach, which made it rather satisfying, I confess.[8]

By Saturday noon, 4 March 1944, we had cleared the last of the basic hurdles specified by regulations and attended to all of the tag-end minutiae. Lieutenant Monteleoni and our other instructor/cademen departed for other duty-assignments or postings, while we were rewarded with weekend passes to Tallahassee, where many of the boys promptly proceeded to soak up much of the booze in North Florida. Since I had drawn KP duty that afternoon (the delayed penalty for having dropped my rifle weeks before) and felt pretty wiped-out by nightfall, I elected to spend the rest of the weekend in camp. My solo celebration on Sunday consisted of reading, doing laundry, and trekking to the Main Post for a chicken dinner and a movie. This turned out to be a blessing in disguise, for when Monday dawned and the technical phase of our schooling commenced, I was one of the few unafflicted by miserable hangovers.[9]

The handful of us who had been selected as apprentice SCR-284 radiomen, among whom were Bennie Weaver, Carl Stegman, and Neal Whitten, had been instructed to report to the School Detachment, ASFTC Headquarters, at the Main Post. Our new billet, in Barracks 1104, was much less crowded than our former digs at Area 2, and had wooden flooring. As it developed, life at the Main Post offered other little gratuities as well. In addition to the metropolitan daily newspapers, books, and magazines readily available in the Service Club, a GI journal, *The Beachcomber,* was published weekly, covering local news and featuring stories of particular interest to amphibian troops, so that we felt as though we had reentered civilized society. Not only were the movie theatre, PX, and restaurant facilities we had been patronizing from afar now close at hand, but an excellent jazz ensemble staged concerts and performed for parties and dances at the Service Club on evenings and weekends. Calling itself "The Swingphibians," and composed of musicians from the 434th ASF Marching Band, it was led by CWO William A. Teason, former trombonist with the Fenton Brothers and Red Nichols bands, and contained some top-flight artists. The lead trumpeter, Sgt. Hogue, was ably backed by another talented brass man, Frank Svoboda, with Frank DeVito on tenor sax, Bernie Kublinski on alto, and clarinetist Francis Rooney, among others. Renditions of their theme song, "Someday I'll Return," still cause my heart to miss a beat whenever I hear them. Parenthetically, one of the enlisted men in the battalion which I was soon to join was an exceptionally-accomplished accordionist. A shy Italian kid from someplace in the North, he crafted lovely variations of popular melodies, and his spur-of-the-moment solos were a potent antidote to ennui and helped keep the blues at bay on crowded troopships and dismal shores. Of all the Terpsichorean legacies from Gordon Johnston days embedded in my psyche, however, the most ineradicable is a rollicking tune entitled "Rose of San Antone," which blared forth incessantly from the Service Club jukebox. For reasons which I still cannot fathom, it was an overriding favorite of the seahorsemen.[10]

So it was that we communications novitiates found our new circumstances relatively idyllic after our formerly quasi-penal lifestyle. Not only were the living quarters less primitive, but the mess hall's cuisine was distinctly more palatable. Admittedly, it was sometimes a drag to sit in one place wearing earphones for hours on end listening to repetitions of "da-da-dit—G," or "dit-da-da-dit—P" in order to memorize the Morse Code, or repetitively tapping out signals on a transmitting key. But this was child's play in comparison to slogging through pelting rain over hellish miles of sand, with acheing shoulders and blistered feet, toting mountains of gear, swatting pestilent insects and dodging clouds of flies, disinfecting malodorous privies, or scrubbing mountains of greasy pots and pans in steamy kitchens at the bidding of surly cooks. Our radio school mentors, Chief Instructor Sgt. O. H. Rodenburg, and his underlings, T/4's Robert A. Spry and Albert L. Obrofta, were patient and helpful. By the end of the first week (10 March 1944), I was in the upper bracket of my class, but then my progress began to lag, and I worried that I would fail the upcoming speed test. It never crossed our minds that we would not be allowed to complete the full 8-week course, but in the middle of our third week, everything came to a screeching halt as we were peremptorily withdrawn from the school and inserted into various units of the 4th Brigade, three or four to a company. Weaver, Whitten (a congenial newly-married draftee in his late twenties from Memphis, Tenn.), and I found ourselves consigned to Shore Company F of 534th EB&SR, while Carl Stegman was sent to the 594th. The official explanation for the abrupt termination of our technical schooling was that 4ESB had just received orders to proceed to a Port of Embarkation (the location of which, along with the brigade's ultimate destination, were closely-guarded military secrets, not to be shared with the likes of us}, and since all units bound overseas were supposed to carry an overstrength of 15%, we were the lucky ninth-hour super-numeraries.[11] (The Boat Battalion of the 594th, had, in fact, already departed Gordon Johnston for Oakland, California, and, ultimately, New Guinea, in three echelons—C Company on 8 February, followed three weeks later by Companies A & B. Not for another month-and-a-half would 594th's "boats" be reunited with their shore colleagues.)[12]

The 534th, inflated by some 40 or so of us ex-RTG'ers, was under the command of a 39-yr.-old West Pointer [Class of 1927] of Indiana origin, Col. Robert H. Naylor. Although I would seldom be in his presence, he impressed me as quiet and somewhat remote, but quite capable and proficient. Like the 594th, our regiment was soon to be shorn of its boat battalion as well, but for a far lengthier period. Our boatmen were about to be diverted to

Balimba, Australia, for duty at a steel-barge-assembly plant, leaving the Headquarters Company, Shore Battalion, and ancillary units with no organic boat element for many months to come.[13]

The brute fact was that we greenhorns were being hustled overseas far faster than any of us could have imagined, given the fact that we had been in active service for a paltry two-and-a-half months. That was the bad news. The good news was that we were to be immediately granted a week's furlough home. To this day I can recall my utter dismay and emotional turmoil at these developments. While jubilant at the prospect of a brief reunion with my family, I felt utterly betrayed by the Army, not only for welching on the ASTP contract, but adding insult to injury by depriving me of any opportunity to fill a specialist slot in my new unit. In reality, however, even had we been able to complete radio school and qualify as operators, all such benefices had long since been preempted by fellows from the brigade's original complement. Now classified simply as "521's" [Engineer Basics], we were more or less permanently relegated to the bottom of the pyramid. ASTP-designates supposedly represented the top 2% among Army personnel in intellectual acuity, and, at the risk of being thought an insufferable snob, it was genuinely ego-deflating to contemplate spending the rest of the war as a buck private in the least-mentally-challenging and most dead-end kind of duty, with little likelihood of transfer or promotion, and a better-than-average chance of not returning home in one piece, if at all. The most stunning aspect of it was that we were being rushed to the war zone with absolutely minimal combat skills, deprived even of the swimming/water-rescue instruction accorded all the other amphibs. (It was a good deal worse, I would later learn, for a great many displaced ASTP'ers army-wide; they would become real cannon-fodder—some had never even fired a rifle before being assigned willy-nilly to infantry replacement pools to beef up divisions already overseas. This fate had befallen a couple of my contemporaries and close postwar associates at the University of North Carolina, who, having been dumped into the infantry, were caught up in the Battle of the Bulge as virtually-untrained privates.) This was not one of the War

Department's more inspired policy decisions, as was later admitted. It was not that we considered ourselves too superior to risk our necks on the front line like anyone else, but that we could have been employed to so much better effect at duties appropriate to our talents.[14]

Thoroughly disgruntled, agitated, and in a veritable fever to get away from Camp Gordon Johnston and everything it symbolized, each of us hurriedly packed a haversack with enough clothes for a week, stuffed the rest in our duffle bags for delivery to our new units, and boarded a bus for Tallahassee's Seaboard Station on Saturday, March 25th. The Carolinians among us secured seats on the 2:50 P.M. eastbound train and arrived in Jacksonville Terminal at 7:20 that evening, in time to catch #108, the northbound *Sun Queen,* to Raleigh, where we alighted at 0630 Sunday morning. While Bennie, Lonnie Squires, and the other Tar Heels made a beeline for their respective hometowns, I caught the next Greyhound bus to Winston-Salem, and showed up at our domicile just after the St. Paul's morning worship had concluded. I calculated that I would have less than six days at home, so I had better make the best of them. When I walked through the front door, there was, needless to say, a very emotional reunion with my parents and little sister, Ruthie (my older sibling, Peggy, was absent, having, as previously noted, taken up residence in Easton, Maryland.) Aside from the cascades of conversation, in which we endlessly swapped reminiscences and observations, and random visitations with old pals and family friends, I remember very little of that turbulent week. I discovered that one of my high-school classmates who had signed on with the Navy V-12 was getting an accelerated college education and would be attending Medical School at the taxpayers' expense, in stark contrast to my own apparently ship-wrecked career. (Following an active-duty hitch as a Naval physician, he was to enter upon a lucrative practice after the war.) Obviously, I told myself, I had made a fool's bargain. I strolled over to Reynolds High one morning to chat with some younger student acquaintances and drop in on a few fondly-remembered teachers, in the course of which I bumped into my former coach, and learned to my secret satisfaction that he had been rejected as physically unfit for military service by reason of a stomach ulcer or something of the sort. It afforded me more than a little ego gratification, I'm ashamed to say, to stand before him in uniform and paratrooper boots, and in top physical condition, and reveal that I was headed overseas.

The remainder of my leave sped by, and on Saturday afternoon, trying rather unsuccessfully to master my pervasive depression, I embraced my loved ones in a gut-wrenching farewell scene at the bus station, and rode away from my vestigial childhood. I made it to Raleigh with time to spare, linking up conveniently with Bennie and another RTG buddy, Foy Brown, at the Seaboard station. We boarded southbound #107 at 9:25 P.M., and for once had no trouble getting seats together. Eleven somber hours later, we changed trains in Jacksonville and were back in Tallahassee by 2:50 P.M. on the gloomy, overcast Sunday of April 2d. The three of us strolled over to the city's U.S.O. Club to savor our last hours of freedom before checking in for bus transport back to camp. I took the opportunity to have a voice recording made to send home to my family. When I listened to the playback—the first time I had ever heard myself—I was appalled at my provincial Carolina accent, vowing then and there to work at acquiring a more universally-American mode of speech. Then I wrote my parents a hasty note assuring them of my safe arrival, and enclosed the phonograph record, so that in case I failed to return from the war, they would have something of me to hold on to. Bennie, Foy, and I reentered the grim precincts of Gordon Johnston around 9:30 that night, and reported in to 534th's Co. F orderly room. The regimental cantonement was in Area 3 at the St. Teresa locale, three or four miles east of our old RTG bivouac.[15]

My introduction to the seahorse fraternity was a genuine downer—the skies were leaden and the rain was falling as I stepped over the threshold of my new barrack. The first individual whom I encountered was a buck sergeant (whom I shall dub "Laird"), a lean, flinty, saturnine, and tattooed New Englander. He appraised me sourly and growled, "Kid, I'm gonna rape you." Needless to say, I was somewhat taken aback, but muttered some response to the effect that if he tried it, one or the other of us would have to resort to homicide. I endured only standard harassment from him thereafter, but this verbal affront revealed what seemed the prevalent attitude evoked by our insertion into Co. F. In a letter to my parents Monday evening, I commented—with an equally-reactive lack of charity—that "It [my barrack] certainly contains a group of morons—the average IQ must be even lower than [that in] the Replacement Training Group, if that is possible—I hate the thought of having to live with them, but I guess I'll have to learn sooner or later." (In my defense, I realized that I could do with some roughening and toughening, but for the moment I was ill-prepared to face the ordeal.)[16]

The lot of a recruit in any outfit whose members have trained and functioned together since its inception is seldom an enviable one. Largely frozen out of informal social groupings (except with fellow rookies), treated with vague contempt, and assigned to the least desireable fatigue details, he must simply grin and bear it, or "suck it up," as we say these days. This exclusion persists for an indeterminate length of time until the "old boys," even hoplites of one's own lowly rank, have tested one's mettle in all sorts of humiliating ways. It amounts to an unofficial version of the West Point "plebe" system.

It was obvious that the regiment was being prepped for overseas duty, because on my first full day in its ranks—during which the rain fell in torrents—everyone was issued a new two-piece backpack of superior design and greater versatility than the old W.W.1-model with which we had originally been equipped; our raincoats were replaced with ponchos which could also serve as groundsheets; and we got brand new shelter-halves (solving my problem in that regard, at least.) Our woolen uniforms had to be turned in to the Supply Room (a clear indication that we would not be campaigning in any regions of frigid or temperate climate), while any extra-issue clothing items one had acquired or other superfluous personal effects had to be disposed of or mailed home. Our Ml Garand rifles were replaced with light-weight (8.55 lb.), shorter-barrelled,

30-cal. carbines having 15-round magazine clips. Though much handier to carry about than the cumbersome M1's, the carbines had a shorter range and were less accurate. Next, we were instructed in the preparation of a Last-Will-and-Testament, along with another legal instrument granting power-of-attorney to a party of one's choice (in my case, my dad.) Several high-priority P.O.M. [Preparation for Overseas Movement] combat-training requirements that the seasoned amphibs had already completed, but to which we rookies had not been exposed, including Street-Fighting and Infiltration courses and the Transition-Firing Range, also had to be satisfied. For the street-fighting bit, we were trucked to the old Harbeson City ruins north of Carrabelle, now rechristened "Schicklegruber's Haven," a cluster of battered shacks and tumble-down houses lining a ruined, cratered street littered with combat debris. The abandoned structures bore corny slogans such as "Hitler's Club (Bring Your Own Clubs)" or "Heydrick Hangout," and included a gallows from which dangled a mock corpse. An "Execution Wall"—which we were required to scale— and an outhouse with Mussolini's visage adorning its wall above the caption "I was born here," were part of the macabre scenery. Our team was supposed to battle its way through these ruins, dodging from one bit of shelter to another and exchanging fire (using blank ammunition) with an opposing team until we had "captured" the village.

The infiltration course was more realistic—and nerve-wracking. We were ordered to crawl on our bellies cradling our carbines across a 100-yard-long muddy battlefield pocked with shell holes, weaving through barbed-wire entanglements and around blasted tree stumps, while machine-gunners fired live ammunition overhead— about 30 inches above ground level—and explosive charges, buried every few feet, were randomly detonated with a terrifying racket, showering us with dirt and debris. When it was over, our filthy carbines, equipment, and clothing had to be thoroughly cleaned, shined, and readied for one of the infernal inspections that were conducted even more obsessively in Co. F than in the RTG. Last of all, we were rotated through the Transition-Firing Range, where live rounds were issued which we were to shoot at a succession of pop-up targets, so that we could become adept at handling our new firearms. This was considerably more fun, and, to my surprise, I scored well enough to qualify as a "sharp-shooter."

In a final letter to my folks written on the night before Easter Sunday (8 April), I advised them not to expect any further correspondence from me for an indeterminate period, and explained that following a final summary inspection the next morning, we would be busy packing and loading regimental impedimenta until we boarded the troop trains.[17] Throughout Easter Day we labored relentlessly in the rain crating equipment and supplies and hoisting it all onto trucks which were then driven up on railway flatcars and lashed down. Monday, the skies were still overcast as we ourselves, uniformed in summer khaki's and buckled into our field equippage and steel helmets, with carbines slung over our shoulders and lugging duffle bags crammed with the rest of our clothing and accoutrements, vacated our barracks and were transported on DUKW's to the railroad sidings at the Main Post, where several trains waited with steam up. While the brigade band played martial airs, we assembled in ranks to file aboard our cars. As I later recorded the event, "There were no beautiful girls to wish us goodbye—only a few seagulls winging overhead and clouds of insects, of which G.J. had an overabundance. The sergeants cursed and the officers raved, but finally we all got into our appointed places in the midst of much confusion." When we were properly grouped and numbered off according to the seating capacities of our assigned cars, I found that I would be occupying a "troop sleeper" at about mid-train.

A word of explanation regarding these carriages is in order here. In 1943, when the number of troops requiring rail transportation had begun to exceed a million a month, stretching the available stock of Pullmans and coaches to the limit, the Government had ordered 1,200 specially-designed troop sleepers and 440 "troop kitchen" cars from the nation's railway-carbuilders. These were adaptations of the standard 50-ft. steel freight box car, modified with steam and communication lines, and mounted on special "full-cushion" high-speed 4-wheel trucks.

With doors in the center of each side like a box car, rather than at the vestibule ends, as on a conventional passenger coach, a troop sleeper, measuring 51 ft., 8-1/2 in. in length, accommodated 30 men in ten three-tiered folding bunks installed crosswise instead of paralleling the center aisle. Ventilation was provided by windows left and right of the center door on the car sides, and by little vents just under the roof-line. Toilets and wash basins were located at the car ends. Operated by the Pullman Co., troop sleepers were stocked with bed linens and other supplies just as on conventional sleepers, and their bunks made up at night by a porter, one to each car. In brief, while these conveyances were a step up from the primitive French 40-&-8's of World-War-I fame, they were a long way shy of the well-appointed standard Pullman cars.[18]

Our troop main's designated commander, who happened to be Company F's Captain (reportedly a former candy-salesman from a small town east of Raleigh, N.C.) and to whom I shall hereinafter refer by the pseudonym of "Wellman," was, in my assessment at least, a petty-minded, mean-spirited individual. He strictly forbade us to raise our car's windows until we were travelling at a good clip (presumably to forestall the disclosure of any classified information to potential enemy agents, or maybe to discourage anyone from jumping off and deserting.) When the train did get up to speed (in a manner of speaking, restricted as it was by the flimsy trackage and antique locomotives of the Carrabelle branch to a breathtaking 25 mph. or so), and we were allowed to throw open the windows, we were soon dusted with smoke and cinders. As we rolled into Tallahassee a couple of hours later—with windows shut again—a lively controversy erupted among the boys as to whether our main would be switched to the tracks heading east toward a port on the Atlantic or to those heading west toward the Pacific. Actually, we clattered across the junction with the Seaboard's east-west line and continued in the same northerly direction (though at a somewhat more lively pace) on the former G.F.& A. branchline into Georgia. Not until we reached the town of Richland late that night was the mystery finally resolved, for there we found ourselves diverted to the westward axis of an intersecting Seaboard line linking

Savannah, Ga., and Montgomery, Alabama. As the night wore on, we entered Alabama—and the Central Time Zone—and well before dawn rolled to a stop in its capital city, first seat of the Confederate government. After a considerable interlude during which the S.A.L. locomotive and crew were exchanged for those of the Louisville & Nashville R.R., our progress resumed at a swifter pace into the sunrise of a second day, now palpably northward, on the L.& N.'s main line via Birmingham and across the broad Tennessee River at Decatur to Nashville, Tennessee. There we veered away from the trunkline to Louisville on a diverging L.& N. stem heading northwest through Evansville, Indiana, on the north bank of the Ohio River.

With the onset of our second night on wheels a'rolling, I was detailed as one of the train guards, standing with my carbine at the door and keeping a lookout. I observed that our course beyond Evansville tended ever more westerly as we crossed the southern tip of Indiana and bisected lower Illinois via Mount Vernon (where my recently-deceased Great-Uncle Sterling Price had made his home and where his remains were now interred.) With the passage of several hours, the glare of coke ovens and the diffused glow of a vast metropolis on the late-night horizon signalled our approach to the Mississippi River and the city of St. Louis on its far shore. After we crept over the bridge, our wheels cooled for a brief spell in the renowned "Gateway to the West." While the troops snored, the railway carmen did their inspections, and engines and crews were swapped again.

We steamed away from the congested St. Louis terminal complex on the tracks of the high-stepping Wabash Railroad, while I, released from guard duty, sank into a sound sleep in my bunk, not to be roused until we chuffed into Moberly, Mo., early the next morning. Here we were ordered off the train for some physical exercise. Although the rising sun brought promise of a gloriously clear day, the air was chill, and we shivered in our lightweight "suntan" khaki's as we formed ranks to jog up and down the streets of Moberly in formation, working out the stiffness in our joints. Once back in the vicinity of the station, we were put through the usual set of morning calisthenics, to the considerable amusement of some of the local yokels who happened to be up and about. I had read somewhere that Moberly's citizenry were the most hospitable to passing troops of any in the land, but, alas, no comely Red Cross lasses or kindly USO ladies were on hand to dispense coffee and doughnuts at that early hour, so after entraining again, we in our car bribed the porter to sprint to a store and buy some candy bars for us. We might as well have spared ourselves the expense and him the trouble, for soon after the train was in motion again it was announced that the troop-kitchen car would be serving breakfast, so that our hunger pangs would be stilled courtesy of Uncle Sam. It was no mean feat to carry a tin tray loaded with hot food and a paper cup full of steaming coffee safely through the swaying vestibules and packed aisles of the intervening cars, especially on the fast-running Wabash, but we were beginning to get the hang of it.

That afternoon we steamed into storied Kansas City with its stockyards and packing houses, and shuddered to a halt at its massive Union Station. Here we sat motionless for what seemed hours during which the Wabash Railway's locomotive was uncoupled and replaced by another with a Chicago, Rock Island & Pacific Lines logo emblazoned on its tender, the train was inspected and serviced, and supplies restocked for the long pull across the remaining half of the continent. Two or three other troop trains occupied tracks parallelling ours at the station platforms, transporting miscellaneous outfits under much more permissive supervision than we. Their occupants freely roamed about or yelled at us from their open coach windows, while we, as always, were forbidden to leave our cars, raise our windows, or communicate with them in any fashion. One might have surmised that we were engaged in the war's most crucial secret mission, when in all probability everyone in North Florida knew more about our peregrinations than we dogfaces in the ranks.

When our main eventually steamed off westward again on the Rock Island Ry. across the Kansas prairies and we settled down to the monotonous spectacle of fields of corn and wheat stretching away into infinity, the sheer immensity of the North American continent began to impact those of us who had never been west of the Appalachians. Into the depths of a star-studded night our iron horse's mournful whistle heralded our arrivals in and departures from such populous communities as Topeka and Manhattan. Through dozens of isolated hamlets huddled at the feet of towering grain elevators, we labored across the length of the Sunflower State on a single-track railway jammed with traffic (as, indeed, were all the other East-West lines at that juncture), compelling us to slow down or stop at frequent intervals to weave our way around other trains travelling in both directions. During the more drawn-out meets or at points where the locomotive tender had to be replenished or maintenance performed, we were allowed to get off for a bout of exercise or to stretch our limbs. I recall one such break in Goodland, Kansas, and another after we were well into Colorado at the junction town of Limon. The farther west we trekked, the more barren and empty the landscape appeared. This stretch of the Great Plains was still recovering from the ravages of the drought which had brought such devastating depopulation during the previous decade as to earn the sobriquet "Dust Bowl."

Not until late afternoon on the fourth day of our odyssey did we reach "The Mile-High City" of Denver at the base of the snow-capped Rockies. It seemed a mirage, so beautiful, clean, and enticing, after the endless miles of sun-baked, dun-colored High Plains. At Denver's Union Station, Red Cross personnel were out in force, feting us royally with cigarettes and candy. Here the Rock Island handed our troop main over to the Union Pacific Railroad, and, towed by two mighty steam engines, we commenced a 100-mile jog northward toward Wyoming on the U.P. line parallelling the towering Front Range of the Rockies through the towns of La Salle and Greeley. After a third locomotive was added to augment our double-header at Carr, our main swung west again on the Borie cutoff at Speer, Wyoming, bypassing the bustling rail center of Cheyenne just to the east. This brought us onto the U.P.'s heavy-duty transcontinental trunkline, the celebrated Overland Route linking Omaha, Nebraska, with San Francisco. These busy tracks climbed over a flattened-out spur of the Rockies known as Sherman Hill (cresting at 8,013 ft. above sea level, the highest point on the entire U.P.)

By now it was much too dark to see the awesome peaks in the middle distance, and soon everything outside was obscured by swirling snowflakes, while we shivered in our blankets. Forever etched in my memory are the thrilling sights that unfolded, as we snaked around sweeping curves, of that trio of mighty steeds ahead, straining to drag us up the grade, their beaming headlights and flashing fireboxes illumining the snowfall. I was ensconced on a second-level bunk, with my head next to an open window, and as I leaned out and drank in the frigid mountain air, the deep, resonant notes of the whistle reverberated from the walls of the cuts and cliffs with singular clarity. Somewhere along the steeper portion of the incline, we halted on a siding for almost two hours while a long parade of Union Pacific's higher-priority limiteds and fast freights bound for West Coast destinations thundered past. Finally, after our turn came to regain the high iron up and over the summit (where the helper engine was dropped), we trailed them westward through Laramie and Rawlins across a vast elevated plateau. Daylight revealed an undulating snow-mantled landscape, with the jagged mountains well behind and to the south of us before we topped the continental divide itself at Creston (elevation 7,102 ft.) in the gently rolling uplands. About noon we jolted to a stop at Green River, a small but strategic railway division point strung along the riverbank, for servicing and crew changes. The world's largest locomotives, the articulated 4-8-8-4 "Big Boys," were based here and at Cheyenne, and I was jubilant at getting my first unobstructed look at these behemouths. The surrounding bluffs and buttes carved out by the river eons ago assumed fantastic shapes, resembling the towers and turrets of medieval castles. Just a few miles to the west, at Granger, the U.P. mainline forked, the right-hand trunk heading northwest to Spokane, Portland, and Seattle via Pocatello, Idaho, while the original transcontinental artery continued due west, penetrating the steep barrier of the Wasatch

Mountains through a succession of narrow defiles, tunnels, and canyons to Ogden, Utah.

As our train drove deeper and deeper into Utah, the scenery was absolutely indescribable, and I was frankly jaded with its ceaseless wonders before our descent into the vital railway nexus at Ogden, ten miles east of the lake shore. Situated in the flattened bowl of the Great Salt Lake, once the bed of a vast prehistoric inland sea, Ogden was the terminus of the U.P. portion of the Overland Route to central California. From this point, our troop main angled southward over the U.P.'s Los Angeles extension as far as Salt Lake City, and our officers finally divulged to the rest of us our stateside destination: Camp Stoneman, at Pittsburgh, California, just east of Oakland. At Salt Lake City, we were to be switched over to the tracks of the Western Pacific Railroad for the remaining 900 miles to the San Francisco Bay area. Our train sped southward over the short 35-mile stretch to the Holy City of the Latter Day Saints, past neat little towns and well-tended farms testifying to the industrious ways of the Mormons, and pulled into the Salt Lake depot about 3:00 P.M. The city itself was something of a disappointment, perhaps because the railway traversed its older, more run-down neighborhoods; it appeared to me one of the grubbier urbs of my experience, though its broad avenues were impressive. A good many of the visible inhabitants (including lots of poverty-stricken Mexican-Americans) seemed rather unkempt and shabby as well. While our train stood in the station, some of the GI's in my car had become so ravenous that they scarfed down watery ice-cream purchased at an exhorbitant price from a couple of dishevelled juvenile hucksters—and afterward could count themselves lucky to have escaped gastric upheavals, I thought. In any case, now in the hands of the Western Pacific R.R. and behind one of its oil-fired steamers, our train surged out of Brigham Young's citadel in handsome style over that carrier's single-track line.

At length we skirted the barren southern extremity of the Great Salt Lake and crossed the vast Bonneville Salt Flats, which were just what the name implies for as far as the eye could see. We were soon deep into a singularly desolate wasteland of barren mountains and arid deserts known to geographers as "The Basin-and-Range" region, inhabited by a few hardy stock-herders and gold-and-silver miners, but virtually noone else. Here the wagon-train pioneers of the last century had faced the grimmest ordeal of their harrowing trek, as they and their oxen trudged with parched tongues across the saline crust to reach a cool spring at the foot of Pilot Peak. It was just west of this remote oasis that the ill-fated Donner Party took their fateful turn onto a more southerly trail, delaying their intended crossing of the Sierras until it was too late in the season, with well-known results. That night we came to the last settlement of any significance in Utah, Wendover, truly in the middle of nowhere. (Although none of us could have known it, the Air Force base here would soon host the 509th Composite Group, whose Col. Paul Tibbets and giant new B-29's would star in the final, fateful act of the war, the culmination of the secret Manhattan Project. From Wendover, in April 1945, Tibbets and his fellow airmen would proceed to Tinian Island in the Pacific, from whose runways they would take off four months later to drop the two atom bombs on Japan, and thereby in all probability preserve the lives of the majority of those aboard our train.)[19]

At this remote depot, our progress was arrested for a time, due to the heavy rail traffic with which our train had to interdigitate. Ninety miles beyond Wendover, at Wells, Nevada, the Western Pacific tracks converged with those of the Southern Pacific Overland Route, and for the ensuing 180 miles to Winnemucca, the two lines were more or less side-by-side. Over this segment, all westbound trains of both carriers ran over the S.P.'s trackage, and all eastbound on the W.P. Thus, our troop main was borne along on S.P. rails for the next several hours that night, but beyond Winnemucca resumed the lonesome trail of the W.P. The latter pursued a course well to the north of the older S.P. line through Sparks and Reno (the former Central Pacific, built eastward by Chinese labor to its celebrated junction with the U.P. at Promontory Point, Utah, in 1869, thereby marking the completion of the nation's first transcontinental.)

With the dawning of our sixth day "on the road," our rumbling conveyance was approaching Beckwourth Pass at the crest of the rugged Sierra Nevadas, after a stiff climb up their eastern ramparts during the night. Just over the western side of the summit, at the railway-shop town of Portola, California, hemmed in by fog-shrouded peaks, we paused in the early morning sunlight to refuel our locomotive, uncouple the helper engine, and take aboard a fresh set of crewmen. Then we commenced a sinuous 112-mile descent down the Pacific slope of the Sierras, first alongside the Middle Fork of the tumbling Feather River, then, via Williams Loop (where the track circled over itself), to the Feather's North Fork, paralleling its tortuous course through majestic gorges and declivities, arguably the most scenic stretch of terrain upon which our eyes had feasted since exiting Camp Gordon Johnston.

Six hours out of Portola and 4,631 ft. closer to sea level, having descended a gradient engineered to a steady 2%, our troop main slid to a stop at Oroville with its brake shoes smoking like chimneys. Beyond Oroville, as the topography abruptly flattened, we raced south during the waning afternoon over the floodplain of the broad Sacramento River and through the capital city of the Golden State to Stockton at the upper end of the adjoining San Joaquin Valley, a veritable Garden of Eden. At the latter point, our train was switched to the Atchison, Topeka, and Santa Fe Railway's trackage for the final 36-mile lap across the hills of the Pacific coastal range to Pittsburgh.

Everything associated with the concluding phase of our overland journey to war is a mere blur in my memory, dazed and disfunctional as we all were after so many days of confinement, motion, and visual stimulation. Moreover, so much of my reserves of psychic energy had been expended enroute in coming to grips with the sea-change in my life and trying to relate to my new companions-in-arms that I was doubly disoriented. We detrained at Camp Stoneman around midnight. The soiled summer khaki's worn since our final hours in Florida's Franklin County afforded scant protection from coastal California's biting chill as we were herded over to our transient barracks.[20]

VI

SAN FRANCISCO TO PAPUA

Camp Stoneman, the Army's staging post for the San Francisco Port of Embarkation, lay about thirty-five miles northeast of San Francisco at the industrial community of Pittsburg in Contra Costa County. The town, on the south bank of the estuary formed by the junction of the Sacramento and San Joaquin rivers, and site of a large Columbia Steel Company plant, was a small-scale replica of its namesake metropolis in Pennsylvania. The military installation, covering 3,242 acres, could accomodate about 40,000 troops. The Civil War-era worthy for whom it was named, Brig. Gen. George A. Stoneman, cavalry officer in William T. Sherman's army and a postwar governor of California, had, incidentally, commanded the only Federal force ever to invade my hometown of Winston-Salem. Stoneman's horsemen, raiding through North Carolina's Piedmont during the final days of the tottering Confederacy in April 1865, had wrought little or no damage in our vicinity, I might add.[1]

We bleary-eyed and road-weary warriors of the 534th wasted no energy dwelling on such historical trivia, however, fixed as our minds were on the vision of a peaceful night's rest on a stationary cot, but it was not to be. The initial round of our processing for overseas service commenced with scarcely a moment's delay. No sooner had we dumped our stuff in our quarters than we were herded to a medical facility, where we were ordered to strip off our clothes and drape ourselves in our ponchos for a short-arm inspection (exactly how the powers-that-be thought any of us could have contracted a social disease on a closely-guarded transcontinental troop movement defied all logic.) Prefatory to this rite, we lined up and shuffled along, shivering, embarrassed, and edgy, for what seemed like hours, and after its performance, received immunizations against small pox and other scourges indigenous to the geographical regions to which we were bound. About 0300 we were mercifully allowed to bed down, only to be roused out by reveille two hours later, an unpromising start to our final fortnight in the land of the free and the home of the brave. There were multiple forms and documents to be filled out and signed, further health screenings to determine combat fitness, and treatment for minor medical or dental conditions that might be troublous in the future. We were lectured on security precautions and on the maintenance of hygiene, and outfitted with assorted items deemed essential to service in a tropical environment, such as machetes, plastic goggles, cans of dubbing to fortify boots against moisture, jungle hammocks (which had waterproof canopies and mosquito netting} and insect bars—small nets to protect the head and neck, and large cubical ones to drape over portable camp cots. We were handed cans of medicated foot powder to ward off skin fungus, expanded first-aid pouches containing sterile dressings and packets of sulfanilamide powder, bottles of atabrine tablets to combat malaria, of salt tablets to counteract desalinization from heavy perspiration, and of halogen tablets for water purification.[2] Everyone's original-issue "windbreaker" field jacket was replaced with a restyled gray-green, water-repellent, thigh-length model having commodious pockets, zip-out wool lining, a drawstring to snug the midriff, and a detachable hood to pull over the head and neck. I acquired at government expense a couple of spare pairs of metal-framed eyeglasses ground to my prescription by the camp's optometry lab. (Unfortunately, perspiration caused their frames to corrode, as I would soon discover, leaving green marks around one's nose and temples.) GI's needing dentures were similarly fitted out gratuitously. The Army's Special Services branch, charged with sustaining troop morale, even proferred free paperback copies of novels and literary classics; I eagerly availed myself of a select few, stuffing them in my backpack alongside the pocket-sized Bible and Prayer Book which had been prized possessions since my Ft.

Bragg days. None of us were permitted to leave the base, which scarcely mattered, since there was precious little free time anyway.

By now the rearmost elements of the brigade had officially closed out at Gordon Johnston, and 4ESB units showed up at intervals throughout our brief Stoneman sojourn. Several of my buddies, including Bennie, drew K.P. at Stoneman, which was exceptionally-onerous duty in P.O.M. installations, where the mess halls were in service twenty-four hours a day, and the preparation and clean-up of meals fast-paced and never-ending. Any self-congratulations I may have harbored at having escaped this drudgery were rudely dispelled when I was nabbed for an advanced shipboard K.P. detail, which meant boarding our troop transport ahead of the other battalion personnel. Accordingly, in the wee hours of Friday, 21 April, I and a small party of other les miserables, clad in fatigues and laden with our arms and all our gear, were ferried over thirty miles of waterway to the Oakland Army Base pier where our vessel was docked, near the eastern end of the San Francisco-Oakland Bay Bridge. I was entranced at the sight of this immense span, opened just before the war, and currently considered one of the world's foremost engineering marvels.[3]

In the pale light of early morning, the ark which was to haul our menagerie across the vast Pacific did not look particularly imposing. It was the first ocean-going ship I had ever seen up close, much less been aboard. Bearing the incongruous name of FAIRLAND, she was one of 2,700 Class EC [Emergency Cargo] "Liberty" ships built during the war, having a length of 469 ft., a beam of 63 ft., a draft of 41-ft., and a gross tonnage of 8,932, propelled by 6,600 h.p. turbines. A hastily-built 1942 product of the Gulf Shipbuilding Company's Chickasaw, Alabama, yards, FAIRLAND and fifteen others, known as EC-2's, had been converted into troopships, accomodating about 700 people. Judging from her scabrous appearance, she had seen hard usage.[4]

Staggering under the weight of our tightly-stuffed duffle-bags and field gear, with steel helmets (upon which the numbers of our designated hold and compartment were chalked) crowning our pates, carbines slung over our shoulders, and cumbersome fully-loaded field packs strapped on our backs (protruding from mine were my newly-acquired paperback books), we stumbled one by one to the foot of the gangplank. Here we had to pass muster under the beady eye of our sour-visaged Captain Wellman. As I drew nigh him, he bellowed, "What the hell you doin' with those goddamn books?" Declaring them non-essential for any "real" soldier, he ordered me to throw them into the bay. When I tried to explain that I had already cleared their portage with his second-in-command (a sensible, mannerly 1st lieutenant named Tompkins as I remember it), who had raised no objection, Wellman brutishly overbore me, so I sullenly but dutifully pitched them into the water.

Once we had struggled up the gangway to the FAIRLAND's main deck, we wove our way along narrow passageways and down several almost vertical flights of steps to our cramped compartment below the waterline. Partway down, I lost my grip on the handrail and, overbalanced by my cumbrous load, fell like a cannonball onto the steel deck below, fortunately landing atop my duffel bag. No noticeable damage resulted, and nothing lost save dignity. From one of five or six tiers of paired canvass bunks hinged to vertical poles—each bunk had a headway of less than two-and-a-half feet— I staked out one just under the ceiling. It was adjacent to a ventilating grill which emitted a stream of frigid air, but I figured that this would be a minor annoyance compared to having someone step on me or my bedding everytime he climbed into or out of a bunk above, or contending with the vomit of some seasick occupant overhead. After stashing my duffle bag and gear into my elevated bunk, I crawled up into it to await developments. At length a mess sergeant came through the compartment and dragooned everyone in the lower tiers, but, being out of his line of sight, I escaped his attention for the time being. When I later awoke from an impromptu nap and began nosing about, I discovered that our entire battalion had mustered on the dock and begun boarding. As bandsmen played and WACs and Red Cross girls performed "Aloha" routines (with which they must have been pretty jaded by that juncture, considering the number of GI's who had preceded us to the far side of the world), I positioned myself on an upper deck in an out-of-the-way spot, leaned over the railing, and observed it all unmolested, with a lump in my throat. It took the better part of the afternoon to load all the personnel and stores aboard. After a time, I crossed over to the ship's starboard quarter and gazed westward across the Bay as the rays of the afternoon sun highlighted the skyscrapers adorning San Francisco's hills on the far shore. The more distant twin towers of the magnificent Golden Gate bridge were sharply etched in the marvelously translucid atmosphere. I mused on the hundreds of thousands of civilian San Franciscans going about their business wholly oblivious to our embarkation and to the fact that many of us might well be departing their precincts for all eternity.[5]

About midnight FAIRLAND cast off, and by daylight (Sunday) we had left the Golden Gate far behind and were plowing westward through the open seas. Although the weather had turned chilly and foggy, a Protestant Worship service was conducted that morning on the open deck by our regimental Chaplain, a Lutheran named Lindeman, a not-particularly-gifted pulpiteer, but a conscientious pastor nontheless. A Roman Catholic chaplain celebrated Mass for the numerous papists in our ranks. The ship was loaded to capacity, and in fair weather her open decks were so crowded that it was hard to find enough space to recline or stretch out. In spite of the best efforts of the ventilating system, the atmosphere in the troop compartments soon turned foul. As the days dragged on and the weather warmed, the holds grew progressively stifling and fetid. We were able to buy chocolate bars from the ship's store until the supply ran out, although they melted almost into soup if not rapidly eaten. Whenever heavy seas were encountered, many of the men became seasick and threw up at random, so that the decks had to be mopped incessantly. The latrines ("heads," in naval terminology) were always crowded, and invariably one had to wait in line to use them. Since the freshwater valves were turned on only during certain hours to conserve the limited quantity of potable water aboard, we also had to qeue up to get a drink or fill our canteens. Aside from sinks, the sole bathing facilities consisted of a pitifully few saltwater showers, under which it was virtually impossible to work up a lather, even with the special salt-water soap the ship provided, so that after a few days, one's dead skin cells began to peel off. No matter how frequently I tried to bathe or how hard I scrubbed, I could not seem to maintain more than a semblance of cleanliness.[6]

If the FAIRLAND's dormer and hygenic facilities were low-grade, so was the provender, except, of course, for that served in the Officers' Mess. Supplies of fresh milk, meat, and vegetables for the enlisted men were soon exhausted, after which our menu consisted mostly of canned bully beef, meat-and-vegetable stew, or spam sandwiches, potatoes (until they ran out, whereupon dehydrated, or, more accurately, rehydrated, spuds were substituted), powdered eggs, and, now and then, an orange or apple. Two daily meals were served, the troops eating in shifts by compartments. The mess area, located somewhere in the bowels of the ship, could be reached only by ascending or descending several tiers of steep stairs or semi-ladders. Here, we ate from our own mess-kits and canteen cups standing at closely-spaced steel trestles or shelves, and because it was mandatory to wear at all times (or at least have close at hand) one of the ship's grimy, bulky life jackets, it was virtually impossible to pass by anyone else without squeezing around him.[7] After dining, since the utensil-washing sinks were on a deck above, one had to carry his dirty kit and any remains up the ladder for disposal and cleansing. Whenever the ship rolled or lurched, it was distressingly easy to lose one's equilibrium and slip or fall, tipping out any contents, so that the floor and steps were more or less chronically coated with grease and droppings.

I had the ill fortune of pulling two stints of K.P. during the cruise. On the first, just a few days out of Frisco, I was ordered by a cook to carry a wooden crate of potato parings and other detritus topside and, in his words, "dump it." I duly manhandled it up the slippery ladders from the galley to the main deck, and, since no one had bothered to inform me that there were garbage bins somewhere about, I carried my crate over to the rail and dumped it into the sea. While making my way back down to the galley, a voice boomed over the loudspeaker, "Now hear this . . . Will the party who dumped garbage over the ship's side report to the bridge immediately!" Instantly aware that I had done something terribly wrong and would be in real trouble if I revealed myself, I prudently retreated into my bunk and stayed there awhile in hopes that the flap would die away, as indeed it did. I later learned that it was a cardinal sin to throw anything overboard on the high seas, especially garbage, as it leaves a trail on the water's surface which enemy submarines can track to its source and launch torpedoes at it. This mishap has heretofore been secretly filed away in my private memory bank as "the time I almost sank the regiment."

My second spell of K.P. duty afloat was even more aggravating than the first. The galley was always as hot as the ante-room of hell, and the wretches who labored there were usually drenched with sweat. I was carrying a kettlefull of hot grease out from the companionway to tip into the sea (considered legitimate in this case, since biodegradable liquids in moderate quantities aren't grossly visible), when the ship suddenly gave a great lurch, and down I went, grease cascading over everything in the vicinity, myself included. There was a redeeming aspect to my gaffe, however; it provided an excuse to loaf the rest of the day on the pretext of having to get cleaned up and change into fresh fatigues. It was such a bother to track anyone down on our crowded ark that no one came to check on me, if indeed I was even missed. As the reader may infer, I was acquiring some expertisse in the old army game of "goofing off"—passive aggression being one of the few emotional releases available to lower ranks when affronted by the mindless abuses of authority so commonplace in the military.[8]

By this stage in the war, the U.S. Navy had made a relatively clean sweep of enemy subs in that part of the Pacific, and it was decreed an acceptable risk for Allied ships to travel singly rather than in convoys except in forward combat zones. Consequently, FAIRLAND pursued her course solo, and so far as I could determine, we never sighted another ship from the time we left the States until we arrived overseas, unless one slipped past in the darkness.[9]

We had been a mere four days at sea when, on the night of April 27-28, the most tragic disaster ever to befall the Amphibian Engineer brotherhood occurred on the opposite side of the world, in Lyme Bay, England, off Slapton Sands, where the Normandy invasion forces were rehearsing their upcoming landings. Some of the units of Col. Eugene Caffey's lst ESB, recently returned from the Italian campaign to prepare for the assault on Utah Beach, were among the troops aboard a flotilla of LST's sailing along the English coast. A covey of German MTB's [Motor Torpedo Boats] struck without warning, torpedoeing three of the vessels and inflicting heavy casualties among their passengers—no one to this day knows precisely how many. A total of 638 were officially declared lost, with lESB and attached units hit hardest of all—413 amphib officers and men were accounted dead or missing, along with l6 wounded.[10] News of the event was suppressed at the time, and we were never told about it. Had the FAIRLAND been similarly smitten, there is little doubt that the vast majority of us would have gone to a watery grave, since only a handful could have gotten topside before the ship foundered. Lying in my bunk, I frequently brooded about such an eventuality, but tried to suppress the thought since there was absolutely nothing anyone could do to avert it.

There was little to occupy us on shipboard other than to sweat in the heat, stand in lines, tidy up the ship's interior, read whatever was at hand, eat, talk, gamble, or write letters (all our correspondence, by the way, was now censored by our company officers, so that no information of possible use to the enemy could be leaked). I soon abandoned my scruples and joined in the blackjack gaming, which, along with poker, dice-throwing, and other games of chance, went on non-stop. On the day the ship crossed the equator, the crew staged what sailors call "King Neptune's Court," a sort of silly ceremonial slapstick cum horseplay, about on a par with pie-throwing or mud-wrestling, for the entertainment of the troops. The event injected some coarse humor into our own increasingly-testy and short-tempered interplay. One day, as we were approaching the far shore, there was a sub alert, and we were ordered to assemble on deck with full canteens, helmets, and, of course, with life jackets buckled and tied, prepared to abandon ship if necessary. Very predictably, it took an eternity to get us all up from the holds, but happily nothing untoward occurred, except that the FAIRLAND's engines quit in the midst of the alert, causing us to drift for some twenty-four hours until the engine-room crew could restart them. The remainder of the trip was uneventful aside from the passage overhead one day of a lone Australian airplane, the only external sign of civilization we encountered enroute.[11]

At long last, after twenty-five days on the bounding main (we had gained a day moving westward with the sun), we glimpsed land on the far horizon. As the FAIRLAND drew nearer, passing a succession of small islands, we closed on the mainland of New Guinea, its mountains looming dead ahead. Under a sun whose rays beat down with ferocious intensity, our sweltering bark navigated slowly into Milne Bay on the fifteenth day of May, 1944, through water as clear and smooth as glass, and dropped anchor, 5,800 nautical miles from San Francisco.[12]

The island of New Guinea is one of the world's largest, second only to Greenland. Embracing about 317,000 square miles, not counting its numerous offshore islets—almost four times the contiguous land area of Great Britain—it is situated less than 100 miles across the Torres Strait from the Cape York Peninsula at the tip of Australia's northern Queensland. It lies on the volcanic rim of the Pacific "ring of fire," in that sector where the northbound Indian-Australian tectonic plate collides with several southbound Pacific plates. As a result, New Guinea's mountains are among the highest in the eastern hemisphere aside from the mighty Himalayas, with many of its peaks exceeding 10,000 ft. and some permanently snow-covered. The huge island contains scores of live volcanoes, subjecting adjacent areas to recurrent earth tremors. The mountainous terrain produces prodigious rainfall in many locales— as much as 300 inches annually—with an overall average of some 60 inches a year. Consequently a dense rainforest blankets the lower elevations and the seacoast, virtually impenetrable, murky, and insect-infested. Some of the island's more remote regions are so inaccessible that they have never been explored.[13]

New Guinea's shape resembles the outline of some huge prehistoric fowl roosting atop Australia, with the top of its head almost grazing the equator and beak pointing westward. Hence, the westernmost portion is called the "Vogelkopf," or bird's head. At the opposite extremity, some 1,600 miles to the southeast, the very tip of the bird's tail, lies Milne Bay, eleven degrees or so below the equator. This bay, twenty miles long and about the same in width at its mouth, soon tapers to a uniform four-mile width as far as its western shoreline. Because of its extraordinary depth, ships can heave to very close inshore for loading and unloading, making it the choice anchorage in the entire region. About two thirds of the way down the New Guinea bird's back there is a knobby protuberance known as the Huon Peninsula from which, across a couple of narrow straits, extend two long slim islands curling back westerly toward the distant Vogelkopf rather like the segmented tail of a terrier dog, or, to put it more fancifully, a decorative plume. The larger of the two, proximal to the Huon Peninsula, is New Britain, and the smaller and more distal, New Ireland. This pair, together with a relatively isolated cluster of neighboring islets farther to the west, the Admiralties, comprise the Bismarck Archipelago, and partially enclose a platter-shaped basin of the Pacific known as the Bismarck Sea. Dribbling off southeastward from New Ireland is a chain of elongated islands known as the Solomons, most prominent among them Bougainville, Choiseul, New Georgia, Santa Isabel, Malaita, Guadalcanal, and San Cristobal. Another body of water, the Solomon Sea, is ringed by Papua New Guinea on the west and south, New Britain on the north, and the Solomon Islands on the east.

At its widest girth, New Guinea itself measures about 430 miles north to south. Soaring mountain ranges run along its length like a jagged spine, the southeastern segment of this cordillera known as the Owen-Stanleys, crowned by 13,363-ft. Mt. Victoria. The loftiest peak in the chain, Mt. Carstensz, at 16,503 ft., lies in its western reaches. Among New Guinea's few redeeming features, aside from its bountiful supply of timber and some mineral deposits, including gold and copper, is that it harbors the world's most stunningly beautiful species of birds—the so-called Bird of Paradise—whose gorgeous plumage provided the most prized adornment of the native male populace. (The aborigines also sported necklasses or pendants of fancy seashells, and many wore the bones of wild pigs inserted through their pierced noses and earlobes.)[14]

New Guinea hosts an incredible range of vegetation and wildlife, including a wealth of reptiles, large and small, many of them extremely venemous. This exotic and challenging environment supported a sparse human population of some 2,870,000, mostly Melanesians only a step up from the stone age in cultural development, some of them practicing ritualistic cannibalism, usually of foes slain in the endless tribal warfare. Although a smattering of Malaysians and Polynesians dwelt along New Guinea's shores, along with a handful of Europeans, Australians, and Chinese, the awesomely-forbidding topography and inhospitable climate have made it one of the most primitive areas on earth. Aside from a few of its highland plateaus, it arguably qualifies as one of the globe's least desireable habitats for our species, not far behind the Sahara Desert or the polar regions, a veritable global purgatory. I can without fear of contradiction testify that it was a genuinely horrific locale in which to wage war. Gen. Douglas MacArthur depicted it accurately in his characteristically rolling prose:

> Few areas in the world present so formidable an obstacle to military operation. The jagged mountains rear their tall peaks amid sudden plunging gorges, towering above the trackless jungle that covers nearly the entire surface of the sprawling island. Swamps of nipa and mangrove pock the lowest areas— 'a stinking jumble of twisted, slime-covered roots and muddy soup.' In the jungle itself, trails were a sea of mud, with little relief from the swollen rivers, and the razor-edged kunai grass that grows in treacherous bunches higher than a man's head. Offshore were dangerous reefs, most of them uncharted, and the existing harbors were poor and

inadequate. Everything about the island and its approaches seemed to hamper combat efforts . . . Nature did not stop with adverse terrain, however. Constant high humidity intensified the unrelenting heat that sapped human energy; the rain came as an unpredictable but frequent blinding deluge. Health conditions matched the world's worse. Malaria could be controlled only by means of an intensive constant regimen of tiresome preventive measures. Dengue fever was widespread, the quickly fatal blackwater fever was also a waiting menace. Both amoebic and bacillary dysentery were continuing threats. Tropic ulcers could develop from a scratch. For the man who relaxed his guard, even for a moment, there waited hookworm, ring—worm, scrub typhus, and the dread yaws. Disease was an unrelenting enemy. And, if only to add an almost intolerable irritation, millions of insects were ever-present, always finding any unguarded spot to bite or sting—mosquitoes, flies, leeches, chiggers, ants, fleas. New Guinea was a background in which almost every threat of nature combined with the sudden and unforeseeable dangers of modern war to provide a miniature of the vast struggle in the Southwest Pacific.[15]

The preponderance of the island's indigenous Melanesians, or "Fuzzy-Wuzzies," as Europeans referred to them, were hunter-gatherers or dependent on subsistence agriculture. Yams, sago, coconuts, and bananas seemed to be the dietary staples, supplemented by fish and pigmeat for protein. Most lived in small isolated villages connected only by foot-trails, and many were head-hunters. Roads were virtually non-existent except in the immediate vicinity of a few coastal towns, and there were no railroads at all. The sole mode of transit aside from watercraft or reliance upon one's feet was by airplane, for which there were precious few landing strips. Consequently, about 750 distinct local languages had developed, according to modern-day linguistic experts. Most of the natives inhabiting the more accessible locales of Papua spoke a lingua franca known as "pidgin," a corrupt form of the colloquial

English introduced by traders and missionaries. The essence of simplicity, it has no unnecessary articles of speech, no pronouns, no prepositions, no plural nouns or verb tenses, and is spelled phonetically. I was continually amused by pidgin terminology: the place where the Kokoda Track crossed the deep gorge of the Kumusi River on a terrifyingly shaky footbridge suspended from a single wire cable was called "Wairopi" (Wire Rope); a refrigerator was a "bokis ais" (icebox); a thumb, a "nambawan pinga" (number one finger); and a wife, a "pella Mary" (fellow Mary). I have read that when Britain's Prince Charles attended the country's independence celebrations in the 1950's, he was popularly referred to as the "nambawan pikinini bilong Misis Kwin" (number one pickaninny belonging to Mrs. Queen.) A "wantok" (one talk) is an individual who speaks your mother tongue, i.e., a member of your family or clan.[16]

The Melanesians were willing hirelings when military stores had to be transported on human backs—or atop heads—as they did on any and all expeditions into the parts of the interior lacking convenient watercourses or landing strips. Some of the natives would serve the Japanese soldiery as readily as they would those of us in the Allied camp, though a good many soon came to regret it after a taste of the sadistic brutality so commonly displayed by the former. The U.S. Army did its best to prepare its personnel to communicate with the Papuans. While we had been on shipboard, phonograph records of repetitive English-Pidgin translations were frequently played over the loudspeakers. A common English phrase would be coupled with its pidgin equivalent, to wit: "What time is it? Bimeby son ee kum ware?" [Bye and bye, sun, he come where?—i.e., what is the position of the sun in relation to the horizon?]; or "toe; Pinga bilong fut" [finger belonging to foot.] I myself never became very adept at pidgin, because the situations in which we functioned seldom gave occasion to employ it.

Not until the latter years of the 19th century was New Guinea deemed worthy of exploitation in the emperialistic scrambles of the European Powers, whereupon it was divided up between the Dutch, the Germans, and the British. The island's western half became Dutch New Guinea, the northeastern quarter, German New Guinea, and the southeastern quarter, British New Guinea. Australia took over the British sector in 1905, renaming it the Territory of Papua (from the Malay word for "Fuzzy-Hairs.") At the outbreak of the First World War, the Australians ousted the Germans from Northeastern New Guinea, and following the cessation of hostilities, were assigned its administration by the League of Nations as a Trust Territory.[17]

When Japan joined the Axis in World War II and her forces lunged southward, all the islands off New Guinea's northeastern coast including the Bismarck Archipelago and the more northerly of the Solomons, along with most of the coast itself, quickly fell into their hands. The Japanese selected the mountain-ringed town of Rabaul, with its deep protected harbor, on the far eastern end of the island of New Britain, as one of the two principal bases for their operations in the South Pacific, the other being Truk in the Carolines, some 900 miles to the north.

In midsummer of 1942, Japanese expansion had reached its limit. Australia still clung to the lower two-thirds of Papua, including Milne Bay, as well as the administrative capital at Port Moresby on the southeastern coast, a bare 340 miles across the Coral Sea from the Australian homeland, and 450 airline miles from Rabaul. Climatically speaking, Port Moresby was an anomaly; it lay in the midst of an atypically dry pocket, with abundant eucalyptus trees, its aridity interrupted by a rainy season lasting only from January until about April, enhancing its utility for Allied air operations.[18]

A trump card of inestimable value to the Allies was their ability to decipher enemy radio transmissions after U.S. military cryptologists in Hawaii succeeded in breaking the Japanese Naval Code. This contributed substantially to two fortuitous American naval triumphs in the early summer of 1942 which probably determined the outcome of the war. The first, in the Coral Sea (the arm of the Pacific Ocean bordering northeastern Australia) on May 4-8, was history's first carrier vs. carrier battle. Though technically a draw, if not a Japanese victory, since three U.S. ships, the flattop

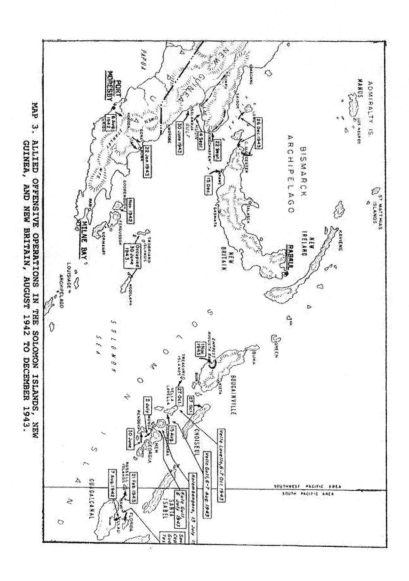

MAP 3. ALLIED OFFENSIVE OPERATIONS IN THE SOLOMON ISLANDS, NEW GUINEA, AND NEW BRITAIN, AUGUST 1942 TO DECEMBER 1943.

LEXINGTON, a destroyer, and a fleet oiler, were sunk, and a second carrier, the YORKTOWN, badly damaged, while five enemy ships, including the light carrier SHOHO, a destroyer, and three auxiliary ships, were lost, this engagement so depleted Japanese naval aircraft strength in that sector that the Empire's most promising effort to invade and conquer Australia was nullified. A second, more decisive confrontation the next month, off Midway Island in the central Pacific (June 4-6), resulted in a clear-cut victory for the United States. No less than four of the enemy's aircraft carriers and a heavy cruiser were sent to the bottom, precluding any further attempts by Japan to enlarge her "Greater East Asia Co-Prosperity Sphere" for the time being, and winning precious time for America to rearm.[19]

Later that summer, however, pressure on the Allies in the southern Pacific was renewed when the Japanese, having occupied Tulagi in the southern Solomons on 3 May, also moved onto Guadalcanal, from which their aircraft could readily choke off Australia's tenuous life-line from North America. Equally ominous was a resumption of the Japanese offensive against the Australian continent in the shape of a two-pronged overland thrust across Papua aimed at Port Moresby.

The Allied High Command reacted swiftly to the first threat by inserting the lst Marine Division under Maj. Gen. Alexander A. Vandegrift on Guadalcanal on 7 August 1942, triggering a long and bitter campaign which eventually ousted the intruders, but only after sucking in three more divisions of American ground troops, the 2d Marine and the Americal and 25th Army divisions. As Naval historian Samuel Eliot Morrison has written, the struggle for control of Guadalcanal was "the most bitterly contested in American history since the Campaign of Northern Virginia in the Civil War," involving "seven major naval engagements, at least ten pitched land battles, and innumerable forays, bombardments, and skirmishes."[20]

Meanwhile, on New Guinea's northeastern coast, where Japanese garrisons were already ensconced at Salamaua and Lae near the base of the Huon Peninsula, 16,000 troops of the "South

Seas Detachment" led by Gen. Tomitaro Horii came ashore on 21 July farther down on the shore of the Solomon Sea at the Papuan villages of Buna and Gona to commence an overland drive on Port Moresby. Horii's column pushed southward on the Kokoda Track, a mere footpath through the suffocating jungle, brushing aside the pitifully few Australian militia units blocking their progress. Crossing the Kumusi River gorge at Wairope, the intruders seized Kokoda at the foot of the towering Owen Stanleys, preparatory to tackling the formidable mountain barrier. To undergird this daring and ill-conceived—if not downright foolhardy—venture, in the following month a smaller Japanese force attempted to wrest from Allied hands the advanced base taking shape on the shores of Milne Bay, with its three vital airstrips and wharf at Gili Gili.[21]

Two of three all-volunteer A.I.F. (Australian Imperial Force) infantry divisions campaigning alongside the British in the Middle East against Erwin Rommel's Afrika Korps were recalled to defend the threatened homeland and reinforce the Aussie militia brigades trying to hold Papua New Guinea. The modest Allied garrison at Milne Bay, consisting of three battalions of militia and 1,300 U.S. Army engineers, known as the "Milne Force," was hurriedly stiffened with a brigade of 7th A.I.F. veterans. On 25 August, under the cover of dense clouds and in pouring rain, 1,200 elite Japanese troops of Vice Adm. Gunichi Mikawa's Special Naval Landing Force from Rabaul were unloaded on Milne Bay's north shore some distance east of the airfield at which they were aiming, and soon blundered into Maj. Gen. Cyril Clowes's more numerous Milne Force. After three incredible weeks of see-saw combat in the sodden jungles fringing the bayshore, Mikawa's invaders, denied reinforcements and supplies from Rabaul by Royal Australian Air Force interdiction, were forced to back out with their "elite" tails between their legs (17 September 1942), handing MacArthur his first land victory.[22]

Simultaneously, across the fearsome wilds to the north, Horii's overland invaders had clawed their way to the crest of the Owen Stanleys and gotten partway down the reverse slopes to Ioribaiwa and Imita Ridge, a mere thirty miles from their goal, before they were stone-walled by fresh Aussie infantry rushed up from Port Moresby. To allow the hard-pressed militiamen on this front some desperately-needed relief and refitting, other brigades of the 7th A.I.F. were committed to that sector. Weeks of savage fighting in incessant rains up and down the saw-tooth terrain followed as the Aussies, led by Maj. Gen. George Vasey, succeeded in shoving Horii's now-exhausted force relentlessly rearward over the all-but-impassable Kokoda trail. It was one of the most nightmarish contests in the annals of modern warfare. As the hunters became the hunted, Horii was slain, and by early November 1942, the Australian pursuers, poorly-nourished, ill-equipped, and close to the limits of human endurance themselves, had driven their emaciated opponents into pockets at Buna, Sananda, and Gona on the northeast coast from whence they had started. Here, however, the undersupplied Allied counteroffensive abruptly stumbled and stalled.

Despite heavy damage inflicted by Allied airmen on Jap convoys bringing additional troops and desperately-needed stores to Buna-Sananda-Gona, enough got through to reinvigorate temporarily the late Horii's chastened invaders, holed up with their backs to the sea in a nexus of expertly-sited and cleverly-camouflaged barricades and machine-gun bunkers. To regain the Allied momentum, especially in the Buna locale, and finish off the job, MacArthur fed in another A.I.F. brigade under Brigadier George F. Wootten, together with two regiments of Maj. Gen. Edwin F. Harding's untried and physically-unconditioned U.S. 32d Division (federalized National Guardsmen from Michigan and Wisconsin.) Bereft of tanks and with little or no artillery, however, even this beefed-up array proved unable to eject the never-say-die Japanese from their asylum. Hunkered down in their earthen-and-palm-log nests, fronted by seemingly impassable insect-and-reptile-infested swamplands, and bolstered by obsolete tanks, the Japanese gunners and riflemen inflicted heavy casualties on the Allied infantry, especially Harding's inexperienced and under-equipped mid-Westerners, who quickly tired of attempting futile frontal assaults. Malaria, scrub typhus, dysentery, and malnutrition steadily eroded the health of all antagonists, friend and foe alike. This sorry state of affairs dashed MacArthur's hopes for a quick and decisive breakthrough in Papua.[23]

Meanwhile, halfway around the world in Washington, Joint Chiefs Marshall, King, and Arnold had approved a long-range strategy to reverse the course of the war against "the slant-eyed sons of heaven," as we GI's liked to call them. The plan called for Nimitz's South Pacific Naval and Marine amphibious forces (with Army appendages) to stage an offensive northward up the Solomon Island chain from Guadalcanal, while MacArthur's Aussies and GI's, backed by Vice Adm. Thomas C. Kinkaid's Seventh Fleet (wryly referred to as "MacArthur's Navy") and its component VII Amphibious Force under Rear Adm. Daniel E. Barbey, would make a parallel advance up the northeastern coast of New Guinea. Not until the Buna-Sananda-Gona redoubt could be erased, however, could MacArthur get his piece of the action underway.

As the disheartened troops of the 32d floundered, sickened, and died in ever-growing numbers in the water-logged lowlands, morale plummetted and discipline slackened. In total frustration, MacArthur ordered Maj. Gen. Robert L. Eichelberger to fly up from Australia and get the faltering 32d off dead center, warning him to "take Buna or don't come back alive!" Only after the injection of a second division of ex-National Guardsmen (from Washington, Oregon, Idaho, and Montana), the 41st, which Eichelberger had been whipping into shape in Australia, could the stalemate be broken.[24]

For political reasons, the command of all Allied ground forces in the SWPA had ostensibly been vested in Australia's senior soldier, Gen. Thomas Blamey. MacArthur, however, had little regard for the fighting qualities of the Aussies, one division of whom, serving under British Lieutenant General Percival in Malaya, had been forced into surrender at Singapore. He therefore arbitrarily grouped his U.S. infantry into a separate "Alamo" task force directly responsible to Lt. Gen. Walter Kreuger, and through Krueger, to himself.[25]

Sacking Harding as C.O. of the 32d, MacArthur shipped in— or flew in—enough artillery, light tanks, and additional reinforcements for Alamo Force to eradicate the Buna stronghold by 9 January 1944, a month after Vasey's Aussies had forced their way into Gona. Although a wretched remnant of the Japanese boxed in at intervening Sananda still held fast, they had reached such desperate straits, not only from battle losses, but from disease and starvation—some had resorted to cannibalizing Allied corpses— that Imperial Japanese Headquarters on 4 January 1943 ordered their evacuation by sea to Salamaua/Lae. (On the same day, incidentally, the last of the 13,000-man Japanese garrison on Guadalcanal were also extricated.) Thus, according to an official SWPA communique, ended the harrowing Papuan Campaign— although an intransigent rear guard at Sananda could not be overborne until 21 January. The price paid by the Aussies and Yanks to suppress Buna-Sananda-Gona had been greater than that exacted for Guadalcanal—3,095 killed, 5,451 wounded, and thousands more permanently disabled by illness, predominantly malaria.[26]

Henceforth, the warfare in the Southwest Pacific would assume a noticeably different character, as Krueger's GI tyros, less intimidated by the myth of Japanese invincibility in jungle combat, acquired confidence and competence. At the same time, improvements in the flow of supplies to the Papuan front were making life less grim for the infantrymen. Nonetheless, Rabaul-based "Zero" fighters and "Betty" bombers continued to hound Allied shipping and pound installations with deadly effect. Admiral Barbey was loath to risk the vessels of his VII Amphibian Force by venturing beyond Milne Bay into the dangerous and unfamiliar waters along New Guinea's northeastern coast. Replenishment of the Allied ground forces inching westward up the Papuan shore was dependent on a scraped-together fleet of shallow-draft fishing boats and luggers who ventured forth only at night and hid out during daylight hours to elude enemy air raiders.

MacArthur, shuttling between his command post in Brisbane and his forward headquarters in Port Moresby, planned to employ the same leap-frogging tactics espoused by his collaborator, Nimitz. This involved a progressive seizure—or "climbing the ladder"—of carefully-selected Japanese bases which could be redeveloped and utilized for his own logistical or air support, and by-passing those not worth the cost of assailing, until the Allies had gained mastery of the entire New Guinea littoral, i.e., as far as the Vogelkopf. MacArthur humorously referred to this stratagem as "hitting 'em where they ain't." The by-passed enemy strongpoints, isolated and deprived of supplies, would simply be left to "wither on the vine." Once the frowning citadel at Rabaul was vanquished or neutralized, the overall offensive scheme called for a reshuffling of forces between MacArthur and Nimitz. The major share of the latter's resources and efforts would thereafter be devoted to the more direct thrust across the Central Pacific from Hawaii via the Gilbert, Marshall, Caroline, and Mariana island chains, aiming either at Mindanao, the southernmost of the Philippine Islands, or at Formosa (the target of choice in the eyes of Chief of Naval Operations Ernest King in Washington.) Though the imprecision in strategic goals was left unresolved at the topmost level for the nonce, there was an underlying presumption that MacArthur would assume primary responsibility for the recovery of the Philippines, while Nimitz would attend to clearing the approaches to the Japanese home islands, more or less as envisioned in prewar plan *ORANGE*.[27]

Accordingly, the opening round of the Allied offensive, dubbed *OPERATION CARTWHEEL*, had as its main objective the suppression of Rabaul, as a preliminary to which the satellite Japanese base at Lae in Northeastern New Guinea would have to be taken and the Huon Peninsula recovered. Blamey's "Diggers" would initially have to bear the brunt of the fighting until the American build-up reached more satisfactory levels. Once this was achieved, MacArthur was determined that U.S. ground forces would "take the point," and the "mopping up" of any residual Japanese concentrations in their rear relegated to the Aussies.

Milne Bay (Base A), currently the logistical funnel for his operations, would be be supplanted by others more proximal to the successive ladder-rungs by which he would mount, such as

Base B, taking shape at Oro Bay, just south of Buna and 211 miles nearer the Philippines. At these entrepots, the cargoes of inbound transoceanic vessels had to be unloaded, sorted out, and either reloaded on smaller coasters or stored ashore until needed. Since New Guinea's harbors were virtually devoid of any but the most primitive docking and warehousing facilities, Allied engineers would be forced to develop useable ports "from scratch." At the war's outset, the sole cargo-handling instrumentality at Milne Bay, for instance, consisted of a single small jetty at Gili Gili, serving a Lever Brothers coconut plantation. More elaborate facilities had to be erected not only at that site, but at others along Milne's northern bayshore such as Waga Waga and Ahioma, where the water's depths reached 35 to 40 ft. The Base A complex eventually included 14 wooden piers, an oil jetty and storage tanks, and even a floating dock and heavy-duty floating crane, along with its three airfields.

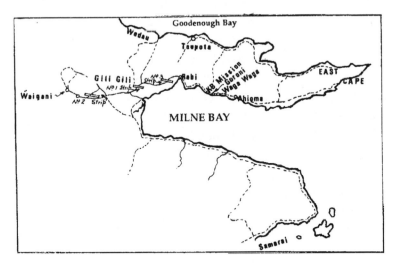

MAP 4. MILNE BAY (BASE A), PAPUA, NEW GUINEA, JULY 1942.

Since the bay's environing real estate was usually too waterlogged for pavement, the airstrips had to be surfaced with steel Marston matting. Even so, while landing or taking off, planes threw up clouds of muddy spray. Ships' ladings deposited on the piers had to be trucked over mired roads or lightered to storehouses or dumps often several miles distant. A chronic shortage of trained cargo-handling personnel was a further detriment to the provision of adequate logistical support for the field forces.[28]

Following the expulsion of the Japanese from the lower Solomons and Papua, there was a temporary pause while MacArthur and Nimitz (headquartered in Honolulu) consolidated the gains in their respective spheres, created more depots and airfields, gathered supplies, equipment, and reenforcements, and assembled their cohorts for the dual offensives. In addition to his Chief-of-Staff, Richard K. Sutherland, and others of the so-called "Bataan Gang" whom he loyally kept at his side, MacArthur had a superbly-talented operations team whom he nicknamed "my three K's," or "my Ku Klux Klan"—Lieutenant Generals Kenney (Fifth Air Force) and Krueger (Sixth Army/Alamo Force), and Rear Admiral Kinkaid (Seventh Fleet.)[29] Nimitz was also blessed with an indefatigable new right-hand man on the Solomon Island scene, Adm. William "Bull" Halsey, who had replaced Vice Adm. Robert L. Ghormley as chief of the South Pacific segment of his Pacific Ocean Areas Command. Halsey, based at Noumea, New Caledonia, worked in surprising harmony with MacArthur—in marked contrast to the Navy's big boss in Washington, Admiral King, who detested "Dougout Doug." Despite the perpetually simmering interservice rivalry emanating from the topmost command level in Washington, the outlook for the Allies in the Pacific was beginning to take on a perceptibly rosier hue.[30]

For the Japanese, on the other hand, the contest in the Southern Seas was assuming a more malignant visage. With their naval air capabilities badly compromised by the heavy attrition of carrier planes and experienced pilots in the Coral Sea and Midway affrays, coupled with the failure of their 8th Area Army to hold its ground in the lower Solomons and Papua, Imperial General Headquarters was forced to revamp its strategy. In anticipation of the Allied offensives, the Japanese war lords swiftly pumped in fresh manpower and shored up their ramparts in New Guinea and the upper Solomons. These efforts availed little, however, in parrying the ever-

more-puissant blows of Kenney's U. S. Fifth and Royal Australian
Air Forces, operating from a multiplicity of dromes in northern
Queensland and eastern Papua in concert with XIII Air Task Force
and Marine Corps air units based in the lower Solomons. On March
3-4, 1943, a large Japanese convoy carrying an abundance of badly-
needed supplies and six thousand troop reinforcements from Rabaul
around New Britain's north coast to Lae was virtually wiped out
by Kenney's bombers and fighter planes (the Battle of the Bismarck
Sea.) This outstanding coup measureably enhanced the prospects
of the Allied ground forces, predominantly Australian, closing in
on the Lae-Salamaua enclave from the south and west. To sink the
enemy vessels, the Allied airmen had employed a new and
phenomenally successful "skip-bombing" technique introduced by
Kenney, whereby the pilot flew in on his target at 200 m.p.h. at
an extremely low, mast-top level before releasing bombs armed
with time-delayed detonating fuses, which would bounce across
the surface of the sea like skimming stones and penetrate the vessel's
hull before exploding.[31] To repair their sagging fortunes, the
Japanese dispatched aircraft by the hundreds from Truk and the
East Indies to Rabaul, and launched a flurry of air sorties, but
could do little to deflate the ballooning capability of the Allied air
arm. Japanese prospects were further dimmed by the death of their
foremost naval stratagist, Fleet Admiral Isoroku Yamamoto, architect
of the Pearl Harbor strike, when his plane was shot down on 16
April 1943 by U.S. fighters from Henderson Field, Guadalcanal.
Recent territorial gains by Halsey in the central Solomons at Vella
Lavella Island and Munda on New Georgia had further expanded
the range of Allied air cover. (The phrase "air cover," implying
blanket mastery of the air space over a specific territory, is somewhat
misleading; a more apt paradigm might be that of a cluster of
overlapping opened-out umbrellas, the handle or stem of each
representing an airfield, and the circumference of the fully-extended
umbrella representing the outermost limit or range of the type of
aircraft based there, bearing in mind that bombers, with their
larger fuel capacity, have a wider range than fighters. Each fresh
stepping stone acquired by Allied ground forces brought an

additional airfield/umbrella, topography and soil conditions permitting).[32]

In late June 1943, the ground action in MacArthur's theatre began to pick up steam, as his forces made an unopposed descent upon the Trobriand Islands of Woodlark and Kiriwina in the Solomon Sea, and airfields were developed on each from which bombers and fighters could assail Rabaul and Lae. At the same time, a small Alamo expedition made an amphibious leap upcoast, landing just sixty miles short of Lae at Nassau Bay near Salamaua.[33]

VII

4ESB'S PRECURSORS:

CARTWHEELING TOWARD RABAUL.

To make much sense of 534th EB&SR's transposition from the Milne Bay "butt" to the tip of the Alamo lance which MacArthur was levelling at the Japanese empire's Philippine underbelly, there is an unavoidable necessity to sketch in the activities of the two Engineer Special Brigades who had preceded us to the SWPA. This presents a daunting challenge, since Army amphib formations did not normally function tactically under brigade control, but typically were attached to AGF units or task forces for specific missions, reverting to ASF-base control upon their completion. Therefore our focus must be upon specific regiments, battalions, even companies. The responsibilities of command at the brigade level were threefold, essentially: (1) procurement of landing craft and other amphibious equipment, parts, and supplies, and their forwarding to its components, (2) provision of a radio net for communication with and between these elements, and (3) consultation with Theatre and Army commanders regarding the planning and execution of joint operations and the deployment of ESB units.[1]

The Nassau Bay initiative, MacArthur's opening gambit in the *OPERATION CARTWHEEL* offensive against Rabasul, marked the combat debut of seahorse soldiers in the SWPA. Its intent was to roll up the eastern flank of Lt. Gen. Hatazo Adachi's 18th Army by capturing Salamaua. The action was notable for the courageous performance of an element of Brig. Gen. William F. Heavey's 2d Engineer Special Brigade.

Stalled at Ft. Ord, Cal., for some two months between late fall of 1942 and early 1943 by the dearth of shipping, 2ESB had dribbled into Australia in considerable disarray during February and March 1943, its constituents deposited randomly at east-coast ports from Sydney to Townsville. Two of its three boat-and-shore regiments, 542d and 592d, were reconcentrated at a locale just north of the city of Rockhampton in Queensland, while its 532d was posted six hundred miles farther north near Cairns. Once things were sorted out, Heavey's amphibs were dismayed to discover that there were scarcely any landing craft for them to work with. The boat-repair specialists of the 411th Base Shop Battalion, dispatched overseas in advance of 2ESB with the urgent mission of reassembling the knocked-down wooden LCVP's shipped from the U.S., had found upon their arrival at Cairns that no physical facilities whatsoever had been made available for the project. Moreover, the components of the LCVP "kits," like 2ESB's personnel, had been offloaded at docks all along the eastern Australian seaboard. Weeks were consumed in locating and gathering together at Cairns all of the Higgins-boat sections, engines, and hardware, a process complicated by the variations in track gauge of the antiquated Australian railways over which they had to be hauled. Having no recourse other than to erect an assembly plant "from scratch," the 411th, with the help of Heavey's newly-arrived 562d Engineer Boat Maintenance Battalion and 532d EB&SR, lost no time in rounding up building materials and constructing a 450-ft. "factory" with three production lines. Once the plant was up and running, the first operable LCVP emerged on 7 April 1943, and soon the amphib artisans were turning out seven each day. When a sufficient quantity had accumulated, 532d's boat-and-shoremen commenced joint training with Australian infantry stationed in the Cairns vicinity, most notably the 9th A.I.F. Division, the famed "Rats of Tobruk," fresh from North Africa.

Down at Rockhampton, pending the acquisition of lighters, the personnel of the 542d and 592d received instruction in infantry tactics and jungle warfare, and sharpened their skills in aircraft recognition, antiaircraft marksmanship, signal-communication, beach reconnaisance, beach-mat installation, boat-repair, and vehicle-waterproofing.[2]

During the first week in May, a detachment of the 562d EBM deck-loaded ten hard-used LCM's on Liberty ships at Brisbane and sailed across the Coral Sea to Port Moresby, thereby becoming the first Army amphibs to set foot on New Guinea. Their mission was to transport supplies from Moresby one hundred miles westward along the island's south coast to the mouth of the Lakekamu River, and up that serpentine stream to Bulldog, deep in the interior. Bulldog was the support base for an Australian force holding the mountain-girt village of Wau, a gold-mining center and airfield a bare 25 miles southwest of Japanese-occupied Salamaua on New Guinea's north coast. The Aussies at Wau were preparing to attack Salamaua from the rear, or landward side, in concert with U.S. 41st Division elements advancing upcoast from Buna-Gona. Scarcely had the 562d amphibs nosed in at Bulldog, however, when torrential rains washed out portions of the tortuous mountain road leading up to Wau, forcing cancellation of the waterborne-resupply attempt, and compelling the Aussies there to rely upon C-47's of the USAAF and RAAF for delivery of supplies, while the EBM detachment sailed their LCM's back to Port Moresby.

The next amphibs to be introduced to New Guinea were from 592d EB&SR's Boat Battalion, assigned lighterage duties at Milne Bay, a dark and dismal locale, as we in the 534th would discover upon our arrival there a year later. The steep, jungle-swathed promontories of the Stirling Range looming above the bay were popularly referred to as the Cloudy Mountains, since their summits were usually shrouded in thick mist or obscured by heavy clouds, spawning precipitation which averaged 200 inches annually and drenching their slopes incessantly, or so it seemed. As though the Milne Bayshore's steamy heat, soupy quagmires, and dripping verdure were not sufficient trial for the human spirit, the area was a malarial pesthole. Earlier in the Papuan campaign, when quinine or chloroquine was in short supply, the rate of infection among personnel stationed there hovered around 4,000 per 1,000, meaning that every individual could expect to suffer four major bouts of malarial chills and fever a year! When atabrine was developed as an anti-protozoal, a daily prophylactic dosage was mandated for every serviceman in SWPA. No antimalarial drug, however, has to this day proven totally effective against all strains, and up to 20% of cases of falciparum malaria, so prevalent in Burma, can be fatal. Despite such environmental hazards, Heavey's 592d boatmen applied themselves assiduously to their harbor tasks, steering around the hulks of bomb-shattered ships and Japanese landing craft sunk in the shallows during the repulse of the previous year's invasion. The seahorsemen raised, repaired, and restored to service several of these derelict barges to supplement their meager flotilla.[3]

In anticipation of the demands soon to be imposed by the pending offensive up the north coast, 300 of the 542d's shoremen at Rockhampton were sent up to construct a staging and boat-repair base on the small island of Samarai just off the mouth of Milne Bay. Scarcely had they completed their task when it became evident that the site was too remote from the developing battle zone, and after a few months, Heavey relocated the facility to Oro Bay, where he eventually established his command post (25 October 1943.) That spring—actually fall in the southern hemisphere—an urgent request for amphib assistance was relayed from Maj. Gen. Horace Fuller, commanding the 41st Infantry Division currently laboring northward up the Papuan coastline from Buna through primeval swamps and slimy, reptile-infested jungles. Not until more LCVP's could be turned out at Cairns, however, could substantive help be tendered.[4] When a sufficient quantity had accumulated, the Higgins boats were brought up on freighters to Milne Bay, put overboard, and navigated by boat crews of 532 EB&SR under cover of darkness through the treacherous passage around New Guinea's eastern tip and up the coast to Oro Bay. (Some 2,000 new lighters would eventually be forwarded over this route for delivery to various amphib units.) For the time being, the constant menace of Japanese air attacks made daytime runs too risky to attempt. Navigation through these uncharted waters was further hampered by the unpredictability of the tides along the Papuan coast—often there was only a single rise-and-fall every twenty-four hours rather than the usual two.[5]

Oro Bay, fifteen miles south of Buna Village, though a much smaller indentation than Milne Bay, was deep enough for use by transoceanic vessels, but had little, if any, wharfage. Here, too, the remains of bombed-out ships poked above the shallows, mementos of the previous year's savage fighting in the vicinity. Chosen by MacArthur's staff as the location for forward Base B, Oro Bay would undergo major transformation beginning in mid-June 1943. Eventually, a half-dozen or more wooden wharfs would line its waterfront, at one of which, 1,500 ft. in length, four Liberty ships could moor simultaneously. With time, Oro Bay would also acquire a floating dock and crane. At neither Base A nor Base B, however, could adequate sheltered storage be provided at the mooring sites, and ladings discharged at the latter had to be trucked as far as twenty miles to facilities such as the vital Dobodura airdromes, mandating widespread road and bridge construction. As MacArthur commented, decrying the lack of pre-existing infrastructure in his theatre, it was an "engineer's war."[6]

Toward the middle of May 1943, the 532d EB&SR, having finally accumulated enough landing barges to do the job for which it had been trained, set up its bivouac at Oro Bay preparatory to its up-coming combat mission in support of Fuller's 41st Division units. On 18 June, the regimental campsite was pasted by enemy bombers, inflicting the first of many casualties which Heavey's units would incur in the course of their extensive campaigning. At the month's end, an advance party of "boats" from 532d's Company A and "shovels" from Company D shoved off in their new LCVP's to cruise up to Morobe village, midway between Oro Bay and Salamaua, and link up with the vanguard of the 41st.

At Morobe, in close proximity to Adachi's lines, not only did the Yanks have to maintain a sharp lookout for Japanese, but for non-human infiltrators as well. On one occasion, a quartet of GI's from the 163d Infantry Regiment were taking a respite by cooling off in brackish water near the mouth of the Morobe River when a ravenous crocodile soundlessly and with the speed of lightening dragged one of their number underwater and completely devoured him, apparently, for none of his remains were ever recovered. (Normally, large natural predators like crocs or sharks tended to shun areas of human activity—alas, the same could not be said of New Guinea's insect denizens, who descended in clouds wherever there was the scent of human flesh.)[7]

The A Company boatmen, tasked with transporting and landing a battalion-sized force of the 162d Infantry Regiment (including an artillery battery), under Col. A. R. MacKechnie, were fated to play center stage in the upcoming Nassau Bay incursion. Returning to Oro Bay for a hasty rehearsal, the amphibs assembled a convoy of thirty-three LCVP's, an LCM, and three former Jap barges, and steered back upcoast to Mageri Point close by Morobe, 55 miles south of Nassau Bay. Here, after taking aboard MacKechnie's 740-man task force, its vehicles, field guns, and a couple of caterpillar dozers, the flotilla, split into three boat sections or "waves," headed out to sea at twenty-minute intervals after darkness fell on 29 June, shepherded by two Navy PT Boats. The high-powered PT's, with a cruising speed of 25 knots, recurrently outran the slower landing craft, limited to a mere 8 knots. To add to their troubles, the three sections sailed into the teeth of an unanticipated tropical storm, bringing mountainous seas, howling winds, and blinding rain, knocking out their radio communications and scattering their formations. Disoriented by the storm and the stygian blackness, one boat wave overshot the designated landing zone and was forced to put about and return to Morobe. The other two made it inshore as planned at 0100 to a beach within the Japanese perimeter about seventeen miles south of Salamaua. Grounding in 10 to 12-ft. surf, the amphib coxswains managed to get all the task force personnel on shore without losing a man. Unfortunately, however, much of their equipment, arms, and stores were ruined as twenty-one of the barges broached and were pounded into wreckage by the crashing waves. While the two bulldozers made it on to the beach before daylight, none of the field guns could be retrieved, and only four of the emptied barges were able to retract and reach safety at Morobe.

The sixty-eight stranded crewmen, armed only with their personal weapons and a few machine guns recovered from their splintered boats, were posted by Colonel MacKechnie on the southern flank of the beachhead. The Japanese in the vicinity, alerted to their presence by the noise of boat and bulldozer engines at full throttle, attacked by the hundreds the next night. The amphibs, frequently in bitter hand-to-hand combat, repelled their assailants, as did MacKechnie's infantry, and the tenuous beachhead was preserved. In recognition of A Company's valorous stand, which cost the lives of two of its officers and seven of its enlisted men, it was later awarded the first of the many battle honors accumulated by 2ESB units. Heavey's feisty seahorsemen had proven their mettle in combat and won their spurs—or spars, as it were.[8]

The Nassau Bay penetration expanded day-by-day as MacKechnie's force linked up with Australian battalions who had battled their way out of the high mountains from Wau. Additional units of the 41st, some hiking up from Morobe, others boated in by the 532d, plunged into the fray as well. Several sticky command disputes between Yanks and Aussies had to be resolved before the Allied aggregation succeeded in battling its way across Mt. Tambu and other ridges barring the way to Salamaua. To replace those lost in the initial landing and accomodate the increasing volume of shore-to-shore traffic from Morobe, sixty-seven new 532d boats and crews, along with shore Company D, were brought in. Night after night, the amphib LCVP's ran a gauntlet of machine-gun and mortar fire to import reinforcements, equipment, and stores— and take off casualties, mail, and evacuees—at a succession of beaches ever closer to the squalid seaside town of Salamaua. Once adequate aerial protection could be provided by Fifth Air Force, the boatmen switched to daytime navigation. While this lightened—and enlightened—their task, it exposed them to heavier and more accurate enemy fire from the shore, reciprocated by the amphibs with the machine-guns mounted on their boats.

In early August, as their casualties and fatigue mounted, the 532d companies were relieved by C and D of the 542d and rejoined the rest of their regiment at Milne Bay for rehearsals with the battle-hardened 9th A.I.F. for another and bigger seaborne assault.

During the first days of September, two months after his forfeiture of Nassau Bay, General Adachi had most of Salamaua's played-out defenders—some 6,000 in mumber—evacuated by barge to Lae, and others taken off by submarine to Madang, after which the ramshackle town was abandoned to Fuller's Yanks and the Aussie "cobbers" (ll September 1943.) This relatively-minor operation, rough and drawn-out though it had been for the participants, had, in the larger scheme of things, been intended only as a diversion, a feint, to confuse and mislead the Japanese. The main objective of the campaign was the suppression of the menacing stronghold at Lae, 60 miles beyond Salamaua, at the angle on the shoreline where the southward-flowing Markham River empties into Huon Gulf. (Lae is familiar to most Americans as the point from which aviatrix Amelia Earhart and her navigator last touched down for refueling on their ill-fated transglobal flight attempt in 1937, ending in their mysterious disappearance in the Pacific Ocean near Howland Island.)

To this end, a far more intricate and larger-scale joint amphibious expedition had been launched from Morobe on 3 September, for which the entire 532d EB&SR and 54 of its remaining LCVP's and LCM's had been requisitioned. The shore-to-shore employment to which Heavey's amphibs had hitherto been accustomed was now expanded to include ship-to-shore lighterage under the direct supervision of "Uncle Dan, the Amphibious Man" Barbey, and in close cooperation with his VII Amphibious Force. At his command were three flotillas of beaching craft—one each of LST's, LCI's, and LCT's—along with a trio of APA's [assault transports], one American and two Australian, an AKA [assault cargo ship], and several high-speed APD transports. (APD's were renovated flush-deck World-War-I-vintage destroyers with two of their four boilers and stacks removed, quarters and mess accomodations for troops installed, and retrofitted with davits for four landing craft.) Cruisers and destroyers provided screening and pre-invasion fire-power. (As the conflict in SWPA wore on, Barbey's amphibious resources would expand, both in numbers and varieties of ships.)

For the Lae operation, which would be VII 'phib's first venture beyond Milne Bay into New Guinea coastal waters, the Barbey/ Heavey combine would carry ashore and sustain Maj. Gen. George A. Wootten's 9th A.I.F., with whom the 532d had been rehearsing. The army and navy amphibs would have to learn to work together amicably, something not easily achieved on first acquaintance, given the latter's patronizing attitude toward the "army landlubbers" or "amateur yachtsmen" whom they perceived as having muscled in on their turf—or surf.[9]

The initial landing, at 0630 4 September, on so-called "Red Beach," twenty miles due east of Lae, went almost flawlessly following a ten-minute barrage by five destroyers. Although the 532d shoremen efficiently funnelled Wootten's troops and materiel across the beachhead despite heavy and persistent hammering by enemy air raiders, Barbey, lacking first-hand experience in shore engineering, complained of what he termed "unsatisfactory" preparation of exits from the beaches and roads to supply dumps. His carping attitude was soon dispelled as he observed the westward progress of the slouch-hatted Diggers, forced to slosh along the trackless shoreline toward Lae through ten days of continuous torrential rainfall. The hard-driven 532d boatmen, unfazed by a paucity of useable intermediate beaches, kept Wootten's column resupplied by lighterage from the beachhead with consistent reliability. One 532d boat team in particular won elaborate plaudits from the Aussies for ferrying their infantry across the flooded mouth of the Buso River for sixty hours without let-up in the face of heavy enemy fire until pontoon bridging could be emplaced. Wootten was fully appreciative of their efforts—he stated afterwards: "Not for one hour has my advance on Lae been held up by failure of the 2d Engineer Special Brigade to deliver troops, supplies, or ammunition at the time and place needed."[10]

The Lae campaign was climaxed by a carefully-rigged trap sprung upon Adachi's befuddled forces. In the first paratrooper drop of the Pacific War, the U.S. llth Airborne Division's 503d Regiment seized an abandoned airstrip at Nadzab, just up the Markham River from Lae. The field was swiftly rehabilitated for the use of Kenney's C-47 transports, who airlifted from Port Moresby a second A.I.F. division, Major General Vasey's 7th. Adachi's legions, caught in a three-way squeeze between the Allied columns converging from Salamaua, Red Beach, and Nadzab, fled the shattered town of Lae on 15 September, just four days after Salamaua had fallen. The toll levied on the 532d by the twelve-day Lae campaign had not been trivial; in landing more than 10,000 tons of cargo and 12,000 troops, 9 seahorsemen had been killed, 66 wounded, and 5 landing craft damaged beyond repair.[11] Only 9,000 of the 28,000 Japanese corralled at Lae managed to slip away into the mountains of the Huon Peninsula before the Allied trap snapped shut.[12]

The way was now cleared for the subsequent pinching off of the entire peninsula, which MacArthur intended to use as a springboard for jumping across Vitiaz and Dampier straits to the island of New Britain and grasping the ultimate prize of Rabaul at its far end. In the wake of the signal victory so adroitly wrought by Blamey and Krueger, Vasey's 7th A.I.F. trudged back inland to Nadzab and advanced up the Markham and Ramu river valleys to seal off the peninsula from the southwest, while their countrymen in Wootten's 9th turned about, slogging and slugging their way along the shore toward the port of Finschaffen at the peninsula's southeastern corner, 64 miles beyond Lae. With its easy accessibility to deep-draft vessels and proximity to New Britain, Finschaffen was a plum which MacArthur was eager to pluck and the Japanese no less determined to retain. The town perched on a narrow half-mile-wide coastal shelf backed by a densely-forrested wall of mountains. To facilitate its capture, a brigade-strength task force of Wootten's division was sea-lifted from Buna and Lae by VII 'phib to a landing on 22 September at a beach designated "Scarlet," six miles north of Finschaffen. To handle the off-loading, 550 boat-

and-shoremen of the 532d sailed over from Lae in their own landing craft.

Wootten's force achieved a firm lodgement at Scarlet, although the brief prefatory naval shelling had not silenced all the Japanese guns concealed in pillboxes overlooking the beach. While their counter-fire inflicted moderate casualties among the landing force, the nuisance was soon eradicated by renewed naval shelling, and the moment the Aussies and their trucks, tanks, cannons, and 850 tons of supplies were well ashore, the invaders surged southward along the constricted coastal bench toward Finschhaven. Anticipating resistance from no more than a few hundred foemen at most, the Diggers found themselves confronted by 5,000, and not until another of Wootten's brigades could be hastily imported from Lae on 532d's boats could the hostiles be driven out of Finschaffen into the surrounding heights (2 October.)[13]

Subsequent Jap attempts to puncture the Finschaffen/Scarlet perimeter forced the shore parties to keep their mitts up. On the rainy night of 17-18 October, some of Adachi's dispossessed soldiery, hoping to sever the Allied dragon's tail, as it were, mounted a seaborne counterattack on Scarlet Beach itself, guarded by a scant two companies of Australians and a contingent of 532d shoremen. The amphibs, having attended with commendable dispatch to the unloading and forwarding of vehicles and supplies from Barbey's second echelon, though frequently strafed and bombed by enemy aircraft, acquitted themselves with distinction in defense of the beachhead during pre-dawn hours of the 18th. About 0400, in pitch darkness and amidst a steady downpour, four enemy barges stealthily approached the shore with engines muffled and ramps partially lowered. The obtruders were within 200 yards of dry land before being spotted by an eagle-eyed 532d artilleryman and the Aussies manning a Bofors anti-aircraft gun. The barrel of the ack-ack gun could not be sufficiently depressed to engage the incoming craft, but the amphib gunner trained the sights of his 37-mm. piece squarely on the leading barge. Holding his fire until its bow struck the sand, he disabled it with his opening round. Though the survivors were quickly rescued by comrades in the other boats, they all came to grief nonetheless after grounding farther down the beach and wading straight into the sights of a camouflaged amphib HMG [50-cal. Heavy Machine Gun] emplaced a few yards from the water's edge. The gunner, a mild-mannered Idaho teenager, Pvt. Nathan "Junior" Van Noy, and his loader, Corp. Stephen Popa, coolly opened fire, felling some in the boat and systematically raking those emerging onto the beach. While a team of Jap flame-throwers in the forefront was mowed down, other assailants dropped to the ground and lobbed hand grenades at the spouting machine-gun, blowing off one of Van Noy's legs and severely wounding Popa. Pinned underneath an adversary whom he had slain with his rifle, Popa was extricated and dragged off to safety by amphibs who had dug themselves in on higher ground to the rear, but Van Noy, despite his own grievous injuries and ignoring entreaties to withdraw, continued firing into the darkness. He exhausted two entire belts of ammunition before slumping over dead with his fingers still gripping the trigger. Daylight revealed heaps of Japanese corpses in front of his gun-barrel. The two machine-gunners had accounted for at least half of the thirty-nine enemy dead strewn along the sands, thereby assuring the safety of the beachhead. For his singular act of heroism, 19-year-old ex-schoolboy Van Noy was awarded a posthumous Congressional Medal of Honor, the war's first to be earned by someone from the ASF or Corps of Engineers, and the Navy named a vessel in his honor, while Popa received a Silver Star for gallantry.[14]

In Allied hands, and after substantial upgrading and expansion of its archaic port facilities, Finschaffen blossomed into one of the SWPA's busiest troop-staging, cargo-transfer, and small-ship-repair depots.[15] Meanwhile, Vasey's 7th A.I.F., having gained Dumpu in the upper Ramu Valley, turned eastward and battled toward the coast across the steep hogbacks crinkling the northern segment of the peninsula. For their part, Wootten's boys laboriously flushed out concentrations of Japanese dug in on the heights above Finschaffen at nearby Sattelburg and elsewhere in the southern reaches of the soaring Finnisterre-Saruwaged-Cromwell Mountain Range. As their quarry withdrew up the rugged coastline toward

the village of Sio fronting on Vitiaz Strait, the "blokes" of 9th
A.I.F. doggedly pursued, alternately sloshing through mangrove
and nipa swamps or inching up cliffs so sheer at places as to require
scaling with ropes, while the 532d amphibs kept pace, scouting
out a succession of landing sites through which Wootten's battalions
could be kept in biscuits and bullets. The Aussies showed their
gratitude by fondly dubbing Heavey's seahorsemen "The Cape
Cod Commandos."[16]

To isolate and "throw a loop of envelopment" (one of
MacArthur's choice phrases) around the Japanese fugitives
congregating in Sio, a regimental task force of the U.S. 32d Division,
conveyed by Barbey's VII 'phib and screened by eight destroyers,
was put ashore in calm seas at Saidor, 70 miles upcoast from Sio,
on 2 January 1944, with the aid of Heavey's 532d and 542d
"commandos." The 542d shore battalion swiftly laid steel matting
across the stony and pebble-carpeted beach over which the offloaded vehicles could trundle. Then, laboring alongside beach
details from the 127th Inf. Regt., the shoremen clinched a new
speed record by emptying a half-dozen of Barbey's cavernous LST's
within a mere three hours, so that they could retract and regain
safe anchorage before enemy aircraft could reach the scene.[17]

Seventy miles or so northwest of Saidor, beyond the far end of
the Huon Peninsula, lay the next sizeable Japanese coastal stronghold
in Northeast New Guinea, Madang, to which General Adachi had
removed his command center after quitting Lae. Here, with his
shrunken and shaken ranks reinforced, reordered, and refitted, he
awaited a chance to strike a counterblow. The 32d Div. GI's who
had splashed ashore at Saidor (their first reentry into combat since
Buna, where 9,000 of their number had been smitten by malaria),
were prevented by drenching monsoon rains from carrying out
with celerity their part of a planned pincer movement on Sio in
cooperation with Wootten's northbound Aussies. Their tardiness
allowed the bedraggled Jap cat to slip out of the bag once more, as
Adachi, commandeering a submarine at Madang and making an
undetected end run past the 32d's beachhead at Saidor, personally
superintended the evacuation of the troops threatened with

ensnarement at Sio. Packing as many as possible on barges for an escape by sea to Madang, he ordered those left behind on the beach to join forces with their confederates fending off the Australians in the adjacent mountains. The embattled highlanders, in turn, were instructed to disengage and, in company with the stranded Sioans—about 14,000 in all—make their way as best they could through the trackless interior wilds to Madang and safety. Having thus done all within his power to salvage this fractured wing of his 18th Army, Adachi reboarded his sub and, eluding patrolling American PT boats, returned whence he came. Four thousand of his cross-country retreatants subsequently perished in the jungle fastness from hunger, fever, and exhaustion. Not until 1 March 1944 would the last faint, famished, and ravaged survivors of the Salama/Lae/Finschaffen debacle drag themselves into Madang.[18]

Wootten's 9th A.I.F. victors eventually joined hands with those of Vasey's 7th, and together they captured Bogadjim, just short of Madang, on 13 April 1944, thereby ensuring Allied mastery of the entire Huon Peninsula.[19] (I have limned the foregoing campaigning in considerable detail, since it appears to me that, aside from the 11th Airborne's drop on Nadzab, it has received far less attention from American journalists than MacArthur's subsequent advance to the Vogelkopf, which was an exclusively Alamo enterprise.)

Meanwhile, if we may regress temporally to the immediate aftermath of Finschaffen's capture, MacArthur's nimble intellect had been weighing his options as to the cheapest and quickest manner of prosecuting the remainder of *CARTWHEEL*. To clear an entryway for Kinkaid's Fleet into the Bismarck Sea through the bottle-neck of the Vitiaz and Dampier straits, he had resolved to descend upon New Britain's southwest coast at Arawe, directly opposite Finschaffen. Arawe had not only a prime airdrome, but a small harbor from which PT squadrons could deny the narrows to enemy maritime traffic. To ensure complete domination of the straits, however, it would be necessary to gain control of the entire western tip of New Britain. In mid-December, therefore, employing tactics similar to those which had proven so fortuitous at Salamaua/

Lae, MacArthur made his opening move onto New Britain at Arawe. This, too, was the first in time, but much the lesser in weight, of a two-part operation, to divert the enemy's attention from the major effort at another point of entry.

Barbey was directed to ship Brig. Gen. Julian W. Cunningham's independent 112th Cavalry Regiment from Goodenough Island for the Arawe landing. Army amphib support, under the direction of Lt. Col. William White (Memphis, Tn.), was entrusted to 592d EB&SR's Company B, with a pair of 2ESB's rocket-Ducks appended. (While in Australia, several of Heavey's LCM's and DUKW's had been retro-fitted with racks of 4.5-in. rocket launchers, whose missiles had a range of 1,100 yards. Forming a so-called "Brigade Support Battery," these were intended to supplement conventional naval fire power on landings or operate independently in constricted or shallow waterways where Barbey's larger gun-ships could not be effectively deployed. Barrages from the two amphib rocket-DUKW's and a similarly-armed Navy LCI would help "pave the way" for the primary assault waves at the two sites selected for the Arawe landing, both on a small peninsula known as Cape Merkus. This would be the first field test of Heavey's rocketry in an amphibious assault.)[20]

Scheduled for the morning of 15 December 1943, the mini-invasion seemed jinxed when, during the pre-dawn hours, a reconnaisance team in fifteen rubber boats, attempting to sneak onto the base of the peninsula, was detected by vigilant Jap pickets and subjected to a murderous crossfire, puncturing all but three of the boats and killing sixteen of the scouts. Aside from this single mishap, however, the landings at daybreak went off better than anyone could have foreseen. After a fifteen-minute barrage laid on by Navy subchasers plus a bit of last-minute aerial bombing and strafing, the amphib rocket-Ducks, launched from LSD CARTER HALL, moved close inshore along with the LCI(R) and fired off their unnerving missiles. Then came the first four assault waves, also from CARTER HALL, in slow-paced but sure-footed LVT's of the 1st Marine Amphibian Tractor Battalion, crossing the barely-submerged coral reefs and attaining the shore without interference.

Amphib scouts had located gaps in the coral through which all but one of Colonel White's LCM's and LCVP's, bringing in follow-up waves from the attack transport H.M.A.S. WESTRALIA, navigated safely to the beaches as well.[21]

Once ashore, the only opposition came in the form of nineteen enemy bombers who dodged past the air cover and briefly disrupted shore party proceedings. On day two, larger formations of Rabaul-based aircraft showed up, sinking an APC "Applecart" [Assault Coastal Transport] just offshore, damaging several smaller vessels, and machine-gunning forty or so survivors floating in the water, among them Colonel White, all of whom were snatched from Neptune's clutches by his boatmen. Enemy air harriers revisited the beachhead for several more days until downed or driven off by AAF fighter planes and ground fire, with at least five kills credited to amphib gunners. A fortnight after the landing, two battalions of Japanese infantry dispatched from far-off Rabaul threw themselves against Cunningham's perimeter, but failed to dent it. All the while, Co. B's boats prowled adjacent coastal waters too shallow for the Navy PT's, in order to forestall any enemy maritime counteractions. Nocturnal patrolling was especially hazardous, since the Japanese craft usually emerged under cover of darkness. Amphib boatmen ferretted out and destroyed numerous hostile craft hidden on nearby islets or in mainland coves. By piggybacking the Rocket-DUKWs on the more stable and heavily-powered LCM's, they were able, upon sighting enemy watercraft, to move in and blast them at close range with the fearsome missiles. By mid-January 1944, the last of the would-be spoilers in the vicinity had withdrawn to more distant precincts and there were no further Japanese attempts to retake Arawe.[22]

To this small parcel of New Britain a bigger chunk was added, as MacArthur brought Maj. Gen. William H. Rubertus's revived 1st Marine Division up from Australia for the main event on 26 December at Cape Gloucester, near the island's northwest tip. Bearing more directly on Dampier Strait and with two enemy-built airstrips, Cape Gloucester afforded even handier basing for aircraft and PT-boats. This intrusion, essentially replicating that at Arawe, though of much larger dimensions, was allotted Barbey's full complement of beaching vessels, screened by a squadron of cruisers and destroyers. Units of 592 EB&SR with no prior exposure to combat were selected to round out the cast of the "Cape caper."[23] The two beaching sites were repeatedly savaged by a three-week-long pre-invasion aerial bombardment. At day-break on the day after Christmas, following an hour's naval shelling and further scourging by the missiles of 2ESB's Support Battery, wave after wave of Marines—thirteen thousand in all—waded ashore with relative impunity from VII 'phib's LCI's, LST's, and APD's (Barbey was reluctant to risk his vulnerable APA transports in such close proximity to the Rabaul hornet's nest). Overhead, U.S. P-38's engaged swarms of hostile aircraft, sending scores of Japan's finest down in flames, though not in time to prevent the bombing and sinking of an escorting destroyer, drowning 108 of those aboard.

While 592d's boats did ship-to-shore transferrals, losing several of their crewmen to aerial strafing, and Heavey's rocket-DUKW's were of further service as itinerant batteries, clobbering inland targets, the well-schooled Marines did their own shore-party work. The ground assault elements, compelled to slog through swampy jungle to reach the coveted airfields, soon came under fire from camouflaged log bunkers. To minimize their casualties on the advance inland, the leathernecks used battle tanks, blasting out, burning up, or entombing their tormenters.

Although three weeks of close-quarter combat under climatic conditions more trying than those on Guadalcanal were required to flush out and eradicate the 10,000 Japanese adversaries, fewer than 300 of Rubertus's men were slain. More insufferable than the fire-fights were nature's elements in this quintessential rain forest, where attempting to sleep in a foxhole was like reclining in an overflowing bathtub. All participants, friend and foe alike, were buffetted and drenched by exceptionally horrific monsoon storms, bringing rainfall of as much as 16 inches a day and kicking up offshore waves as high as 20 ft. Lashed mercilessly by these natural furies, the 592d and Support Battery crews were stretched to their limit running resupply missions and patrolling the angry watercourses off the beaches against counterattacks. While a number of amphib lighters were capsized or swamped in the process, no crewmen were drowned, although several seahorse casualties and boat losses resulted from Japanese air strikes, and, more regrettably, from the blunders of a few U.S. pilots who mistook 592d craft for those of the enemy. When the Cape Gloucester operation stabilized, PT-base construction and airfield renovations commenced, and the Marine perimeter was expanded until it melded with that of Cunningham's troopers at Arawe, assuring American dominance of the entire western end of the island.[24]

In a third, but less consequential, amphibious initiative on the same date as that on Cape Gloucester, a company-sized task force of 592d shoremen, travelling on Navy PT-boats from Finschaffen across 105 miles of storm-tossed sea, made an unmolested landing on Long Island at the head of Vitiaz Strait, using rubber rafts. In their wake, LCM's and LCVP's from 592d's Boat Battalion brought in a detachment of Aussie radiomen and equippage for the purpose of monitoring enemy traffic through the straits. Known for its spectacular volcanic lake nestled between twin mountain peaks, the islet had been ignored by the Japanese. Its occupation was merely temporary and escaped enemy notice, but provided valuable intelligence.[25]

Shark-shaped New Britain, measuring some 300 airline miles from end to end, is dominated throughout by a range of lofty, precipitous mountains broken by deep gorges and fast-flowing streams, and smothered in tangled verdure. On its eastern extremity, where several active volcanoes smudge the skies, lay the picturesque port of Rabaul. Since 1942, the Japanese had been busily fortifying the heights ringing its semicircular harbor, and here their 8th Area Army (embracing both Gen. Harukichi Hyakutaka's 17th Army in the Solomons and Adachi's 18th in eastern New Guinea) was headquartered. An impregnable underground redout had been created, honeycombed with miles of interconnecting tunnels and caverns, replete with barracks, hospitals, anti-aircraft and heavy artillery bunkers, machine-shops, and storage rooms crammed with enough supplies and munitions to sustain its 100,000-man garrison for years. Rabaul boasted five airfields, its harbor was heavily mined, and its roads cleverly camouflaged. So unassailable had it become, in the opinion of the Pentagon Chiefs, that at their August 1943 Quebec Conference they had advised MacArthur and Nimitz to sidestep it and pounce on softer prey such as Kavieng on nearby New Ireland or Manus in the Admiralty Islands farther to the west.[26]

While MacArthur's cohorts had made impressive gains toward their *CARTWHEEL* objective as per the original plan, equally gratifying progress had been achieved in Halsey's domain. By November 1943, Maj. Gen. Allen Turnage's 3d Marine Div. (backed up by the Army's 37th and Americal divisions) had carved out a sizeable beachhead at Torokina on Bougainville's Empress Augusta Bay. The largest of the northern Solomons, Bougainville was only a short hop from Rabaul. Despite ferocious counterattacks (March 9-17) by elements of General Hyakutaka's 65,000-strong 17th Army, smarting from their less-than-creditable performance on Guadalcanal, "Bull" Halsey's interlopers were not to be evicted, nor even rocked back on their heels. Behind the bristling Yankee ramparts, Navy Seabees transformed this newly-won acreage at Bougainville's narrow waist into a major air base, from which fighters as well as bombers of the "Airsols" (Air Command Solomons, a melange of Army, Navy, Marine, Australian, and New Zealand squadrons) could readily "maul Rabaul." For the remainder of the war, Hyakutaka's minions on Bougainville would remain helplessly immured beyond the Yankee wire, gnashing their teeth while Allied airmen demolished everything above ground at Rabaul.[27]

As the new year of 1944 unfolded, Japanese Imperial Headquarters were compelled to redeploy the hard-pressed aggregations manning their south seas flank along a contracted frontier stretching from Madang and Wewak in eastern New Guinea through Rabaul and the Carolines, Marshalls, and Gilberts in the Central Pacific, to Wake Island. Thanks primarily to America's burgeoning air and naval might, Nippon's fortunes and those of the Allies had undeniably reversed. Driven from the Aleutians at the end of the previous summer, Japan had begun to feel the effects of relentless submarine and aerial attacks on her lines of supply and communication, crippling her ability to sustain and reinforce her forward positions.

As of mid-March 1943, by order of Admiral King, the three fleets operating in the Asiatic-Pacific had been redesignated numerically rather than by sector, with Halsey's thereafter known as the Third, and its counterpart under Vice Adm. Raymond A. Spruance in the Central Pacific, the Fifth, while Kinkaid's Seventh and its constituent VII 'phib continued to serve with MacArthur. Upgraded with new state-of-the-art big carriers, fast battleships, and 2,100-ton destroyers, Fifth Fleet was rounded out five months later with the creation of a subsidiary V Amphibious Force commanded by Rear Adm. R. Kelly Turner, its ground force element, V Amphibious Corps, in the hands of Marine Maj. Gen. Holland M. ("Howlin' Mad") Smith. Wielding this intrepid mallet, Nimitz had cracked the tough nuts of Makin and Tarawa in the Gilberts in November 1943, and less than three months later had taken Kwajalein and Eniwetok atolls in the Marshalls, tearing great rents in Japan's diminished shield. With Halsey's Third Fleet no longer tied down in the South Pacific area and now available for employment in his westward drive toward Japan, Nimitz reshuffled his upper echelon command structure in the spring of 1944. Spruance's Fifth Fleet and Turner's V 'phib would henceforth take missions alternately with Halsey's Third Fleet and Rear Adm. Theodore Wilkinson's III 'phib (with its ground force component under Marine Maj. Gen. Roy S. Geiger.) Rear Adm. Marc Mitscher's Fast Carrier Force, serving both fleets, would be designated TF-58 [Task Force 58] when working under Spruance, and TF-38 when under Halsey. In other words, while one Fleet Admiral's staff-and-command team was conducting invasive activities, the other's was ashore planning the next operation. As Samuel Eliot Morison explains it, "This arrangement may be compared to a change of quarterbacks in a football game, while the line and the rest of the backfield stay in; the line in this case being the fire support ships and the backfield, Fast Carrier Forces Pacific

Fleet."[28] This new format would govern Naval operations for the rest of the Pacific war.

In northeastern New Guinea, Adachi's slimmed-down ranks, along with those of Lt. Gen. Fesataro Teshimo's 2d Army farther to the west at Wakde/Sarmi, Biak, and the Vogelkopf, were tasked with defending Japan's vestigial holdings with whatever human and material resources they had at hand. Scoured and scorched night and day by Allied bombs, Rabaul no longer provided a safe haven for the Imperial Naval forces based there, and they were extricated to Truk Atoll in the Carolines, 900 miles to the north, home of the Combined Fleet. By the same token, what remained of Rabaul's once lavish stock of ground-based aircraft had been sent off to Hollandia in formerly Dutch New Guinea. In its turn, Truk itself now began to shudder under the concentrated blows of Mitscher's TF-58.[29] Japan's naval lords, in full awareness of Truk's vulnerability, had begun withdrawing their investments from that bank as well, above all, the Combined Fleet. In February, 1944, 265 of the aircraft stashed there were destroyed, 140,000 tons of shipping sunk, and many of its installations flattened, and on 29/30 April, TF-58's hawks finished off what was left. Under the lancets of Kenney's burgeoning Fifth Air Force and Halsey's Airsols, the hemorrhaging of Japan's aerial strength in MacArthur's Southwest Pacific area continued unrelentingly as well, despite sporadic tranfusions from other parts of her empire.[30]

The amphibious capabilities of MacArthur's Alamo were boosted in January and February of 1944 with the belated arrival in the theatre of Brig. Gen. David A. D. Ogden's 3ESB, released from its six months' detention in the comparatively posh environs of Ft. Ord, California, by virtue of the ever-expanding productivity of America's ship-builders. Consigned to Goodenough Island just off Papua's lower east coast not far from Milne Bay, its components, like those of Heavey's 2ESB, were soon scattered hither and yon across the theatre. The 563d EBM and part of the 543d EB&SR, for example, were sent over to Milne Bay for a turn at the LCM-reassembly plant, while 533d EB&SR's Shore Battalion was ordered forthwith to Finschaffen to replace one of Heavey's units at stevedoring duty, where it was soon joined by its mating boat battalion. Shortly thereafter, Ogden shifted his command post from Goodenough to Finschaffen as well. Toward February's end, the 533d, save for one boat company detached to Cairns for joint training with the Australians, was ordered to New Britain to assist the thinly-stretched 592d in servicing the 1st Marine Division beachhead. On 3 March, another of 533d's boat companies landed elements of the 32d Division in good order and against scant enemy resistance at Yalau Plantation on the New Guinea shore above Saidor, and commenced coastal patrolling. Last but not least, Ogden's third EB&SR, the 593d, would be quickly pressed into action even farther afield.[31]

With his feet now planted solidly on New Britain's western-most reaches, MacArthur took another long stride toward Rabaul in early March by having Hubertus send some of his 1st Marines from Cape Gloucester to seize Talasea, located on the Willaumez Peninsula which juts out like a dorsal fin two-fifths of the way along the island's north coast. For this largely-redundant exercise, the unblooded boatmen of 593d EB&SR were teamed with a section of Heavey's battle-wise 592d old-timers. The feeble enemy reaction provoked by the Talasea interposition was easily brushed aside and another airstrip pocketed cheaply, bespeaking the utter impotence of the huge garrison pent up at Rabaul and validating its erasure from further consideration by Allied strategists. One final desideratum would ensure Rabaul's total eclipse, namely, Allied control of the Bismarck Sea itself, the only corridor through which it could still collaborate with the larger "Co-Prosperity Sphere" beyond.[32]

VIII

4ESB'S PRECURSORS;

BROADJUMPING TO THE VOGELKOPF.

Emboldened by his recent triumphs, MacArthur could scarcely contain his compulsion to erase the stain of Bataan. As he stated in his memoirs, "I was still about 1,600 miles from the Philippines, and 2,100 miles from Manila."[1] All that now stood in his path were the remaining enemy hives along New Guinea's north coast, sited so as to bracket virtually every mile from Madang to Manokwari on the Vogelkopf. Foremost among them was Hollandia, lying just beyond the invisible border separating Northeastern New Guinea from Dutch New Guinea, so near and yet so far! The Rabaul beast may have been caged, even defanged, but the back door to the cage was unlocked, in the sense that Nippon's soldiery still occupied New Ireland and the Admiralty Islands, framing the Bismarck Sea on the north, thereby threatening Alamo's flank were any further westward movement to be attempted. As MacArthur pondered this conundrum, a possible resolution suddenly presented itself; B-25 pilots reported on 24 February that the Admiralties, the more remote and westerly of the hostile northern sentinels, appeared virtually devoid of Japanese. He decided to check it out forthwith.

The cluster of islands known as the Admiralties consists of 1,200-square-mile Manus, mostly primeval wilderness, a miniscule sister on its east, Los Negros (the two, separated by a 3-mile-long, 1,000-foot-wide slot of water, resembling a supine cat with a bushy curving tail), and a wreath of tiny satellites. In what eventuated as

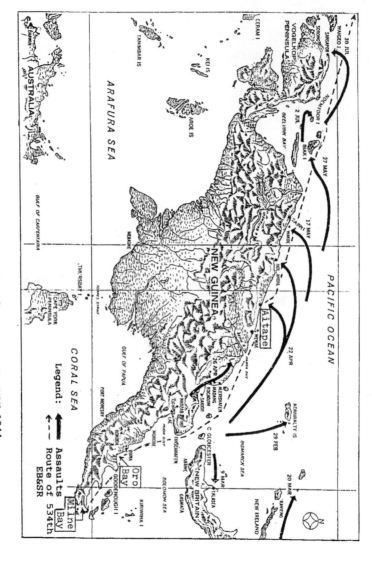

Map 5. Allied Progress Toward the Vogelkopf, March–July 1944.

one of the most brilliant coup de mains of his career, MacArthur ordered that a "reconnaisance in force" be made on Los Negros on 29 February 1944 by a 1,000-man task force from Maj. Gen. Ennis P. Swift's 1st Cavalry Division, Special. (Having no equine mounts and organized into two brigades, each with two regiments, this division was scarcely what its name implied, but simply a mobile or light infantry formation, the only one of its kind in the entire U.S. Army.) Led by Brig. Gen. William P. Chase, the recon force, to which was appended a company-sized boat detachment of 592d EB&SR and some of Heavey's Support Battery watercraft, was swiftly sealifted from Oro Bay by a hastily-rounded-up squadron of VII 'phib APD's screened by destroyers and two light cruisers, PHOENIX and NASHVILLE. (The firepower of the amphib Support Battery had recently been enhanced by the accrual of several formidably-armed "flak boats"—LCM's mounted with four ex-Martin-airplane turrets of twin 50-calibre MG's, plus a couple of 20-mm. guns and a 37-mm. cannon, in addition to their 4.5-rocket launchers. Rigged up by the 162d Ordnance Maintenance Company, the flak boats were referred to, only partly in jest, as "General Heavey's battleships.")[2]

MacArthur opted to go along aboard NASHVILLE to assess the situation for himself. Under ample air cover, the modest convoy sailed northwest through the Vitiaz Strait and across the Bismarck Sea to Los Negros. Although the landing per se, at Hyane Harbor on that island's eastern shore, went off smoothly enough on 29 February, there were in fact some 4,000 Japanese positioned under cover on its opposite side, fronting on Seeadler Sound, who made their presence known that night. Recognizing that Chase's rec force was heavily outnumbered, MacArthur made a snap judgement; rather than withdraw them, he would summon reinforcements pronto, calculating that the inevitable enemy counterattacks would be delivered in piecemeal fashion—in manageable increments, so to speak—as the Japanese were wont to do, and so it proved to be. Beginning about 0300 on their second night ashore, the landing party fended off substantial assaults on their perimeter's right flank by some 1,500 of the enemy. An hour after daybreak, there was a final suicidal charge by fifty seemingly-demented disputants singing "Deep In The Heart Of Texas!" A count of the enemy dead strewn in front of the perimeter totalled almost 200.[3]

The same day, March 2d, to everyone's immense relief, a half-dozen LST's sailed in with 1,500 additional lst Cav. troopers, along with 400 Navy Seabees and contingents of artillery, armor, and 592d amphib reinforcements cum barges. Enlarging and realigning their beachhead to enclose the island's covetted Momote airfield with its 5,000-ft. runway, the Yanks quickly turned the tables on their assailants. As soon as Japanese mortar and machine-gun fire slackened under the weight of the Yankee firepower, the intrepid seabees set to work repairing and enlarging the Momote drome. The mastery of Los Negros was no longer in doubt after Chase had part of his force sail around to Seeadler Sound and descend upon its defenders from the rear. (Seeadler, partially enclosed by Manus and Los Negros, was one of the largest, deepest, and, for Allied purposes, most convenient semi-protected anchorages in the entire South Pacific; it would serve thereafter as a superb staging and support base for the avenging octopus whose tentacles would soon be choking off the Philippines and reaching for the Japanese home islands.)

Having thrashed or trashed the hostiles on Los Negros and adjacent islets—at least those who had not hastily decamped to Manus—the lst Cavalrymen were ferried by Barbey's ships and Heavey's barges across Seeadler Harbor to the northern shore of the larger island near the village of Lorengau. Here, with heavy reliance on tanks, artillery, bulldozers, and dynamite, they reduced Manus's 340 pillboxes and bunkers to rubble—and their occupants to charred corpses—and gained another prime airfield in addition to Momote on Los Negros. After a bit of mopping up, the aim of the audacious mini-campaign in the Admiralties was fully realized, the dromes made serviceable for Allied fighters and bombers, and the real estate for a future naval sally port secured. Kenney now had a superb launching pad from which his planes could waste Truk, Kinkaid an incomparable berth for his fleet, and Krueger an inside track for his Vogelkopf express.[4]

Thus, at one fell stroke, the Bismarck Sea was transmuted into an Allied lake, and Rabaul (along with its heavily-fortified outpost at Kavieng on New Ireland) locked in, its swollen garrison hors de combat, its airfields cratered, and its harbor floor a graveyard of sunken vessels. On the Bismarck Sea's New Guinea shore, Adachi's refuge at Madang was rendered untenable, forcing his unstrung 18th Army to endure another weary wilderness trek upcoast, this time to Hansa Bay at the mouth of the mighty Sepik River and the town of Wewak beyond.

Inspired by congratulatory missives from Winston Churchill and George Marshall, MacArthur resolved to vault over Adachi's latest fallback lair at Hansa Bay/Wewak and land squarely on Hollandia in Dutch New Guinea, 580 miles closer to his cherished goal. The Joint Chiefs quickly sanctioned his scheme for an accelerated advance to the Vogelkopf and Mindanao, the southernmost island in the Philippine archipelago. The new scenario called for Nimitz's Central Pacific forces to neutralize in thorough fashion the already-badly-battered Imperial naval base at Truk in the Carolines, occupy the Mariannas, and capture Yap and the Palau Islands, 600 miles east of Mindanao, by mid-September. In furtherance of this up-dated strategy, the Washington authorities redrew the theatre boundaries, alloting what had formerly been Halsey's South Pacific domain to MacArthur's jurisdiction and reshuffling their respective forces. The Australians would take over in the Solomons and New Britain, whittling away at the isolated enemy pockets left behind, while MacArthur gained control of the Army elements previously assigned there (the 25th, 37th, 40th, 43d, 93d, and Americal divisions), with Halsey's naval appanage and Marine divisions redeployed for Nimitz's more direct drive across the western Pacific. The scope of Kenney's aerial command was similarly expanded and redesignated the Far East Air Forces, an amalgam of the Fifth Air Force and what had been XIII Army Air Task Force based in the Solomons, now upgraded to a new Thirteenth Air Force. Maj. Gen. St. Clair Streett took command of the Thirteenth, while Kenney's deputy, Ennis Whitehead, with a second star now affixed to his collar, took over the venerable Fifth. At the same time, Nimitz was instructed to lend MacArthur sufficient carriers to guarantee air coverage for the pending Hollandia operation. It was all beginning to come together rather nicely, or so it seemed at the time.[5]

With the passing of March 1944, Blamey's Aussies closed in on Madang, while Adachi's 18th Army completed its withdrawal westward to Hansa Bay and Wewak for resuscitation and regrouping, only to see his airdromes at those locales promptly savaged by Kenney's fighters and bombers, disabling more than 100 parked planes, and his seafront installations and watercraft walloped by Kinkaid's cruisers and destroyers. With scarcely any of their warbirds left intact, the personnel of the Japanese Fourth Air Army at Wewak were sent 225 miles farther upcoast to Hollandia, where they might be of more use. Persuaded by all the fireworks at Hansa Bay/Wewak that the next blow of the Allied hammer would surely fall there, Adachi was caught completely by surprise when it became evident that MacArthur's sights were set upon Hollandia instead.[6]

Between 30 March and 3 April 1944, like thunderbolts out of the blue, Fifth Air Force bombers rained destruction on Hollandia's airfields, reducing the 300 Japanese aircraft sequestered there to junk. Lt. Gen. Robert Eichelberger, assigned overall command of the Hollandia assault force, assembled its components in the Admiralties, from whose Seeadler Harbor they set sail in mid-April with a more-than-adequate naval escort. Besides aircraft carriers, Admiral Nimitz supplied Kinkaid and Barbey with whatever extra shipping was needed for the sealift. Figuratively speaking, the plan called for Eichelberger's 50,000-man phalanx (code-named *RECKLESS*) to swoop down on Hollandia like a great hawk, while a lesser raptor (dubbed *PERSECUTION*) was simultaneously jabbing its beak into Aitape, 125 miles closer to Adachi's nest at Wewak. Aitape's Tadji airdrome would be needed as a refueling station for Whitehead's limited-range fighters and bombers, which, along with Nimitz's carrier aircraft, were to provide the umbrella for the Hollandia operation. Possession of Aitape would also protect Eichelberger's beachheads from any interference by Adachi from the east.[7]

The town of Hollandia (known today as Jayapura), prewar territorial capital of Dutch New Guinea (now West Irian), was situated on Humboldt Bay, which, along with Tanamerah Bay twenty-two miles to the west, provided the only two protected deep-water anchorages along the entire north coast short of Geelvinck Bay at the Vogelkopf. Inland from Hollandia, along the northern shore of fishhook-shaped Lake Sentani, sequestered from the seafront by the Cyclops mountain range, rearing up to 6,000 feet and stretching from one bay to the other, the Japanese had built three airfields. For this operation, Alamo's largest thus far, Barbey's VII 'phib would land two regiments of Maj. Gen. Horace Fuller's 41st Division, forming the left-hand talon of *RECKLESS*, on 22 April at Humboldt Bay, close by Hollandia, and Maj. Gen. Frederick Irving's 24th Division, the right-hand talon, at Tanamerah Bay, each to be supported by one of Heavey's EB&SR's.

At the same time, the adjuvant *PERSECUTION* team, built around Fuller's third regiment, led by Brig. Gen. Jens A. Doe, and sealifted by Capt. Al Nobles' squadron of VII 'phib, would be inserted downcoast at Aitape, with the support of 543d EB&SR. Once ashore, Doe would be reinforced by a regiment of Gill's 32d Division from Saidor.[8]

The Aitape sideshow was a pushover; the Tadji airdrome was in American hands by 1245 on the 22d, and the 1,000-man Japanese garrison, mostly unemployed air-support and service troops, was smothered within 24 hours. As soon as Yank airfield engineers had their machinery off-loaded, repairs on Tadji were rushed through, enabling Kenney's planes to touch down, gas up, and take off for Hollandia, freeing Nimitz's carriers for duty elsewhere.

The two-pronged main event came off almost as easily—the ll,000 Japanese troops in the Hollandia/Lake Sentani vicinity, the majority of whom were non-combat technical personnel, put up amazingly little resistance. At both the Humboldt and Tanamerah bayfronts, however, the narrow strands on which Barbey's vessels grounded, pocked with shellholes from Kinkaid's gunfire and 2ESB's Support Battery rocketry, proved far from ideal topographically. Mere ribbons of sand for the most part, they were separated from the mainland by long stretches of unfordable mangrove swamp, precluding the establishment of proper dump sites for the mounds of cargo discharged from Barbey's ships. Nevertheless, the debarkations of troops and stores proceeded as scheduled. Heavey's well-seasoned 532d and 542d seahorsemen, using more than 250 of their own LCM's and LCVP's as well as Navy amphtraks, worked their respective sectors as smoothly as the unsatisfactory waterfront terrain permitted. On the following day, a lone Jap plane, eluding the air cover and anti-aircraft fire, dropped three bombs directly on Humboldt Bay's congested White Beach (nearest Hollandia), one of which touched off a huge explosion and fire in an ex-Japanese munition and fuel dump, quickly igniting adjacent piles of newly-deposited American stores. The awesome conflagration raged for two days, consuming the ladings of a dozen LST's—or about 40% of the provisions needed to sustain the two regiments pushing inland in that sector, and restricting their troops to half-rations for a week or so. Heavey's amphibs won high praise for their courageous efforts to confine the damage, and the Collecting Platoon of 262d Medical Battalion's Company B was awarded battle honors for heroism in rescuing those injured. In the larger scheme of things, however, this mishap was only a minor glitch, soon remedied by the delivery of emergency supplies by USAAF cargo planes to a nearby airstrip.[9]

Within four days of their landing, Eichelberger's dual infantry columns, whose combat engineers were forced to bulldoze and corduroy twisting roads around each end of the Cyclops Mountains, converged on the Lake Sentani airfields (26 April.) To speed things along, 2ESB boatmen, using the Navy LTV's, ferried the foremost assault elements across the lake. The airfields were soon overrun and 600 Japanese captives rounded up, while the rest of the 7,000-man garrison fled into the jungles in hopes of reaching Sarmi, 145 miles westward (only about 500 ever made it through.) American fatalities for the entire operation totalled a modest 155. Under Eichelberger's close supervision, the Hollandia complex was rapidly reshaped into one of SWPA's foremost logistical bases, rivalling

Finshaffen and supplanting those at Milne Bay and Oro Bay, now far to the rear. For the comfort and convenience of MacArther and his staff, an elaborate new advanced general headquarters layout was created on picturesque high ground above Lake Sentani.[10]

It had been Air Chieftan Kenney's assumption that, after hasty refurbishing, the Lake Sentani airdromes would assure Allied air supremacy as far as the next objective, the island of Biak, 340 miles farther west, dominating the skinny neck of the New Guinea bird. It soon became apparent, however, that without much more thorough-going and time-consuming repairs, their spongy runways would not bear the weight of the big bombers needed for the intrusion at Biak. As things stood, the heavies could operate only from Nadzab, 440 miles to the east, or rear, of Hollandia, or, alternatively, from the equally remote Admiralties. And not until Biak's more substantially-constructed dromes were secured could Kenney protect the next long jump across the waters toward the Philippines. In the interim, however, lesser enemy airfields could be had for the taking 125 miles closer to Hollandia just east of Sarmi at Maffin Bay and on a nearby islet known as Insoeomar. (The latter, together with a tiny sister, Insoemanai, on its inshore side, constitute the Wakde Islands, leading to the custom of referring to Insoemoar itself as Wakde, a source of considerable confusion to historians; hence, for clarity's sake, Insoemoar will hereinafter be called Wakde.) From the Wakde/Sarmi airfields, lighter and shorter-range U.S. aircraft could readily protect a Biak invasion. MacArthur reasoned that his most plausible move, therefore, would be to glom on to Wakde/Sarmi without delay, and then go all out for Biak. A task force known as TORNADO, consisting of Jens Doe's 163d RCT of General Fuller's 41st Div. at Aitape (with 593d EB&SR's Shore Battalion and 542d's Boat Company A tacked on) was hastily formed to descend upon Wakde/Sarmi, while Fuller and his two regiments from Hollandia would tackle Biak ten days later.

The TORNADO team was hurriedly shipped up by a VII 'phib flotilla to a landing at the seaside village of Arare (not to be confused with Arawe on New Britain), the point most proximal to Wakde Island, twenty miles short of the subtantially-garrisoned enemy post at Sarmi. As the "Doe-boys" were soon to discover to their sorrow, the Japanese troops occupying the Wakde/Sarmi area, under Gen. Hachiro Tagami, were well-nourished and in fine fighting trim, an altogether tougher breed than those so easily chased from Hollandia. They were also present in vastly greater numbers than MacArthur's Intelligence staff had calculated—in fact, another entire infantry division had recently arrived from China, doubling Tagami's strength. At daylight, 17 May, Doe's troops attained the foreshore at Arare almost unmolested, and the 593d shore amphibs, despite rough surf and a shallow seafloor, had jetties bulldozed out to the beaching vessels within an hour. By 0930 the last of the infantry, motorized equipment, and guns had been offloaded, and the beachhead was in rough order, with heavy artillery emplaced to shell Wakde preparatory to its invasion the next day. Doe quickly extended both ends of his beachhead, one eastward toward the Tementoe River, the other in the opposite direction toward the Tor River, beyond which lay the main enemy forces occupying Sarmi and its airfields. Wakde, whose well-graded airstrip covered a large portion of its 540-acres, had already been worked over for twelve days by Whitehead's planes and Naval gunships.[11]

At daylight, 18 May, after subjecting the island to one last pounding by fire-support ships and Doe's 105-mm. guns on the mainland, six waves of 542d A Company's LCVP's, laden with assault troops and four tanks, headed across for the landing. As they neared their objective—a constricted beach requiring a lateral approach—the leading craft were cruelly raked with fire from concealed MG's. The infantrymen, huddled below the gunwales, were spared injury, but not so the exposed amphib coxwains and deckmen, three of whom were slain and twenty-eight wounded— 33 percent of A Company's roster. None of their boats, no matter how bullet-riddled, failed to land, however, and Doe's troops, once afoot on Wakde—or on their bellies, more likely—brought their tanks into play, wearing down, rooting out, and largely annihilating the stubborn 140-man garrison. Despite desperate infiltrators who damaged some of the shore-party's vehicles and machinery, Doe had the island fully in hand within a couple of days, while his industrious airfield engineers quickly patched up its airdrome to accomodate Fifth Air Force's medium bombers and fighters.[12]

TORNADO's complimentary thrust, toward the airfields around Sarmi, came close to being a total washout, alas. Even after augmentation by Brig. Gen. Edwin D. Patrick's independent 158th Regimental Combat Team (imported from Arawe, New Britain), the units inching westward beyond the Tor River found themselves blocked by heavily-manned Japanese redoubts on heights just inshore from Maffin Bay, one known as "Lone Tree Hill" in particular, arresting further progress for almost two months! Doe's own team, as we shall shortly see, was soon pulled away to stiffen the rest of the 41st, now heavily engaged on Biak. This left the faltering Sarmi enterprise entirely in the hands of Patrick's 158th, which subsequently wore itself thin in vain attempts to dislodge their obdurate foes, now numbering in excess of 10,000. The situation deteriorated seriously when Japanese formations turned the tables and began to lap around the overstretched Yank perimeter—now extending for twelve miles along the coast— exerting such pressure that it began to disintegrate. Quickly readjusting to a defensive stance, Patrick contracted his imperiled holdings into some eight waterfront enclaves, whereupon Alamo Chief Krueger replaced the hard-pressed, outnumbered 158th with an entire division of regulars, Maj. Gen. Franklin C. Sibert's 6th (14 June.) Sibert, deploying his superior forces with studied deliberation, soon restored cohesion to the perimeter, and, by having the amphibs land one of his regiments on the Maffin bayshore to the rear of Lone Tree Hill and adjacent heights, outflanked the occupants.[13]

Thanks to this stratagem and to relentless strafing and napalming of the elevated enemy positions by P-47's from Wakde, this barrier was finally cleared (30 June.) Within a week or so the Japanese were swept from the remaining heights above the bayfront, after which Krueger, with time running out, and needing the services of the 6th elsewhere, extracted it in exchange for the 31st "Dixie" Division (Maj. Gen. John C. Persons.) By now 1,900 American casualties had been sustained in the effort to seize Sarmi, and after closer scrutiny revealed that its airstrips were so inferior as to be of only marginal utility anyway, MacArthur wisely called a halt to further exertions in that direction. The 31st "Sons of the South" henceforth had little more to do than help their precursors load their dunnage on the ships, patrol the perimeter, and erase a few troublesome outposts. By 6 February 1945, the 31st, all its belongings, and everything else of any value within its lines, would be pulled out as well, allowing Tagami's legions to roost unmolested at Sarmi for the duration of the war. Wakde Island's drome would be retained thereafter solely for emergency landings by crippled aircraft, its safekeeping entrusted to a company of the 93d Infantry Division.[14]

The seahorsemen had taken their share of punishment during the protracted Wakde/Sarmi operation. The 593d shore engineers working the mainland beachhead had withstood repeated Banzai attacks, and in one of several fire-fights, perduring for fourteen hours, were driven from their anti-aircraft guns, only to regain them undamaged. Boat Company A of 542d, so badly bruised going into Wakde (for which it was later awarded a Distinguished Unit Citation), and subsequently tasked with landing and supplying Sibert's men at Maffin Bay, had been shelled by the 75-mm. field guns and mortars atop the infamous Lone Tree Hill, absorbing further casualties.[15]

With Wakde's drome functional, MacArthur, grown a bit too overconfident, quickly drew a bead on Biak, the largest of the Schouten Islands partially enclosing Geelvinck Bay at the scrawny neck of the New Guinea bird. Just inland from Biak's reef-obstructed southeastern coast, the Japanese had scraped out three airfields. The island's jungled surface, like a thickly-bearded face pitted with acne, was scarred by eroded coral outcroppings, terraced ridges, and arid, scrubby flats, making it an especially forbidding arena for combat. Its invasion, code-named *HURRICANE*, was hastily arranged for execution on 27 May by the two regiments of Fuller's "Jungleers" (as the boys of the 41st liked to call themselves) not participating in the Wakde/Sarmi venture. Heavey's 542d EB&SR and Support Battery (now with 54 LVT's of their own) were handed this assignment. In retrospect, considering the Biak campaign's long-drawn-out devolution, *WALKING CANE* might have been a more apt moniker.[16]

The action opened on a surprisingly-subdued note in light of the mischief-making potential of Biak's 10,400 enemy occupiers and their exceptionally able commander, Col. Naoyuki Kuzume. After the customary preliminary naval shelling and bombing by fifty or so AAF Liberators, Rear Adm. W. M. Fechteler's VII 'phib (Barbey himself was off on other business at the time) had little trouble depositing Fuller's units at the island's only settlement of note, Bosnek, where the Japanese had created a couple of coral-rock jetties. There was a modicum of confusion at the outself when one of the assault battalions was carried well to the west of its assigned landing site by adverse currents and with visibility obscured by smoke from white phosphorous shells used in the prefatory bombardment. The first waves, on 2ESB's Buffaloes, got ashore intact, but their successors, whose LCVP's and LCM's grounded on a coral reef, had to wade some distance to terra firma. Some of 542d's thoroughly-waterproofed bulldozers were able to chug to the beach (through water up to their operators' shoulders) and improve the deteriorated Japanese jetties at which Fechteler's LST's could discharge other tracked and wheeled vehicles. A pair of causeways fashioned from steel pontoons were extended over the reef into deeper water (the first use of this technique in SWPA) to accomodate two more LST's, and an LCVP/LCM shuttle was organized for offloading the remainder of the beaching craft, transports, and cargo ships.

Enemy reaction against the Bosnek beachhead was negligeable, by and large, aside from some strafing and bombing by five planes appearing out of nowhere just before sunset, one of which singled out the LST on whose deck General Heavey and his aide, Capt. Barron G. Collier, Jr. (son of the multi-millionaire enterpreneur for whom my Dad had once worked), were huddled with some Navy confreres. Luckily, the plane's bomb failed to detonate, though Collier was struck by a few fragments from friendly anti-aircraft shellbursts. Another Jap bomb took out an LCVP alongside, and a third struck the stern of a patrol boat, causing several casualties. While none of the five aerial predators survived the Yank AA fire, more such visitations occurred over the next fifteen days, though with scant effect on ground operations. On D+1, Mars showed his uglier face as one of Fuller's regiments surged westward in searing 100-degree heat down the road leading to Mokmer, the nearest of the island's three airdromes, while another dug in on the beachhead and began to clear the heights behind the town of sources of harassing fire.

When the vanguard of the strung-out column driving toward Mokmer drome reached Parai defile, a narrow sea-side shelf beneath cliffs graduating upward like ball-park bleachers, some two miles short of its goal, it was abruptly assailed by heavy enemy fire and tank-led counterattacks and recoiled in some disorder. Fuller's Shermans rolled to the forefront and made short work of the outgunned and under-armored Japanese crawlers, while his disconcerted infantry backed out of the defile, leaving some units cut off and requiring hazardous extraction by Heavey's LCM's and LVT's.

Kuzume had painstakingly deployed most of his mixed force of combat and service troops on, within, and among the rugged coral ridges dominating the airfields. From a multiplex of caverns and recesses amply stocked with ammunition, rations, water (of which Biak had scant natural sources), and generators for electricity, his MG's, howitzers, AA guns, and even a few unshipped 6-in. naval guns, had been preregistered on all likely avenues of approach, with overlapping fields of fire. Thus disadvantaged, Fuller was forced to call in his third regiment from Wakde/Sarmi before he could resume his advance. Upon its arrival, he dispatched a second column toward Mokmer through the barren, parched interior on an axis paralleling the coastal road. This team gained access to the airfield by 7 June, only to find itself isolated and pinned down by artillery and mortar fire from the surrounding ridges. Another regiment was then injected by sea onto the shore nearest to Mokmer drome, proceeding inland and linking up with the isolates, thereby outflanking the hostiles at Parai defile. The combined force undertook a reduction of the enemy positions infilading the airfield along with those at Parai, a slow, tedious, and sanguinary business.[17]

Fuller's inability to secure the dromes in timely fashion for use by long-range bombers compelled an embarrassed MacArthur to renege on a solemn promise to Nimitz of Biak-based air support for the latter's invasion of Saipan in the Mariannas, scheduled for 15 June. As the theatre commander exhorted Alamo boss Krueger to hurry things along, Krueger in turn rudely prodded Fuller, neither superior bothering to come and see for himself the nature and extent of the impediments with which the 41st was having to contend. The result was a replay of the shabby drama back at Buna, as Eichelberger, "the Fireman of the SWPA," was sent in once again to take over and get things moving, whereupon the indignant Fuller submitted his resignation, with the divisional command devolving upon Jens Doe, his former deputy. Methodically reengineering Fuller's basically sound tactical approach, Eichelberger imported reinforcements in the form of a regimental combat team of the 24th Division, which for the moment did little to rev up the lagging operation.[18]

So unnerving to the Naval section of Japanese Imperial Headquarters was the prospective loss of Biak's airdromes that three successive attempts were made to reinforce Kuzume's beleaguered cohorts by sea—and providentially foiled, though not before another 1,200 of Hirohito's soldiery had been surreptitiously barged onto the island. Despite their infusion, Kuzume's redoubts and caverns were successively sealed off, blown in, and incinerated one-by-one, while on nearby Owi Island, Yank airfield engineers bulldozed a new airstrip from which fighters could soar aloft to swat pestiferous enemy air raiders. Not until 22 June was Mokmer drome rendered secure and serviceable, and by early August, its two sisters had been repaired and expanded as well. The last sparks of resistance on Biak were stamped out on August 20th. *HURRICANE* had swept away more than four hundred American lives, left 2,300 disabled by wounds, and another 7,200 so severely stricken by illnesses—mostly scrub typhus, other malignant fevers, and dysentery, plus an astounding 423 psychiatric cases—as to require lengthy hospitalization. The medics staffing temporary hospitals on Owi Island were stretched to their limits by this tidal wave of invalids.[19]

Throughout the operation, the 542d shoremen working the Bosnek waterfront had contrived to keep the logistical necessities flowing in satisfactorily, while the boat units and Support Battery "Buffaloes" and flak boats took extraordinary risks hauling personnel and supplies to exposed positions or removing evacuees. Heavey's gunboats also contributed their firepower to the sealing of cave entrances and the supression of coastal strongholds. As an indicator of their unstinting dedication to their missions, when the Biak action ceased, only 7 of the Support Battery's 54 Amphtraks were still operable; the unit's services were lauded by a Distinguished Unit Citation.[20]

On the opposite side of the ledger, a mere 220 of Kuzume's warriors were taken alive, leaving behind 4,700 of their number as corpses, and he himself driven to suicide. Their rotting remains, together with those of thousands more who had succumbed to malnutrition and disease, made of the island's more fought-over acreage an abominable pesthouse for a time. Of all MacArthur's initiatives (with the sole exception of the Kokoda Trail/Buna-Gona counteroffensive), the Biak foray ranked among the most anguishing for every participant, friend or foe, high and low. Whitewashing it as best he could, MacArthur rewarded Eichelberger with the command of the newly-formed Eighth Army, which would soon be in spirited competition with Krueger's Sixth for the honor of recapturing the Philippines.

In broad outline, having roughly sketched in the largely-unpublicized contribution of the amphibian engineers, this is how the land war in the Southwestern Pacific had progressed—or, in Japan's case, regressed—as of summer's end, 1944. The Allied forces had made a remarkable comeback after the ignominious and humiliating capitulations at Singapore and Bataan. A long, hard road, nonetheless, still stretched to the horizon—or the Land of the Rising Sun—and thus far the pace had been much too glacial to satisfy the restless MacArthur. The thin array of demoralized and poorly-equipped Australian militia, green U.S. National Guardsmen, and random assortment of airmen and support troops at his disposal upon Wainwright's surrender at Corregidor had been massively augmented and lavishly re-equipped during the two intervening years. In addition to Blamey's now-numerous brigades, Kenney's burgeoning air forces, and Kinkaid's ever-expanding armada, MacArthur currently fielded a powerful combat-tested Sixth Army (along with an emergent Eighth) embracing eleven or so divisions of infantry, airborne troops, and "foot-cavalry," as well as three independent regimental combat teams. Supporting them, in addition to our trio of Engineer Special Brigades, were a wealth of other engineer, medical, ordnance, quartermaster, signal, and technical units. In short, having everything of which any army group in Eisenhower's theatre could boast (except for a full contingent of armor, which was of only limited use in jungle warfare), MacArthur could no longer complain with any legitimacy of being short-changed. American industry was now generating limitless quantities of high-quality armament and aircraft, while the radical innovations in ship-building technology pioneered by Henry Kaiser and his associates had brought a mind-boggling expansion of trans-Pacific shipping capacity. The successful conclusion of the six-months-long Papuan Campaign early in 1943 had laid to rest any anxieties regarding Australia's security. With Rabaul's encapsulation and the capitulations of Manus, Hollandia, and Biak, the end of the New Guinea Campaign was clearly in sight, and the final stage of the long march back to the Philippines about to kick in.

Only two items yet remained to be crossed off the Chief's New Guinea agenda, Noemfoor and Sansapor. Situated 50 miles west of Biak, the ovoid 30-mile-wide island of Noemfoor contained another trio of Japanese airfields, one of which, Kamiri, had a 5,300-ft. hard-surfaced runway which Allied airmen itched to get their hands—or their bombers—on. Its capture was entrusted to Patrick's 158th Regimental Combat Team, dubbed *CYCLONE*. Rested and refitted after its gruelling stint at Sarmi, the 158th was undergirded by two of Ogden's units, the shore battalion of 593d

EB&SR and a boat company of the 533d, along with the bravos of 2ESB's Support Battery and their LVT's. Heading the amphib contingent was Col. Oliver W. Van den Berg (whom I met later on Luzon and considered an unusually impressive, competent, and cultured gentleman.) Van den Berg's Buffaloes were the only conveyances by which the assault waves could get across the coral belt wholly encircling the island like a wedding ring around a finger. At the last moment, another boat company—A of 543d EB&SR—also weighed in, having spent twelve hectic days aboard its LCM's with engines at full throttle to cover the 700 watery miles from Finschaffen in time to get in on the action.[21]

Whitehead's airmen had hammered the landing area so frightfully with 1,000-lb. bombs that Noemfoor's entrenched protectors—at least those not blown to kingdom come—were stunned into insensibility as Patrick's battalions emerged from their transports and took to the LVT Buffaloes and DUKW's on the morning of 2 July. The leading elements gained the shore with reasonable alacrity, though the undersides of Van den Berg's Ducks took a beating in the ebb tide, having to be dragged across the reef in wholesale numbers by the LVT's, while his dozers shaped temporary causeways over it and demolition teams breached it to admit his lighters. The *CYCLONE* team was accorded extra, but as it turned out, quite superfluous, clout by troopers of the 503d Parachute Infantry Regiment, 1,400 of whom were dropped from C-47's that day on Kamiri's hard main runway. Through someone's egregious error, the troop carriers levelled out at less than 400 feet, leaving almost 10% of the jumpers disabled upon impact. Next day, the members of another airborne battalion, deplaning from a higher altitude, got aground without mishap, thankfully.

On their first night ashore, having hacked out a perimeter encompassing Kamiri drome and the landing beaches, Patrick's GI's hunkered down under a brisk fire from enemy mountain guns and 37-mm. field pieces on coral terraces just beyond the airdrome. A spirited counterattack on D+1 failed to arrest further inland penetration by the infantry and paratroopers. The amphib Support Battery's thin-sided Buffaloes doubled as battle tanks, suppressing counterfire and enabling the invaders to close in on enemy bunkers and caves, for which Patrick paid them special tribute in his after-battle report. Over the next ten days or so, notwithstanding the desperate courage displayed in multiple fire-fights by fragments of the heavily-outnumbered 2,000-man garrison, all but a corporal's guard were swept up by the *CYCLONE* force at a total cost of 400 American casualties. The outcome was hardly surprising, especially in light of their opponents' advanced state of malnutrition—some of the more loose-lipped among the handful of captured Japanese disclosed that Formosan laborers on the island had been cannibalized by their famished masters. One P.O.W. averred that a Captain Sugahara, who was both medical officer and mess officer, had dissected the corpses and cubed and cooked their flesh with such expertisse that it resembled pork and was as tasty as "any other meat." The mopping-up of scattered pockets of starveling resistors took until the end of August.[22]

Once done with their ship-to-shore lightering, Van den Berg's boat units switched to a shore-to-shore modality on Noemfoor, freighting in ton upon ton of supplies from Biak, while the 593d shoremen built substantial jetties and pipelines, graded roads, and created an auxiliary airstrip. In mid-July, the tired-out Support Battery amphibs reboarded LST's and returned to Wakde for a brief rest. Before July's end, all of Noemfoor's airfields were serviceable, clearing the way for the seizure of Sansapor-Mar on the Vogelkopf's Cape Sansapor, the last hunk of the New Guinea bird for which MacArthur had any use.[23]

Just as the curtains were about to close on the New Guinea campaign, 470 miles or so to the rear a heavy enemy counterpunch smote Alamo's Hollandia outposting at Aitape, where a regiment of Maj. Gen. William H. Gill's 32d Division had been standing guard. The maleficent pugilist, General Hatazo Adachi, having recomposed and resuscitated his frazzled 18th Army at Hansa Bay-Wewak (to the degree that his depleted stores permitted), had been ordered to kick up such a ruckus that any further Allied progress toward the Philippines would be retarded, if not reversed. In April, rallying his patched-up and fever-wracked legions, Adachi had led 20,000 of his fittest westward through the bush. Bereft of anti-malarial drugs, subsisting on the barest of rations, and weighed down by field guns and ammunition that had to be dragged over every mile, they had spent more than a month reaching the Driniumor River, bordering Aitape on the east. Here they halted to rest their weary bones and reorganize before attacking the Yanks manning the river line.[24]

To summarize the complicated sequence of battle actions which ensued there, the current XI Corps commandant at Hollandia, Maj. Gen. Charles P. Hall, forewarned by radio intercepts of Adachi's approach, sent in the 112th Cavalry Regiment to reinforce Gill's formations. In the latter half of May, nonetheless, the Japanese succeeded in puncturing the American lines at the Driniumor. Falling back a few miles to secondary positions along the X-Ray River, Gill's veterans recomposed and redisposed themselves, while Hall himself came down from Hollandia to call the plays. At length Hall ordered a series of counterattacks, until his men had largely regained their original positions, whereupon Adachi tried battering through the southern end of the American defenses near the hill village of Afua. There, and along the Driniumor, the two antagonists remained locked in savage conflict for another fortnight, neither prevailing, until, at July's end, Hall resorted to a flanking maneuver, striking east along the coast, then turning south to entrap his foe, while a fresh division, the 43d, called up from New Zealand in early August, took over along the river line. By then, Adachi had apparently had enough; twenty-five days of relentless combat had bled off almost half of his effectives and exhausted his meagre supplies. Hall soon discovered that his quarry had quit the field and withdrawn to the far bank of the Dandriwad River, some fifteen miles eastward.[25]

After pausing to lick their wounds, Adachi's played-out minions, screened by a rear guard, like Napoleon's shrivelled Grand Armee after recrossing the Berezina, resumed their retreat in earnest—all the way back to their bomb-shattered den at Wewak, from whence they would never again emerge (except to melt into the surrounding bush when the Australians finally shouldered their way into the town ten months later, in May 1945.) When Japan surrendered, Adachi and his scarecrows were still impounded in their green prison, surviving on whatever provender they could raise or scrounge from the native populace; after ordering his men to lay down their arms, Adachi committed hara-kiri rather than face the disgrace of a war-crimes trial.[26]

Even as the terminal lunge of the doomed 18th Army— Adachi's last adagio, one might say—was unravelling, MacArthur's final touchdown of the New Guinea series was consummated at Mar and Cape Sansapor on the Vogelkopf's north coast, to gain airfields more proximal to the Philippines. This ploy, involving an end run around the sizeable enemy garrison at Manokwari, was brought off at July's end by units of Seibert's 6th Division, released from their Hansa Bay/Sarmi exertions. Sealifted by a VII 'phib groupment under Fechteler, one of Siebert's regiments was landed uneventfully at the fishing village of Mar and its airstrip overrun on the 30th. The next day, to confound the enemy, 543 EB&SR carried a battalion onto an unlikely strand at nearby Sansapor where offshore waves reached heights of 12 to 15 ft. and a 5-ft. surf crashed upon the sands, subjecting the amphib landing craft to a cruel battering and creating multiple problems for 543d's boat-maintenance specialists. This, however, was the only fly in the ointment, so to speak, since the small body of Japanese 2d Army soldiery stationed around the two villages, short on food and ammunition, had betaken themselves to less perilous parts before the invaders had even set foot on their turf. As soon as airfield engineers had their apparatus ashore at Mar, rehabilitation of the airfield commenced, and at the same time, a new fighter strip was created on the offlying island of Middleburg. The moment these were useable, Thirteenth Air Force personnel flew in, set up shop, and prepped their birds for the opening round of the Philippine offensive. Though Sansapor-Mar had been taken with virtually no loss of lives, a virulent strain of scrub tyhus indigenous to the area, carried by rodent-borne mites, spread rapidly among the GI interlopers, producing a notably higher rate of fatalities than at Biak, for reasons that no one could discern. Fortuitously, the dispossessed Japanese, bereft of provender, either melted into the Vogelkopf's jungles, to remain largely dormant thereafter, or joined their by-passed brothers at Manokwari, where they languished for the rest of the war.[27]

Sixth Army's broad kangaroo-hops from Papua to New Guinea's western extremity had been a testimony not only to MacArthur's genius and the valor of his infantry, but to the adaptability and versatility of the Army amphibs—and the foresight of Noce and Trudeau. Heavey's tried-and-true 2ESB, still headquartered back at Oro Bay, had been, and until the final redemption of the Philippines, would continue to be, on the cutting edge of it all. His seahorsemen and Barbey's seafarers had earned one another's full respect, and now functioned smoothly in unison. Ogden's 3ESB amphibs had been admitted to that select fraternity as well, and we of 4ESB would soon be catching up with them.

Let us now pause and survey contemporaneous developments on the larger Asiatic-Pacific scene. Ever since the glory days of the late Admiral Yamamoto, the overlords of Japan's powerful naval arm had been thirsting for a show-down with Nimitz's Pacific Fleet, which they schemed to bring off in June, 1944, in the vicinity of the Palau Islands or the western Carolines. For the execution of this plan, known as A-Go, Adm. Soemu Toyoda, master of the Combined Fleet (recently redesignated the First Mobile Fleet), had instructed Vice Adm. Jisaburo Ozawa to assemble in Philippine waters a formidable strike force, including several newly-commissioned aircraft carriers, and lead it forth. Ozawa had feared that his gathering armada would be exposed to surveillance and attack by Kenney's long-range bombers from Biak, were MacArthur's intrusion there to succeed. This had been the rationale for the Mobile Fleet's three abortive attempts to reinforce and rescue Kuzume's beleaguered garrison. The final effort, had it been carried through, might well have proven disastrous for the *HURRICANE* forces, since the relief squadron had been heavily-muscled with the YAMATO and the MUSASHI, the most powerful battleships on earth, whose 18.1-inch guns could smash anything or anyone above ground, or floating on water, for that matter. Fortunately for

Eichelberger, just as this fearsome flotilla was getting underway, Toyoda and Ozawa had been alerted to the arrival in the Mariannas of Nimitz's huge Fifth Fleet array, with its fifteen big carriers, shielding the mid-June invasion of Saipan by Marine Lt. Gen. Holland M. Smith's V Amhibious Corps.[28]

Abruptly recasting his plan and reconcentrating all his squadrons, Ozawa rushed his battle fleet northeastward, touching off the giant melee known as the Battle of the Philippine Sea (19-21 June.} Destined to go down in the books as the greatest carrier clash of the war, this action matched forces more than three times those engaged in the Battle of Midway. In what the Americans would afterwards call "The Great Mariannas Turkey Shoot," one-third of Ozawa's carriers and all but 35 of his carefully-hoarded planes were lost. Although the Mobile Fleet had suffered a shattering setback, it had escaped annihilation, and steamed off to fight again another day.[29]

Meanwhile, on Saipan, Gen. Yoshitsugo Saito's defenses had been worn away and obliterated by three weeks of "Howlin' Mad" Smith's ferocious hammering, in the course of which the lives of 3,426 leathernecks and GI's and almost eight times as many Japanese servicemen had been consumed, to say nothing of thousands of civilians who had hurled themselves into the sea from the island's steep cliffs. At the end, Saito ritually disemboweled himself, and Admiral Nagumo, one-time commander of the Pearl Harbor attack force, put a pistol to his head. In Japan, on 18 June, the day Saipan's loss was announced, Prime Minister Hideki Tojo and his cabinet submitted their resignations. The more distal island of Guam, southernmost of the Mariannas, proved a no-less-maddeningly obdurate prize when its number came up on 21 July. Not until the sun had risen and set on another nineteen days of wastage and at the sacrifice of 1,435 more young Americans could that island's guardians be brought to extermination. Saipan's neighboring atoll, Tinian, by contrast, assailed by other elements of V Amphibious Corps on 24 July, was mastered with textbook efficiency in only half that time and at quite moderate cost. These key acquisitions brought the Japanese home islands for the first time within range of Airman "Hap" Arnold's new B-29 superfortresses.[30]

This mid-summer conjunction of victories in the far Pacific forced the Joint Chiefs in Washington to settle once and for all the thorny and long-deferred issue of strategic goals. Admiral King urged that the recovery of the Philippines take a back seat to an invasion of Formosa, with the final thrust at Japan's heart staged either from bases there or in the Ryukyus. General MacArthur, implacably set as always on liberating the Philippines first and foremost, and promoting Luzon as the most feasible springboard to Japan, was ordered by General Marshall to present himself for a conference at Pearl Harbor on 26 July. Upon his arrival and reunion with his counterpart, Admiral Nimitz, the two were ushered into the presence of President Roosevelt himself, who had travelled from Washington in secret to settle the issue. When FDR solicited their respective views on the matter, the eloquent MacArthur made a convincing case for his newly-evolved strategy of "Leyte, then Luzon," arguing that America had a moral committment to the Filipino people that could not be dishonored. King's proposal, on the other hand, was compromised by the fact that most of China's coast had recently fallen to the Japanese, rendering Luzon preferable to an outflanked Formosa as the more feasible platform from which to launch the knockout blow. Roosevelt declared himself quite won over by MacArthur's presentation, whereupon the latter returned to his arena feeling fully affirmed. While in the strictest sense, this resolution was more in the nature of an understanding than a hard-and-fast directive, Admiral King had no recourse other than to go along with it, doubtless with smouldering resentment. Accordingly, the Combined Chiefs of Staff at the Quebec Conference in September drew up a fresh timetable calling for MacArthur to take Morotai, and Nimitz to take Pelelieu, that month, and in October, Nimitz to take Yap in the Carolines, then Ulithi, then Talaud. In November, MacArthur would hit on Mindanao, and in December, he and Nimitz would invade Leyte conjointly. Whether the last objective, once attained, would be followed by a landing on Luzon, or alternatively on Formosa, was yet to be determined. Within a week, this plan underwent modification by the Joint Chiefs in Washington, who directed a speed-up and a revision of the intermediate goals. MacArthur and Nimitz were now to invade Leyte on 20 October, by-passing Mindanao, and the Yap seizure was scratched, while the Morotai and Pelelieu expeditions, preparations for which were too far advanced to be cancelled, would proceed as originally scheduled.[31]

IX

THE 534TH, FROM MILNE TO MORTY;
REAR TO FRONT.

On 23 May 1944 (four days before the 41st Jungleers were splashing ashore to do battle at Biak, and eight days after we in the 534th had been introduced to Milne Bay), General Hutchings opened 4ESB's command post at Oro Bay, where Colonel Crume's 544th and the Shore Battalion of Colonel Falkner's 594th were put ashore after a protracted passage from Oakland. That same week, 1,350 miles to the south, in Brisbane, Australia, the boatmen of our regiment were rolling up their sleeves to begin fabricating steel barges for the Transportation Corps at the Balimba assembly plant, where they would remain sidetracked for months to come. The 594th's Boat Battalion, sent over to SWPA well in advance of 4ESB's other units, had already spent a month practicing the arts of welding and rivetting, but on a different project, and in far-less-felicitous surroundings, at Milne Bay.[1]

By now, the LCVP-assembly plant at Cairns, Australia, had largely fulfilled its purpose, having knocked together 901 of the wooden Higgins boats, thereby satisfying not only the requisitions of all three ESB's for this type, but equipping harbor-craft units, the Navy, and the Australian services as well. For the remainder of the war, the landing craft most in demand would be the larger, more durable, steel-hulled LCM's. Following manufacture and testing by Higgins in New Orleans, they were being transported by rail to the West Coast, where, to conserve deck space, their engines and hardware were removed and crated, and hulls cut into four or five sections, for shipment overseas. In early June 1943, a detachment of the 411th Base Shop Battalion at the Cairns plant had been sent up to Milne Bay to lay the groundwork for an LCM-reassembly installation there. The Milne plant had been completed and put into operation by the 563d EBM of Ogden's brigade, dispatched to New Guinea in September 1943 ahead of 3ESB's other units for this purpose. The plant team had been enhanced two months later by the newly-arrived Shore Battalion of 543d EB&SR (Col. Gerald E. Galloway.)

Once acclimatized to "miserable Milne," Galloway's shoremen were soon turning out 150 "Love Charley Mikes"—or "Mikes," for short—each month, for delivery by his boatmen to 2ESB and 3ESB units deployed across the SWPA.[2]

In early April 1944, the 594th Boat Battalion took over the Mike reassembly-and-delivery enterprise from the 543d. None of Galloway's boys, I suspect, were at all displeased at their replacement by the "fresher meat" of the 594th so that they could "take up the sword"—or, less fancifully, the shovel—where the real action was going on. Falkner's boatmen, pitching their tents at Hawalia Point, Milne Bay, and determined not to be outdone by their predecessors, went at their task with a will, Company A alone producing 171 Mikes between 5 April and 20 July 1944. (At summer's end, the reassembly operation would be taken over by a new "Boat Building Command.")[3]

Up at Oro Bay, meanwhile, their counterparts in 594th's shore battalion, just in from the States, having unloaded their equipment, set up camp along the bayshore, where some of their number commenced stevedoring and others constructed thirty-five barracks intended for WAAC [Women's Auxilliary Army Corps] occupancy. Energized no doubt by the prospect of interaction with the future tenants, the barrack-builders completed their task in only six weeks, then underwent jungle-warfare schooling at Buna or rebuilt dilapidated piers. In their off-duty hours, they erected for themselves a commodious recreation hall, known as "The Beachcomber," reputedly the largest in all of New Guinea. In early August, the 594th was reunited as its boat battalion, having produced enough

LCM's to equip itself, was released from its servitude at Milne Bay and sailed in its new craft to Oro Bay. The mariners, alas, had little or no time to sample the delights of "The Beachcomber," for B Company was promptly ordered across the waters to Cape Gloucester and Arawe on New Britain to replace 543d's Company C for a brief spell, then remanded to Finschaffen to inaugurate a weekly round-trip convoy service from that point to Madang (with intermediate stops at Long Island, Sio, and Saidor.) Company C of 594th, meanwhile, joined the llth Airborne Division, just in from the States, for four weeks of intensive amphibious training. In September, A Company was ordered to relieve the 3ESB units lightering cargo and patrolling farther up the New Guinea coast. It also manned refuelling stations at Finschaffen and Madang, and boated small assault parties of the 40th Division from Arawe to Gasmata and elsewhere along New Britain's southe rn shores, helping to draw the noose ever tighter around Rabaul.[4]

Crume's 544th EB&SR at Oro Bay was equally active; as soon as its quota of newly-fabricated LCM's could be brought up from Milne Bay, it was divided into three boat-company/shore-company teams, each paired for landing practice with a battalion of the 31st "Dixie" Division, bivouacked at nearby Dobodura and soon to replace the 6th Division at Wakde/Sarmi.[5]

In late June, the last 4ESB unit to depart the U.S., 564th Engineer Boat Maintenance Battalion, arrived at Oro Bay after a brief stopover in Australia, and from its ranks, a new heavy shop company was formed and opened up for business on the beach, while its other companies (3015th, 3016th, and 3017th) were parcelled out among the brigade's boat elements. No more seahorsemen would be serving in the Asiatic-Pacific until forces were being amassed a year later for the assault on Saipan and the projected invasion of Japan itself.[6]

In sum, most of us 4ESB tail-enders, "boats" and "shovels" alike, were for the moment so far removed from the "front" that our only casualties seemed likely to result from accidents, pestilence, dementia, or more probably, sheer boredom. Sooner than any of us imagined, however, we too would be warriors in deed as well as word. In fact, at this stage of the great crusade against the Fascisti, Emperor Hirohito would have been well advised to throw in the towel, for the pugilists of the mighty FOURTH were about to climb into the center ring, rhetorically speaking!

And climb we of 534th did on that Monday in mid-May, 1944, from FAIRLAND's gangway into DUKW's to be taxied to dry land—if one could ever call it that at Milne Bay. We were dropped off in a muddy field beside a fast-flowing creek in the lee of a towering wall of mountains. Dragging our gear off the vehicles and into the muck, we took stock of our new surroundings. The brush had been haphazardly cleared and sagging pyramidal tents hastily thrown up by some other party (probably a detail of 594th boatmen), in which we stowed our stuff and set up our folding cots and mosquito bars. It wasn't long before the darkening skies began to release incredible torrents of rain, while we tried to square up the center poles of the tents, drive their wobbly pegs deeper into the ground, and tighten up their slack ropes. The prodigious precipitation did not let up for the rest of that day, nor throughout the ensuing week. In fact, the hovering clouds continued their copious weeping throughout most of our residence in that God-forsaken place. The creek quickly overflowed and the morass in which we slopped about was soon knee-deep, if not thigh-deep, while our cots threatened to sink out of sight. It was obvious that we were going to have to do some fast ditching, throw up mounds and dikes, and construct elevated platforms if we were to avoid drowning. We hastily cut down some palm trees for pilings and drove them into the goo, rounded up scrap lumber, and knocked together makeshift framework and flooring atop the pilings to raise ourselves out of the muck. The officers' tents, as well as those for the orderly room, supply room, mess, and dispensary, got first dibs, of course. That week ranks at the top of the list of "superlatively miserable" in my lifetime (though for my older sister Peggy, ironically, it was probably her most ecstatic, for on Saturday, 20 May, at St. John's Episcopal Church, in Trappe, Maryland, she was wed to her Coast-Guardsman fiancee, Boatswain's Mate Second

Class William P. Wales, of St. Michael's, Md., on leave while his ship, the USCG GALLUP, was in drydock.)[7]

It soon became dismayingly evident that all of our possessions, supplies, and equipment were going to succumb in short order to mildew, mould, rot, rust, and decay unless prompt remedial measures were taken. All our spare moments had to be devoted henceforth to what the military calls "first echelon maintenance," a vexing business in view of the fact that our skin surfaces, clothing, and footgear were perpetually saturated with an unholy blend of rainwater and copious sweat, to the point that everyone's body odor alone was enough to drive us all to the brink of madness. To expunge the mud from our persons, we often simply sat in the creek fully clothed and scrubbed away. Even the roads at Milne Bay were a glutinous soup through which vehicles spun their wheels or splashed like boats. Though I tried to clean and oil my carbine twice each day, a thin film of rust reappeared in a matter of hours. Preyed upon by swarms of super-sized flying bugs and slithering vermin, we were ordered to keep our sleeves rolled down and our shirts buttoned up at all times, and to spray insect-repellant on all exposed body parts. An insecticide was liberally sprayed around the premises daily, and diesel oil poured on any pooled water to kill larvae. As soon as one retired to his sack at night, and tucked the edges of his mosquito net under his blanket, the mist from small insecticide bombs had to be sprayed about to quell the winged wildlife trapped therein. Wooden latrine boxes had to be constructed atop high mounds of earth to prevent the runoff from contaminating everything in the vicinity. A revolting stench hung about the premises anyway because the soil was permeated with rotting vegetation, as indeed in all the coastal regions and lower elevations of New Guinea at large.[8]

The shores of Milne Bay resembled a vast city dump, with huge mounds of deteriorating stores scattered all along the "roads." I never realized until then how horribly wasteful war is. Stockpiled there were tens of thousands of crates of rations, boxes of munitions, stacks of defective machine or vehicle parts, drums of POL [Petroleum, Oil, Lubricants], and acres of damaged engineering equipment, plus a myriad of other items, much of it beyond recycling or salvaging. In fact, labor crews went about incinerating heaps of spoiled rations. A number of ships were anchored in the harbor, some of which had been there for months, in effect serving as floating storehouses (a major factor, incidentally, in the trans-Pacific shipping shortage), for lack of adequate wharfage and roofed storage facilities, aggravated by a chronic shortage of skilled longshore labor and cargo-handling machinery. Formerly the primary base for the Allies' Papuan and New Guinea campaigns, Milne Bay had now been superceded by the newer depots at Finschaffen and Hollandia, and was in palpable decline.[9]

We in F Company were put to work on Docks #1 and #2 unloading cargoes in eight-hour shifts, one shift assigned to each of the battalion's three companies. Our initial shift lasted from 1600 to 2400, and moving the huge crates and sacks about was back-breaking. One night I was on a stevedoring detail working down in the hold of an elderly rust-encrusted Dutch freighter anchored out in the bay and loaded with aviation bombs topped off by drums of gasoline. The footing was precarious as we inserted the "dog hooks" at the ends of cables to the rims of the drums. A winch operator on the ship's deck manipulated a lever controlling the motor which wound up or played out the cable, which was suspended from an overhanging arm of the mast, hauling the drums up three at a time from the hold, swinging them over the ship's railing, and lowering them into a lighter bobbing up and down at the ship's side. It was dirty, dangerous work, especially for amateurs like me. The procedure was governed by the hand signals of a foreman perched on the rim of the hatch, who mediated between us and the winch operator. The winch, like everything else on the old tub, had seen better days, and its brake was faulty, causing it to slip at intervals. Things began to get interesting when a storm suddenly blew up, the wind rose, and lightening began to strike. As the ship rocked and rolled, some of the suspended drums swung like a pendulum against the bulkheads, denting and gashing a few so that gasoline began to spurt out. I had terrifying visions of a flash of lightening igniting the gasoline and touching off the bombs, which would certainly have blown the ship and all of us to smithereens and gouged out a new crater on the floor of Milne Bay. After a few minutes, it occurred to the dimwits in charge that we had best be taken off the ship until things calmed down. It was an enormous relief to be ordered aboard a lighter and ferried back to the wharf until the storm blew itself out, though afterwards we still had to go back out and finish the job.[10]

On another occasion I was one of a pier gang alongside a moored cargo ship. We were unloading pallets of carboys (large jug-like containers of liquid, braced or framed in wood}, which were being winched out of the hold and lowered onto the bed of a two-and-a-half-ton truck. I was standing on the planked dock underneath one of the pallets preparing to guide it to its resting place when I observed large drops of liquid splattering on the dock-floor near my feet and giving off smoke. While removing the shackles from the pallet, I noted that the containers were stenciled with medical corps symbols and the words, "Danger—Carbolic Acid." It didn't take many turns at this duty to persuade me that stevedoring was definitely not my calling! A number of the northeasterners in the battalion had been civilian longshoremen, and deemed it their God-given right to pilfer any goods passing through their hands. One evening, some of them had been handling crates of PX stores (items sold in Post Exchanges), and had "liberated" quantities of sundries such as razors, pocket knives, fountain pens, and sunglasses. As we lined up waiting for the evening vittles to be ladled into our messkits, these individuals magnanimously distributed their surplus loot to the rest of us. It created something of a moral dilemma for me, because I abhor thievery, but to spurn the proferred items was to incur the contempt or suspicion of some extremely tough and somewhat emotionally unstable or even sociopathic characters upon whose good will my life might soon depend. I dodged the problem by insisting that I already had enough of whatever they were passing around. I don't know why the officers didn't wise up to the scam and quickly put a stop to it, though I don't remember it happening again, so perhaps they did. (In Australia, by the way, the free-wheeling civilian dockworkers who by their government's edict handled all cargoes at homeland ports had raised pilferage to a fine art, and huge quantities of purloined American stores simply had to be charged off by our military officials in the interests of inter-Allied harmony.)[11]

Company F at that juncture seemed to me a rather psychologically-dysfunctional outfit, though in retrospect I suppose that my standards were absurdly lofty. The tone of an army unit is set not only by its commander and other commissioned officers, but perhaps moreso by its non-coms, and those in F Company were certainly a mixed bag. Enough has already been said of the churlish company commander; his lieutenants, Tompkins, Curtin, and Budd (a green college boy from somewhere in the South), seemed decent enough. (Budd, so I was later told, dealt with one insubordinate trouble-maker in his platoon—a Polish ex-coalminer—by stripping to the waist, and, in a toe-to-toe slug-match, beating the culprit roundly.) Of the non-coms whom I can still identify after all these years, the most considerate was a jovial Boston Irishman, Sergeant McGarrity, who was later killed in action. The mess sergeant, Amatelli, seemed an affable fellow as well. Of quite another ilk were a couple of the older three-stripers, both profane, over-bearing long-termers of New England origin, to one of whom, "Laird," I have previously made reference when recounting my introduction to the company at Camp Gordon Johnston; the other, who later became the "Top Kick" [First Sergeant], and whom I shall call "Jacobs," was only slightly less menacing. One of the more rational and humane non-coms—a corporal, as I recollect—was a handsome West-Coast native bearing a strong resemblance to present-day movie star Fess Parker, with beautiful diction and a deep base voice. At a later stage in our compaigning, he was caught, or so it was alleged, in flagrante delicto, having sexual congress with a teen-aged private on the edge of the jungle, for which he was court-martialed and sent to a military prison in Australia. Among the younger privates was an awkward and shambling, though highly intelligent, Jewish lad from New York City, son of Central European immigrants, who consistently neglected his personal hygiene until he became so offensive to those around him that our platoon sergeant ordered him taken to the creek and thoroughly scrubbed with a stiff GI brush. What he needed was psychotherapy, not punishment, and it must have been an excruciatingly painful, humiliating ordeal for him, but I am ashamed to admit that I was too spiritually deflated at the time to dare to speak up in his defense.[12]

A couple of weeks or so after we had commenced stevedoring, my pal Ben Weaver was stricken with acute appendicitis and carried to the 125th Station Hospital for an appendectomy. The operation was successful, there were no complications, and Bennie's affability and charm won him many instant friends among the ward staff and patients. He had a swift recovery, and after his return, was given light duty for awhile as a cargo checker. Although we were all heartened to learn of Eisenhower's Normandy invasion on 6 June, our euphoria was subdued. After eight weeks of existing like a neanderthal at Milne Bay, I was beginning to resonate with Captain Bligh's sailors in *Mutiny On The Bounty,* ready to follow a Fletcher Christian anywhere, when orders were passed down that we were to pack up and load aboard LCM's for transport to Oro Bay. (Negro port battalions eventually took over the stevedoring duties at many of the SWPA bases, though there were never enough to fill the need. I have had a profound appreciation ever since for their unsung contribution to the war effort.)[13]

Seldom have men in the ranks shown more prompt, willing, and cheerful compliance with an order than we of the 534th, as we stowed our stuff, dismantled our soggy encampment, crated and loaded the regimental dunnage, strapped on our accoutrements, and were trucked to the waterfront to take our places in LCM's for transit away from Milne Bay. We mouthed fervent orations of gratitude to the Almighty as each boat cast off its lines and bounced across the choppy surface of the harbor in a cloud of diesel exhaust. When we gained the open waters, many of the boys became seasick as our little steel galleons were slapped around by ocean waves during the 211-mile voyage around East Cape and up the coast to Oro Bay and Buna. Still, it was a blessed relief to take off our shirts, breathe fresh air, soak up some of Ole Sol's rays, and loll about freed from the scrutiny of officers. We put in to shore on or about Wednesday, 12 July 1944, and found our new surroundings a welcome change from our previous habitat. If my predominant impression of Milne Bay had been one of dismal gloom, that of Oro Bay was one of brilliance, at least at that season. Our bivouac fronted a long expanse of white sandy beach, replete with waving palms, blue sea, and overwhelming sunshine, at first glance, the Hollywood version of the South Seas. In reality, it too was a swamp-girdled, odious pesthole, and a few hundred yards back from the beach and the belt of coconut palms, the fetid jungle commenced. Clearly visible above the treetops to the west was Mt. Lamington, an ominously-smoking volcano (whose catastrophic eruption in 1951 would devastate the entire region, snuffing out the lives of some 3,000 Papuans.) Its effusions provided some spectacular visual effects at sunrise and sunset. We put up our tents at the edge of the tree line on a mud flat, and it was like living in a sauna—one day, the thermometer registered 120 degrees! The rank vegetation had already smothered much of the debris from the desperate battling around Buna/Sananda/Gona in late 1942 and early 1943.[14]

The brigade's mobile and heavy equipment had been offloaded here rather than at Milne Bay—jeeps, trailers, trucks, prime movers, cranes, bulldozers, roadscrapers, ambulances, generators, mobile shops, antiaircraft HMG's, 37-mm. antitank guns, etc. Those of us who were "fillers," with the M.O.S. classification of "Engineer, Basic," were detailed to knock apart the huge crates in which machinery and parts had been encased upon our departure from Gordon Johnston. Off-duty, we took refreshing dips in the ocean, and on one occasion, a few of us explored one of the shallow streams emptying into the bay. Wading upstream a couple of miles or so, we were deep into the dense foliage forming a canopy overhead when I happened to glance over to the right bank. There, keeping pace with us and gliding silently along through tangled branches and vines, was a great boa constrictor, fifteen or twenty feet in length. Although he made no aggressive moves toward us, we vacated the spot with celerity—in fact, I moved downstream so fast that I doubt that my feet touched bottom till I got back to familiar territory!

As oven-hot coastal New Guinea goes, Oro Bay at that season was relatively habitable and life had its little rewards. We soon had our electrical generators up and running, with wires strung about the bivouac, and a light bulb hanging from the pole of each tent— a welcome change from the flickering candles, smoky kerosene lamps, and fading flashlights that had provided our only nighttime illumination at Milne Bay. Not only could literature be read and letters written with far less eyestrain, but we could listen to radio broadcasts, including those of Japanese propagandist "Tokyo Rose" (who, by the way, specifically welcomed our brigade to the war zone), and the morale officer arranged for the showing of outdoor movies. Two thousand of us crowded the 594th's open-air theatre one night to be entertained by Hollywood humorist Jack Benny and his troupe.

On one memorable Sunday, 16 July, having no duties, I slept late (until 0800.) After a hearty breakfast, I showered, donned clean khaki's, and relished a visit with two old RTG buddies serving in another company, Privates Squires and Hannahan (a former Charleston, S.C., insurance agent and sportsman), both urbane gentlemen of a stripe rarely encountered in the ranks. The three of us attended Protestant worship in the regimental chapel. Chaplain Lindemann's sermon, on Our Lord's injunction to "Be not afraid, for I am with you always," put me in a theologically reflective mood for the rest of day. That afternoon, Bennie, Carl Stegman, and I took a long swim in the bay, and, when darkness fell, attended a better-than-average movie, *The Adventures of Mark Twain*. Later that evening, in an extraordinarily expansive frame of mind, I composed a letter to my parents, observing that "Somehow, things never turn out as planned . . . this strange, all-powerful destiny— some call it fate, some the will of God—I prefer the latter—seems to fashion and shape the lives of each of us in wonderful ways. Our tastes and moods are so inconsistent and changeable that life often seems a hopeless hodge-podge, yet the things which perturb us most seem always to work out for the best in the end." This was a more than casually-prophetic musing, at least in my case, as the reader will soon discern.

In fact, my fortunes underwent a change for the better almost immediately. Having befriended some fellows in the regimental medical detachment, I learned that it might be possible to transfer into that unit as an aid man, or, as we would say these days, a paramedic, which seemed to offer some distinct advantages over the kind of dead-end grunt work to which I had fallen heir in Company F; I quickly sought an appointment with the battalion surgeon and medical officer-in-charge, Maj. Silvio J. Caserta. After I made my case, he arranged the switch for me, and I forthwith became a medic. In a few days, Bennie followed my lead and got himself enrolled in the detachment as well, much to my joy. On the first day in our new billet, a class was held on the diagnosis and treatment of dysentery, after which some of us learned how to draw blood with a syringe by practicing on one another. Soldiering with the medics was distinctly more challenging for someone of my tastes and disposition; I acquired many useful skills and valuable insights, and derived greater satisfaction from treating the ills and wounds of humankind than from inflicting them. (Someone told me many years later that after our names were removed from Company F's roster, its C.O., Captain Wellman, was struck by a falling tree at Buna—or maybe during a subsequent landing—incurring severe injuries; whether or not he was permanently impaired, I can't say, but in any event, I think he was evacuated to the States and consigned to the military hospital in Memphis, Tenn.)

The Regimental Medical Detachment had a complement of six officers and fifty-five enlisted men, and I would become very well acquainted with—and fondly relate to—most of them as I was integrated into the team and together we acquired the savvy requisite for survival in the SWPA. Major Caserta soon departed for reasons unknown to me, and the detachment command passed to Maj. Byron S. Knapp (Ecorse, Michigan.) The vast majority of my new companions-in-arms were from the northeastern or midwestern U.S., 6 hailing from New York City alone. Only 10 of us were Southerners, 4 from North Carolina, and 1 each from Georgia, Alabama, Mississippi, Louisiana, Tennessee, and Arkansas.

We of the Dixie minority were generally referred to by our colleagues from above the Mason-Dixon line as the "f—g rebels."[15]

Each of an ESB's three regimental medical detachments staffed a dispensary/aid station where primary care was tendered for any and all ills. Sick Call was sounded after unit assemblies each morning, at which anyone needing medical or dental attention reported to the dispensary, where the physicians (and dentist) rendered diagnoses, prescribed therapies, and supervised treatment of the more routine cases. Military medicine functions on a triage modality; i.e., the mildly disabled are treated first so that they can quickly return to duty, then the more seriously, but not severely, incapacitated, whose cases are amenable to short-term outpatient treatment, and last of all, the critically ill or injured, who are stabilized and made as comfortable as possible until they can be evacuated for specialized treatment at higher and safer levels of the medical institutional heirarchy. To put it in somewhat different terms, at the lowest level, the seriously ill or wounded were given superficial treatment—their symptoms alleviated, exsanguination arrested, pain anaesthetized, wounds debrided, sutured, and bandaged, and broken bones reset and stabilized—pending referral if necessary to other facilities affording more sophisticated and extended therapy. At or close to the battle front, a casualty, having received whatever hasty treatment could be provided on the spot, was carried—or, if ambulatory, walked—to the nearest aid or clearing station. The seriously impaired were sent on to an evacuation or field surgical facility, from which they were relayed to a hospital vessel or a general hospital.

During the initial phase of an invasion, the Navy assumed charge of seriously-disabled personnel at the waterline, whereupon they were channelled in accordance with naval procedures and systems. Although the Navy had several superbly-equipped hospital ships, the Army, at least in the SWPA, had none at this stage, to my knowledge, and on a beachhead, evacuees usually were taken aboard an LST (a few of which were rigged up to treat casualties), and transported to the most convenient and appropriate facility. Personnel stationed in the Z.I. [Zone of the Interior] or in rear areas who became seriously ill or injured were sent to the nearest station or general hospital. Our detachment had a field ambulance to transport patients to and from the battalion aid station, or on up to the next rung in the therapeutic ladder. If ambulances or other vehicles were unavailable, immobile casualties had to be carried on litters or on someone's back. Depending on the terrain, from two to four men were required for a litter party. In the campaigning across swampy or mountainous Papua and those parts of New Guinea where roads were non-existent or casualties had to carried over considerable distances, the hardy natives were often hired for this (as well as for the portage of ammo and stores.) If far inland, the infirm and injured were usually evacuated on DC-3 transport planes. If we were in combat, an aid man accompanied whatever platoon or small unit to which he was assigned, treated casualties on the spot, and saw that the incapacitated were gotten as quickly as possible to the nearest battalion aid station.

Not only did I routinely work sick calls at the dispensary tent in our battalion encampment, but, having been to college and thereby assumed to be more than passably literate, and possessing some typing skill, I was also appointed to assist the Detachment Clerk, T/4 Hugh Riley (Fayetteville, Arkansas), in the orderly room, with record-keeping, reports, and administrative correspondence. In the field, each aid man carried, along with all his usual combat gear, one or two medical kit bags containing such basics as morphine sulfate ampules, bandages, tape, sulfanilamide powder, and plasma bags, plus tubes of burn ointment and bottles of peroxide, merthiolate, gentian violet, calomine lotion, medical alcohol, terpin hydrate, paregoric-and-bizmuth, and APC [Aspirin/Phenacetin/Caffeine] tablets or capsules, all of which had to be kept as dry and sterile as possible. Unlike medics in other theatres, we carried firearms and wore no Red Cross brassards on our sleeves or markings on our helmets, since the Japanese did not observe the rules of the Geneva Convention and indiscriminately, if not deliberately, shot or bayonetted medical personnel and patients, bombed or shelled ambulances and treatment facilities, and attacked hospital ships.

Throughout our service in the equatorial tropics, the vast majority of presenting cases consisted of "jungle rot" (a generic term covering a variety of skin eruptions, lesions, abscesses, and ulcerations); of fevers and upper respiratory illnesses of assorted origin; and of gastro-intestinal maladies and parasitic infestations, besides the usual burns, lacerations, puncture wounds, concussions, battle traumas, sprains, and broken bones, all exascerbated by the extreme heat and dampness. In this extraordinarily unhygenic environment with its noxious flora and fauna, any breaks in the skin became easily infected. In bivouac, potable water was chlorinated, stored, and dispensed from water trailers or lister bags. Latrines had to be carefully sited and the effluent burned out every day or so with quicklime and covered over with dirt. Under combat conditions, hallogen tablets were used to purify the water in our canteens if it was suspect, and when one needed to defecate, he dug a hole, quickly filling it in afterwards for obvious reasons, but especially to avoid attracting flies and insects, who would otherwise descend en masse and contaminate everything in the vicinity. If one had to relieve himself while hiding in a foxhole, he used any disposable container at hand or even his steel helmet, throwing the contents as distally as possible.

Most prevalent among the pathologies rampant in SWPA were malaria, typhus, and dysentery. Dengue (or "Breakbone") fever, cholera, pneumonia, hepatitis, and parasitic infestations were also distressingly common. Dwelling in slit trenches and foxholes where the soil was contaminated with pathogens, parasitic ova, or chemicals made it urgent to wash one's hands before eating and to avoid going about barefoot if at all possible. And of course, one had to be constantly wary of the venemous reptiles, scorpions, arachnids, and other toxiferous vermin, rodents, and plants abounding in those regions. Despite their youthful vigor, many GI's became so acutely disabled from these "natural" enemies that they had to be evacuated from the war zone or discharged from the service, and diseases accounted for a far larger percentage of losses than battle traumas. For instance, soon after 594th Shore Battalion's arrival at Oro Bay, the officer commanding its Company D became so disabled by a severe tropical illness that he had to be sent back to the States, and during its subsequent posting to Cape Gloucester, five of its enlisted men contracted fulminating skin diseases of such severity as to mandate evacuation.[16] All of us had to contend with fungal eruptions in armpits, crotch, ears, scalp, or feet. In some of the more-long-embattled infantry units, dysentery was so pandemic that many people simply cut out the seats of their pants to facilitate chronic defecation, or, as the Japanese and their P.O.W.'s frequently did, wore improvised diapers. I shall leave it to the reader's imagination how the premises they had been occupying looked and smelled! Healthwise, the only positive thing about serving in these largely uninhabited jungle climes was that the rate of new venereal infections declined to virtually zero.

. . . .

Two regiments of our brigade, the 534th (less its boat battalion) and 544th (less one boat company) had been selected for the upcoming Morotai invasion (code-named *INTERLUDE*, and the task force to execute it, *TRADEWIND*.) My mates and I were now going to "see the elephant," as the boys in the Civil War used to say of their initial battle action!

On 8 August 1944, our regimental headquarters at Oro Bay received orders via telegraph specifying that the 534th would first proceed 500 miles westward to Aitape, where part of the *TRADEWIND* force would stage. The 28,000-man assault force, to be led by Maj. Gen. Charles P. Hall, XI Corps commander, would consist of Maj. Gen. Clarence P. Martin's 31st Division, whose 155th and 167th regiments were currently at Wakde and Maffin Bay, and its third, the 124th, at Aitape (along with the 126th RCT of Gill's 32d Division, designated as the Task Force Reserve.) The operation was scheduled for 15 September, with our 534th supporting the 124th Regiment, landing on White Beach, while Colonel Crume's 544th would go in with the 155th and 167th on Red Beach. Two EBM battalions, the 3015th and

3017th would accompany us. The staging for this operation would be complicated because the accompanying airfield-construction and service units were scattered all the way from Finschafen to Wakde.[17]

The very next day, 9 August, we began decamping, packing our dunnage, and loading everything aboard trucks. Our tracked and wheeled equipment, having been prepped and waterproofed, was then "combat-loaded" aboard LST's and LCT's, i.e., in inverse order of need, "first on, last off." This procedure called for drivers to shift their vehicles into reverse gear and back them into the beached vessels in accordance with a carefully-studied sequence, so that DUKW's and "Cats" could be driven off first, ahead of the jeeps, trucks, prime movers, and towed trailers and artillery, behind which were stowed the road-scrapers, cranes, power-shovels, air compressors, generators, etc. We ourselves boarded the troopship U.S.S. MEXICO for the hop to Aitape, where we would hook up with the 124th. The equipment-laden beaching vessels would follow us at their own slower pace. The MEXICO, a 1932 product of the Newport News Shipbuilding yards, was a 5,235-ton former luxury liner designed for the Caribbean and South American trade, and while somewhat smaller than the FAIRLAND, was the finest transport I ever took passage on. Though crowded, as were all troopers, she was less so than most. Our transit was swift and uneventful, and I had little to do other than sleep, read, and play cards. The food was relatively good, the weather mild, and the only memorable events of the journey were passing within sight of Finschafen (where Heavey's boys and Wootten's Aussies had aquitted themselves so valiantly ten months previously), and Wewak, still in Jap hands.

The 544th, having wrapped up its amphibious exercises at Oro Bay, was already afloat—its boatmen had sailed off aboard their own craft, its shoremen on LST's and LCI's, bound for Wakde/Maffin Bay, about 900 miles westward, where Crume's boys would stage for the Morotai show with their 31st teammates. With stops only to take on fuel and water, 544th Boat Battalion's voyage-by-lighter was probably the lengthiest ever undertaken for a combat operation by any unit in small boats throughout the entire war![18]

After our own brief and relaxed cruise on the good ship MEXICO, we in 534th's Shore Battalion disembarked at Aitape and camped out temporarily in a jungle clearing along the perimeter. Since we were to be there for only a fortnight while all of TRADEWIND's components were assembling, our bivouac was minimalist. We dug foxholes, sheltered in pup tents, bathed and shaved out of steel helmets, subsisted on field rations, and relieved ourselves in shallow slit trenches. Less than two weeks previously, the bulk of Adachi's forces had vacated this vicinity, leaving some of their number behind to mask the withdrawal, and the area was still classified as a combat zone. Maj. Gen. Leonard F. Wing's 43d Division, shipped in from New Zealand in late July and early August, was taking over the task of mopping up the Aitape sector teamed. (In November, Wing's boys would in turn hand that job over to 6th A.I.F. Aussies, who would be contending with hostiles thereabout until the war ended.)

We surrounded our bivouac with two-man V-shaped foxholes to repel infiltrators, and posted a double guard. This not only enabled paired-off members of the guard details to keep a lookout in two directions, but each individual could communicate silently with his partner by kicking the other's feet. We had been briefed on the standard Japanese practice of stealing in after dark and quietly knifeing or garrotting the unwary. It was impermissible to move about freely after nightfall, make unnecessary noise, or show any lights. One evening, when I was paired with "Whitey" Reuther (Norwalk, Conn.) on guard duty, we found ourselves occupying the last foxhole at the extremity of the perimeter. Having never before been in close proximity to the enemy, Whitey and I had no trouble staying awake, and, happily, my less-than-proficient knife-fighting skills did not have to be exercized during our long nocturnal vigil.[19]

At sunrise one day, we all awakened to the revolting revelation that our bodies and blankets or groundsheets were crawling with maggots which had hatched out while we slept. (New Guinea was rife with such apparitions. It was not uncommon, for example, after wading through swamps or streams, to find oneself infested with leeches; they were usually detached by touching them with lit cigarettes—simply trying to pull them free caused their heads to break off and remain burrowed in the dermal tissue, becoming prime sources of infection.) Little, if any, rain fell during our two weeks or so at Aitape, and by the time we left, we were a pretty unsavory and unkempt lot, liberally coated in dust and sweat, and everyone's deeply sunburnt skin was tinged with yellow from the atabrine we had been ingesting daily.[20]

While thus roughing it, we busily prepared for what Morotai might hold in store for us. In addition to helmet, carbine, web-gear, entrenching tool, bayonet-knife, machete, aid-kits, and backpack (containing mess-kit, poncho, shelter-half, blanket, toilet articles, spare fatigues, underwear and socks), each of us would be carrying a three-day supply of combat rations ("C"-type, containing 3 cans of pre-cooked meat and vegetables, 3 cans of hard crackers, and packets of soluble sugar and coffee; and "D"-type, 3 four-ounce bars of dessicated "tropical" chocolate), along with two canteens of water and five clips of .30-Cal. ammo.

On 4 September, after the beaching vessels with our mobile equipment and stores had put in from Oro Bay, and the 124th had loaded, a hasty landing rehearsal was held. All available amphibs, including medics, had to lend a hand in this, since speedy and systematic offloading would be essential to *INTERLUDE*'s success. A beached LST with its bow gates ajar bore a striking resemblance to a supine whale with its mouth open. Forming two parallel human chains out to its maw, we filled and passed along sandbags, tossing them into the water to help create a dry jetty over which the vehicles could be driven. The procedure could be carried out only in relatively calm surf, and the more gradual the slope off the beach, of course, the farther the jetty had to extend. Steel pontoon sections had been brought along by some of the LST's so that in the event that the groundings were too far out (as at Biak), they could be dropped overboard and lashed together to bridge the gap. Standard landing practice called for shore-party amphibs to be boated in with the foremost assault waves, discharging their own machinery and necessities first, then assist in the offloading of the infantry and subsequent echelons, while simultaneously organizing the beachhead, preparing exits to the interior, and setting up beach defenses.

To conform to the tight schedule, the rehearsal was called off at midday, and as the partially-emptied beached vessels were hurriedly reloaded, retracted, and maneuvered into position to form the convoy, we in the shore battalion and regimental headquarters were lightered out to board an APA transport, H.M.A.S. [His Majesty's Australian Ship] KANIMBLA. As with *TRADEWIND*'s other APA's, she carried suspended from davits her own LCVP's, which would land us on the hostile beach. Hundreds more LCVP's/LCM's were either lashed to the decks of Barbey's other vessels or reposed in the well of the huge LSD [Landing Ship, Dock—essentially a self-propelled floating dry dock] accompanying us. When her quota of landing craft had been floated in through her stern aperture, the gates were closed and the dock pumped dry for the duration of the voyage to Morotai, where it would be reflooded and the lighters regurgitated to navigate under their own power to the beach.[21]

Weighing anchor, KANIMBLA took her position in Barbey's "Beach White" convoy, with his flagship WASATCH in the lead, and all got underway. Our westward course to Morotai, laid over the most direct route, carried us within sight of several enemy-held sectors along the New Guinea coast. Off Wakde/Sarmi, Fechteler's vessels, crammed with 31st Div. troops and impedimenta, plus the 544th and its equipment and watercraft, fell in astern of us. The combined consist included, in addition to WASATCH, KANIMBLA, and another Aussie APA (MANOORA, I think), 5 APD's, 45 LST's, 24 LCI's, 20 LCT's, and the LSD, all strung out over the ocean as far as the eye could see. Off the Vogelkopf on 13 September, we picked up the cruisers, destroyers, DE's [Destroyer, Escort], minesweepers, and six CVE's [Aircraft Carrier, Escort] of Admiral Berkey's covering force, including light cruiser NASHVILLE bearing General MacArthur. Among the minesweepers in Berkey's squadron was the USCG GALLUP, with my new brother-in-law, Bill Wales, aboard, although I was quite unaware of it at the time.[22]

While not as cushy as the MEXICO, KANIMBLA was not bad as troop transports go; what I remember most about her was the dress and customs of her crew, all of whom wore white shorts, short-sleeved shirts, knee socks, and British-Navy-style caps. Whenever one of her officers entered our troop compartment, he was preceded by a bosun blowing what we called his "peanut whistle," at which we were expected to jump to attention and maintain silence. This became rather irksome, and we began to refer derisively to the intruder as "The Peanut Man." On one occasion, he overheard us, at which the hold commander, an amphib lieutenant, was reprimanded for our slack discipline. This incensed our officer, who retorted that his men "could lick the hell" out of any Aussie unit, even if we were not strong on spit-and-polish parade-ground soldiering. Nothing came of the incident, and the rest of the trip was quite routine until the night before the landing, by which time we were all wound up as tightly as steel springs.

Lying ten miles off Cape Djodjefa, Halmahera's northernmost promontory, Morotai measures about 44 miles from north to south and 25 miles in width. Elliptical in shape, it is sweltering, mountainous, and jungle-swathed. A tiny flat peninsula known as Gila protrudes from its narrow southwestern coastal plain like the tail on a tadpole. At the base of this peninsula, near the minisicule native village of Pitoe, lay our prime objective, an unfinished enemy airstrip. Although no more than 1,000 Japanese were believed to occupy the island, 30 miles or so across the water at Galela and Waisile on Halmahera, large enemy troop concentrations were stationed, with small watercraft aplenty. Our landings were to take place just west of the base of Gila Peninsula at the two beaches designated Red and White, the former to the left, and the latter to the right of the end of the unfinished Pitoe runway which angled off from the shoreline to the northeast at about 45 degrees.

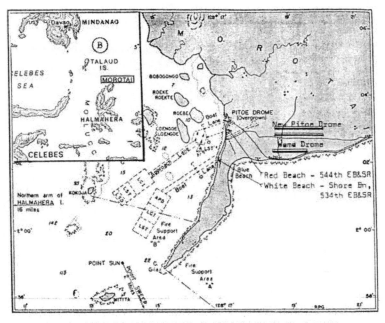

MAP 6. INVASION OF MOROTAI, NETHERLANDS EAST INDIES,
15 SEPTEMBER 1944.

Rear Admiral Fechteler would oversee the Red Beach
proceedings, while his superior Barbey would superintend those
on White Beach, where we of the 534th and the 124th RCT
were to land. Fire-support was to be provided by Rear Adm. R.
S. Berkey's group, including, in addition to his flagship
PHOENIX, two other U.S. light cruisers and two Australian
heavy cruisers, along with eight U.S. and two Aussie destroyers.
Kenney's planes from Biak and Noemfoor would suppress enemy
air activity from Halmahera and patrol the sea corridor between
Geelvink Bay and Morotai. Two days prior to the landing, six of
Rear Adm. Thomas S. Sprague's CVE's, or "Jeep" carriers, would
rendezvous with Barbey's fleet to handle antisubmarine patrolling
and provide extra air coverage enroute. For added security on "A-

Day" [Assault Day, so-called to distinguish it from the much-touted "D-Day" on Normandy] and A+1, a Naval fast-carrier task group would strike enemy airfields in the Celebes northwest of Morotai.[23]

A-Day, Friday, 15 September 1944, began for us about 0300 when we were rousted out of our bunks. Few of us had been able to sleep anyhow—I myself had spent most of the night in profound meditation and fervent prayer. I think that it was the first time in my eighteen years of existence that I had known mortal fear. Everyone else in the battalion, I suspect, was similarly quaking on the inside. In the ship's mess, the cooks served one of the best breakfasts to which we had been treated since leaving the States, including, as I recall, fresh eggs, toast, and sausages. I didn't have much appetite for it, sad to say, but it all looked, smelled, and tasted delectable. Afterward, returning to our troop quarters, and visiting the "head" to empty overactive bowels and bladders— most of us had queasy stomachs and a few were so agitated that they vomitted—we buckled on our packs, aid kits, and combat gear, snatched up carbines, and, at the loud speaker's injunction, "All Army personnel board your landing craft," assembled on deck at our boat stations to await debarkation. Even those among us who normally were irrepressibly loquacious were subdued and indrawn. The skies above were partially overcast, though clearing. From his more august perspective, Naval historian Samuel Eliot Morrison, writing in 1958, summarized the preliminaries to the drama:

> At 0510 Admiral Berkey's cruisers, including NASHVILLE with General MacArthur embarked, pulled out [from the covering force] to bombard the Japanese strongpoint on Galela, across the Strait. An hour's shooting provoked no reply. The cruisers then recrossed the Strait to Cape Gila, where Admiral Barbey and General Hall boarded NASHVILLE to report to General MacArthur. Thereafter the cruisers steamed about southward of Morotai, ready to provide gunfire support, which was never required.[24]

Our approach apparently had gone undetected by enemy aircraft, and at 0620 the main convoy slowed to a halt, five miles short of the channel between Cape Gila and Mitita Island through which it had to pass. The LST's which had towed the shallower-draft LCT's across the open seas now cast off their tow-lines, while GALLUP and the other minesweepers went ahead to rig their vanes and clear the passage of mines (of which there were none.) At 0630 Barbey's ships, forming a single column, steamed through in the wake of the minesweepers, while the Australian cruisers and two destroyers took station off the eastern flank of the Gila Peninsula and began to shell the landing beaches and other targets close by. For the first time in any Pacific campaigning, the terrain planned for seizure had just been drenched in DDT by U.S. C-47's to suppress the insect vectors of malaria and the scrub typhus which had afflicted so many troops on Biak and Sansapor.[25]

Only later was it learned that there were only 500 enemy on Morotai at the time—four companies of the 2d Raiding Unit, mostly Formosans, under Maj. Takenobu Kawashima. His superiors on Halmahera had planned, in what they considered the unlikely event of an assault on Morotai, to mount a counterattack from the bigger island, but many of the watercraft and most of the aircraft at their immediate disposal had been destroyed by Kenney's preemptive air strikes. Our ever-resourceful foe had, however, managed to reconstruct a half-dozen or so operable aircraft out of parts salvaged from damaged planes, and within a few hours, would unleash them upon us, soon followed by others from more distal bases on Borneo and elsewhere in the East Indies. For the moment, though, our airplane jockeys were in sole possession of the skies overhead.

Barely masking our trepidation, we of the leading assault element from KANIMBLA made our way three or four at a time down the swaying rope landing nets suspended from her lofty main deck to the LCVP's bobbing up and down beneath (having already been launched and circling off the ship's stern until it was their turn to load, then steered alongside.) Getting safely into them was a dicey business, given the weight and constriction of our

packs and accoutrements, and there had been no opportunity to
practice. It was fatally easy to slip and fall between the ship and
the barge and drown, or become crushed. One had to pick precisely
the right moment to release his grip and drop onto the LCVP to
avoid breaking a limb or being struck by the fellows descending
from overhead. As soon as each boat was filled to capacity, its
coxswain steered it away to join its predecessors circling off the
ship's bow until all eight or so of those comprising a designated
wave were at hand, whereupon they peeled off to form a line
parallelling the beach. Then each turned 90 degrees, and all headed
more or less abreast to the line of departure, from which, at the
designated moment, they churned shoreward. These maneuvers
took about twenty minutes. We were the third boat wave to head
in, and everyone rode crouched below the gunwales for what seemed
like hours until shortly after 0830, when our craft abruptly
grounded and its ramp was cranked down. The first man off plunged
into unexpectedly deep water, as did all of us behind. The boat,
running upon some unseen obstacle, had grounded prematurely,
leaving the Aussie sailor manning the helm no choice but to leave
us floundering in the drink and retract or risk losing his boat.[26]

While awaiting my turn to jump off, I surveyed the scene and
realized that we were still a long way from the shore. On either
side of us, other similarly-impeded craft were disgorging troops
who struggled in crooked lines toward the land's edge where the
two preceding waves of sodden GI's were pushing into the jungle.
Pre-invasion air reconnaisance photos had conveyed the false
impression that the seafloor here was sandy and sloped out
uniformly. Thus misinformed by Intelligence briefings, the
coxswains had unwittingly run upon a belt of invisible coral
upthrusts, on the inshore side of which the waters were not only
relatively deep, but underlain by a mat of tangled seaweed topping
three or four feet of viscous grey mud interspersed with potholes.
Consequently we had to make our way through saltwater that was
chest-deep at best, even for six-footers such as I. At intervals,
weighted down and unbalanced by our accoutrements, one of us
would break through the vegetation and sink into the glutinous

mud or stumble into a hole, often to the point of complete submergence. The men of shorter stature especially were in grave danger of drowning. I tried desperately to keep my aid kits and carbine dry by holding them over my head, but at least twice I went under and had to be helped up by a buddy who had his footing for the moment and could extend his carbine toward me so that by grabbing its barrel, I could regain my balance, and I in turn did the same for others, until we finally attained the shallows. Thanks to the sheer grace of God and my teammates, I reached dry land with my gear soaked but intact, and so eventually did almost everyone else. Had the Japs been present in large numbers and opened any significant volume of fire, it is doubtful that many of us could have survived, but to our enormous relief, there was no hostile reaction of note. Hence, our "baptism of fire" turned out instead to be "baptism by total immersion." Apparently, only a handful of Kawashima's soldiery had been keeping an eye on things in our vicinity, and I saw no signs of habitation nearby, though there were two or three fishing villages somewhere along the shore and a leper colony back in the interior—indeed, I don't remember sighting a native throughout my entire stay on the island.

Having gained terra firma at White Beach, our first concern was to get our equipment ashore while the infantrymen on our front and those to our left pushed on inland to secure a two-and-a-half by three-and-a-half-mile perimeter encompassing the beachhead and the airstrip. Vehicle offloading came within an ace of being an almost total foul-up. On Red Beach, the first three waves of 31st Div. assault troops, having the good fortune to be riding in on Amphtraks, had reached shore right on schedule, but the two succeeding waves, stepping off from ocean-going LCI's, had to contend with the same obstacles we in KANIMBLA's LCVP's had faced at White Beach. Still more disconcerting, the equipment-laden beaching vessels approaching in our wake were brought to a standstill even farther out from the shoreline—LCT's could get no closer than 80 yards, and LST's, 100 yards. Five of 534th's eight bulldozers clanking off into the water from LST's promptly drowned out or sank into the mud, as did almost three-fourths of the LCT-borne vehicles. At length a pontoon causeway was rigged into White Beach over which the remaining bulldozers could be driven to shore and used to extricate the bogged-down wheeled-and-tracked machinery. All subsequent LST traffic inbound to Red Beach was blocked until it could be diverted to some more favorable strand. There, on A+1, access to shore from the foremost LST's was created by lashing together a pair of shallower-draft LCT's end-to-end and filling them with sandbags.

The LST's had difficulty retracting as well; one, No. 452, stuck fast and could be dislodged only with the help of a sister, 459. Standard beaching procedure for these big flat-bottomed ships (whose ballast tanks were kept filled while at sea to keep them stable) called for dropping the stern anchor on the approach and paying out its cable until the anchor was at least 100 yards astern when the ship slid up on the beach. Then, when emptied and ready to retract, it was rendered more bouyant by pumping out the ballast tanks, and its anchor reeled in while its starboard and port engines were alternately run "full speed astern," thus rocking the ship from side to side enough to "waltz" it off into deeper water, taking great care not to foul the screws by overrunning the anchor cable. In this instance, LST 459 steered to the rear of 452 and passed a stout eight-inch hawser to the former's stern, then, backing off until the line was taut, the engines of both were reversed at full while 452 simultaneously reeled in her cable; in this manner, and with additional aid from a tugboat, 452 was finally refloated. (LST skippers were anxious to retract from beacheads as expeditiously as possible, because, while immobilized, they were easy targets for enemy planes and artillery. They were especially leary of remaining beached overnight, given the predeliction of Japanese airmen for making their raids at dusk or at first light when less visibility was afforded Yank antiaircraft gunners.)

In our White Beach sector, things went marginally better due to the time and effort invested in careful combat-loading at Oro Bay and Aitape and the fact that more of our Caterpillar tractors were able to made it ashore initially and could winch or tow the bogged-down equipment from the briny. Our amphib hydrographic surveyors soon discovered a less-obstructed beaching site about 1,500 yards to the south, or right, of our strand, to which LST's were diverted, and by the day's end, 6,000 troops and 7,200 tons of supplies had been unloaded there. The next day an even better stretch of shore on the opposite side of the Gila Peninsula was scouted out; designated Blue, and having clearer approaches and more favorable offlying slope and seabed, it was swiftly put to use. There is general agreement among analysts of joint operations in SWPA that the initial beaching conditions at Morotai were probably the worst encountered anywhere during the entire war.

We in 534th, of course, with our boat unit thousands of miles to the rear in Australia, had no LCM's and LCVP's of our own to facilitate the ship-to-shore portage of vehicles and cargo. Although most of 544th's 185 organic craft were at hand, they were of little help in untangling the general mess for two or three days, having been preassigned to the lighterage of radar, antiaircraft artillery, and small tactical units to off-lying islets. In brief, everyone along the entire beachfront was stretched to the limit until more satisfactory off-loading could be achieved and things on the cluttered strands sorted out.[27]

On A-Day, two hours after those of us in the leading assault waves had landed, MacArthur came ashore in person to make a brief survey and confer with his subordinates. He, too, stepped off into water up to his chest when his Higgins Boat hung up on the coral just as ours had. When he had concluded his business and was reboarding his craft at a more accessible spot, his clothing still damp, he paused and gazed wistfully to the northwest, according to one observer, "almost as though he could already see through the mist the rugged lines of Bataan and Corregidor . . . 'They are waiting for me there,' he mused; 'It has been a long time.'" His LCVP then returned him forthwith to cruiser NASHVILLE, which sped him back across the bounding main to his new Hollandia headquarters to map out his next moves.[28]

In response to reports that a large enemy amphibious force from Singapore was enroute to Morotai to take us in flank or rear, the heavy weapons sections of the 534th and 544th lost no time in emplacing and barricading their 37-mm. cannon and HMG's, facing seaward. Thanks to the intervention of Allied airmen, however, the would-be retributors were deflected, or so we were told, freeing everyone for the tasks of jetty-and-road-building, beachhead reorganization, etc. Once we medics had an aid station installed, we lent a hand where needed; filling and throwing those infernal sandbags for the jetties was exhausting in the equatorial heat, but no one could be spared until all the high-priority machinery and materiel had been offloaded. One of our boys, Pvt. Joseph Betesh (Brooklyn, N.Y.) I believe it was, found by chance a copy of a recently-dated Japanese field order directing the evacuation of most of Morotai's garrison to Halmahera, whereon the *TRADEWIND* hammer had been expected to fall.

By sundown of our first day on "Morty," a semblance of order had begun to emerge from the jumble on the beachhead. The three infantry assault teams had reached their objectives and joined up to form a seamless perimeter. (The reader might infer from this that we were now sheltered behind a continuous line of hasty entrenchments, but in jungle campaigning, an established perimeter implied nothing more elaborate than a string of more or less contiguous clusters of mutually-supporting foxholes.) A feeble "banzai" attack that night was easily repelled, but no serious enemy countermeasures had yet materialized. Friendly casualties thus far were limited to a couple of dead and a handful of wounded, as over against twelve Japanese killed and one captured.

During the ensuing days, thousands of additional combat and service troops, including three battalions of USAAF airfield engineers and two RAAF construction squadrons, streamed ashore to solidify our gains, with a plethora of vehicles, artillery, heavy machinery, and stores. Heavy rains hampered operations from 20 to 30 September, making life miserable for everyone, while infantry patrols penetrated more distant parts of the densely-jungled island, dispersing small parties of the enemy. On A+20, 4 October, General Krueger declared *INTERLUDE* officially concluded, by which date a total of 117 enemy troops had been liquidated or captured at the modest cost of 31

Americans slain or unaccounted for and 85 wounded. Patrolling Navy PT boats intercepted and sank several Japanese barges full of troops trying to escape to Halmahera, adding another 200 or so to the toll of enemy dead. The smouldering embers of opposition would flare up again, however, as covert enemy water-crossings from the opposite direction commenced, until by mid-December, an entire infantry regiment, Col. Kisou Ouchi's 211th, had sneaked onto Morotai with the aim of driving us into the sea. Positioned well to the north of our perimeter in an area beyond the Pilowo River known as Hill 40, their efforts were initially limited to patrolling and harassment, but as their numbers increased, they became a substantial menace. To eradicate them and release the 31st for more urgent business elsewhere, Clarkson's 33d "Golden Cross" Division was imported from Finschaffen just prior to Christmas. After twenty days of sharp fighting in the steaming jungles (the so-called Second Battle of Morotai, ending on 14 January 1945), most of Ouchi's intruders were ferretted out and slain by units of the 33d, and the remainder dispersed, inflating to 150 the American lives expended in securing the island (five fatalities occurred when a GI triggered a mine, taking four companions into eternity with him.) Ultimately, the lives of 870 of the emperor's loyal subjects were squandered in the futile counter-effort, and only 10 taken prisoner. In 1945, long after we in the 534th had moved on to another field of action, a handful of enemy fugitives still hiding out in Morotai's more remote parts were flushed out by the 25th Infantry Regiment of the 93d Division (the only Negro combat outfit serving in the Southwest Pacific.) Among the prey they snared was Colonel Ouchi himself, one of the highest-ranking P.O.W.'s to be taken during the course of the war.[29]

During our first three weeks on Morotai, we of the Medical Detachment, when not absorbed in shore party labors or treating the disabled, grabbed what fitful rest we could in foxholes or the pup tents we pitched alongside our burrows. The airfield engineers worked at a frantic pace to improve the primitive Japanese airstrip and to hack out of the bush, grade, and surface (with crushed coral rock dredged from the sea) two new runways of sufficient length and durability to accomodate the B-17's, B-24's, and B-25's which the Fifth and Thirteenth Air Forces were anxious to base there. The Jap-built field proved to have such poor drainage that further efforts to rehabilitate it for fighter planes were dropped and construction of a third strip initiated in its stead. Within forty days, all three dromes were substantially completed, and in short order, their bays became crowded with Kenney's planes, while Navy Catalina float-planes operated from three tenders anchored out in the roadstead. As soon as there were parking-bays to accommodate them, Liberators of the "Bomber Barons" and "Long Rangers" squadrons began routinely taking to the skies from Morotai to hammer enemy positions in the southern Philippines. To sustain this intense aerial activity, other engineer units created access roadways and erected a temporary hospital, fuel-storage tanks, a couple of floating wharves, and a pile dock for the moorage of Liberty ships. Our battalion was coopted for several of these projects, and supplied hatch-and-dock crews to empty the freighters.[30]

In full awareness of what our seizure of Morotai and the development of its dromes portended, the Japanese subjected us to a seemingly-endless succession of bombing and strafing raids, mostly nocturnal, beginning on our first night ashore and lasting until mid-March 1945. Though typically carried out by only one or two planes, at times there were as many as twelve. The mini-raids accomplished little in the way of significant destruction, aside from cratered runways, which were usually repaired within a couple of hours. Occasionally, however, large numbers of parked planes and airfield structures were damaged or demolished, and ammunition and fuel dumps ignited, transforming the sable skies into a lurid semblance of dawn. The raiders tried to evade our radar by coming in low over the water, but for the most part they were quickly pinpointed and tracked by big portable searchlights whose beams began crisscrossing the heavens the moment their approach was detected, whereupon antiaircraft batteries would throw up an intense curtain of fire, stitched with tracers, exposing those of us on the periphery of the dromes to greater danger from raining shell fragments than from bomb blasts. When our gunners hit their mark, it would usually plunge to earth like a fiery comet and explode upon impact, to our great glee. They came at all hours of the night, but more often than not in the wee hours of the morning. Our sleep was thus rudely and persistently interrupted, compelling us to douse all lights, cram on helmets, and dive into foxholes until the all-clear sounded. As soon as the racket subsided, virtually everyone in the battalion would emerge from his hole and stumble to the edge of the jungle to urinate before bedding down again, so that the raiders quickly earned the moniker "Piss-call Charley,"[31]

At length we staked out a habitable bivouac in a grove of palm trees some distance from our original diggings, yet still close enough to the shoreline to catch cooling breezes. Once ensconced in our pyramidal tents, we began to savor some of the delights of civilization, including shower baths, proper field latrines, and decently-cooked balanced meals. Numerous injuries were treated in our aid station, among them a youngster who had stepped on a land mine, hideously mangling his lower extremities; sadly, he expired before we could pass him on to more appropriate reparative agencies, an unsettling experience for all, to say the least. Though few amphibs contracted the scrub typhus afflicting several units on Morotai, other illnesses, predominantly skin infections, fevers, and gastro-intestinal disorders, rather than battle wounds, demanded most of our attention throughout our sojourn there. My therapeutic skills, such as drawing blood, giving shots, or cleaning, bandaging, and medicating injuries and lesions, improved with practice, as did my clerical and typing competencies. In my spare time, I buried my nose in books, devouring such classics as Nordhoff and Hall's *The Hurricane* and Thomas Wolfe's *You Can't Go Home Again* and *The Web and the Rock*. (Wolfe, a fellow Tar Heel, had attended the University of North Carolina at Chapel Hill, where, as a post-war student, I would occupy for a year or so a run-down rented room in which he was reputed to have dwelt.) Mail was delivered with some regularity, and I was able to dash off letters to my relatives almost daily. Aside from the ennervating equatorial heat and occasional mild bouts of nasopharyngitis, fever, diarrhea, and nausea with which most of us had to cope, the quality of life on Morotai was more tolerable than in New Guinea.

I, along with many others, harbored a nagging guilt at having escaped the carnage accompanying so many other amphibious operations, one in particular which had taken place in the adjoining theatre on the same date as ours. While the scheduled assault on Yap Island had been cancelled, Nimitz had insisted, against the advice of his subordinate Halsey, on proceeding with the invasion of the Palau Islands, 450 miles due east of Mindanao, concurrently with that of Morotai. A task force of lst Marines and 81st Division troops led by Marine Maj. Gen. William H. Rupertus drew the onerous task of prying loose the principal islands in that chain, primarily Peleliu, for supplementary air-basing. Instead of the easy pickings anticipated, the campaign devolved into a hideous bloodbath. The Tokyo war-lords were now wedded to a tactic of compelling the lavishly-armed-and-supplied Yankee aggressors to pay such an extravagant toll in lives for each yard of territory gained that the American public would react negatively to any further offensive strategies and pressure Roosevelt for a negotiated settlement. At Biak, resort to this semi-suicidal policy of defense-in-depth had bought the Japanese precious time. Now, on the accursed island of Peleliu, shaped like a backward "J" with its long spine corrugated by ravines and limestone ridges, the garrison commander had raised these tactics to a fine art. He planned for a mere token resistance on the beaches while concealing his main forces and heavy firepower within elevated warrens virtually impervious to aerial bombardment or offshore shelling, from which he could counterattack under optimal conditions. After a ferocious two-day naval cannonade, which signally failed to blunt the antagonist's capability, Rupertus's troops stormed ashore and grabbed Peleliu's airfield without untoward losses, only to see their prospects rapidly deteriorate. The Japanese, burrowed into the high Umurbrogol Ridge, stymied every attempt by the Marines to break out from their congested beachhead. A singularly nasty eight-week orgy of attrition ensued, devouring the lives of l,950 young Marines and soldiers, and disabling another 5,000 in the agonizingly slow process of pulverizing and incinerating each of the infernal dens, notwithstanding the use of newly-introduced tank-mounted long-range flame-throwers. Within days of the Peleliu landing, Angaur Island five miles to the south was invaded by 81st Division GI's and speedily pacified with remarkably less effort and fewer casualties, while Ulithi atoll on the northeast was taken without a shot being fired, its defenders having vamoosed to Yap. As a bitter footnote to the Peleliu bloodletting, there was an emerging consensus that the enemy's retention of the Palaus would have been inconsequential, given the drastic diminution of his pool of skilled pilots and aircraft.[32]

. . . .

Similarly dampening any elation which we on Morotai may have entertained at our almost-uncontested intrusion was sobering news from the European Theatre in late September of the virtual annihilation of the British 1st Airborne Division by Hitler's S.S. Panzers at Arnhem in ill-starred Operation *MARKET GARDEN.*[33] Although it seemed indubitable that the Axis coalition would be vanquished in the not-too-distant future, given the heartening Soviet gains on the eastern front, the depletion of manpower reserves and decline in quality of life within the Western Democracies was approaching the limits of popular tolerance.

Robert Meredith Watson, Sr.

Ruth Adelaide Cadman Watson

The Watson Kids
(Clockwise):
"Peggy"
"Bobby"
"Ruthie"

Robert M. Watson, Jr. (left)
in parade of Civil Defense
Volunteers, Winston-Salem,
N.C., 1943

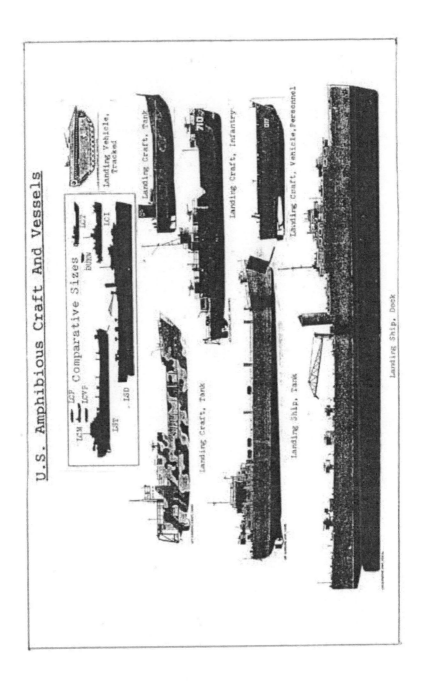

U.S. Amphibious Craft And Vessels

LCVP - Landing Craft, Vehicle,
Personnel.

LCM - Landing Craft, Mechanized
[Equipment].

DUKW ["Duck"]

Maj. Gen.
Daniel Noce
[founder, EAC]

Brig. Gen.
Wm. F. Heavey
[C.O., 2ESB]

Brig. Gen.
David Ogden
[C.O., 3ESB]

Brig. Gen.
H. Hutchings, Jr.
[C.O., 4ESB]

Amphibian Engineer
Uniform Breast
Pocket Patch

Combined Operations
Uniform Shoulder
Patch

Hastily-Constructed Buildings,
Camp Gordon Johnston, Fla.

(L. to R.) Pvts. Benjamin R. Weaver, Robert M. Watson, Jr., and Carl Stegman, Radio School, Camp Gordon Johnston, Fla.

THE TROOP SLEEPER

Top: Exterior.
Bottom: Interior:
left, Set-up for
Day Use, Each
Seat Accomoda-
ting Three Men;
Right, Pullman
Porter Preparing
Three-tier Bunks
For Sleeping.

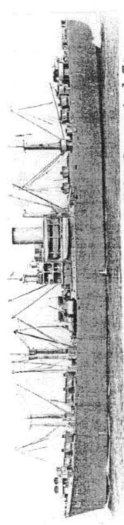

FAIRLAND – C-2 "Liberty" Cargo Ship Converted To Troop Carrier.

GENERAL H. W. BUTNER – AP 113, P-2 Troopship.

594th EB&SR Shoremen Unloading
LCM's At Unknown Location, SWPA.

31st Division Assault Troops
Wading Ashore From LCI's On
Red Beach, Morotai, N.E.I.,
15 September 1944.

Clutter of Drowned-out Wheeled
And Tracked Vehicles Off
Morotai Beachhead.

4ESB Bulldozer Mired Down Off
Morotai Beachhead.

2ESB Shore Engineers Constructing
Jetties Out To LST's At Leyte
Beachhead.

L. to R. (kneeling), D. Hanson,
C. Vadorsky; (standing) R. Watson,
R. Bridges, B. Weaver, after island
patrol, off Morotai, N.E.I.,
November 1944

L. to R., B. Weaver, J. Bannister,
R. Watson, in camp, Morotai, N.E.I.,
November 1944

Loaded Top Deck Of An LST Enroute
To An Invasion In The Asiatic
Pacific Theatre.

Main Street, Dagupan, Luzon,
P.I., 1945.

Ruins of Legislature Building,
Manila, P.I., 1945

Manila, P.I., February 1945, Ruins
Of The Bureau Of Commerce Building.

Burnt-out Shell Of Gen. MacArthur's
Luxurious Hotel Apartment In Manila.

2d Battalion, 534th EB&SR, bivouac,
San Fernando, La Union, P.I., looking
toward China Sea, June 1945

Medical Detachment section, 534th
bivouac, San Fernando, La Union, P.I.
(author's tent top left)

R. Watson, San Fernando, La Union,
P.I., June 1945

Medical Detachment clerical staff
(L. to R.), L. Russell, H. Riley,
R. Watson, San Fernando, La Union,
P.I., June 1945

Ruined city center, Baguio, Luzon,
P.I., August 1945

Medical Detachment Group, San Fabian,
Luzon, P.I., August 1945: (L. to R.)
front, G. Ruderman, R. Hoffer, S. Frielich, B. Goodstein (?), M. Tiejero;
rear, G. Manke, W. Benasek, R. Watson

Congested Shipping At South Harbor, Manila, P.I., After The Bay Had Been Cleared of Sunken Vessels.

534th EB&SR Barracks, Nagoya, Japan.

B. Weaver, R. Watson, Nagoya, Japan,
November 1945

S/Sgt. R. M. Watson, Nagoya,
Japan, December 1945.

T/Sgt. R. M. Watson (With Japanese
Infantry Rifle), Nagoya, Japan,
January 1946.

(L. to R.) B. Weaver, Japanese friend,
R. Watson, Daidacho, Nagoya, Japan,
6 January 1946

X

OPENING THE DOOR TO THE PHILIPPINES

North of Morotai, the dual Allied offensives were about to converge on the Philippines preparatory to a unitary thrust into Japan's home waters via the Ryukyus. Admiral Halsey was convinced that the Japanese grip on the archipelago was feeble at best, and on his and Nimitz's recommendation—and with MacArthur's concurrence—the Joint Chiefs authorized an acceleration of their invasion by two months, the target date now set for 20 October. Another revision of strategic objectives was also sanctioned, with the initial blow now to fall upon Leyte in the Visayan group of the central Philippines, rather than upon Mindanao, the southernmost island. Luzon remained the primary goal, bordering as it did upon the vital South China Sea lanes by which alone Japan could still access her rich larder of raw materials in the Dutch East Indies, Malaya, and Indochina. With Luzon's retrieval, most Pentagon theorists had now come to believe, the Japanese homeland could rapidly be starved into submission and her war industries skeletonized. American submarines had already reduced the flow of petroleum to Japan so severely that her oil-fired naval vessels were being kept close to their home ports to conserve fuel, and her aeronautic replacements were training in flight simulators instead of aloft.[1]

Leyte, resembling, as William Manchester has suggested, an extracted molar with its roots pointing southward, is separated by a thin slit of water, San Juanico Strait, from her somewhat larger companion on the east, Samar. This duo, like the rest of the Visayas, are interposed between the archipelago's two principal islands, Luzon to the north, roughly equivalent to England in land area, and

Mindanao to the south, comparable to Ireland. Access to the major anchorage in the Leyte/Samar vicinity, Leyte Gulf, can be attained from the Philippine Sea on the east only through two passages, San Bernardino Strait separating Samar and Luzon, and Surigao Strait between Leyte and Mindanao. These, in fact, provide the sole east-west apertures along the entire length of the archipelago.

Halsey and MacArthur were persuaded that the substitution of Leyte for Mindanao offered two distinct advantages; not only could it be captured speedily because of its pattern of roads, but, given its proximity to Luzon, its airstrips, clustered for the most part on its east coast around Tacloban and Dulag, would enable Kenney's P-38 and P-47 fighter planes to control the air-space above any likely invasion site on the primary objective. For the moment, however, the as-yet-unfinished dromes on Morotai remained the only ones from which the pending Leyte landings could be afforded ground-based aerial coverage. Thus, until Morotai's strips were fully operable, MacArthur, though leary as always of relying solely upon carrier-borne aircraft, had no other choice, for time was running short.[2]

Morotai had been in our hands for less than a month when a gargantuan fleet of 738 ships was pulled together by Admiral Kinkaid at Manus's Seeadler Harbor and Hollandia's Humboldt Bay for the descent upon Leyte, which would be MacArthur's most ambitious undertaking thus far. (Among Kinkaid's amphibious assets, incidentally, were twelve of the latest design in beaching craft, the Landing Ship, Medium [LSM], 203 ft. in length, filling a gap between the LCT and LST classes. Speedier and of shallower draft than an LST, yet more comfortable and seaworthy than an LCT, it carried a crew of 4 officers and 55 men.) Backed by "Bull" Halsey's nearby Third Fleet with its 6 new battleships, 17 cruisers, and 64 destroyers, topped off by the 16 fast carriers of Task Force 38 under Vice Adm. Marc Mitscher, Kinkaid's Seventh—"MacArthur's Navy"—would have at its immediate disposal the 18 "Jeep" carriers of TG 77.4 (Rear Adm. Thomas L. Sprague.) The Seventh Fleet armada was to take aboard two full corps of Krueger's Sixth Army—Franklin Sibert's X (1st Cavalry and 24th Infantry division), and John Hodge's XXIV (7th and 96th Infantry divisions, fresh from the Central Pacific)—

and insert them onto Leyte's east coast, fronting on Leyte Gulf. [Map M7]

Like a fork with two tines, this operation, to be known as *KING II*, would be binary, with Rear Admiral Barbey's TF-78 "Northern Attack Force" (X Corps) landing close to Tacloban, Leyte's capital, and Vice Adm. Theodore Wilkinson's TF-79 "Southern Attack Force" (XXIV Corps), fourteen miles downcoast near Dulag. The plan had its drawbacks; the island's airfields, situated on the rainier east coast in the vicinity of these two towns, lay atop poorly-drained soil, rendering their utility for Kenney's aircraft problematical with the monsoon season in the offing, and promising wretched weather for ground operations and engineering projects. Ton upon ton of Marston steel matting would have to be hurriedly laid to make the squishy runways useable until they could be resurfaced, and Tacloban possessed the only pier at which an ocean freighter could dock.

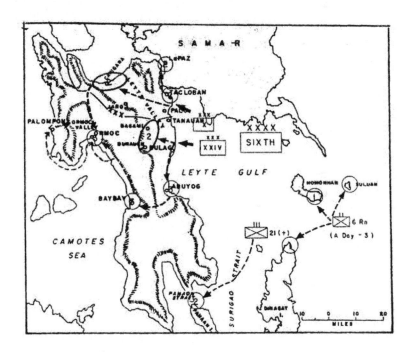

MAP 7. SIXTH ARMY'S LEYTE CAMPAIGN,
20 OCTOBER–25 DECEMBER 1944.

On the other hand, Krueger's two corps could expect to confront no more than 21,000 antagonists, at least by the optimistic reckoning of Maj. Gen. Charles A. Willoughby, MacArthur's Intelligence Chief. This was a gross miscalculation, for in actuality, 35,000 currently lay in wait on Leyte, sharpening their long bayonets, sighting their field-pieces and knee-mortars, and polishing their Nambu MG's, and more were on the way, it being Tokyo's intent to wage the decisive contest for mastery of the Philippines there rather than on Luzon.

Recently appointed to the command of Japan's Fourteenth Area Army, i.e., all ground forces in the Philippines, was Lt. Gen. Tomoyuki Yamashita, the "Tiger of Malaya," widely-acclaimed conqueror of Singapore in 1942 and an exceptionally-gifted strategist and tactician. Strongly convinced that his main defense should be made on Luzon instead of Leyte, Yamashita had resisted any dispersal of the forces amassed on the former, but had been overruled by Field Marshall Count Hisaichi Terauchi in Saigon, master of all "Southern Area" armies. Accordingly, Yamashita's Leyte field army, under Lt. Gen. Sosaku Suzuki, had already been substantially enlarged at the expense of the Luzon garrison, and thousands more would shortly be fed in, so that Krueger's two corps would ultimately find themselves crossing swords with 80,000 seasoned fighters, many coming directly from China and elsewhere in Southeast Asia. Willoughby's egregious error had not yet surfaced, however, as the awesomely-puissant American expedition got underway.[3]

KING II's extended troop list had originally included Ogden's entire 3ESB, widely dispersed across New Britain and New Guinea, and with its command post now at Biak, but at the last minute, under the press of time, Heavey's hard-worked 2ESB had been substituted, simply because its units were located nearer the staging areas. To help his "Cape Cod Commando" boat units gear up for the strenuous work ahead, one hundred of their battered landing craft were exchanged for newer ones of the 3d and 4th brigades, who also shared their precious stock of spare parts, always in short supply. Leyte was 1,200 miles distant even from 2ESB's closest deployments, and given the high probability of encountering monsoon-bred storms enroute, all of Heavey's 400 lighters would have to be piggybacked on VII 'phib's vessels, leaving his 2 tugboats, 4 fuel barges, 4 crash boats, and 2 small freighters to navigate under their own power, arriving at the beachhead a week behind the assault force.[4]

As Kinkaid's main *KING II* convoy labored northward through the seas toward Leyte, its foregoing minesweepers and vessels, carrying scouts and underwater-demolition teams along with the elements of 6th Ranger Battalion charged with securing the islets at the entrance to Leyte Gulf, were roughed up by a strong but brief typhoon. The storm had, however, conveniently dissipated by L-Day, 20 October, bequeathing sunny skies and placid waters. As soon as Sprague's carrier planes and Kinkaid's fire-support ships had flayed the shores, the two assault forces closed in on their respective beaching sites, none of which were obstructed by coral reefs. The landings were challenged only at Red Beach, the more southerly of the two at Tacloban, where Heavey's boats and Kinkaid's LST's were taken under fire by field artillery, damaging several of each, but sinking none. The spearheading troops in both prongs of Krueger's 104,000-man phalanx clambered ashore with comparative ease, thanks not only to the now-calm surf, but to the close teamwork of the Army-Navy amphibs. The only complications occurred on the two X Corps strands, especially at Red Beach, where the LST's were blocked by shallows until pontoon cubes could be imported from the Dulag sector. At White Beach, an unmapped sand spit forced the deposition of bulk cargoes on the runway of the sole available airstrip in the vicinity, which parallelled the seafront, precluding its immediate use by the AAF, to the utter chagrin of the airmen.[5]

At 1300 that afternoon, MacArthur, accompanied by Sergio Osmena, president-designate of the Philippine Republic, and his influential political crony, Carlos Romulo, waded dramatically from one of 2ESB's barges onto the sacred soil near Tacloban as the news cameras clicked, and announced over the airwaves to the world at large the redemption of his solemn pledge to strike the shackles from Filipino wrists. In a matter of hours, both the provincial capital and Dulag were in American hands, and in due course, MacArthur established his advanced headquarters in a Tacloban mansion. The offloading of X and XXIV corps—along with some 200,000 tons of supplies—was swiftly accomplished, and their divisions surged inland, to the immense relief of Nimitz, so many of whose assets had been temporarily committed to this operation. Vice Adm. Marc Mitscher's TF-38, in collusion with USAAF XX Bomber Command from mainland China, had already done their bit by two weeks of massive preemptive raids on Okinawan, Formosan, and Luzonian airfields, eliminating more than 600 Japanese aircraft which could potentially have made a bloody shambles of *KING II*.

With Krueger's force safely landed, Halsey's warships and carriers promptly steamed off to forestall any interference from the enemy's partially-rehabilitated Mobile Fleet. Their departure gave surviving Japanese land-based aircraft from Luzon and other nearby islands a brief "window of opportunity" to pummel Krueger's beachheads of which they took full advantage until redirected to the more critical mission of covering three fast-approaching retaliatory Imperial naval squadrons and convoys bearing reinforcemens and supplies for Susuki's army.[6]

Heavey's brigade, now toting all Northern Attack Force's ship-to-shore traffic, would remain in the Visayas sustaining Krueger's offensive throughout the ensuing campaign.[7] Leyte's highways were a bonus to the invaders, but it was soon apparent that its reconquest would be no walkover. While the terrain in the island's northeastern quadrant was predominantly level, its western half was dominated by rugged mountains, punctuated only along the upper western coast by the broad Ormoc Valley, carved out by the southward-flowing Pagsangahan River, its estuary forming a gum-line cavity in the molar, as it were. Near the river's mouth, at approximately the same latitude as Dulag, lay Leyte's major port, Ormoc, through which Susuki's main force, positioned within and behind the mountain ramparts, drew the bulk of its provisions and reinforcements. As Krueger's infantry took to the roads running across the island's upper half, one segment of XXIV Corps swinging south to Abuyog, then west toward Baybay on the opposite coast below Ormoc, another driving directly west to grab the airfields clustered around Burauen at the base of the mountains, while X Corps lunged toward the north coast town of Carigara, the weather turned more foul than the meteorologists had predicted. Drenched by almost continual downpours, the GI's met ever stiffer resistance as they advanced into the higher terrain. The lightly-surfaced roads across the rice paddies in the flatlands soon became virtually impassable, imposing upon Heavey's lighters and DUKW's an increased burden of troop movement and resupply, not only as coasters, but up inland streams and across bogs as well.[8]

The key to victory was the town of Ormoc and the valley above, which Krueger aimed to envelop from north and south. Until Leyte's spongy east-coast airstrips could be more firmly compacted or new ones built, however, none of Kenney's planes were available to choke off Suzuki's main sea artery from Luzon. By 2 November Sibert's troops had taken Carigara, and the 7th Division had reached Baybay, but weeks passed before the Japanese dispositions in the mountains enwrapping the Ormoc Valley could be overpowered. Meanwhile, to the northeast, 2ESB amphibs boated elements of 1st Cavalry Division over to Samar, while Hodges's XXIV Corps units fanned out over southern Leyte, and the 6th Rangers and Filipino guerillas sanitized the last of the small islands in Leyte Gulf.

Calling up three fresh reserve divisions (32d and 77th Infantry and 11th Airborne), Krueger had Maj. Gen. Andrew D. Bruce's 77th sea-lifted by Rear Adm. A. D. Struble's TG-78.3 from Tacloban to a landing near Ormoc on 7 December—the third anniversary of the Pearl Harbor attack. Though Struble lost two destroyers to Kamikazes, Bruce's regiments got ashore scot free, assisted by Heavey's LCM's and rocket-and-flak boats. Three days later, having taken the town and choked off Suzuki's provenance, the 77th's GI's, in tandem with those of the 7th, pushed into Ormoc Valley from the south, while the 1st Cavalry, 11th Airborne, and 24th and 32d Infantry divisions pressed in from the north and east. As Christmas approached and Krueger's clamps tightened down on the 40,000 of Susuki's stalwarts still holding fast in the valley, Yamashita in Manila concluded that the Leyte campaign, having bled off 55,000 casualties, was beyond redemption, and that no further depletion of his manpower could be tolerated. Informing Suzuki that Leyte would have to be written off in order to sustain the defense of Luzon, "The Tiger" consoled himself with the thought that his subordinate's tenacious stand had compelled Sixth Army to postpone its descent upon the more crucial island from 20 December 1944 to 9 January 1945.

On the day after Christmas, MacArthur issued a semi-mendacious communique announcing the victorious conclusion of the Leyte Campaign, aside from some "minor mopping-up." Foisting upon Eichelberger and his new Eighth Army (to which Hodge's XXIV Corps was transferred) the task of suppressing whatever opposition remained on Leyte/Samar, MacArthur ordered Krueger to redirect his energies and reposition Sixth Army toward the invasion of Luzon without further delay.[9]

On Leyte's environing waters, meanwhile, even as the curtain had first risen on *KING II*, the greatest sea battle in the annals of human history had raged, from 23 through 26 October. As soon as word of the Leyte invasion had reached Imperial headquarters in Tokyo, the widely-dispersed, battle-scarred components of Admiral Toyoda's fleet had been regrouped to parry this most recent knife-thrust at Japan's jugular. Three separate naval strike forces were dispatched at top speed to the Central Philippines—two from the homeland and a third from Singapore via Borneo—to smite Kinkaid's squadrons and cripple Nimitz's fleet in what would indubitably be the war's climactic maritime showdown. Until Toyoda's avengers could reach the critical scene, all Nipponese aircraft within range were loosed on Seventh Fleet and the beachheads.

Of the two enemy flotillas sortieing from the home islands, the first, entrusted to Vice Admiral Ozawa and built around four aircraft carriers virtually denuded of planes and two hybrid battleship/carriers (dreadnaughts altered abaft their stacks to accomodate short flight-decks), was tasked with decoying Halsey's fast carriers and upscale warships as far away as possible from the environs of Leyte Gulf. The second, under Vice Adm. Kiyohide Shima, was charged with providing back-up for the third (and by far the most dangerous) assemblage sailing east from Lingga Roads, Singapore, commanded by Vice Adm. Takeo Kurita, intent upon knocking out Kinkaid's Seventh Fleet as it was shielding and sustaining Krueger's beachhead on Leyte. The complicated Japanese battle plan, fraught with possibilities for miscommunication and malcoordination, issued in four distinct clashes, known collectively as the Battle of Leyte Gulf.

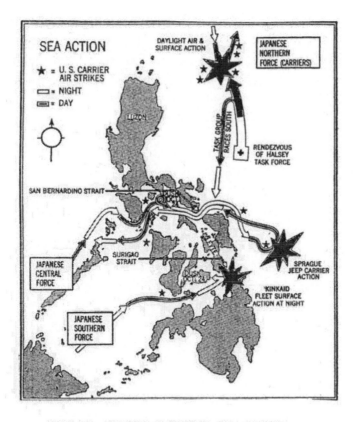

MAP 8. NAVAL BATTLE OF LEYTE GULF, 23–26 OCTOBER 1944.

To summarize the sequelae in more or less chronological order, Kurita's big armada from Singapore, after pausing at Brunei, Borneo, for refuelling, split shortly before midday of 22 October, with its smaller segment, Vice Adm. Shoji Nishimura's "Southern Force," heading south to enter Leyte Gulf via Surigao Strait, where Shima's squadron from Japan was supposed to hook onto its tail for an attack on Seventh Fleet. The remainder of Kurita's "Center Force," namely, the two 68,000-ton super-battleships MUSASHI and YAMATO, three older battleships, ten heavy cruisers, two light cruisers, and more than a dozen destroyers, would proceed from the South China Sea, thread its way through the Sibuyan Sea and San Bernardino Strait into the Philippine Sea, and turn south down Samar's outer coast to penetrate Leyte Gulf via its upper, or eastern, entrance. The idea was to grind up Kinkaid's fleet between the jaws of Kurita's brawny Center Force and that of Nishimura, strengthened by Shima's squadron from Japan.

In the wee hours of 23 October, off Palawan, a couple of American subs sighted Kurita's formation heading eastward, picked off two of its cruisers, and disabled a third. Two days later, in Sibuyan waters, Halsey's planes further savaged Center Force, sending the mighty MUSASHI to the bottom, crippling still another cruiser, and inflicting serious damage on several other vessels (the Battle of the Sibuyan Sea.) The skittish Kurita then reversed course, his withdrawal deluding Halsey into rashly taking Ozawa's bait and sending his Third Fleet on a chase after the latter's virtually-planeless carriers northward through the Philippine Sea, leaving San Bernardino Strait unguarded. Halsey's departure emboldened Kurita to turn his chastened Center Force about once again, slip undetected through the strait, and veer south as originally planned along Samar's east coast to rendezvous with his collaborators Nishimura and Shima at Leyte Gulf.

As the still-formidable Center Force steamed down toward the gulf's eastern entrance, Nishimura's "Southern Force" detachment, followed by Shima's so-called "Second Striking Force" from Japan, passed into Surigao Strait, the western or lower entrance to Leyte Gulf. Forewarned of his danger, Kinkaid deployed Rear Adm. Jesse

Oldendorf's six battlewagons and three heavy cruisers across the upper neck of Surigao Strait, while sending destroyers and PT boats to inflict what damage they could upon Nishimura's squadron as it entered the lower part of the strait. At the outset of this second round of the titanic title match, near midnight of 24/25 October, Nishimura's force was thinned-out by Kinkaid's destroyer/PT boat outriders, yet forged ahead regardless, only to suffer virtual extinction a few hours later from the big guns of Oldendorf's heavyweights. This, modern warfare's last Old-West-style shoot-out between surface battle fleets, erased all but two of Southern Force's assets, a cruiser and a destroyer. When Shima's trailing squadron came upon the scene belatedly about 0420 in search of Nishimura's formation, it sighted two of Oldendorf's battle cruisers on the horizon and let fly with torpedoes, none of which struck home. Shima then prudently turned tail and ran, with Nishimura's hardy pair of survivors tagging along in his wake. Oldendorf pursued for a spell, finishing off the rearmost cruiser before calling off the chase. Shima, realizing how narrowly he had escaped Nishimura's fate, raced away to refuge at Brunei, Borneo, thereby preserving his own two heavy cruisers and quartet of destroyers, along with the single destroyer remaining from the wiped-out Southern Force. Thus ended the second bout, the Battle of Surigao Strait.

The third round opened early on 25 October after an American patrol plane spotted and took fire from some of Kurita's warships ploughing southward off Samar. Thus forewarned, the only U.S. surface force anywhere around, and a puny one at that, Rear Adm. Clifton Sprague's six escort carriers and screening destroyers, probing northward off Samar, realigned itself for what was sure to be an absurdly-uneven scrap. By a fortuitous combination of favorable winds, exceptionally-adroit maneuvering, and all-or-nothing aerial bombing and torpedo strikes, Sprague's outgunned underdogs managed to inflict so many deep bites on the still-awesome Center Force that three more of Kurita's heavy cruisers slid to the bottom of the sea. In the immediate aftermath of this lop-sided contest, the Sons of Heaven had their revenge by springing the first organized Kamikaze raid of the war upon

Sprague's jeep carriers, sinking the ST. LO and mauling four of her sisters. Kurita, assuming that he had run up against part of Halsey's main fleet, broke off the action by turning his mangled marauders about for the third time and withdrawing rearward through San Bernardino Strait, thereby ending what would officially be known as "the Battle off Samar," the next-to-last bout of the title match. The cost to the U.S. Navy of Sprague's feisty stand had not been cheap, with the erasure of two escort carriers, two destroyers, and a destroyer-escort, plus heavy damage to several other vessels. More tragically, a thousand of its brave bluejackets and naval aviators had gone to a watery grave, and almost as many disabled.

At about the same time, the fourth and final round erupted far to the north, some two hundred miles off Luzon's Cape Engano, in the wee hours of 25 October, as Halsey's search planes finally sighted the rearmost of Ozawa's 17-ship Northern Force, with its empty carriers, "hermaphrodite" carrier/battle-ships, light cruisers, destroyers, and oilers. At daybreak, Third Fleet fighters, torpedo bombers, and dive bombers commenced a series of masssive aerial strikes, unfazed by intense, well-directed fire thrown up by Ozawa's antiaircraft gunners. All four of Northern Force's carriers, including ZUIKAKU, the sole remaining flattop of those which had once scourged Pearl Harbor, were sunk, along with a destroyer. Belatedly peeling off a task group under Vice Adm. John S. McCain to snare Kurita's fugitives in San Bernardino Strait—the posse was too tardy by three hours—Halsey steamed on northward at top speed to overhaul Ozawa and finish him off. Although his mastiffs caught up with their prey in time to pick off two more Jap destroyers and a light cruiser, the foxxy Ozawa darted away to the Ryukyus with the remainder, satisfied that he had fulfilled his part, at least, of Toyoda's overly-ambitious challenge with consummate skill.

The net result of it all was a catastrophic wipe-out of Hirohito's Navy, with the subtraction of thirty-four of its ships over and above those sunk four months previously in the Philippine Sea embroglio, including 4 carriers, 3 battleships, among them MUSASHI, pride of the fleet, 10 cruisers, 13 destroyers, and 5 submarines. Though American aircraft and shipping losses in the Leyte Gulf actions were by no means insignificant, they could be readily replaced, as Japan's could not, and her permanent eclipse as a naval power was now beyond dispute.[10]

. . . .

In light of these pivotal developments to our north, we in the 534th anticipated an immiment redeployment. As the Allied offensive regained momentum and hard-surfaced airdromes on Leyte became available, the by-now-fully-serviceable and heavily-trafficked airfields on our small lily-pad and those to our rear in New Guinea and the Admiralties would find their status altered. Morotai would continue to serve as a way-station for USAAF flights to and from the Philippines and as a base for Navy PT-boat squadrons stalking maritime quarry in the Celebes. But with Japan's hoarding of her fast-shrivelling aerial reserves for an all-out stand on Luzon and in the Ryukus, air operations from Morotai would take on more of an Aussie accent. It would soon became the hub of Air Vice Marshall William Bostock's RAAF Command's expanded venue in western New Guinea as well as the staging point for an Australian invasion of oil-rich Borneo. Maj. Gen. St. Clair Streett's Thirteenth AAF squadrons would move up to the central Philippines to cover Eichelberger's Eighth Army ventures, while Ennis Whitehead's Fifth would work hand-in-hand with the Navy in policing the skies over Sixth Army's postponed landing on Luzon. At the moment, however, the completion of the dromes under development on Leyte and Samar was still lagging far behind schedule due to the inclement weather and saturated terrain, and Kenney had to look elsewhere for basing to suppress the enemy hives on Luzon.[11]

Two-hundred-and-fifty miles northwest of Leyte, athwart the southern approaches to Luzon, lay the lightly-garrisoned island of Mindoro; airfields in its drier, flatter southwestern corner around the city of San Jose would be less susceptible to the vagaries of the weather. Hence, Mindoro became the next morsel to be plucked, an appetizer before the main course, as it were. For its conquest, a

Seventh Fleet "Visayan Attack Force" under Rear Adm. A. D. Struble was hurriedly organized at Leyte Gulf to sealift 12,000 men of the 503d Parachute and 19th Infantry (24th Division) regiments, together with the 532d EB&SR, 6,000 service troops, and 10,000 USAAF personnel. The weather, for a change, was bland, and upon arrival in the San Jose vicinity on 15 December, the landing force met with little or no interference groundwise, the small enemy garrison having fading into the interior. By Christmas Day, the requisite portions of Mindoro were well in hand, at a bargain price of only 200 Army casualties, endowing MacArthur with the sorely-needed airfield sites as well as PT-Boat bases. (In addition to discharging their beachhead duties, the 532d shoremen demonstrated their versatility by the rehabilitation and short-term operation of a narrow-gauge railway.) The dromes were readied just in time to ensure Fifth Air Force coverage of the Luzon invasion armada poised to sail past the island's outer shores.[12]

There is a darker side to the Mindoro story, however, for the Navy paid dearly for this Yuletide present. The Japanese had loosed upon Struble's ships the most deadly instrument in their arsenal, mass Kamikazes. The Kamikaze Corps had only recently been organized to compensate for the empire's irremediable losses of skilled pilots and carrier aircraft. The USAAF XXI Bomber Command's B-29 forays from the Mariannas had not yet succeeded in seriously impairing Japan's domestic aircraft productivity, and newly-manufactured warbirds were still being rushed to the Philippines, but her output lagged far behind that of the U.S., while the Yank pilots with their now-technologically-superior fighter planes were becoming ever more adept at interception. Moreover, our anti-aircraft shells were tipped with proximity fuses, making it extremely hazardous for conventional Japanese bombers to home in tightly enough on a radar-equipped vessel spouting AA-fire to score a hit. (Huge quantities of these fuses were being produced by Winston-Salem's Western Electric plant.)

The Japanese term "Kamikaze," meaning Divine or Heavenly Wind, derived from an historic incident in 1570, when the homeland had been miraculously saved from conquest by a typhoon which wrecked a huge fleet of Chinese invaders. "Diabolic Wind" would have been a more appropriate appellation for this fiendish tactic, whereby a manned aircraft with fully-fuelled tanks and armed with bombs was deliberately rammed at top speed into a targetted ship, ideally aiming at the bridge or stack, triggering a huge explosion and a raging conflagration fed by the gasoline spraying from its ruptured tanks. Even if its pilot had already been slain in the air, the plane's momentum would, more often than not, drive it into a ship's bowels with appalling accuracy, causing severe and widespread damage, multiple deaths, and hideous burn casualties. Though obviously fatal for the airman, only minimal training for the job was required, and thousands of Japanese youths, under intense psychological pressure, volunteered to sacrifice their lives to sink or mangle ships of the otherwise-indomitable U.S. Navy. The tactic had a further advantage in that obsolete aircraft, such as slower bi-planes or those with non-retractable landing gear, could satisfactorily serve this purpose. No Allied air coverage was impermeable by these humanly-guided missles, whose strikes were usually timed during the first and last hours of daylight when visibility was minimal. The only defense was to direct a concentrated stream of antiaircraft fire directly at the incoming malefactor in hopes that it would disintegrate before it impacted. The AA gunners aboard the targetted ships had to be almost as gutsy as the Kami pilots themselves.[13]

Even before Struble's invasion convoy had gotten halfway to Mindoro, his flagship NASHVILLE had been struck and set aflame, killing 133 (including the Admiral's chief of staff and his army counterpart), and wounding 190, one of whom was Brig. Gen. William C. Dunckel, the ground force commander, forcing her return to Leyte as soon as her fires could be quenched. Destroyer DASHIELL was bashed so severely that she too had to turn back, with 14 dead and 24 injured. And this was only the beginning; fresh waves of suicidal assailants crashed other vessels at their San Jose anchorage and ravaged resupply echelons enroute. Before the deviltry ceased, five Liberty ships and three LST's had been sunk, a number of other vessels badly damaged, and more than 1,000 sailors killed or wounded. Freighter LEWIS L. DYCHE, chock full of ammunition when she was hit, exploded with such force that everyone aboard was blown to bits, and two torpedo-boats a quarter of a mile distant were lifted clear out of the water! It was a nightmarish foretaste of things to come.

In a final desperate effort to nullify the Mindoro landing, a pathetic remnant of the Imperial Fleet—two cruisers and six destroyers, under Rear Admiral Kimura—steamed in on December 26th to wreak further havoc. Although the only deterrents at hand were a score of motor torpedo boats and 105 of Kenney's planes which had just been flown in from Leyte, they were more than enough to thwart Kimura, sinking one of his destroyers and crippling so many others that next day he and his jackals slunk away to safer precincts.[14]

. . . .

Refocussing our narrative upon Morotai and the 534th, and rolling back the clock a month or so, before the monsoon season had yet obscured the skies, I had a day to myself after nocturnal guard duty or something of the sort, and, hankering for a swim, betook myself to the seashore. While everyone else was engrossed in their labors, I waded out into what appeared to be fairly manageable surf. The tide was receding more swiftly than I had anticipated, and there was an unusually strong long-shore current. Before I realized what I had gotten myself into, I was pulled inexorably into deeper water and carried laterally from my point of entry. No one else was about, and no matter how hard I attempted to swim back into shallow water, I was drawn as if by a huge magnet toward the stern of an LCT unloading stores some 400 yards down the beach, its propellors churning the waters furiously to keep her nosed in at a 90-degree angle to the shoreline. When a crewman on her stern yelled at me to keep away, I retorted that I couldn't, and needed help. Just as I was about to be sucked down into the deadly screws, he threw me a line, the end of which, by sheer Divine providence, I managed to clutch by one hand in a vice-like grip, and by it the sailor hauled me up on the deck. I was so traumatized that I must have lain there dazed and panting for a full five minutes before I could thank my benefactor and stagger off to shore. Never thereafter did I make the mistake of swimming alone in the sea. This incident marked the second of several close calls that I experienced in the course of my mostly-humdrum military career, with others no less harrowing soon to follow.

In early October, I was unexpectedly promoted to Private First Class, and could not have been more puffed up had I been named Theatre Commander, since it meant a whopping raise of $4.86 in my monthly pay. Equally welcome, at least at their onset, were the cooling rains which began to fall on the 23d of that month, notwithstanding the sudden revelation that our tent leaked badly at the seams and through shrapnel holes above our cots, drenching our bedding and belongings. The precipitation was part of the same immoderate weather system that was soaking the combatants on Leyte so mercilessly. My tentmates and I shivered throughout several long nights until we could do some effective patching and mending. On the other hand, at about the same juncture, Lady Luck favored me in a Bingo game with three cartons of Camel cigarettes and a pack of playing cards. I had the good sense to bestow the smokes upon some addicted comrades, thereby storing up a bit of extra goodwill upon which I drew later, and by practicing with the cards, I overcame my fumbling ineptitude at shuffling and dealing. I also took advantage of the relatively slack times to prevail upon our dentist, Capt. Milton Nimaroff (a New Jerseyite of Russian ethnicity), to give my teeth a good cleansing, repair a cavity or two, and extract a couple of molars too far gone for restoration. As the rains increased in volume and frequency and the winds rose, tent-dwelling became genuinely unpleasant, forcing us to crowd our cots together in the middle to avoid being soaked. Our shelter had been pitched on a mild slope, and we had lacked sufficient foresight to dig adequate drainage ditches, so that water cascaded over its dirt floor like a swollen river, saturating all our belongings. Nature's bounties seemed always excessive in those alien climes.

I formed a friendship with an ex-lumberman from Northern Queensland named Griffith, serving in one of the RAAF engineer units. He was older than I, in his mid-thirties, and, like so many of his countrymen, a very upbeat and entertaining companion. He had been campaigning in the wilds a lot longer than I, and whenever I appeared morose, he would say, "Cheer up, myte, you'll get 'ome!" Griffith and I enjoyed hours of lively conversation; I shared some rations and PX stores with him, and he reciprocated with a couple of items of Aussie-issue clothing, a wide-brimmed slouch hat and light-weight battle jacket. He also presented me with a letter opener he had crafted from a small shell-casing and a ring fashioned from a florin (an Australian coin equivalent to 32 cents in U.S. currency), both of which I mailed home to my younger sister, Ruthie. As a result of our many philosophic dialogues exploring the nature and destiny of humankind, I developed a profound respect and esteem for the Aussies, and have held them in high regard ever since. Sad to say, Griffith and I lost contact after we left Morotai.[15]

We had been there little more than a month when preparations for the Luzon invasion began to stir; our mates in the 544th and 3017th were alerted on 20 October (the day of the Leyte landing) for a move back to Bougainville, 2,000 miles eastward, to stage with the 37th Infantry Division. Their extraction indicated that our turn would surely be coming up in short order.

Almost-nightly single-plane visitations by Charlie continued through 11 October; then, for some odd reason, we had a blessed 12-day respite until the 23d. That night, and on the three thereafter, he reappeared at about 2100 or so, doing little harm except on the 24th, when twenty men were injured by a couple of heavy phosphorous bombs dropped near the dock before our ack-ack guns could open up. There was another cessation lasting five days and nights until 0530 on the 31st, when six fighters and a "Betty" bomber strafed and dropped incendiaries, barely missing several parked B-24's, and losing four of their number to ground fire. Monsoon storms prevented further hostile aerial activity until 5 November, when a flock of five zoomed in at daybreak, causing little or no damage. Every night from then on, however, throughout half of November, we were hit during the wee hours by from one to four raiders, resulting in the destruction of two Navy PB4Y's, two B-25's, and a P-40, and damage to a dozen other planes on the ground. Silence reigned again during the third week of November, but at 2000 on the 22nd, the day following my nineteenth birthday, another series of aerial assaults opened with a vengeance as we were gathered at the theatre for a movie; a loner roared in low with his lights on, followed by eleven more, one after another, over the next two-and-a-half hours, raining bombs on the airdromes and camp areas, while every AA gun on the island opened up. As we scrambled for cover, the fires and explosions wiped out no less than 15 parked aircraft, disabled another 23, killed 3 people, and injured at least 8. Two nights later, at 0330, 4 Jap buzzards swooped in, wrecking 3 more of our planes, heavily damaging several others, and inflicting 3 fatalities and 11 injuries. Fourteen hours later, we were struck again, this time by 9 assailants, who scored direct hits on 2 additional planes. For the rest of November, two-to-four-plane raids occurred nightly, smashing up another half-dozen of our birds. (This tally was compiled by Fred Hitchcock, Jr. of Sudbury, Mass., serving with the 79th Airdrome Squadron on Morotai.)[16]

Aside from enduring this recurrent ruination and watching the fireworks and dogfights in the skies, there was not a great deal to occupy the 927 of us in the 534th as 1944 faded. The other 4ESB elements far to our rear, however, were on the move. At Oro Bay, General Hutchings and his headquarters personnel were about to embark for the Big Show on LSD OAK HALL, from which they would have to transact business for an entire month while all of Sixth Army's elements assembled. On New Britain, at Borgen Bay, Colonel Falkner's 594th had been pulling together its widely-dispersed constituency from Arawe, Talasea, and more distal Oro Bay/Buna, to stage with the 40th Division troops who had been keeping the Japs boxed in at Rabaul, a chore now falling to the Australians of 5th AIF. Boat Company B of 594th would perforce stay behind at Arawe at the bidding of the Aussies, who knew a good thing when they saw it, and there, like lost sheep, they would remain for months to come, running various shore-to-shore errands. As soon as Falkner's shoremen had constructed jetties and approach roads at Borgen Bay for the boarding of their own and the infantry's equippage, the 40th/594th team would be shipping out to Lae, New Guinea, for a rehearsal before proceeding on to Manus in the Admiralties, where they would join up with the corresponding 37th/544th team from Bougainville. Two regiments of Ogden's 3ESB, the 533d and 543d, had also been coopted for the Luzon invasion. The 533rd, at Aitape, was momentarily assisting with the debarkation of the 6th AIF diggers who would be replacing its soon-to-be teammates in the 43d Division. The 543d, some at Sansapor and others at Biak (to which Ogden's command post had been relocated), still engaged in lighterage and shore-to-shore resupply, had begun refurbishing their hard-used landing craft preparatory to staging with the 6th U.S. Division. In short, the three 4ESB infantry/amphib match-ups would be complemented by two others involving 3ESB regiments, namely, 43d/533d and 6th/543d, for the 9 January Luzon descent.[17]

While biding our time on Morotai, we "pill pushers" (as our web-foot brothers often referred to us) were ordered to upgrade our slovenly bivouac, which seemed rather absurd, in view of our pending exit; it may, however, have been for the benefit of the GI's or Aussies who would be the island's next tenants. At any rate, starting with the officers' club tent (as one might suspect), we fashioned and painted wooden walls, levelled sand floors, cut back bush, smoothed and lined pathways with rocks, and raked the premises. One of my chores was to spray used diesel oil around the latrines and mess tent to inhibit insect-breeding, therewith thoroughly impregnating my faded fatigues, so that even after repeated scrubbings, they looked disreputable. The soles on one of my pairs of prized para-boots had become so badly worn that I turned them in for repair, which I quickly came to regret, since they were never returned. By way of compensation, I was issued brogans of the rough-out kind which would not take a shine, and canvas puttees which were more bothersome to keep clean and lace up. On the brighter side, we drew our first overseas pay—in the paper guilders and Dutch coins that were legal tender in the Netherlands East Indies—a portion of which I arranged to have sent to my parents to subsidize the lean family exchequer. (They had recently purchased a house on Jersey Avenue in Winston-Salem, just downhill from St. Paul's Church, for which my father was tightly stretched to keep up the mortgage payments. He was still defraying the costs of treatment for his ruptured appendix during the Depression, and now had the added burden of nursing home expenses for my enfeebled grandparents.)

In the open-air theatre nearest our neatened encampment, regular evening film-showings had resumed, featuring such hits as *Dragonseed,* based on the Pearl Buck novel dramatizing the horrors of the Japanese occupation of China, and the mindless comedy *Abroad With Two Yanks,* along with newsreels depicting the progress of the Allied armies across the globe. The valorous achievements of the Navy and Air Force were endlessly touted—or so it appeared to us—with lavish portrayals of the exploits of the elite Marine Corps in the Pacific campaigns, but little footage was devoted to us grunts in MacArthur's theatre. We were kept informed on late-breaking news through radio transcripts (which I was asked to read over a microphone while the movie reels were being changed.) A touring U.S.O. troupe highlighting Bob Hope, Frances Langford, and Jerry Colonna also performed for us. Hope's opening line, as he leered at the lightly-clad, shapely Miss Langford, was "Take a good look, boys—this is what you've been fighting for! I've been fighting for it ever since we left Frisco."[18]

To use up our energy and hone our martial skills, units of our battalion were assigned a bit of combat patrolling on offshore islets. During one memorable two-day junket, I had to tote a heavy machine-gun tripod through the bush for hours on end. As we toiled along a faint trace through the thick, vine-choked jungle, I walked hunched over with two legs of the tripod over my shoulders and the third thudding against my butt, making my back ache as though I had polio. Those of us not burdened with ammo, rations, or heavy weapons had to take turns on the point, cutting back the thick vines, branches, and undergrowth with machetes, so the exercise was extremely wearing on everyone. The heat, as usual, was fierce, our canteens were soon drained, and always there was the nagging fear that some son of Heaven might slip up on you from the rear with knife in hand or, from concealment up in a tree, had you in his rifle sights. Eventually we circled back without mishap to a rendezvous with the LCM that had brought us out, thus ending one of my infrequent exposures to the hazards of close-up jungle combat.

The cuisine in our mess was improving; on Thanksgiving Day, we were served a tasty turkey pie, and one Sunday we enjoyed the luxury of ice cream (though it melted into slush before it could be spooned up.) I tried to attend church services every Sabbath, and read a passage from my Bible each evening, as was my custom throughout the war. We had been isolated in the bush for so many months that our limited diversions were wearing thin, and irregularity in mail deliveries was an increasing irritant. The favorite slogan making the rounds was "Stick with Mac (MacArthur) and you'll never get back!" The daily monotony was leavened by episodic training lectures and demonstrations, inspections in ranks, or hikes into the bush to keep us fit, and in off-duty hours I labored at a correspondence course in *Railway Traffic Management*. The Japanese air raids, though unrelenting during December, with one or two exceptions, seemed more symbolic than serious, aside from one at Christmas. This was our first Yule overseas, and while the circumstances hardly lent themselves to unfeigned celebration, as one might imagine, the receipt of several letters and an intact fruit cake from my parents was a godsend, and our leadership did what they could to brighten our gloom by some very considerate special touches. The evening of 22 December was unmarred by any enemy aerial disturbance, and the Chaplain put together a program of Christmas carols and delivered a homily on "The Meaning of the Incarnation." Afterward, the movie *One Foot in Heaven* was shown, starring Frederick March and Martha Scott, a tender portrayal of the trials and tribulations of a Methodist pastor and his mate. Two nights later, on Christmas Eve (which fell on Sunday that year), the Mess Sergeant served a tasty supper of canned turkey and green peas. The mess tent, chapel, and dispensary were adorned with evergreens and paper decorations, and while dining, we were entertained with renditions of well-known Christmas hymns and popular tunes by the regiment's instrumental quartet (saxophonist, trumpeter, violinist, and accordionist.) I had received a second gift package from home that day containing socks, candy, books, and stationery, and after dark, we had a film presentation featuring Greer Garson and Walter Pidgeon in *Mrs. Parkington*. About halfway through, it was interrupted by an exceptionally intense three-plane raid, with bombs dropping so close to our bivouac that I became distinctly uneasy, to put it mildly. A B-24 and a P-47 were destroyed in their revettments, but RAAF Spitfire night-fighters soon soared aloft to engage the heathens, two of whom were sent down in flames. Although the mayhem abated for ahile at midnight, in time for the chaplains to offer their Christmas Holy Communion liturgies (the Protestant version of which I gratefully attended), the despoilers reappeared two or three more times before sunup. While a lot of our boys partied on some potent home-brewed "jungle juice" throughout that noisome night, I begged off, having not yet (with the emphasis on "yet") acquired a taste for alcohol, on the excuse that I had early duty preparing the daily Morning Report (at which Hugh Riley and I took turns.) Christmas morning, the cooks served up a hearty holiday breakfast of cream of wheat, powdered eggs, and toast with genuine creamery butter, which I greedily devoured, and later I attended another Narivity worship service. At lunch, all the K.P. chores were performed voluntarily by the ranking N.C.O.'s, a genuinely touching gesture. Small Red Cross cartons containing candy, chewing gum, cigarettes, and a paper-back novel were distributed, and that afternoon, some of us took a relaxing swim in the ocean. All things considered, it was as fulfilling an observance of Our Lord's birth as one could wish, given the enemy harassment, the remoteness of our station, and the separation from those dearest to us. The moon shown so brightly Christmas night that a raider coming over about 2230 was clearly visible; several of his bombs exploded close by our bivouac before he banked sharply and made his escape unscathed by the scanty and belated AA fire— the gunners were undoubtedly partying like everyone else.[19]

Within twenty-four hours, our orders came to mount up for the invasion (we knew only that it would take place somewhere on Luzon.) Thereafter, we had no time to listen to radio reports of the fighting in

Belgium's Ardennes Forest (where Nazi Panzers had sprung their surprise offensive in what would become the critical Battle of the Bulge), nor to write letters home until we were aboard ship. We hastily packed everything in boxes, from toilet paper and wood saws to typewriters and shovels, and loaded them on our trucks, with the stretchers and medical stores we would be needing in combat stowed where they could be most easily retrieved. The kitchen utensils and rations, except for the ingredients of our final two meals before boarding, were among the last to go. Our personal duffle bags containing spare clothing and non-essentials were sent off, omitting only those short-term survival items which would have to be carried on our backs into battle. Last of all, the tents were struck, tied up, and stowed on the vehicles, the latrines burned out and filled in, and the area swept clean. Then we ate our final meal ashore, buckled on our field gear, and hiked to the beach. It took a couple of days to load all the battalion's impedimenta and equipment aboard the two LST's (66 and 170), which would carry us to Sixth Army's point of entry on Luzon.

Alongside ours, eleven other LST's were drawn up on the sands loading out airfield engineer and technical units, and out in the roadstead awaited the three sleek "greyhounds of the sea" [destroyers, in Naval parlance], McDERMUT, McGOWAN, and MERTZ, who would be the guardians of our flock. To convey something of the volume and complexion of the colossal stream of shipping to which ours was merely a minute tributary, the Morotai LST unit (Cdr. L. A. Drexler) was one of six such rivulets pooled in LST Flotilla 3 (Cdr. A. A. Ageton) carrying assorted troop formations from all across the SWPA. Ageton's flotilla was itself only a fraction of TG-77.9 REINFORCEMENT GROUP (Rear Adm. R. L. Connolly), sealifting the 158th Regimental Combat Team which we were to support, and Sixth Army's Floating Reserve, the 25th "Tropic Lightening" Division, together with all their attached units.[2]

Connolly's TG-77.9 would be trailing Vice Admiral Kinkaid's main convoy, LUZON ATTACK FORCE TF-77, which would carry Krue-ger's assault troops in on S-Day, 9 January 1945. Integral to TF-77 was TG-77.1 FLEET FLAGSHIP GROUP (including cruisers WASATCH, Kinkaid's flag-ship, bearing Krueger and his staff, and

BOISE with MacArthur aboard), and its two major components, Vice Admiral Barbey's TF-78, SAN FABIAN ATTACK FORCE, and Vice Admiral Wilkinson's TF-79, LINGAYEN ATTACK FORCE, named for the points on Lingayen Gulf's southeastern shore at which they would land. On 11 January, or S+2, Connolly's TG-77.9 REINFORCEMENT GROUP would go ashore on Barbey's San Fabian sector of the beachhead, except for that portion of Ageton's Flotilla 3 lifting our 158th/534th team, which was to insert us 35 miles farther upcoast at San Fernando, La Union. A major problem inherent in this extremely intricate enterprise, as in most joint operations in every theatre throughout World War II, was the insufficiency of amphibious shipping. As an indication of the staggering number of vessels required for an expedition of this magnitude, a single full-strength standard infantry division at this stage of the war embraced 14,000 men, 1,390 vehicles, and 123 artillery pieces, to say nothing of the attached artillery, engineer, signal, transportation, medical, quartermaster, and other specialized units, with all their necessities. On S-Day, four divisions would have to be placed ashore simultaneously at Lingayen Gulf. Enormous though Kinkaid's fleet was, the shortage of suitable vessels would compel these units to reserve most of their allocated shipping space for the assault echelons and short-term supplies, along with deck space for the landing craft (including the amphibs' LCM's and the Navy's LCT's), and leave behind in the staging areas many of their organic vehicles and even such high-priority ancillary equipment as construction machinery, Marston matting, or portable bridging, to be brought up in subsequent echelons. This meant that once landed, not only would there be a serious deficiency in motor transport at the outset, but that multiple follow-up convoys (including merchant ships by the dozens), would have to be scheduled at close intervals, mandating speedy unloading and swift turn-arounds by the vessels of the spearhead.[21]

This gargantuan assemblage, under Kinkaid's overall control, would rely for close coverage on the waters and in the skies primarily upon Seventh Fleet warships and CVE Carriers, plus the Fifth Air Force planes from Mindoro. Back-up surface-and-air shielding for the whole operation would be provided by Halsey's powerful Third Fleet and its TF-38 Fast Carrier arm, based at Ulithi and currently hovering northeast of Luzon. Out ahead of Kinkaid's TF-77 would be TG-77.2, Vice Admiral Oldendorf's big BOMBARDMENT AND FIRE SUPPORT GROUP (with his flag on battleship CALIFORNIA), fronted by Commander W. R. Loud's TG-77.6 MINESWEEPING AND HYDROGRAPHIC GROUP. The operation plan called for Oldendorf's warships, "jeep" carriers, oilers, and auxiliary vessels, sortieing from Leyte, to arrive at Lingayen Gulf three days in advance of TF-77 to allow plenty of time for surveying the beaches, clearing the bay of mines, and laying on a thorough pre-invasion bombardment.

Admiral Kinkaid's responsibility on S-Day was to ensure the orderly and timely landing of two Army corps abreast: on the left, in the San Fabian sector, Maj. Gen. Innis Swift's I Corps (43d and 6th Divisions), and on the right, in the Lingayen sector, Maj. Gen. Oscar W. Griswold's XIV Corps (40th and 37th Divisions.} Two days later, on ll January, the first follow-up echelon, Connolly's TG-77.9, would bring in the 25th Division, 13th Armored Group, and 6th Ranger Battalion, for use as needed, along with our l58th RCT/534th EB&SR. Coordinating a movement of these dimensions across such long distances on short advance notice made the elaborate cross-channel transport arrangements for the Normandy invasion seem like child's play in comparison.

As in the assembly of an intricate jigsaw puzzle, the randomly-scattered pieces began to cohere on 3 January, when the nucleus of Barbey's TF-78, having gathered up and rehearsed with each of the two I Corps divisions and their 3ESB boat-and-shore attachments from Aitape, Hollandia, Biak, and Sansapor, converged at sea near the Palaus with Wilkinson's TF-79 from Manus, laden with the two XIV Corps divisions and 4ESB regiments originating at Bougainvile and New Britain. The consolidated convoy then proceeded to the expedition's primary concentration point, Leyte Gulf, arriving 4 January 1945. Here TF-78 added not only the vessels carrying assorted troop units from Leyte, but its guard-dogs, Rear Adm. C. T. Durgin's ESCORT CARRIER GROUP and Rear Adm. R. S. Berkey's CLOSE COVERING GROUP of destroyers and light cruisers (among them BOISE and WASATCH hosting the top brass.)[22]

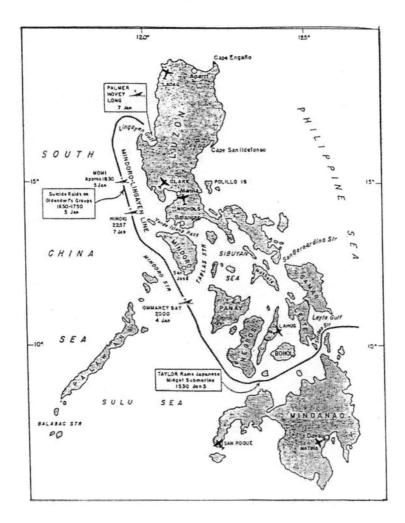

MAP 9. TRACK OF ALLIED INVASION FLEET, LEYTE GULF TO LINGAYEN
GULF, LUZON, JANUARY 1945.

From Leyte Gulf, the composite TF-77 (with Barbey's TF-78 leading Wilkinson's TF-79) tracked Oldendorf's warships to its rendezvous with destiny at Lingayen Gulf, Luzon. Exiting through Surigao Strait, the entire entourage steered southwestward through the Bohol Sea skirting Mindanao's north coast, circled around the southern tip of Negros into the Sulu Sea, and took a northern heading alongside Panay and through Mindoro Strait into the South China Sea, thence up the western coast of Mindoro and Luzon past the mouth of Manila Bay to Lingayen Gulf. The nucleus of Connolly's trailing TG-77.9 REINFORCEMENT GROUP, comprising the APA troopships, AKA freighters, and other fast transports and cargo vessels carrying 25th Division (which had no attached Army amphibs) from far-off Noumea, New Caledonia, headed northwest, with a pause at Guadalcanal for rehearsal, to Manus in the Admiralties. Here it absorbed the smaller flotilla bearing our colleagues in the 158th RCT from Noemfoor, and set sail for Leyte on 2 January. Ageton's LST Flotilla 3, comprised of slower beaching craft and freighters, having gathered in its core components at Hollandia from as far away as Bougainville and Oro Bay, steamed off westward for Leyte on 30 December, picking up sub-units at Noemfoor and Sansapor before adding ours at Morotai. At Leyte, Ageton's flotilla appended still more LST's laden with the 6th Ranger Battalion and 13th Armored Group, and took its place in Connolly's 77.9 convoy tailing Kinkaid's immense TF-77 northward to land two days after the main I & XIV Corps assault forces. Kinkaid's armada in front of us, strung out over forty miles from end to end, the wakes of its ships suggesting endless files of sea snakes, would have presented a stunning spectacle to the eyes of an imaginary observer in the stratosphere![23]

There was insufficient room in the jammed well deck of our LST to accomodate everyone, and many of us had to camp out on its exposed upper deck, in whatever niche we could find, between, under, or on top of the vehicles lashed down there. At first, I roosted under the running board of a deuce-and-a-half next to the ship's railing. A narrow passageway had been left alongside for access aft to the mess and toilet facilities and the messkit-washing cans. After one or two meals, the deck became so greasy that people kept sliding into my little stake-out, so I scouted out a 3-by-6-ft. space on top of the canvass cover of another truck amidship and settled myself and my gear there. To get to and from my aerie perch, I had to run an obstacle course, but it was safer, tidier, and more private there than on the surface of the deck, and I had a grandstand seat from which to observe God's universe. But this spot, too, had its drawbacks—the sun beat down cruelly, scorching my already-bronzed hide. I licked that problem by rigging up a sort of pup shelter, which helped considerably. My nest was, of course, a breezy one at best, and during a rain storm a night or so later, the raging wind tore down my frail little structure, thoroughly soaking me and all my stuff, and I began to shiver as though I were at the North Pole. With the return of daylight, however, my metabolism regained its balance and everything dried out promptly in the sun's warming rays and the stiff breeze; I redesigned my shelter and anchored it more securely, which largely did the trick. My companions who had made their beds beneath trucks regretted their choice when it rained and they found themselves bathed in mud and lubricants dripping from overhead. The LST's galley and mess facilities were overcrowded like everything else, and only two daily meals were served, but the food was plenteous and palatable, as Navy chow usually was. The toilet facilities, by contrast, were grossly inadequate, and one usually had to stand in line to use them. I was unable to wash my face for a couple of days because I could not get to the tap before the daily allotment of fresh water, of which the ship's tanks held only a limited volume, was turned off. Seawater showers were available, if one could fight his way to them, but, as on the FAIRLAND, the soap wouldn't lather, so that not much grime could be laved off. They were cooling, however, and left an illusion of cleanliness. Within two or three days we were all rather odorous and grubby, but in a perverse sort of way, I found most of the trip rather pleasant, for no authorities pestered us, and I could read and nap to my heart's content. At night, everything was totally blacked-out, even the ship's running lights. During the ten days we were aboard her, I devoured Sinclair Lewis's *Babbit* and a biography of St. Paul entitled *The Apostle*, together with a selection of short stories, and frittered away a good many hours playing blackjack with my shipmates. As we entered the South China Sea, the waters grew rougher and the LST began to pitch and roll so violently that I had to vacate my perch and relocate aft.[24]

The closer we drew to our destination, however, the calmer the seas became, though not our nerves, and for good reason; far ahead of the troop convoys, like motorcycle cops fronting a parade, Oldendorf's 164-ship Bombardment and Fire-Support Group had barely emerged into the open waters before they were beset by Kamikazes. The first organized Kamikaze attacks on record had occurred on 25 October 1944 during the Battle off Samar when several vessels had been crashed and the escort carrier ST. LO sunk, and again at the Ormoc landing in early December, where they had snuffed out two destroyers. Less than two weeks later, as the reader will recall, they had mutilated the convoys to and from Mindoro, sinking at least ten ships. Now the Luzon invasion force would have to deal with them in larger numbers, and it was a terrifying prospect, especially for those of us on crowded troopships.

Commander Loud's mine-sweeper/recon group, TG-77.2's front-runners, departing Leyte Gulf on 2 January 1945, had scarcely gotten underway when, early the following morning, a lone Kamikaze dove upon one of its oilers, killing two crewmen, but doing only slight structural damage. As Oldendorf's Fire-support flotilla, coming on behind, was steaming across the Sulu Sea, it was spotted by Japanese aerial observers and set upon by a swarm of conventional enemy fighters from Luzon, most of whom were downed by his Jeep-carrier eagles or Thirteeenth Air Force fighters from Tacloban. Late in the afternoon of 4 January off Panay, however, a Kami struck CVE OMMANEY BAY's flight deck, causing such a fiery explosion on the hangar deck beneath that 93 personnel aboard were killed and 65 wounded, and she had to be scuttled. Next day, as Loud's squadron was ploughing along 100 miles off the mouth of Manila Bay, the score was evened somewhat; a pair of Japanese destroyers enroute from Manila to Formosa were sighted and chased by one of his greyhounds and a couple of his Aussie frigates. After an inconclusive exchange of gunfire, the pursuers had to break off to resume their convoy duties, and the chase was taken over by CVE Wildcats and torpedo-bombers, who soon sank one of the fugitive "tin cans." The other slipped back under cover of darkness to safe harbor at Manila, from which it attempted to steal forth again two days later, only to meet the same fate as her sister. This, however, was of only passing comfort to Oldendorf's tars, for at 1650 that same afternoon, 5 January, 16 suicidal vultures with 4 fighter escorts vented their rage by diving en masse and crashing no fewer than 9 of TF-77.2's ships, prominent among them cruisers LOUISVILLE and H.M.A.S. AUSTRALIA, escort destroyer STAFFORD, and CVE MANILA BAY, all of which sustained damage in varying degrees. Although none of the stricken vessels were prevented from continuing on their course, 63 of their seamen were slain and 195 suffered injuries. Those of us in Ageton's group far astern knew nothing of this havoc at the time, but we were about to become enlightened.[25]

XI

UNDER THE GUN AT LINGAYEN GULF

As Kinkaid's TF-77 steamed northward past Negros on 5 January, cruiser BOISE, bearing his eminence, Douglas MacArthur, narrowly averted disaster by dodging a midget submarine's torpedoes. Two days later, shortly before dawn, she came within a hair's breadth of being smacked by an enemy vulture's poorly-aimed bomb, followed within minutes by the appearance of another aerial desperado who was repelled just in time. As the convoy emerged from Mindoro Strait, Kami lightening struck escorting carriers KADISHAN BAY and, later, KITKUN BAY, holing each at the waterline, and inflicting 56 casualties (mostly on KITKUN BAY), yet both kept underway.[1]

Early Saturday morning, 6 January 1945, when point-man Oldendorf's roughed-up TG-77.2 entered Lingayen Gulf and commenced shore bombardment, the tempo of death's dance quickened. This would become the day of all days for Kami-wrought wastage. For an opener, ten "Zekes" zoomed in for the kill, but before claiming any victims, half were shot down by Durgin's CVE hawks and the remainder turned tail and ran. So far, so good, but around 1130, the Kamikazes began swarming in more single-mindedly, one grazing destroyer RICHARD P. LEARY, while another, already ablaze from antiaircraft fire, crashed into the port wing of battleship NEW MEXICO's navigating bridge, instantly killing her skipper, along with Lt. Gen. Herbert Lumsden (Churchill's liaison officer at SouWesPac headquarters), his aide, and 26 others, among them a *TIME* Magazine correspondent, and wounding 87. Destroyer WALKE was singled out by 4 devil-birds, 2 of which were gunned down before impacting, only to have a third strike her bridge, drenching her skipper with gasoline and torching him. Another careened into destroyer ALLEN M. SUMMER's deckhouse and torpedo mounts, leaving her aft magazine flooded, while a suicidal companion crashed minesweeper LONG on her port side, setting her ablaze. The luckless LONG, struck again in late afternoon, broke in two, capsized, and sank. Destroyer Transport BROOKS, smitten as well, suffered extensive damage, yet remained afloat. An hour or so later, cruiser COLUMBIA barely escaped destruction when a Kami, passing between her masts, sprayed her decks with gasoline that somehow failed to ignite. But she was to enjoy only a brief reprieve, for as the grim afternoon wore on, she was dealt a shattering blow from a second humanly-guided missile which penetrated three decks before exploding. To contain the ensuing fires, damage-control personnel flooded her magazine and by heroic effort extinguished them within an hour. Three more maniacal buzzards, bent on disabling Heavy cruiser MINNEAPOLIS, destroyer O'BRIEN, and seaplane tender ORCA, succeeded in inflicting only minor harm. Just before sundown, another five flew in on "Oley's" fire-support ships from astern, striking flagship CALIFORNIA at the base of her foremast, snuffing out the lives of 45 of her crewmen, and wounding 151. In the fading light, H.M.A.S. AUSTRALIA endured another bashing, adding 14 dead and 26 injured to her lengthy casualty list of the previous day, while cruiser LOUISVILLE, on this, her thirteenth birthday, was put out of action when her bridge structure was rammed, leaving her captain and 31 shipmates dead and 56 others wounded. Destroyer NEWCOMB and minesweeper SOUTHARD were hit as well, but only moderately damaged. When the curtain of darkness mercifully closed on this fourth day following TG-77.2's departure from Leyte, its aggregate losses thus far amounted to 2 ships sunk and 23 disabled to a greater or lesser degree, plus 325 seamen slain and 763 wounded, with the invasion itself still three days in the future! So dismaying had been the spoliation and carnage that some among the naval command questioned the wisdom of continuing the operation as scheduled, and urgently besought Kenney and Halsey to step up their onslaughts upon the Manila and Clark Field airdromes.[2]

Although within a few days, thanks to the redoubled efforts of the airmen of the Fifth and those of Vice Adm. John S. McCain's TF-38 (and, needless to say, the unmitigated self-destructiveness of their adversaries), scarcely fifty of Japan's Luzon-based aircraft remained operable, the Divine Wind had not yet blown itself out. At 0430 on S-2, 7 January, two enemy birds streaked out of the moonlit darkness upon minesweeper HOVEY, one of whom sank her with an aerial torpedo. The return of daylight and the resumption of 77.2's mine-sweeping and shore bombardment brought forth no further marauders until dusk, when a second minesweeper, PALMER, fell victim to a lone enemy bomber's eggs which hit her amidships near the waterline, killing 18 of her men, flooded her engine rooms, and sent her to the bottom within a mere 6 minutes. On S-l, the fiery breath of the Divine Wind barely ruffled the waters of the Gulf, and though hardy old H.M.A.S. AUSTRALIA, a favorite target, was scorched twice more, her afflictions did not prevent her from bravely "soldiering on" regardless. Far to the rear in Mindoro Strait that day, 8 January, a half-dozen of Barbey's and Wilkinson's oncoming vessels were also waylaid, but emerged relatively unscathed for the most part, although APA CALLAWAY took a hit on the wing of her bridge, losing 29 of her people, and an LCI, H.M.A.S. WESTRALIA, incurred minor damage.[3]

As the sun of 9 January, the long-awaited S-Day, spread its rays across Lingayen Gulf and the weary gunners on the fire-support vessels returned to their tasks, a Kamikaze dove on destroyer escort HODGES, collapsing her foremast and splashing just offboard, while another, aiming itself at

Wilkinson's flagship MOUNT OLYMPUS, was knocked aside by accurate AA fire. A third crashed COLUMBIA once again, inflicting 92 more casualties among her people; as soon as her flames were quenched, however, the redoubtable "Gem of the Ocean" stolidly resumed her shelling duties. LUZON ATTACK FORCE, having now arrived on the scene in full force, was neither distracted nor delayed in carrying out its mission. More than 800 TF-77 ships, freighted with some 191,000 troops, crowded the Gulf as the landings, scheduled for 0930, got underway. MacArthur (a five-star General of the Army as of 18 December 1944, with date of rank slightly behind that of George Marshall and ahead of Dwight Eisenhower), having slept quite unperturbably through the antecedent mayhem on the high seas, rose confidantly from his bed to behold in the smokey sunlight the opening of the largest land campaign of the Pacific War. Before its conclusion, more GI's would fight under his direction on Luzon than had campaigned in either North Africa, Italy, or southern France![4]

The irregularly-shaped 40,420-square-mile main island of the Philippine Republic vaguely resembles an upright sack of beans cinched in at the midriff, Lingayen Gulf on the South China Sea forming the western indentation, and Baler Bay on the Philippine Sea, the eastern. From the sack's lower right corner, a lumpy appendage, the Bicol peninsula, dangles off eastward and southward like a kite's tail down to San Bernardino Strait. In 1945, Luzon was home to about 50% of the former Commonwealth's 17 million inhabitants, of whom a million or so were crowded into Manila, the capital city. The mountain-studded island is graced with a broad and fertile corridor, some 40 miles in width, the so-called Central Plains, running north-south for 120 miles from Lingayen Gulf to Manila Bay, one of the finest harbors in the Orient, on whose eastern shore reposes the city of Manila. The loftiest of its mountain ranges are the Cordillera Central, bordering the South China Sea as far south as Lingayen Gulf, and the Sierra Madres, lining the opposite, or eastern, coast all the way down to the tip of the Bicol Peninsula. Just above Luzon's cinched waist, the Caraballo Mountains laterally connect the Cordillera Central and the Sierra Madres, thereby walling in the the Central Plains on the north, while below Lingayen Gulf, the Zambales Mountains continue down the South China seacoast. The southern segment of the latter range, jutting into Manila Bay, forms the Bataan Peninsula. Thus the Central Plains are defined by the Cordillera Central/Caraballo Mountains on the north, the Sierra Madres on the east, and the Zambales Mountains on the west. Two major rivers meander through the Plains, both having their headwaters in the northern mountains, the Agno, looping across the flatlands to flow into Lingayen Gulf, and, farther south, the Pampanga, emptying into Manila Bay. In Luzon's rugged northern quarter between the Cordillera Central and the Sierra Madres, a lesser, narrower valley carved out by the northward-flowing Carrigara River opens on to the sea at Aparri on the island's north coast (at the top of the bag.)

The tracks of the narrow-gauge Manila Railroad, commencing at the port of San Fernando, La Union, at the northern entrance to Lingayen Gulf, ran southward through Manila to the end of the kite's tail. The railway, along with a loose web of paved two-lane highways and graded dirt roads whose threads stretched to the island's extremities, endowed Luzon with the most extensive ground transportation infrastructure to be found on any of the western Pacific islands except for Japan itself. After three years of enemy occupation, neglected maintenance, guerilla sabotage, and Allied bombing, however, these vital arteries were in a sad state of disrepair.

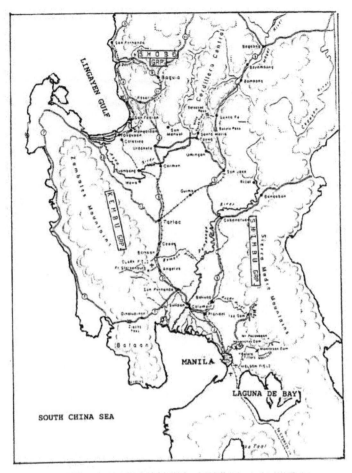

MAP 10. JAPANESE SHOBU, SHIMBU, AND KEMBU
ARMY GROUPS IN CENTRAL LUZON ON THE EVE
OF SIXTH ARMY'S INVASION.

The Manila Railroad edged the shore of Lingayen Gulf, serving
the towns of Damortis, San Fabian, and Dagupan, then swung
inland down the western side of the Central Plains, crossed the
Agno River at Byambang, skirted Clark Field near Bamban, and
bridged the Pampanga River at Calumpit to attain its namesake
city. South of Manila, it hugged the western shore of a large land-

locked lake, Laguna de Bay, and jogged eastward to enter the upper Bicol Peninsula, down which it continued as far as Luzon's southernmost port, Legaspi, on the Philippine Sea. Diverging from the railway's main stem were a stub to Fort Stotsenburg at Clark Field and three branches, two of them running northward up the center of the plains, one from Tarlac through Guimba to San Jose, the other from just south of Plaridel to Cabanatuan, and the third diverging from the main near Laguna de Bay to serve the west coast port of Batangas below Manila Bay.

The primary threads of the road net were hard-surfaced highways 3, 5, 7, and 13. Number 3, originating at Aparri at the top of the island, headed west, then south, in conformity with the upper South China Seashore and the Lingayen Gulfshore through San Fernando to Damortis, from whence it bore inland for five miles as far as Rosario before angling south across the Central Plains, and, after crossing the Agno River, ran alongside the railroad to Manila. A second highway from Aparri, #5, ran almost due south up the Cagayan Valley, crossed the Caballo Mountains over Balete Pass at the valley head, and debouched into the plains at San Jose, continuing down through Cabanatuan to a junction with Highway 3 near Plaridel, 25 miles or so north of Manila. A third, Highway 7, stemmed from Highway 3 at Damortis, followed the U-shaped shoreline of Lingayen Gulf through San Fabian, Dagupan, and Lingayen all the way up to its southern entrance on the South China Sea, then circled south along the seaside as far as Subic Bay before turning eastward across the Zambales Mountains over Zigzag Pass to rejoin Highway 3 at San Fernando, Pampangas (not to be confused with the aforementioned seaport town of San Fernando, La Union.) The fourth major highway, 13, afforded an alternative route southward from the gulfshore town of Lingayen down the upper plains corridor to a junction with Highway 3 at Tarlac, about two-fifths of the way to Manila. These pathways would define the tactical pattern of the campaigning on Luzon and impose significant changes in the style of warfare hitherto prevalent in SWPA, now that it was to be conducted across a relatively thickly populated and urbanized land mass, at least in the more level regions.

General Yamashita had recently relocated his headquarters to the new seat of Jose Laurel's puppet government, the pleasant mountain resort town of Baguio, the Philippine Commonwealth's traditional summertime capital, cradled high up in the Cordillera Central northeast of Lingayen Gulf. He had cannily divided his depleted Fourteenth Area Army into three separate commands within enclaves well-suited for static defense. The 30,000-strong KEMBU Group was emplaced along the eastern edge of the Zambales Mountains overlooking the plains and Clark Field. A much more numerous SHIMBU Group of 80,000 occupied the Sierra Madres east of Manila (where dammed-up streams supplied the city's water) and guarded southern Luzon and the Bicol Peninsula. His principal force, SHOBU Group, 152,000-strong, was stationed in the high mountains north of the Central Plains. The composition of these groupings were by no means all seasoned combat troops, and in general they were badly undersupplied, particularly as to foodstuffs, since many, if not most, of their stores were still stockpiled in Manila. Yamashita's immediate concern was to transfer as much of this provender and materiel as possible northward over the dilapidated railway and highways to his SHOBU redoubt before their severance by the invaders. Calculating that his preponderant numbers there could as a last resort subsist on the harvest of the rice-lands in the mountain-girt Cagayan Valley, he had no intention of squandering Japanese lives or resources by seriously contesting the landings at Lingayen or by attempting to retain Manila with its hordes of famished civilians. In full awareness that Japan's back was to the wall, his overriding strategic aim was simply to tie down MacArthur's forces as long as possible to allow the maximal build-up of homeland defenses. He proposed therefore to evacuate all his effectives from the metropolis except for a small contingent who would extract the remains of its cache (its cash, too, no doubt) via railway to Cabanatuan and up Highway 5 beyond to his mountain stronghold, before themselves withdrawing northward, demolishing the bridges behind them to retard the American advance.[5]

Contrariwise, MacArthur's grand plan, once his beachhead was stabilized, called for a rapid drive by Griswold's XIV Corps down the Central Plains, shouldering KEMBU aside, seizing Clark Field, and capturing Manila and the fortified islands in Manila Bay. Simultaneously, Swift's I Corps would thrust southeast toward the opposite coast to isolate SHOBU from SHIMBU. The subjugation of the remainder of Luzon and the by-passed portions of the archipelago would follow, leaving the conquest of Borneo and the East Indies to the Australians and/or British. Once these movements were well underway, Maj. Gen. Charles P. Hall's XI Corps of Eighth Army would be brought up from the Visayas to Subic Bay on Luzon's west coast, drive eastward into the plains corridor, and link up with Griswold's forces, thereby splitting KEMBU and isolating its elements holding the Bataan Peninsula. Yamashita's attention would be distracted, hopefully, by the insertion of our 158th RCT/534th EB&SR team at the port of San Fernando, La Union, a bare 25 miles or so from his SHOBU nest at Baguio. After Filipino guerillas reported that strong enemy forces occupied the San Fernando area, however, there was a last-minute change in our point of entry—while we were at sea, in fact—to a site just north of Barbey's San Fabian beachhead near the barrios of Mabilao and Alacan. As previously noted, Highway 7 along the concave Gulf shore converged with north-south highway 3 at Damortis (some eight miles north of San Fabian), where the latter bent eastward to Rosario before resuming its course down to Manila. Just east of Rosario, Highway 3 was joined by feeder highway 11 descending from Baguio, 5,000 ft. above sealevel. Highway 3 was selected as one of two routes over which XIV Corps would make its southward advance to the capital city, the other being Highway 13. Possession of the Damortis-Rosario stretch of Highway 3 was no less essential to I Corps in its lateral drive toward the opposite coast.[6]

The revised mission of Brig. Gen. Hanford MacNider's 158th RCT, to whose support we were committed on its 11 January landing, was to push northward up Highway 7 to Damortis, then, swinging east on Highway 3, proceed in concert with the 43d Division to Rosario and the nearby junction with highway ll from Baguio. The 3/11 intersection was one of two key positions at which Yamashita could be expected to attack Sixth Army's flank, and from which, at a later date, the SHOBU redoubt could itself be assailed. Meanwhile, Krueger's ready reserve, the 25th Division, l3th Armored Group, and 6th Ranger Battalion, landing on the San Fabian beaches at the same time as we to their north, could be inserted whenever and wherever needed. For further backup, lst Cavalry and 32d Infantry divisions would be shipped in from Leyte two weeks later (26-27 January.) The 33d Division at Morotai, l,200 miles to the rear, and the 41st at Biak, even more distal, were to be held in readiness as theatre reserves. Since the three regiments of 4ESB (and the two 3ESB attachments under its control) were supporting all the Lingayen Gulf landings, General Hutchings would set up his headquarters near San Fabian on S-Day and serve as Krueger's special staff officer for landing-craft allocation and shore-party deployment to ensure efficient logistical flow. Working in close liaison with 4ESB's boats would be 24 of the Navy's LCT's and 44 of its self-propelled barges.[7]

The tidal variations were minimal in the Gulf, and the slopes off its southern beaches quite gradual, aside from those off to the far left of Admiral Barbey's (I Corps) sector where the coastal shelf narrowed as the steep Ilocos Mountains of the Cordillera Central impinged on the shoreline. The hinterland behind the XIV Corps strands was flat and in part marshy; here the meandering Dagupan and Calmay Rivers described a wide, twisting "H," the crossbar of which parallelled the bayshore, with the towns of Dagupan and Lingayen at its eastern and western ends. The beaches on which Barbey would land I Corps would be more exposed to enemy artillery fire, since Yamashita had numerous outpostings in the barren foothills and heights just north of San Fabian.[8]

To present a coherent overview—and reconcile the often-confusing and fragmentary accounts—of an operation of this magnitude, most particularly those aspects of it which I did not personally witness, is a daunting task. It exemplified vividly what military historians refer to as "the fog of war," and fog it assuredly was, both figuratively and literally. Smoke generators were widely employed both at sunrise and sunset on S-Day and for several days thereafter to blindfold Jap airmen and artillery spotters. Although Seventh Fleet's escort-carrier aircraft were very much in evidence, along with Fifth Air Force squadrons from Leyte and Mindoro, affording reasonably-adequate protection against enemy air sorties (excepting, of course, the diabolical Kamikazes), a dwindling number of Jap planes dodged in from time to time to bomb and strafe the beaches.

Scanning the S-Day landings from east to west—or, from the invaders' perspective, clockwise, from left to right—as they developed across the two Corps sectors (separated by the Dagupan River estuary), starting with those of I Corps in the San Fabian vicinity, 43d Div./533d EB&SR came in under Barbey's own supervision on White Beaches 1, 2, & 3, while 6th Div./543d EB&SR took Blue Beaches 1 & 2, controlled by his subordinate, Fechteler. In Wilkinson's XIV Corps sector (only half as wide as Barbey's), 37th Div./544th EB&SR landed on Crimson I & II and Yellow I & II Beaches (Rear Adm. I. N. Kiland), and at the far right, 40th Div./594th EB&SR on Green I & II and Orange I & II Beaches (Rear Adm. F. B. Royal), just east of the mouth of the Agno River. Each of these thirteen "colored" strands was from 625 to 1,000 yards wide, the entire crescent-shaped beachhead extending almost twenty miles from end to end (including the six-mile gap between the Corps sectors.)

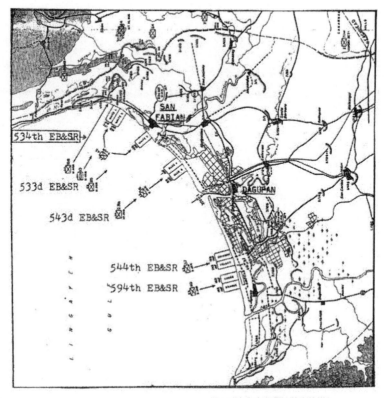

MAP 11. SIXTH ARMY LANDINGS AT LINGAYEN GULF,
9-11 JANUARY 1945.

After the Navy's gunships had blasted the shore from deeper water for a couple of hours, and LCI(R)'s [having rocket-launchers] and LCI(M)'s [with 4.2-inch mortars] had further raked the sands from closer in, they took station beyond the landing lanes to provide supporting fire upon request. On the left, off San Fabian, about 0930, the first two waves, LVT's [amphtracs] bearing the vanguard of Maj. Gen. Leonard F. Wing's 43d Division infantry, easily attained the White beaches, where the surf was moderate. While Wing's boys walked off, formed up, and headed warily toward the hills to their front, there was some confusion when the coxswains of the LCVP's boating his third and succeeding assault waves (along with the 533d shoremen) lost their bearings in the smoke and dust kicked up by the preinvasion barrage and veered into the wrong lanes, but their passengers emerged without wetting their feet unduly. Other than scattered mortar fire, no opposition reared its head until they were 300 yards inland. As the LCT's, LSM's, and LST's coming in behind disgorged motorized equipment unto the firmly-packed sand, the 533d shore-partymen took a few casualties from one or two Jap aerial strafers. On White III, where the larger beaching craft struck bottom farther out, this traffic was soon shifted over to Whites I & II to save time.

At the nearby Blue Beaches, the incursion of Patrick's 6th Division assault waves was similarly uncontested, although a few rounds were squeezed off by Jap riflemen before fleeing the scene. Here, the seafloor's gradient was too slight to allow dry landings from any craft other than the tracked LVT's of the initial waves. Most of the LCVP's and LCM's in their wake struck bottom 100 yards out, from which they either had to chew their way to the water's edge and retract in similar fashion, abrading screws and bending driveshafts, or discharge their motor vehicles into the shallows, where many choked out. While the shore parties working Whites I & II caught a bit of random shellfire from enemy mortars and 75-mm. guns behind the lower ridges to the northeast, the Jap artillerymen soon redirected their sights upon the more easily-targetted larger beaching craft and fire-support ships. Destroyer JENKINS was hit by a 75-mm. shell, killing 3 of her crew and injuring 10 others, and later in the day, enemy artillery fire from the ridges struck 3 LSM's and 3 LST's, killing 12 more people and wounding another 39, but doing scant damage to the ships themselves. Some of Oldendorf's warships off to the north of Barbey's landing-lanes were shelled as well, causing additional casualties. Although the volume of incoming fire increased as daylight waned, its effect on tactical operations was only marginal. Three of 533d's LCS's [Landing Craft, Support—heavily-armed and armored LCM's] entered the shallow Bued River at San Fabian and silenced several enemy guns menacing the 103d Infantry Regiment's flank.

Off the two Blue beaches, about 1300, four Kamikazes and

escorting fighters streaked in low and crashed H.M.A.S. AUSTRALIA yet again, slicing off the top of her smokestack; battleship MISSISSIPPI was smacked as well, losing 23 of her bluejackets and leaving 60 or so wounded, but neither vessel was seriously impaired. To guard against counterattacks on the White and Blue strands, the heavy-weapons sections of 533d and 543d Shore Battalions dug in their 37-mm. field guns and 50-cal. HMG's, while dozers shaped exit roads and carved out dumps and bunkers to accomodate the swelling influx of stores. To speed along bulk-cargo discharge from Barbey's APA's and AKA's and release the first-echelon shipping ASAP ["as soon as possible"], powered pontoon barges did haulage as far shoreward as possible, with LCM's covering the remaining distance to dry land. In this manner, virtually all of Barbey's LSD's and assault transports, and several fast freighters, were emptied by sundown, after which the first return convoy formed up and departed for Leyte.[9]

On Wilkinson's right-hand strands near Lingayen, where higher winds and surf were anticipated, and the flat terrain behind the beaches was criss-crossed by streams and obstructed by rice paddies, fish ponds, salt pans, and tidal swamps, larger numbers of amphtracs and DUKW's were employed than at San Fabian, not only to transfer troops to the shoreline but inland as well. Fortunately, here, too, the early morning winds were light and the waters tranquil save for a gently-heaving ground swell, enabling the personnel of the assault waves to gain their immediate objectives unvexed aside from a bit of sniper fire. Those coming in behind on landing barges, however, had to do considerable wading. The gently-inclining seafloor off all the XIV Corps strands prevented most LCVP's from grounding nearer than 20 to 30 yards from the water's edge, or 50 yards in the case of LCM's, and 75 to 80 yards for LCT's. The majority of LST's, including those bearing the 544th and 594th shore battalions and their equipment, ran upon a previously-undetected shoal some 130 to 200 yards out between the 2-fathom and 3-fathom lines. Since deeper water inshore from the shoal prevented vehicle debarkation, pontoon-cubes were launched to form floating causeways, while the few waterproofed bulldozers which could make it to shore shaped earthen ramps from the opposite direction until connections were made, a process delaying offloading until 1100.

Because of the general shipping shortage, much of the amphibs' badly-needed machinery—motorized cranes, scrapers, road-graders, etc.—had perforce been left behind in the staging areas for later importation. Problems quickly arose for the 544th shoremen as trucked cargo poured in on the Yellow and Crimson Beaches; about 35 feet inshore from the low-water line, there was a 7-to-10-ft. sand dune, confining materiel removed from lighters to an extremely narrow and constricted space, so that off-loaded vehicles had to be routed laterally along the beach, compounding the congestion. The failure of the units pushing inland to return emptied trucks promptly, if at all, further hampered the transfer of supplies. Nonetheless, by nightfall, some 15,400 tons of XIV Corps equipment and stores had been dumped on the sands, and at 1730 a convoy of vacated transports and escorting destroyers, plus three Kamikaze-ravaged cruisers and the battered CVE KADASHAN BAY, steamed off to Leyte Gulf from Wilkinson's sector.

Maj. Gen. Robert S. Beightler's 37th GI's had made commendable progress toward their initial objectives, seizing the town of Dagupan and a couple of intact bridges needed to consolidate the beachhead. Farther to the right (or west), Maj. Gen. Rapp Brush's 40th easily secured the 5,000-ft. airstrip behind Green and Orange Beaches and occupied the town of Lingayen just beyond, and by sunset controlled a 6,000-by-9,000-yard hunk of territory.[10]

With the descent of night's curtain and the realization that some 65,000 of his troops and 30,000 tons of materiel had been safely deposited on Luzonian soil on S-Day, Krueger could breathe a sigh of relief. While a token remnant of the Kamikaze fraternity streaked in low over the water once again, in hopes of erasing more shipping in the Gulf, their efforts were fruitless. One splashed into the sea just off destroyer BUSH's fantail, and shell fragments from the fusillades of nerve-jangled AA gunners on nearby vessels rained down on LSM-66, wounding three of her crewmen. In the confusion, battleship COLORADO was hit by a "friendly" 5-inch shell, wiping out her air-defense control facilities and 18 of her crew, and injuring another 51. Shortly after midnight of 9-10 January, an enemy 320-mm. howitzer in a ravine east of Damortis began lobbing rounds haphazardly onto Whites I & II, causing less damage than annoyance.

In the wee hours of S+1, a more lethal surprise was sprung on Kinkaid's anchored fleet in the form of midget suicide boats. Seventy or so of these 18-&-1/2-ft. plywood craft, hitherto hidden at Port Sual on the Gulf's western shore, each mounting a machine-gun and carrying a couple of 260-lb. depth charges or magnetized mines, and manned by two or three soldier-volunteers, sallied forth at intervals, in an attempt to penetrate the fleet's inner screen. An alarm was quickly sounded, however, and the first of the lot was reduced to splinters by the guns of its intended target; two more of the miniature malefactors soon suffered a similar fate. This in no wise discouraged their successors, whose modus operandi was to slip up under a ship's stern in the darkness and heave short-timed depth charges overboard or clamp mines to a hull, then speed away before they detonated. Before the night's end, LCI(M)-974 had been sunk, and transport WARHAWK's hull punctured below the waterline by an outboard explosion, flooding one of her holds. LST-925 was also breached, disabling her starboard engine, and a sister's bottom similarly holed, admitting seawater to her engine room. Two additional LST's sustained damage, while LCI(G)-365 was wrecked to the extent that she had to be abandoned by her crew. Thankfully, with the return of daylight, virtually all of the midgets had been reduced to driftwood; thereafter LINGAYEN FORCE was spared further such visitations.[11]

At sunrise S+1, smoke generators again spread a heavy pall over the fleet and beachhead, but the Kami's largely stayed their hand. Off Santiago Island, a loner dove upon upon and barely missed Destroyer DASHIEL, while outside the Gulf, another smashed into LeRAY WILSON, a DE on antisubmarine station, mangling her severely, and reducing her roster by 13. The remainder of the day brought no further terror from the skies, but then nature took up where the Kami's left off—high westerly winds built up heavy ground swells off Wilkinson's beaches, buckling the pontoon causeways installed the day before and rendering the beaching of small craft increasingly perilous. As if this were not enough misery, the 544th shore parties could not lay hands on a sufficient quantity of steel matting to pave some of the muddier exits from the beach, further retarding the rate of cargo discharge as trucks became mired up to their axles until towed free by the few available cats and tractors. When the afternoon surf on Yellow Beach rose to 10-ft. heights, numerous Navy LCVP's broached, some damaged beyond recovery, forcing the beachmaster to halt all unloading at 1630, even though as yet none of the hardier, more seaworthy LCM's had foundered. On S+2, after LCM/LCT/LSM traffic into Yellow-Crimson was diverted to more sheltered sites along the banks of the Dagupan and Calmay rivers, the pace of operations was palpably boosted.

Off the Blue beaches on S+1, where the surf was topping 6 feet, one retracting LST fouled the cable of a second, causing it to broach sideways, forcing others out of position and wrecking their pontoon causeways. Three LST's stuck fast, and even LCM's became unmanageable. The task of salvaging and resetting the causeways could not be completed for another twenty-four hours or so, and DUKW's were useless in the extremely choppy waters. That afternoon (10 January), both Blue Beaches and White III had to be closed down until the crashing waves subsided. The 28 LCM's assigned to Blue Beach II had taken such a rough beating that by nightfall of S+2, only 18 were still operational. As the traffic from the three embargoed strands funnelled into still-viable Whites I & II, they too become clogged, overburdening the shore parties and compelling them to draft personnel from other units and employ every able-bodied Filipino they could hire. Adding to the stress was the resumption of sporadic enemy mortar and 75-mm. fire, which perdured for several more days, as well as, for a night or two, some 21 rounds from a 240-mm. gun, taking the lives of two shoremen, wounding 21, and puncturing several "Mikes" above their waterlines.

Filipino civilian idlers began to descend upon Wilkinson's beaches on S+1 "like a swarm of locusts, to fraternize, beg, and pilfer" the supplies which had been piled in some places down to very edge of the high-water mark. The 544th and 594th shoremen took advantage of the temporary suspension of incoming traffic on their respective strands to manhandle the unsorted bulk cargo piled along the water's edge further inshore and distribute it among the proper dumps, pending the establishment of permanent depots. It was exhausting work, even with the help of the additional military muscle and that of Filipino hirelings. Notwithstanding all mother nature's disruptions, by late afternoon of the second day, enough beaching craft, troopships, and cargo vessels had been emptied to form two additional departure convoys which steamed off southward during the night hours. An outbound AKA, DU PAGE, while maneuvering into position, was crashed by a Kamikaze on her navigation bridge, igniting blazes and inflicting 32 deaths and 157 injuries, but not forestalling her departure.[12]

There were no further enemy encroachments in the roadstead that evening (S+1), and as Connolly's TG-77.9 REINFORCEMENT GROUP sailed into the Gulf early the following morning, 11 January, the angry surf had abated, and the Kami tag-ends laid low. Approaching the landing zones, our flotilla split three ways, one portion freighted with airfield engineer and technical troops veering off to the XIV Corps strands, as I remember it. The fifteen transports toting the 25th Infantry and other elements of the floating reserve hove to off the San Fabian beaches, while our band of outcasts was steered into an isolated strand dubbed Red Beach, a couple of miles north of the I Corps sector. As far as I could tell, TG-77.9 at the rear of Kinkaid's big parade had made the entire journey unmolested and trouble-free, aside from a minor collision between two 25th Division transports while maneuvering into their anchorage off San Fabian. The words of Psalm 91 came to mind: "A thousand shall fall beside thee, and ten thousand at thy right hand; but it shall not come nigh thee." Once again the 534th had been blessed by Divine Providence (or

Lady Luck, or the Inscrutable Fates, or whatever metaphysical agency to which one prefers to attribute such favors.)

About 0900, after MacNider's 158th ground-pounders had begun boating in from their PA's and APA's, our LST's shoved their bows upon the sands of Red Beach, opened their maws, and lowered their ramps. Stepping off like the seasoned vets we now thought we were, the Shore Battalion hoplites pitched into their respective tasks, while we scions of Hippocrates excavated a hole for a temporary aid station, roofed it over with a tarpaulin, and layed out the tools of our trade, or addressed other primary concerns. I was then assigned along with five others to unload medical stores a quarter of a mile down-beach from the aid station. Once our stuff was stashed on the sands, everyone dug himself a hole for the coming night and broke out the new-style "ten-in-one" ration-packets we had been given, whose contents were far tastier than the old stand-by C-ration of canned "dog biscuits and Aussie mutton."

At dusk, a long-range Jap 240-mm. cannon began shelling us at five-minute intervals, continuing throughout the entire night. We were told later that this was an American gun which the Japs had captured at Corregidor, mounted on a railway car, and sited where a stretch of track emerged from a tunnel. The cannoneers would shove the mobile monster out from the mouth of the tunnel, fire a round, and then, to evade the counterfire of our warships and fighter-bombers, pull it back inside for sponging and reloading before running it out again for another go. We could see the muzzle flash in the distance, and a couple of seconds later, hear a dull report, followed by a deafening crash as the shell exploded. Needless to say, there was no sleeping, and, as some wit observed, "The society for the improvement of foxholes gained new members by the minute." I certainly burrowed in like a frenzied mole, especially after 0100 as the range shortened and the shellbursts crept nearer and nearer until they were in extremely close proximity to my refuge. As the hours passed, an ammunition truck parked nearby was hit; there was an ear-splitting explosion, with metal fragments flying all about, lighting up the sky like midday. One of our shoremen, Exstine by name, seeking rest on the deck of a beached LST, was badly wounded by a piece of shrapnel from this gun which gouged a hole the size of a half-dollar in his side. Several other LST's received direct hits, causing considerable casualties among those aboard. (Our tormentor was put out of commission a few days later by some of Wing's 43d chaps; I have since learned that Red Beach that night was the recipient of more "incoming mail"—as GI's refer to hostile shellfire—than any of the other Lingayen strands during the entire operation.) About dawn, a twin-engined Betty swooped down through the smoke screen and dropped a large bomb right by my hole. By some miracle, it failed to detonate, but spewed a greenish-yellow chemical of some sort over the surrounding sand. Had it not been a dud, no doubt I and everyone else in the immediate vicinity would have been blown to bits. Out in the Gulf, at about the same hour, the few surviving Kamikazes were back at their dirty work, one ramming itself into Destroyer Escort GILLIGAN, triggering a tremendous eruption and conflagration, and inflicting 25 casualties. Another splashed so close to Destroyer-Escort RICHARD W. SUESENS while she was rescuing sailors blown overboard from GILLIGAN that ll of her own crew were injured. At sundown the previous evening, a few Jap bombs had fallen on the Blue beaches, and at dawn on S+3, one scored a direct hit on the naval beachmaster's command post, killing several people but doing slight collateral damage.[13]

We spent the ensuing day, 12 January (S+3), helping the shore party unload bulk supplies and ammunition from LST's, forming human chains and using portable rollers, and when darkness once more enveloped the beach, I was so fatigued that I slept as though I were dead, and would not have cared whether the Japs offed me or not. By now the Kami wind had almost exhausted itself, at least in our neck of the woods, although early that morning one of a quartet of "Tonys" trying to nail Wilkinson's transports had broken formation and hit AVD [seaplane tender] BELKNAP, completely demolishing her #2 stack and killing 38 of her people. An inbound resupply convoy laboring up the coast had also been smitten, crippling a couple of its Liberties. Two of Connolly's emptied vessels,

LST-700 and APA ZEILIN, were attacked while getting underway early the following morning, 13 January, doing extensive damage to both, and leaving 10 of their crewmen dead and 34 wounded. The last successful Kamikaze blow to be dealt in Philippine waters fell upon escort carrier SALAMAUA a few minutes later at 0858 off the mouth of the Gulf, blasting her flight and hangar decks, and opening her side; she survived her injuries, though not so 15 of her personnel, and 88 more were wounded. During the single month since their first deadly onslaught at Mindoro, the Kami's had sunk a total of 20 ships, badly crippled 24, and damaged 35 to lesser degrees. Most popular historical accounts of the Lingayen Gulf invasion have airily dismissed it as an "easy" landing—it was anything but that for some of our army amphibs and a hideous trial for too many of our seafaring brothers-in-arms.[14]

As MacNider's three battalions began their advance to Rabon and Damortis, each was accompanied by a mine-clearing and demolition section of 534th's D Company. An independent unit with no organic combat-engineer component, the 158th had to rely upon the seahorsemen for these chores. One of Co. D's sections undertook to sneak through enemy lines and destroy an ammo dump, which it duly accomplished, though at the price of one amphib death and several injuries, earning for its members decorations for their "heroism in the face of the enemy."[15]

All things considered, despite the unpredictable foul-ups that had marred the Lingayen landings, the seahorsemen must have done their jobs faithfully, diligently, and commendably, so much so that Admiral Barbey appended to his after-action report, "It is believed that the Engineer Special Brigade as organized in the Southwest Pacific Area is the most efficient Shore Party organization now functioning in amphibious warfare and that the permanent organization of these [brigades has] contributed in large measure to the success of amphibious operations in this theatre." This encomium was endorsed by General MacArthur, and even the dour Krueger, who was not one to indulge in hyperbole, opined that everyone "did as well as could have been expected under existing conditions."[16]

After all the gunfire died away on Red Beach and we had things sorted out after a fashion, the 534th pitched camp on the sands, and everyone was able to bathe, eat some substantial meals, and scope out the surroundings before being ordered southward down the beachhead to the town of Dagupan. Some gruesome evidence of Japanese atrocities surfaced in a nearby barrio—an entire family of civilians, women and children included, had been slaughtered while at their dining table, and other bodies were found hanging in the hallway of the home. Several corpses were strewn about the yards of adjacent dwellings, and a number of unburied Japanese dead lay nearby.[17]

To prevent the Imperial Navy from taking another swipe with its withered arm at Sixth Army's vulnerable lifeline from Leyte (as had been attempted in December at Mindoro), Admiral Halsey and most of his Third Fleet ventured west into the South China Sea on 10 January on a ten-day search-and-destroy sweep. Though there were few, if any, enemy warships to engage, Vice Adm. John S. McCain's TF-38 fast-carrier planes had profitable hunting nonetheless, sinking 44 merchant ships and pounding airfields at Hong Kong and Camranh Bay on the coast of Indo-China. As a passing gesture, they savaged Formosan airfields on the way out and back, for which the Kamikazes in those parts retaliated by ramming themselves into flattops LANGLEY and TICONDEROGA and an accompanying destroyer. All three vessels remained afloat to fight again another day, but 205 more names were appended to the ever-growing list of U.S. Navy fatalities. Still, the arithmetic of carnage was far from unfavorable, since TF-38 had scratched off another half-thousand enemy aircraft at a cost of 201 of its own planes. At January's end, by which time scarcely a single Jap crate was to be found throughout the entire Philippine archipelago, Halsey's force returned to Ulithi for rest and refitting, preparatory to renewed exertions, under the mantle of Fifth Fleet and the direction of Admiral Spruance, at Iwo Jima and Okinawa.[18]

At Lingayen Gulf, following an S-Day lunch aboard BOISE, MacArthur and several of his staff had boarded an LCM and, ignoring a special ramp which had been constructed for their convenience, made another dramatic "wet-leg" landing near San Fabian, splashing through two feet of water while movie cameras rolled and a crowd of cheering Filipinos shouted "Mabuhay" (the Tagalog word for "Welcome.") After a couple of hours shmoozing with civilians and his troops, the Generalissimo returned to his command ship. Four days later, he moved ashore, establishing his advance headquarters in a secondary school in the town of Santa Barbara until Manila should be taken.[19] Airfield engineers worked tirelessly to upgrade and resurface the crude Lingayen airstrip with steel matting (which 594th's shoremen had almost broken their backs to offload expeditiously), and another was improvised at Mangaldan (near San Fabian), so that Fifth Air Force could begin to assume the task of close combat support and release Kinkaid's CVE's for operations nearer Japan. At best, these strips were too few and primitive to accomodate the number of squadrons required for full coverage of the widening land campaign; nothing less than the multiple runways of Clark Field and Manila's Nichols and Nielson fields would suffice. By the same token, more sheltered anchorages and elaborate port facilities than those at Lingayen Gulf would be required for the long-term sustenance of Sixth Army. Only Manila's superb harbor and wharves would be equal to that task.

On 19 January, 4ESB reverted from Corps and Division control back to that of Sixth Army Service Command, with the exception of the 534th, which had been attached to I Corps six days earlier. While our D Company remained at Red Beach improving the roads to Damortis and rendering other services in behalf of 158th RCT, the remainder of the battalion (Medical Detachment included) sidled west down the beachhead to the Blue Beaches for a brief stint of longshoring before proceeding on to Dagupan to apply its skills to the rehabilitation and enhancement of utilities and communications for what was to become Sub-base 2, where our colleagues of the 544th were employed in lighterage and cargo-discharge. The 594th continued its activities at Lingayen (soon to become Sub-base 3), with some of its shoremen assigned to road-construction and the fabrication of fuel tanks. The two 3ESB regiments worked the San Fabian beaches (Sub-base 1) until recalled to the southern Philippines for the support of Eighth Army's invasion and pacification of Mindanao, the 543d departing on 9 February, and the 533d on 25 March. At their newly-installed boat-repair yard on the Dagupan River's west bank, the 564th boat-maintenance specialists worked around the clock restoring the scores of disabled landing craft, stretching their modest stock of spare parts to the limit. At Sixth Army's behest, they also provided a pool of LCVP's and LCM's for reconnaissance, river ferrying, and tactical missions.[20]

In the 534th's Dagupan bivouac, I myself, after 48 hours of guard and fatigue duty, spent Tuesday evening, 16 January, composing a letter to my parents—my first from Luzon. I found it hard to gather my thoughts, since a number of the boys were congregated in our tent singing discordantly, the Polacks stomping out their frenetic polkas versus the hillbillies wailing their lugubrious country-and-western ballads. After the din subsided, I finished my letter and hit the sack, and for the next two nights worked the graveyard shift in the aid tent, trying to catch some rest during the torrid daytime hours. Toward the end of that week, I was sent off as aid-man/clerk with seven other medics and one of our surgeons to a shore company encamped on the edge of Dagupan. Having no duties on Sunday, 21 January, several of us went into the town and attended services at its Methodist Church, a medium-sized, steepled edifice, its tin roof riddled with bullet and shrapnel holes, with crude benches for seating, and the barest of furnishings and ornamentation. There were so many congregants, two-thirds of them GI's, that we had to sit on the floor. Among the civilian worshippers were numerous females, dressed in their finest and looking quite fetching in their colorful frocks and high-heel shoes. The white-robed choir of eight girls and two men, ranged behind the clergyman's chair, performed quite commendably a selection of typical Protestant hymns, including the old standard, "I Need Thee Every Hour." This part of the formalities, it seemed, was the Sunday School hour, and when the offering plate was passed at its conclusion, I put in 50 centavos. Then, at the ensuing worship service, the plate was passed again, and I contributed a peso (which I could ill afford, but it was all I had left in my pocket, and since the church obviously needed funds to refurbish its sanctuary, I didn't begrudge it. My companions must have felt as I did, for the plates, when presented at the altar, were running over with money.) The liturgy was exactly as I remembered it from my boyhood when attending Danville's Mount Vernon Methodist Church, and the pastor, who spoke excellent English, wore a spic-and-span black suit with a white clerical collar. His sermon, on "Patience," was quite moving, and the atmosphere of piety contrasted starkly to the tone set by our untidy field dress, helmets, and rifles, against the background noise of constant military traffic on the road outside. That afternoon, there was a welcoming parade down Dagupan's main street, replete with city officials, firemen, policemen, hospital staff, and members of civic organizations such as the Rotary Club and Masonic lodge. The day had been officially declared "Liberation Day," and the mayor delivered a rousing speech. That afternoon, several of us took a walking tour of the town, which had about 10,000 residents. Its two-and-three-storied buildings, shops, and restaurants were largely undamaged, though a bit shell-pocked and in a sad state of maintenance. This was our first reintroduction to urban civilization after nine months in the wilds of New Guinea and Morotai, and we took full advantage of it. The kids in town saluted us by holding up two fingers to form a "V" and shouting "Veectoree, Joe!" I wandered into a leather-goods store and engaged a craftsman to fashion a new strap for my wrist-watch, which he completed in about twenty minutes, while some of my pals went to a bistro and freely sampled the nipa whiskey (brewed from rice.)

The Filipinos were generally small in stature, with fine features and clear complexions, and few of the males had facial hair. The women were quite petite and comely—to us, of course, virtually anyone of the opposite sex, regardless of pulchritude, would have seemed ravishing. Though the citizenry by and large were clean and neat in their persons and dress, their habitations (most of which were built of bamboo or wood, raised on pilings, and with thatched roofs) left much to be desired in that regard, at least by American standards. Pigs and chickens roved freely about the grounds underneath, and little effort seemed invested in keeping open spaces and streets clear of offal from the ubiquitous carabaos, donkeys, and horses. Battered bicycles and pedicabs were evidently the principle means of urban transit. A laundry-woman whom I hired for a few centavos and some spare rations to scrub my clothes returned them spotless and meticulously ironed. (In the Philippines, we could exchange our money for, and received our pay in, American-issue pesos at a rate of about two per dollar. Millions in Japanese-occupation paper currency floated about, but it was quite worthless, for no one would accept it as legal tender.)

The following Friday, the town sponsored a dance for their GI deliverers, at which the female attendees were outnumbered five-to-one, but it was a grand event nonetheless. Bennie and I were eager participants, and the family of two very out-going teenaged girls upon whom we centered our attentions invited us to dine at their home the following Wednesday. Their elderly parents were relatively literate and affluent local land-owners, the father a onetime government official prior to the Japanese occupation. They showered kindnesses upon us and made us feel as though we were members of the family, remarking that I was too young to be in the army and that I reminded them of their son who had died on Bataan in 1942.

We revisited the church the following Sunday, but found it even more packed, the benches placed so closely together that my cramped legs distracted my attention to the service and sermon. The sun outside was glaring and the temperature soaring; in fact, I don't recall that any "rain fell on the plain" to mitigate the heat or settle the dust for months thereafter. After lunch I repaired to our oven-like office tent to type a letter home, but it was so uncomfortable that after two or three false starts, I gave it up and retreated to my cot until Sergeant Hoffer nailed me for a labor detail. We rode a truck some fifteen miles to fetch a load of lumber, which shot the rest of the day. Monday brought the usual spate of dispensary and paper work, except during the noon break, when I carried some aspirin out to one of our new female friends who was suffering from a toothache, and after supper, Bennie and I visited their home again for an evening's conversation. The matriarch graciously presented me with a delicate wooden folding fan adorned with her name as a gift for my mother. My next day's duties were light, and that evening I went to the dispensary tent, which had the only electric illumination in our bivouac, to type a voluminous epistle to my parents. Each of our tents had been wired for electricity, but most of our stock of light-bulbs had been broken in the course of recent moves, and we had reverted to lanterns and candles. I had just received a couple of letters from home, the most recent dated 5 December, our first mail since Morotai. My tentmates, Weaver and Hanson, and I impulsively purchased a hen and rooster, thinking that they might produce some eggs (which were in great demand), and tethered them to a rock outside. At the end of the workday, upon returning to our tent, we found the fowls roosting on our beds, which dissuaded us from persisting in our poultry enterprise, so we passed them on to some penurious Filipino acquaintances.[21]

XII

MANILA, CRUSHED PEARL

OF THE ORIENT.

The Manila offensive by XIV Corps had been planned as a three-phase process: first, consolidation of the beachhead and development of ground and air basing for the support of subsequent moves; second, advancement to and across the looping Agno River, the primary natural obstacle in its immediate path; and third, seizure of Clark Field, suppression of remaining interference in the Central Plain, and capture of the city itself. Within a week after S-day, the Lingayen dromes were ready for use by Ennis Whitehead's aircraft, and Sixth Army had established a sixty-mile-long crescent-shaped perimeter stretching from Damortis on the left through the towns of Binalonin and Aguilar to Sual on the right. There had been no substantial opposition except on the northeastern front where Swift's I Corps, now stiffened by the 25th Division (Maj. Gen. Charles L. Mullins, Jr.), butted heads repeatedly with SHOBU elements in a succession of low ridges tailing off from the Cordillera Central. Many days were consumed and casualties taken in shouldering these aside and clearing the vital stretch of Highway 3 from Damortis to Rosario and Binalonin. On the right of the I Corps sector, regiments of Patrick's 6th Division spent some ten days smothering an obdurate enemy outpost about ten miles inland at an outcropping of low hills known as the Cabaruans. Griswold's XIV Corps, meanwhile, readied itself for the thrust down the western side of the Central Plains.[1]

Krueger's seemingly-obsessive caution in protecting his vulnerable beachhead and shielding his advance from the SHOBU hordes threatening his upper left flank iritated MacArthur, who nudged him repeatedly to get to Manila by 5 February, within four weeks of the landing (as the Joint Chiefs in Washington had been led to expect.) Krueger, who would not be rushed until I Corps was further strengthened, nonetheless did his utmost to get Griswold's two divisions underway, both hampered by the paucity of motor transport. Brush's 40th Division column proceeded down Highway 13 along the left bank (or, from their perspective, the right bank) of the westerly-then-northerly-flowing Agno River, while Beightler's 37th pursued a roughly parallel course along the Manila Railroad on the river's east. As soon as breaks in the railroad had been repaired, it too was utilized to supply the forward units. Despite an insufficiency of portable Bailey bridging, two partially-wrecked spans over the broad Agno were rebuilt, one carrying the railroad at Bayambang, the other, Highway 3 at Carmen.

The offensive gained momentum with the importation of more vehicles from the staging areas and the augmentation of the railway's meager and dilapidated rolling stock by new locomotives and cars from the U.S. The bayshore's hastily-improvised LST causeways were upgraded and two new 2,700-ft. jetties were built out from White Beach 2, one with tracks for offloading the railway equipment, the other for a pipeline terminal from which fuel could be pumped inland from tankers, and at which ships could replenish their freshwater stores. A 450-ft. riverside dock was erected at Dagupan to accomodate smaller cargo vessels. By mid-February, enough port-battalion, DUKW, harborcraft, marine-maintenance, and base-depot units were on hand to hugely enhance the capability of Base "M" (as the Lingayen Gulf logistical complex was now designated.) These improvements and accretions, however, were merely expediential, pending the acquisition of more satisfactory protected anchorages at San Fernando (La Union), Subic Bay, and, above all, Manila, where pre-existing docking facilities afforded berthing for large vessels. Until then, 4ESB's ship-to-shore services at Lingayen Gulf, where larger freighters could anchor no closer than a half-mile from the shoreline, would remain indispensable to Sixth Army's buildup and subsistence.[2]

At Tarlac, where highway 13 from Lingayen and Aguilar joined highway 3 from Rosario and Binalonan, Griswold's two southbound infantry divisions converged, aiming for Clark Field, twenty miles beyond. By S+15, XIV Corps units had reached the town of Bamban, halfway to Manila and just short of the sprawling Clark Field complex. Here, they encountered Maj. Gen. Rikichi Tsukada's KEMBU force, and after a week of slam-bang fighting, overran the airfields and their guardian Fort Stotsenburg, shoving their foe westward into well-prepared positions along the ridgeline of the Zambales Mountains. While one of 37th's regiments drove on south as far as the Pampanga River crossing at Calumpit, a mere 25 miles from Manila, 40th Division turned aside to concentrate its efforts upon wearing down KEMBU.[3]

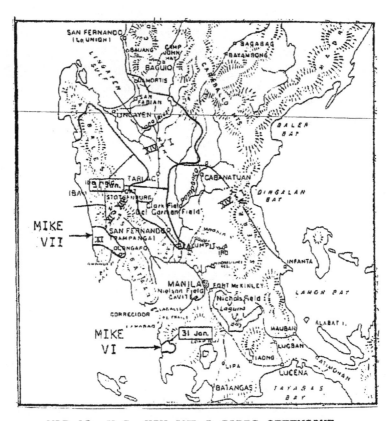

MAP 12. U.S. XIV AND I CORPS OFFENSIVE,
AND <u>MIKE VII</u> AND <u>MIKE VI</u> INTERPOSITIONS,
31 JANUARY 1945.

MacArthur's plans called for a secondary amphibious interposition, *MIKE VII*, on 29 January, by 40,000 troops of XI Corps (38th Division and one regiment of 24th Division) under Lt. Gen. Charles P. Hall, supported by 592 EB&SR, and brought up from Leyte by VII 'Phib Group 9 (Rear Adm. A. W. Struble.) They were to land on the coast of Zambales Province near San Antonio, just north of the Bataan Peninsula, capture the port of Olangapo on Subic Bay's north shore, and push eastward over Highway 7 toward San Fernando, Pampangas, for a link-up with XIV Corps, thereby bottling up KEMBU Force and isolating its elements on Bataan. The landing itself was readily accomplished without any prefatory bombardment, Struble having been assured by Filipino guerillas that no Japanese were in the vicinity. Hall's men were greeted on the beach with open arms, and their sole casualty was a GI gored by a carabao (the notoriously ill-tempered long-horned water buffaloes used by Filipinos to pull carts and plough rice paddies.)[4]

Swift's I Corps, further strengthened at January's end by two more Eighth Army divisions from Leyte, 32d Infantry (Maj. Gen. William H. Gill) and 1st Cavalry (Maj. Gen. Vernon Mudge), continued clawing its way southeast against fierce resistance. The 32d was inserted along Swift's ever-lengthening front near San Nicolas, while 1st Cavalry was deployed to Guimba, in the center of the Plains, 42 miles from Base M. Fuming at Krueger's studiedly-deliberate pace, and anxious to release Jonathan Wainwright's long-abused boys from their imprisonment, MacArthur hit upon another of his artful schemes. (Actually, all the "able-bodied" among the POW's had recently been shipped to Japan to help alleviate the labor gap created by the Imperial Army's sweeping conscription of male Japanese not previously considered for military service. Only the most incapacitated and useless prisoners remained incarcerated at Cabanatuan and other compounds on Luzon and its sister islands still under Japanese control. Hordes of Allied civilians were also interned at various sites in the archipelago, including some 4,000 at Manila's Santo Tomas University.) As a diversionary tactic, MacArthur would insert still another, but smaller, detachment from Eighth Army, the 11th Airborne Division (Maj. Gen. Joseph M. Swing), below Manila, and for good measure, provoke a race between Beightler's 37th and Mudge's lst Cavalry for the honor of being the first to enter the city.[5]

Eichelberger, hungering for a larger share of the more lustrous action developing on Luzon, was eagerly complicit, and quickly arranged for Fechteler's Group 8 of VII 'phib to ship two of Swing's glider regiments from Leyte to a landing at Nasugbu, 40 miles southwest of Manila, on 31 January. Eichelberger himself chose to accompany this so-called *MIKE VI* intrusion. The sea was calm, the sky cloudless, and the pre-landing air and naval bombardment proved superfluous, for there were no signs of enemy presence, but the slope of the chosen beach, like most of those at Lingayen, was inconveniently gentle. The troopers boated in on LCP(R)'s from their high-speed transports landed as scheduled, but many of Fechteler's LCI's and LST's were hindered by an offlying sandbar, from which they had to retract and ram through before being brought to a standstill 50 feet short of the water's edge. Despite the consequent vehicle-towing, all of Swing's formations eventually got ashore serenely, the only hostile reaction appearing after nightfall in the form of midget "Q-Boat" (torpedo boat) attacks on Group 8's vessels. Six of the pests were sunk by the screening destroyers and the remainder driven off, though in the darkness and confusion, two American PT boats were smashed up by friendly shellfire.

Despite the fact that the airborne troops had only minimal motor transport and no artillery other than 75-mm. pack-howitzers, Eichelberger had in mind a swift drive up Route l7 across the narrow neck of land between Manila Bay and Laguna de Bay into the city itself (an initiative not explicitly authorized by MacArthur.) To help clear the path northward, Swing's third (parachute infantry) regiment was dropped three days later on Tagaytay Ridge ten miles inland from Nasugbu. Additional backup was fed in on 10 February in the shape of a 24th Division RCT assisted by 592d EB&SR's Co. C with 40 LCM's and 2 of Heavey's rocket-and-flak boats. Besides providing lighterage and tactical services, the amphib boatmen hunted down and sank seven more Q-boats lurking along the shore.[6]

Although both the *MIKE VII* and *MIKE VI* sideshows got off to a heartening start, the 38th Division expended 1,400 casualties and two ghastly weeks battling over well-defended Zigzag Pass before connecting with Brush's 40th, and on Swing's front, enemy resistance stiffened the closer his paratroopers came to Manila until they were brought to a halt for almost a week at the "Genko Line" two miles short of Nichols Field on the city's southern edge.[7] Meanwhile, from Vernon Mudge's now-mechanized lst Cavalry, having disembarked at Lingayen on 27 January and ridden their tanks, armored cars, half-tracks, and trucks down to Guimba, two "flying columns" were formed on MacArthur's direct orders to race down Highway 5 to Manila. At the same time, the 37th Division units on their right near Clark Field, still short on transport, trekked toward the city down Highway 3.[8]

At Dagupan, on the last day of January, as Krueger's spearhead divisions were closing on Manila, I was assigned as aid-man/clerk to a twenty-one-man subdetachment officered by Capt. Joseph M. Lee (Leeds, Ala.), one of our battalion surgeons, and lst Lt. Roy E. Marengo (Highland Park, Mich.) of the Medical Administrative Corps, both considerate gentlemen whom I held in high regard. We were to be attached to, and provide health care for, the 413 men of the 564th EBM, situated on the far side of the Dagupan River. This foiled my plans to accompany Ben and the girls to a fete to be held in town that night in celebration of President Roosevelt's birthday, and he alone had to escort the ladies in my absence. Bennie and I, incidentally, had just received Good Conduct ribbons for one year's "honorable service" (no big deal, since virtually everyone except chronic malefactors or AWOL's was similarly recognized), and he, too, had just been made Pfc., so I could no longer pull rank on him.

The first order of business at our new posting was to get our dispensary and quarters tents rigged up, and not until this was accomplished could I attend to my clerical chores, whereupon I discovered that the people previously responsible for 564th's health maintenance had left the medical records in total disarray. It took me two days to compile the data for the weekly report to higher headquarters, which I hastily prepared and submitted in what I thought to be acceptable form. The report was tardy and not in exact conformity with S.O.P. [Standard Operating Procedure], for which I was censured—a valuable learning experience in the niggling ways of Army bureaucracy. On Saturday of that week, everyone was given booster shots for typhoid and tetanus immunization, and Sunday afternoon, I got a pass to town, caught a boat to the opposite shore, and met up with Ben to pay another call on our Filipino friends. After wiling away the hours in pleasant chitchat at their home, we were treated to a sumptuous repast of chicken, fish, shrimp, crabmeat, sweet potatoes, rice-and-gravy, and coconut candy, upon which I gorged until I could hardly waddle. I lost track of the time and almost missed the last LCM crossing the river—it had already put off from shore and was chugging into midstream when I hailed it, but the coxswain kindly put about and picked me up. One of the girls had knitted a colorful handbag for my kid sister, and after my return to camp, as I was wrapping it for mailing, my buddies warned me facetiously that it was an ominous sign when females start bestowing presents upon you, for they invariably have marriage in mind.

Some twelve hours later, Bennie and the main medical detachment, along with the rest of the battalion, pulled up stakes and retraced their steps to Sub Base 1 at San Fabian, where the 534th had been ordered to take over shore duties from the departing 543d amphibs, and I would not see many of my friends for months to come. My gloom was somewhat assuaged that night by watching a William Bendix flick, *The Hairy Ape*, on the 564th's screen. For the next three weeks (during which the 11th Airborne overran Nichols Field, the Marines invaded Iwo Jima, and RAF and USAAF planes firebombed the German city of Dresden at the request of the Russians, killing no less than 35,000 people—*not* one of Democracy's finest hours), we worked diligently to alleviate the ills and injuries of the over-stretched boat-maintenance boys. More of our long-lost mail caught up with us; on a single day, I recieved no fewer than seven letters from home, a great morale-booster. My physical vitality, however, seemed to be ebbing, and by mid-February, I was dragging around with a fever of 102.8 and suffering severe stomach cramps, nausea, and diarrhea. I was ordered to bed for a couple of days, after which the symptoms abated somewhat, though I was losing weight rapidly, and my pals observed that I looked like "death warmed over." Lieutenant Marengo, concerned about my emaciation, cooked an egg for me (a very thoughtful gesture, as they were very hard to come by), which I promptly vomitted up, to my disgust.[9]

Just as our activities were settling back into a routine pattern, on Monday, 19 February, the 564th and our subdetachment, along with the 594th EB&SR (in which Carl Stegman, one of my pals at Gordon Johnston's Radio School, was serving), were ordered down to Manila, the "boats" travelling aboard their watercraft, the rest of us by road.[10] To set our sudden transplantation within the larger scheme of things, Sixth Army's traumatic recapture of the city requires narration in some detail. One of the highlights of XIV Corps' southward drive had been a daring raid on Cabanatuan's notorious P.O.W. camp on 30 January by a company of 6th Rangers and 280 Filipino guerillas, who had rescued 500 frail survivors of the Bataan death march and hustled them back to safety. The raid's resounding success had been one of the factors prompting MacArthur to send two units of 1st Cavalry under Brig. Gen. William C. Chase knifing through enemy-held territory to release the civilian internees at Santo Tomas University in northern Manila. With close support from Marine Corps SBD's [fighter-bombers], Chase's twin columns sped down the axis of Highway 5, detouring around one another wherever resistance had to be quelled or swept aside, and dashing over bridges still intact or fording shallow streams where spans were collapsed. Outrunning Beightler's 37th Division foot-sloggers on their west (slowed by blown bridges over unfordable rivers just north of the city), they roared into Manila's outskirts and down Quezon Boulevard to Santo Tomas at dusk on Saturday, 3 February. The foremost speedsters crashed through the gates, rounded up most of the startled Japanese guards, and liberated the tattered and starving inmates except for a separate group of 267— mostly women and children—who were held as hostages. After a day of tense bargaining, the hostage-takers were allowed to march out and rejoin the city's garrison in exchange for their prisoners' freedom. A few hours later (3-4 February), Beightler's infantry also penetrated Manila's northern precincts and released another 1,300 Allied military and civilian personnel incarcerated in Bilibid Prison. Many of the Yank foot-sloggers, tipped off by sympathetic citizenry, took a quick time-out to slake their thirst from the vats of the Balintawak Brewery; thus refreshed, if slightly tipsy, they resumed their piece of the action with renewed spirit(s).

Other regiments of 1st Cavalry, trailing Chase's "flying columns" at a less furious pace, secured the Novaliches Dam and reservoir and the Balara Water Filters supplying much of Manila's potable water, and drove through the city's northeastern quarter, seizing Malacanan Palace (the Philippine White House.) Crossing the Pasig River, they turned east and circled around the outer fringes of the metropolis into its southern suburbs. This bold tactic isolated the enemy forces within the city, cutting them off from SHIMBU Group and its detachments occupying southern Luzon and the Bicol Peninsula. Yamashita had intended to evacuate the entire Manila garrison and declare it an "open city," as had MacArthur in 1942, to spare its buildings and populace, but fanatical Rear Adm. Sanji Iwabuchi insisted that his own 17,000 marine infantry of the "Manila Naval Defense Force" and the 4,000 soldiery alongside them remain to the bitter end to scuttle the ships trapped within the bay and ensure the destruction of all the port's naval installations and stores. Iwabuchi's usurpation of authority was soon expanded to include areas of the city nominally under Japanese Army control, and as Beightler's infantry punched deeper into northern Manila, they found themselves facing a foe committed to an all-out defense, the streets strewn with mines and obstructed by barbed-wire entanglements, overturned trucks, and trolley cars. Building entrances were sandbagged and booby-trapped, countless machinegun nests concealed behind walls and in upper stories, and field artillery and large-calibre guns from scuttled warships emplaced at major street intersections. The port facilities were dynamited, municipal electric power and sewerage systems wrecked, and many of the water mains and valves ruined. Even the aqueducts from the reservoirs into the city were ruptured in places. The bridges over the Pasig River snaking through the city were demolished, except for one or two over which Iwabuchi's troops could withdraw before blowing them up. The waterfront blasts set off fires, whipped up by stiff breezes, which quickly spread into the blocks of bamboo and wooden houses adjoining the dock area, until much of northern Manila was aflame, the smoke visible for fifty mies. Not only was this the most densely-populated quarter, but it contained the majority of the city's retail stores, movie theatres, restaurants, and commercial establishments, as well as industrial plants. The better residential districts lay to the east or on the yonder side of the Pasig River in South Manila, showcase of the metropolis, whose bayfront facilities, known as the South Port, included four large finger piers, one of which, reputedly the world's longest, could berth seven ocean-liners. This, the city's most historic as well as most modern precinct, had undergone extensive redevelopment under American hegemony, particularly during the interwar years, and contained impressive government edifices and parks modelled on those in Washington, D.C.[11]

As the troops of the 37th battled southward toward the river, street-by-street, house-by-house, and even room-by-room, they also attempted to arrest the spreading conflagration by levelling buildings to create firebreaks, but not until the winds shifted could the fires be contained or burn themselves out. MacArthur had forbidden aerial bombing of the city, and Beightler had to obtain permission before employing artillery to knock down the blockades and strongholds, in which he had little choice if his casualties were to be kept low. Between the devastation wrought on Iwabuchi's orders and that resulting from the fires and the shelling by both sides, regrettably, much of Manila was eventually reduced to ruins, and tens of thousands of her helpless citizens slain.

By 7 February, the forward elements of the 37th had reached the Pasig and crossed over in assault boats to carve out a small lodgement on its southern bank. Within a week or so, the river island of Provisor with its municipal power-generating plant had been captured and the Paco railway station secured. While 1st Cavalry completed the circuit around the city's eastern rim to the southside and the bayshore, one segment splitting off to connect with Beightler's GI's, the redisposed 11th Airborne took Paranaque, broke through the enemy's Gengko Line, overran Nichols Field, and joined up with the cavalrymen to take Fort McKinley. Iwabuchi's forces were now inescapably backed into a shrinking enclave with the historic Intramuros at its core, bounded on the north by the lower Pasig River and on the west by the South Harbor bayfront.

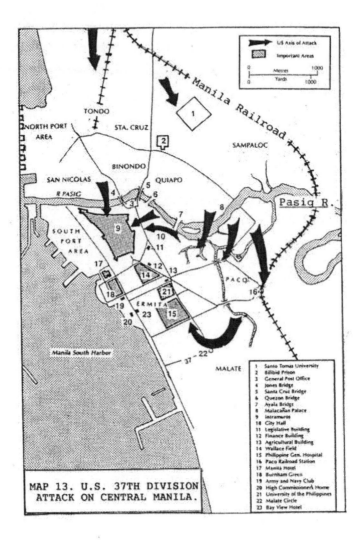

MAP 13. U.S. 37TH DIVISION ATTACK ON CENTRAL MANILA.

Guarded along its river flank only by a low seawall, the Intramuros was the original citadel built by the Spaniards in the 16th century, anchored at its northwest corner by Fort Santiago with its casemates, gunports, tunnels, and subterranean dungeons.

Forming an irregular quadrangle, along whose three landward sides ran massive stone-block walls, some of them 40 ft. thick at their base and rearing up l6 to 25 ft., the 150-acre Intramuros enclosure contained masonry churches, convents, schools, and dwellings. Here Iwabuchi would make his final stand. As his troops withdrew toward this bastion, they engaged in a mass orgy of looting, rape, and pillage, torturing and murdering Filipino and Caucasian civilians by the hundreds on suspicion of giving aid and comfort to the Yanks.[12]

The three converging U.S. divisions, infantry, cavalry, and airborne, under the aegis of XIV Corps and General Griswold, slowly tightened their choke-hold on South Manila, where the Japanese had transformed many of the substantial modern structures into mini-fortresses. These included earthquake-proof reinforced-concrete government buildings in spacious grounds near the Intramuros, most prominently, the General Post Office, City Hall, New Police Station, and the Legislative, Finance, and Agriculture Buildings. All were heavily damaged in the conflict, several systematically reduced to enormous heaps of rubble by the point-blank fire of American tanks and heavy artillery. While part of Beightler's infantry and artillery dodged heavy counter-fire to eradicate these individual strong-points, others pressed on south and east into the Ermita District, expelling obstinate quarry from the Philippine General Hospital and the University of the Philippines.[13]

Meanwhile, the tankmen and troopers of lst Cavalry, advancing northward along the bayshore through the Pasay suburb, corralled a contingent of Iwabuchi's butchers within an ovoid sac surrounding the Manila Yacht Club, Rizal Baseball Stadium, La Salle University, and Santa Scholastica College, and in a bruising struggle, overpowered them. Weighing in alongside Beightler's infantry, the cavalrymen penetrated the South Port area, wresting the Army-Navy Club, Manila Hotel, and Customs House from their maddened Nipponese tenants. MacArthur entered the city on February 7th, and fifteen days later personally witnessed the bitter struggle for mastery of the elegant Manila Hotel, from the ground floor up to his luxurious pre-war penthouse apartment, repository of his most treasured possessions, most of which had been torched. The slaughter and spoliation climaxed with the 37th's investment of the Intramuros itself, harboring hundreds of Iwabuchi's naval troops and 4,000 Filipino hostages. Loudspeaker pleas from General Griswold to surrender honorably and release the captives went unheeded. When no white flag was raised and none of the impounded civilians emerged, Griswold loosed upon it a withering two-day cannonade, using tank guns, 105-mm., 155-mm., and 8-inch howitzers, even 240-mm. mortars. This was followed up on 23 February by dual infantry assaults, one from across the river and over the seawall, the other through breaches or gates in the eastern ramparts. Many of the besieged, caught in the open, were slain by small-arms and automatic-weaponry fire, but against the diehards in the inner recesses, resort was had to more-indiscriminate hand grenades, bazookas, and flame-throwers, putting the hostages at unavoidable risk. There was a brief respite as 3,000 starved and terrified women and children emerged by permission of their captors, but once these were safely beyond the walls, the Yankee pressure was reapplied ruthlessly until resistance collapsed on 24 February and a handful of surviving bitter-enders emerged with their hands in the air. Virtually all of the male hostages had been brutally executed. Thereafter, the remaining vandal nests in the Intramuros environs had to be systematically erased. On March 3d, one month after the opening round of the battle for Manila, from inside the gutted, blackened shell that had once been the Finance Building, a final burst of fire from maniacal troglodytes died away into silence.[14]

The Japanese occupants of Bataan Peninsula and the island fortresses guarding the mouth of Manila Bay now had to be reckoned with. On 27 February, a glider infantry regiment of 11th Airborne and guerilla auxilliaries pressed into the area along the bay's south rim, where 1,350 or so of Iwabuchi's marine soldiery, having abandoned the Cavite naval base, were now concentrated at Ternate, opposite Corregidor. By 3 March, after 350 of the "terminators" at Ternate had themselves been terminated by the paras with the help of artillery, tanks, and Fifth Air Force A-20's, the remnant had hastily taken to the hills on the south or east, leaving behind three-score "Q" boats and long-range guns intended for the annihilation of any Allied shipping attempting entrance into the bay.

At the same time as the southern bayshore was undergoing sanitization, elements of Hall's XI Corps were securing Bataan and Corregidor across the narrows. Three task groups, dubbed East Force, South Force, and Rock Force, had been assembled for this purpose from the 24th and 38th divisions by William C. Chase, star of the race for Manila and newly-installed commander of the latter. East Force stepped off southward from Dinalupihan on 12 February, taking the same road along Bataan's eastern shore over which the defeated American and Filipino troops had been herded in the infamous "Death March" three years before. Repelling a spirited but brief enemy counterstrike at Orion, it advanced to Pilar, splitting off one component to turn due west across the peninsula's midriff to the South China Seacoast, while the other continued south. Meanwhile, South Force and Rock Force, with companies of 592d EB&SR attached, sailed down the seacoast from Olangapo on Subic Bay aboard Rear Admiral Struble's LST's, LSM's, and LCI's—and in the amphib LCM's—and landed on 16 February at Mariveles. While the Japanese thereabout gave little trouble save for some artillery fire and an ineffectual infantry counterattack, the naval mines strewn so prodigally around Mariveles harbor did, sinking one of Struble's LST's, while the slight off-shore gradient held all his beaching and landing craft far enough "at bay" to retard unloading. Once the ground forces were ashore, the harbor cleared of mines, and the handful of hovering Japanese chased away, South Force units took to the roads up each side of the peninsula and joined the two prongs of East Force to confine Bataan's 1,400 forlorn defenders within its jungled mountains, where most eventually perished of fever and famine.

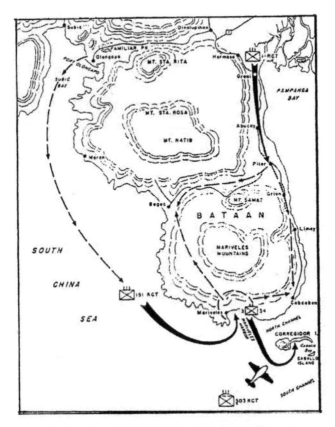

MAP 14. RETRIEVAL OF BATAAN
BY EAST FORCE AND SOUTH FORCE.

With Bataan now incontestably neutralized, Mariveles became
the catapult for a waterborne invasion of Corregidor,"The Rock,"
by Chase's third, or Rock, Force. The fortified island, lying just
across two-mile-wide North Channel from Mariveles, was
garrisoned by the 5,000 naval infantry of Capt. Akira Natagaki's
"Manila Bay Entrance Force," whose numbers Krueger's
Intelligence had grossly underestimated at no more than 850, one-
sixth its actual size. After a ferocious pummelling by AAF bombers
and Admiral Berkey's gunships, Corregidor, three-and-one-half-
miles long and shaped like a tadpole, was descended upon on 16

February, not only nautically by Rock Force, but vertically by a battalion of 503d Airborne Regiment parachutists from Mindoro, in a carefully-timed-and-coordinated operation. The 503d troopers were dropped upon a few level acres known as "Topside," crowning the tadpole's bulbous head, formerly a parade-ground, small golf-course, and barracks, now a bombed-out ruin. Alhough the airdrop was extremely dicey in light of the debris-littered, constricted landing zone, precipitous seafront cliffs, and the unsuspected numerical superiority of the foe, the paratroopers brought it off neatly, by and large, quickly securing Topside and its environs. The utterly-dumbfounded Natagaki, who had anticipated only an amphibious assault, was slain by jumpers near his cliffside observation post, dooming the Rock's defense to incoherence. Two hours later, the Rock Force battalion combat team and 592d's Shore Company D, brought over from Mariveles in A Company's LCM's, landed under a hail of enemy machinegun-fire on heavily-mined northside beaches at the shallow base of the tadpole's tail, or "Bottom-side," just west of Malinta Hill. Linking up with the airborne battalion on their right and climbing to the summit of Malinta on their left, the Rock Force infantry joined the paras in mopping-up—or more accurately, plugging up—lethal enemy pillboxes, cave entrances, and tunnel-mouths. The 592d boatmen not only contributed their fire-power to this endeavor, but picked off anyone attempting to escape by sea. Two thousand or so of Natagaki's fanatics, holed up in the same Malinta tunnel complex that had once sheltered Wainwright's forsaken legion, detonated— either by accident or design—tons of stored explosives. The resultant eruption killed or entombed hundreds of their own and six Americans (21 February.) As the Yank intruders overran the eastern end of the island five days later, a second subterranean arsenal blew up under their feet with no less deadly effects, concluding the operation on a gruesomely tragic note and raising the price of Corregidor's recovery to a final tally of 1,200 American casualties, as over against approximately 4,500 Japanese. For their valorous actions in support of the Rock's redemption, the participating 592d companies were subsequently awarded "Distinguished Unit" citations. On 2 March, MacArthur and his "Bataan gang" coterie sailed over from Manila in a PT-Boat and had the stars and stripes run up a scarred ship's mast standing amid the Topside ruins to herald the renewal of American hegemony and the restoration of her honor.[15]

Other task groups were organized to retake the three lesser island outposts at the entrance to the Bay. The first and nearest, Caballo Island, one mile long and 500 yards wide, just off the tadpole's tail, after merciless aerial strafing, bombing, and napalming, and shelling by naval gunnery and artillery on Corregidor, was assaulted on 27 March by an infantry battalion boated over on 592d's LCM's. They met only minimal interference until approaching some knolls within whose tunnels and mortar pits lurked 400 heavily-armed Japanese. All attempts to extirpate them came to naught until someone thought of converting an LCM into a floating flamethrower by the installation of a powerful pump and fuel tanks holding 3,400 gallons of a highly-flammable mixture of diesel oil and gasoline. The barge was then steered beneath a seaside cliff adjacent to the core enemy haven, an 800-ft. pipeline run aloft, and the volatile fluid was pumped into apertures and ignited with incendiary grenades, cremating many of the beseiged. When opposition persisted, the procedure was repeated; on the third try, the quantity of fuel was doubled and activated by a bigger charge, touching off an underground ammo dump. The cliff was virtually torn asunder and nothing more was heard from the poor eremites within.

On the opposite side of the South Channel lay Fort Drum, or El Fraile, the more formidable of the two remaining guardians; it had been erected by U.S. Army engineers prior to the war on a rock formation protruding from the water. Both in shape and essence it was a stable concrete battleship, topped by two naval gun turrets. The only entryway through its impermeable vertical walls was a ramp which had been thickly mined and sighted for cross-fire by the occupants' machineguns. On the morning of 13 April, El Fraile was socked and pocked by Navy gunships and Air Force bombers, after which an LSM was navigated alongside, from whose conning tower a swinging gangplank or retractible bridge was extended up to the fort's level roofdeck. While the LSM was held in place in the choppy waters by four LCVP's, and the nearby gunships kept the 70-man force within buttoned up with covering fire, agile engineers, like marauding pirates of olden times, clambered across the bridge, dragging a hose from the same tanker-LCM which had been employed at Caballo, and inserted it into a stairwell on the fort's roofdeck. Although the turbulent seas parted the hose after only 400 gallons of the fuel mixture had been pumped inside, repairs were quickly effected, and another 2,200 gallons pumped down a ventilator shaft. A 500-pound TNT charge with fuze timed for 30 minutes was lowered into the aperture, whereupon the riggers retreated with celerity to the LCM and all watercraft withdrew to a safe distance. The consequent ear-splitting detonation cracked the fort wide open, hurling chunks of concrete and pieces of steel hundreds of feet into the air. Those inside either went instantly to their eternal reward or subsequently expired from the asphyxiating smoke which poured from every vent and turret for hours thereafter.

The final bit of enemy-held real estate at the Bay's entrance, Carabao Island, one mile off the Ternate shore, was expurgated for good measure on 16 April. This entailed breaching an enveloping concrete seawall with aerial bombs and the gunfire of cruiser PHOENIX and two destroyers, after which a landing force rushed ashore from 592d's boats, only to find that the 350-man garrison had eloped to the mainland, leaving behind one badly-shaken-up pig. The Japs left another, less benign, memento—a cache of underground explosives with a delayed-time triggering mechanism, which erupted one hour later in a mighty upheaval, inflicting several casualties.[16]

Manila Bay, though littered with wrecked vessels and liberally sewn with naval mines, all of which would have to be removed, was thus opened to Allied bottoms, and the shattered port, once renovated, would be put to excellent use. Except for Warsaw, Poland, the metropolis itself had been more thoroughly devastated than any other Allied capital city during all of World War II. At least

100,000 of its inhabitants and more than 1,000 American combatants had been slain in the process of its recovery, to say nothing of 16,000 Japanese—a ratio of six civilians for every serviceman slain on both sides!

The brutal melee on the south side of the Pasig River was still raging when the 564th EBM and those of us in Captain Lee's subdetachment from Dagupan stepped down from our trucks on or about 21 February in a partially-burned-out slum section of north Manila known as Tondo, and pitched our tents amid the rubble. The nauseating odor emanating from overflowing sewage, rotting garbage, and the burnt and putrifying corpses amid the ruins was almost intolerable. It took a week or so to get our habitation in order, and to unpack and reopen our aid post for business. Within a few days, to my pleasant surprise, Bennie Weaver was transferred down to us.[17]

Unfortunately, my fever and gastro-intestinal misery recurred here almost immediately in acute form, and I had to drag myself to the latrine with lamentable frequency. The standard nostrum of paregoric-and-bizmuth taken orally would stem the cramps and diarrhea for twenty-four hours or so, but there was an inevitable relapse, and each day I was becoming more debilitated. Dr. Lee finally dosed me with ten sulfaguanadine pills daily which kept me ambulatory for awhile longer.

A more convenient and suitable location for the 564th had been selected near the mouth of the Pasig River to which we soon repaired, and with time we had floored tents, a commodious mess hall, and even a recreation center, all screened to keep out the ubiquitous flies and mosquitoes. The quality of food served in the 564th mess was distinctly superior to that in the 534th, though I was in no condition to enjoy it. For the first time since coming overseas, we could dine on fresh legumes, vegetables and fruits— potatoes, lettuce, tomatoes, cucumbers, watermelons—even creamery butter. Not until the second week in March was there any time for letter-writing. On days when I could keep a tight sphincter, I explored the noxious neighborhood with my confreres, some of the more lustful of whom took full advantage of the city's

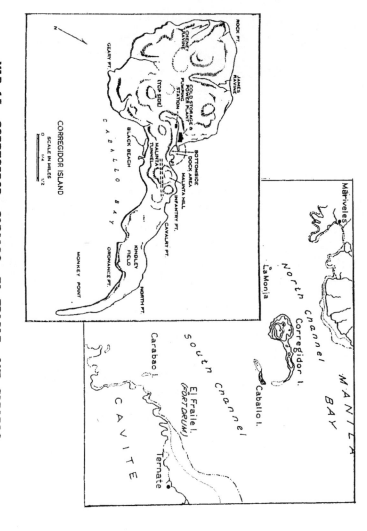

MAP 15. CORREGIDOR, CABALLO, EL FRAILE, AND CARABAO ISLANDS GUARDING ENTRANCE TO MANILA BAY.

plenitude of whores. My respect for Filipinos underwent a marked revision in this urban context; hordes of young, able-bodied, demoralized males hung around our cantonement seeking handouts, seemingly unwilling to perform any labor unless well-rewarded, and making no effort on their own to clean up the debris and filth in the stricken city. Army stores were shame-lessly pilfered, and many of the "Flips," as we now called them, claiming to be guerillas, spent most of their energies parading about in brand-new GI khaki's, boots, and helmet-liners. Three of us got passes into the city one day, taking our aid kits along with the intention of setting up shop in the poorest section and doing what we could to bind up the wounds and treat the symptoms of any sufferers who showed up. Malnutrition and deprivation were all-pervasive, and we had a quantity of medical supplies that had become slightly soiled or dampened in the process of our landing and multiple relocations, and while not totally sterile, sufficed for this purpose. Posting ourselves on the sidewalk in front of a ramshackle hovel, we cleaned, medicated, and bandaged the cuts, abrasions, and ulcers of scores of children and adults until our stock was exhausted. If nothing else, our efforts kept the flies and dirt out of their lesions for a few days, and maybe was of some help psychologically. I felt utterly wiped out when we got back to camp.[18]

At the end of February and during the first week in March, General Hutchings, his headquarters personnel, and the 544th EB&SR moved down from Lingayen Gulf to join the 594th/564th in operating the port of Manila. While the boat battalions did harbor lighterage, the shoremen repaired dock facilities and renovated the North Harbor piers (designed to accomodate smaller coastal vessels) for mechanized as well as manual cargo handling. Open areas along the bayfront and the Pasig River had to be cleared of debris for the discharge of ramped vessels and the anchorage and maintenance of smaller landing craft. Armies of skilled and unskilled civilians were hired to do long-shore labor—at peak, some 8,000. Even in such numbers, however, their high rate of absenteeism and turnover created severe labor shortages at times.[19]

Our medical workload was heavy as well, due in part to a

steeply-rising incidence of filth-bred diseases, venereal infections, and injuries, both job-related and from drunken brawling. Nevertheless, I managed to keep current on my reports (and won a compliment for their neatness and correct form), and somehow mustered enough energy to clean off all my personal gear, for which there had been no opportunity since our landing, and build myself a locker box to stow it in. Here I also had to serve as mail clerk, responsible not only for deliveries and postings, but ensuring that all outgoing correspondence was censored by an officer. There were film-showings every evening in the 564th open-air theatre—*Powers Girl, Pittsburgh, Passage To Suez, The Petrified Forest,* and *Up In Mabel's Room* were some that I recall. As on Morotai, I was delegated to announce the news during reel-changes, and found my voice projection and enunciation improving as I became less self-conscious. A Christmas-gift package from my step-grandmother Emily arrived in pretty sad shape, with all its edibles spoiled, but some items salvageable—a writing pad and envelopes, a couple of photographs of my deceased grandfather, a tube of toothpaste, soap, shaving cream, and razor blades. Not only was it comforting to renew my friendship with my old sidekick Carl Stegman of the 594th, but among my more recent acquaintances in the 564th was an older enlisted man from Winston-Salem, Paul Sappenfield, one-time custodian of the hunting dogs owned by my father's wealthy business partner, Thomas Ruffin. Paul informed me that a couple of hometown Baptist missionaries, Mr. and Mrs. Robert Dyer, were among the internees recently released in Manila, but before I could contact them, they had been repatriated.

The operation of the rehabilitated Manila railroad had been taken over by the Transportation Corps' 775th Railway Grand Division, and regular train service to and from San Fabian restored, with eight scheduled trains arriving and departing the city daily. The main depot was not far from our encampment, and the echoing locomotive bells and whistles evoked waves of nostalgia. Another poignant reminder of old days at home were our battalion softball games; I fielded for our medic team, though my contribution was admittedly marginal, given my lack of pep and somewhat primitive level of skill. In my more optimistic moments when it seemed that I might last out the conflict, I gave some thought to my postwar education, and toyed with the idea of applying someday to the University of Pennsylvania's Wharton School of Finance and Business, then preeminent in the nation. Bennie and I made several new friends among the Manilans, and sustained our spiritual nurturance by more or less regular attendance at the worship services offered in the 594th's bivouac (the 564th had no assigned chaplain), where I found the sermons among the best I had heard in the Army. Among the USO shows staged from time to time at the battalion theatre was a memorable performance by Jack Benny and Carol Landis, and there were also entertainments by local talent—dancers, musical soloists, and orchestras. One hot, dusty day succeeded another, and, on rare occasions, there was some cloud cover and cooling breezes, bringing promise of rain, but no actualization.[20]

On the other side of the world, Eisenhower's armies in Europe had crossed the Rhine at Remagen and were approaching Berlin from the west, as were the Russians from the east. The death of former British Prime Minister David Lloyd George on 26 March 1945 was only the latest of several subtractions from the ranks of elder statesmen and celebrities which had occurred since our departure from home, among them Al Smith, Wendell Wilkie, McKensie King, John D. Rockefeller, and Kennesaw Landis. Lloyd George's demise provoked long thoughts regarding the brevity and uncertainty of human existence in general, and the distinct possibility of my own violent demise in the near future. One Sunday, a group of us attended Mass at the city's largest intact Roman Catholic Church, offered of course in Latin, little of which could I comprehend, but nonetheless found impressive, with the homily delivered by one of our brigade chaplains. The nave and sanctuary were dirty, dusty, and cobwebbed, like everything else in Manila. Its altar and reredos were strikingly ornate, the statuary plaster-cast, and the floors painted to resemble inlaid marble. That evening, Whitey Ruether, one of my tentmates, and I went sightseeing downtown, and patronized the cleanest cafe we could find, ordering tea with limes, lemonade, buttered toast, and chop suey. When my bill was presented, it came to a whopping seven pesos, putting a big dent in my assets, and restricting my dining thereafter to the mess hall.

All of us were shocked to learn of Franklin D. Roosevelt's demise at Warm Springs, Georgia, on 12 April, plunging everyone into deep gloom. Our national colors, like the others in the city, were lowered to half-mast, people were strangely silent, and there was a pervasive anxiety regarding the capabilities of the virtually-unknown Harry S. Truman, the new arbiter of our destinies. The command structure in the Pacific was simplified by the Joint Chiefs that month, giving MacArthur control of all U.S. Army forces in the Asiatic-Pacifict (henceforth termed AFPAC) and placing Nimitz over all naval elements. A long-delayed Christmas package from my ailing Watson grandparents arrived on 16 April containing handkerchiefs and a pocket bible to replace the crumbling New Testament I had carried since Ft. Bragg days. At a mid-month softball game, our team, by some bizarre fluke, trounced the battalion champions, much to the disgust of their company commander, reputedly a multi-millionaire ex-Wall Street broker, who ordered their coach to field nine new players immediately. This individual, according to the scuttle-butt, had his own private hacienda somewhere in the city, complete with running water, the latest in shower and toilet appurtenances, a wet bar, an electric refrigerator, and all the other comforts of home, so I suppose he had scant patience in the face of life's little disappointments.[21]

Since the vast majority of Filipinos harbored intestinal parasites and many complained incessantly of stomach and bowel dysfunctions, those employed in our kitchen and mess hall were required to submit stool samples at regular intervals to the nearest hospital lab for testing; I decided to do likewise, in light of my chronicly-recurring symptoms; to my distress, the report came back positive for hookworm. When it was confirmed by a second test, I was sent for treatment to the 49th General Hospital and admitted as an inpatient on Saturday, 21 April. The hospital was situated in South Manila's Pasay suburb, in Rizal Baseball Stadium at the intersection of Dakota Avenue and Vita Cruz Street, east of Harrison Park, and near La Salle University. The ballpark, a replica of a typical mid-sized major-league facility in the U.S., was part of an athletic complex, including a football stadium, indoor coliseum, tennis courts, and swimming pool, built just before the war for the Olympics. During the Battle of Manila, the Japanese 2d Naval Battalion had hunkered down in many of these facilities. They had dug bunkers in Rizal's left field and sandbagged the rooms under the bleachers near the third-base left-field foul-line, from which they had been ousted by the tanks and flame-throwers of the 5th Cavalry Squadron after two days of savage combat on 15-16 February. The rooms under the concrete stands had been patched up and cleansed to serve as medical and surgical wards and operating rooms. I was issued a pair of pyjamas, assigned a cot with a mattress and clean white sheets, put on a soft diet, and was free to nap whenever I wished, as though I were royalty! The cuisine was excellent, Red Cross ladies handed out candy and a free pack of cigarettes daily, and the nursing staff, med techs, and Filipina aides were most attentive.[22]

Within a day or two, I was visited by our ranking non-com, S/ Sgt. William McCulloch, and T/4 Willie Novak, who brought my mail. When further testing confirmed the tentative diagnosis of ancylostomiasis, treatment with oral medications was begun. Since some of the city's major water sources were still in Japanese hands, or the distribution facilities under repair, consumption of water was restricted and it had to used sparingly. Each day began with breakfast at 0630—typically, oatmeal, eggs, and canned peaches. Dinner, frequently canned chicken and potatoes and some especially tasty canned milk, was served at 1130, and supper, often featuring steak, at 1630.

By the month's end, my parasites had apparently been flushed out, but the lab found evidence of amoebic dysentery, a more pernicious malady. My hospitalization was extended for several weeks, and a new therapeutic regimen imposed; I was given daily injections of emetine and carbarsone in the buttocks, placed on a more restricted diet, with meals delivered to my bedside on a tray, and confined to bed except to visit the toilet. My bowels soon calmed down, but I was dreadfully weak. The patients on my ward were kept in such strict isolation that we called ourselves "The Untouchables." While thus indisposed, I received a couple of packages from home containing items for which I had asked months before—T-shirts and my college English-Lit textbook of readings. The weather had grown increasingly humid and oppressive, and most of my daylight hours were spent reading or answering correspondence. I had no lack of companionship, for several other amphibs were confined in the 49th General, one of whom, Foy Brown, an old RTG pal, was on my ward.

By this juncture, Adolf Hitler had committed suicide in his Berlin Bunker, and the war in Europe was almost at an end. A compassionate young Filipina named Luminada whose family lived nearby visited Foy and me every other day or so, bringing presents of food (which I accepted out of courtesy, but discretely discarded from fear of becoming reinfected.) Sgt. McCulloch, Cpl. Joseph Buckley, Jack Bannister, and other pals on the outside regularly delivered my mail and shared their magazines, and Captain Lee brought my correspondence course materials so that I could stay current on my lessons. Although the attending physicians had warned me to stay abed, I slipped off to the hospital library one day to brouse among the books, only to become violently nauseated from the powerful drugs I was taking; thereafter I was content to remain in the prone position reading Thomas Wolfe's *Look Homeward, Angel* and William Saroyan's *My Name Is Aram*. A musicale was presented on the ward one evening by string instrumentalists and vocalists of the Philippine Symphony Orchestra, featuring Spanish folksongs, selections from Franz Lizt, and popular semi-classical offerings. Their full orchestral performances, suspended during the Japanese occupation, had recently been revived, and were being broadcast over the radio—I especially enjoyed their rendition of Beethoven's "Eroica". On the lighter side, strolling guitarists and banjoists frequently appeared on the ward, and one evening a pair of quite talented five-year-old Filipino twins put on a song-and-dance act for our amusement.

On the afternoon of May 6, at long last, a brief but deliciously-cooling rain fell, and two days later, another. The latter date was the more memorable, however, for other reasons: not only did it bring the last of my injections, but of far greater moment, Truman and Churchill had officially proclaimed it VE-Day, sending us all into orbit and sparking wild speculation about when the Japanese would come to their senses and call it quits. I could now walk about, and made some new friends among still-bed-ridden fellow patients, one an Atlanta boy of my age, John Cook, and another, Richard Johnson, from Little Rock, Arkansas. Much of my time was spent in conversation with a more mature and sophisticated Australian on the ward, son of the Solicitor-General of Queensland. While serving with the Red Cross, his plane had been shot down over the China Sea, leaving him afloat in an open boat for 48 hours before being rescued. Another wardmate, occupying a nearby bed, was a very frail and ill 47-year-old Navy Lieutenant Commander, who had survived long imprisonment by the Japs, first in Shanghai and then in one of the Manila pens, from which he had recently been released. He had insisted on being placed on an enlisted men's ward rather than with the officers, which endeared him to the rest of us. To our great sorrow, he expired while in our midst, as did another patient at the far end of the ward, a young GI harboring some mysterious lung disease who had importuned our nurses to inform his parents that he had no fear of dying.

In mid-May, I was extremely distressed to learn that my beloved grandmother Watson, confined to a nursing home near Winston-Salem, was on the brink of death. The onset of overcast skies and regular afternoon showers did little to elevate my sombre mood. My therapy had almost run its course, and the physicians warned me that amoebiasis was a dangerous and tricky malady with such a high chance of recurrence that I should avoid any over-exertion for a time. They added that, since the pathogen was still communicable, they would advise that my name be stricken from the KP roster. I was released from the hospital on Sunday, 20 May, and reported in to the 564th Battalion Headquarters, where the duty officer informed me that our subdetachment had been reassigned to the 534th EB&SR and had already gone back to Lingayen Gulf. He told me to take it easy for a couple of days until my orders could be cut and transportation arranged. Since the 564th cantonement had a new Red Cross clubhouse, furnished with padded chairs, a phonograph, and a lending library, plenty of games and magazines, and staffed by two resident hostesses who provided free coffee, cokes, and cookies, I was quite content to loll about there until my departure, though nagged with guilt at the thought of the guys up at the front dodging bullets, living in mud and filth, and subsisting on C-rations.[23]

General Hutchings and 4ESB remained in sole charge of all Manila port operations until superseded on 3 March by a Transportation Corps Port Command with its own harborcraft and stevedoring units. Much had been accomplished in raising, buoying, or cutting up the 500 or more sunken ships in the harbor, ranging from barges and tugs to an 18,000-ton liner—the greatest salvage job in history, according to Navy Commodore William A. Sullivan, who was directing the procedure. Tens of thousands of mines had been swept up, and millions of tons of silt and debris dredged from the channels. The first Allied cargo vessel to enter the harbor, laden with military supplies and food and clothing for civilian relief, had anchored on 1 March, but not for another 16 days could any of the larger freighters moor at the docks. Throughout the ensuing weeks the thin trickle of inbound shipping had widened to a mighty flood, and by April's end, 10,713 military personnel were on port duty. Roughly half of these represented 4ESB units, whose services could not be spared as long as so much of the cargo transfer still required lighterage, and until the damaged wharfs and piers were fully rehabilitated. Not until mid-March had electricity been restored in the city, and it would be July before all the piers were illuminated for night work. Our brigade would remain in Manila under the control of the Port Command until June, when it would be recalled to northern Luzon to stage for the climactic invasion of Japan. Most of our landing craft had seen hard usage in New Guinea and at Lingayen Gulf, compelling the 564th to continue laboring 24 hours a day, seven days a week, to keep them operable. Manila was to be the major base for the end game, and the ever-expanding volume of military personnel and tonnage it transfused would not top out until November 1945, three months after Japan's surrender.[24]

XIII

TO THE BRINK OF ARMAGEDDON

While Sixth Army's XIV Corps had been wrenching Manila from Iwabuchi's iron grip and its XI Corps had been dismembering KEMBU, the 6th and 25th divisions of Swift's I Corps to the north had made hard-won progress southeastward along the base of the mountain wall, punching through Yamashita's forward SHOBU dispositions and smashing up his armor, much of it emplaced as static pill-boxes for lack of petroleum. By February 4, SHOBU forces had been expelled from the towns of Munoz and San Jose, the Highway 5 gateway to the Cagayan Valley and terminus of the railway branch from Tarlac. Patrick's 6th Division had then surged on to Baler and Dingalen Bays on the east coast, sundering SHOBU's ties to Lt. Gen. Shizuo Yokoyma's SHIMBU. Though now isolated, those still-formidable concentrations were by no means close to capitulation, and for months to come, their reduction and strangulation would preempt Krueger's energies. A northward offensive against the SHOBU redoubt was held in abeyance until Yokoyama's minions could be dislodged from their well-entrenched positions along the edge of the Sierra Madres east and northeast of Manila, enclosing the two dams whose lakes had supplied the city's water. The first, Wawa Dam, impounded the Marikina River where it emerged from the mountains to flow westward into the plains as a tributary to the Pasig River, while the other, Ipo Dam, twelve miles north of Wawa, restrained another westerly-flowing stream, the Angat, which emptied into the Pampangas River above Manila.[1]

On 14 February, 6th Division was reassigned to Griswold's XIV Corps and aligned with a brigade of 1st Cavalry to strike east-ward, capture Wawa, then Ipo, and shove the SHIMBU forces deeper into the inhospitable southern Sierras. Sixth Army's Intelligence Staff estimated the enemy's strength on that front at only two-thirds of their actual 30,000. The cavalrymen, attacking in the southern sector, advanced across a level expanse of ricelands to the edge of the highlands until forced to an abrupt halt at Yokoyama's outerworks, a complex of interlaced caves and saps which his tunnel-rats had had ample opportunity to render virtually impervious to Yankee bombing and shelling. The concealed entrances, spouting fire from machine-guns, mortars, and fieldpieces, had to be taken out one by one, a nasty, but not-unfamiliar business for old SWPA hands. On the cavalry's left, a corollary effort by the 6th Division brought few gains and many casualties, among them Patrick himself, who fell mortally wounded, his command passing to Maj. Gen. Charles E. Hurdis. After a month's bruising struggle, the weary cavalry troops on the right were replaced by Leonard "Red" Wing's 43d Infantry Division, and the entire operation handed off to Hall's XI Corps. Then, quite unexpectedly, Yokoyama redeployed the formations manning the southern portion of his line to a more compact position closer to Wawa dam. Following them up into the heights, the GI's of the 43d had no choice other than to repeat their predecessors' disappointingly low-yield tactics. Not until mid-April did MacArthur and Krueger learn from city engineers that the pipeline from Wawa had been disconnected since 1938, and in a quick revision of priorities, ordered the 43d to undertake an all-out attack on the more vital Ipo dam to the north, handing over to Hurdis's thinly-spread 6th the less-imperative task of wearing down Wawa's defenders. At April's end, the 6th, its capabilities sapped by combat losses, illness, and battle fatigue, was relieved from the Wawa front by Chase's 38th Division.

With the American effort now concentrated upon Ipo's seizure, Yokoyama's subordinate in that sector, Maj. Gen. Osamu Kawashima, posted his troops in a wide arc blocking Highway 52, the most feasible approach to the dam, to fend off the encroaching 43d. Rather than attempting an assault up the final convoluted stretch of highway, Wing gambled on a more direct approach from the south over unscouted terrain, setting his column in motion after nightfall, 6 May, in synchronization with Col. Marcos Agustin's guerillas who were sweeping around through the mountains to descend upon Ipo from the north. Kawashima, ordered by his superior to detach part of his forces for a counterthrust against the 38th near Wawa (an error compounded by their miscommunication), was thrown completely off balance by the Wing/Agustin double envelopment. Once alerted to his peril, Kawashima reformed and contracted his lines, but was unable to prevent the 43d from breaking through and capturing a hill just three-quarters-of-a-mile south of Ipo. Wing, bringing his artillery partway up Highway 52, loosed it upon the shrunken Japanese perimeter, while Fifth Air Force planes rained bombs and napalm on the dam's near approaches. Kawashima, finding his position no longer tenable, abruptly withdrew his forces eastward into the mountain fastnesses—so hasty was their departure, in fact, that they neglected to set off the pre-laid demolition charges under the dam. On 17 May, elements of the 43d and Agustin's irregulars, cautiously descending upon their objective from opposite sides of the river, captured the unbreached dam, thereby resolving the water crisis afflicting those of us in Manila.

Meanwhile, on the Wawa front, 38th Division engineers carved out new roads over which flame-thrower tanks and half-tracks could close in and plug up the remaining enemy tunnel appertures, giving Chase's infantry sufficient room for maneuver to crack Yokoyama's left-wing palisade. By 27 May (one week after my release from the hospital), the disjointed SHIMBU's Wawa sector defenses had been forsaken, its tenants retreating deeper into the heart of the Sierras.[2]

While XI Corps' rams had been butting SHIMBU rearward, a fundamental redirection of strategic effort and reallocation of forces had taken effect within the Philippine arena at large. With Luzon's Central Plains and Manila now firmly in Sixth Army's grasp,

MacArthur had sensed that the moment was propitious for expelling the Japanese from the by-passed lower islands. The Joint Chiefs at the Pentagon had preferred that this enterprise be left to the army of the reinstated Philippine government and the resident guerillas, so that the full weight of American resources could be brought to bear upon the Japanese homeland without further delay. MacArthur maintained, however, that for the U.S. not to finish the job throughout the entire archipelago would be a shameful breach of his promise to strike the shackles off all their long-suffering incumbents. In truth, it was not unlikely that the Filipino civilians and the P.O.W.'s still squirming under the heel of the embittered Japanese in the southern islands were now at greater risk than ever. Moreover, many of these locations could provide close-by land basing for an aerial canopy over the planned Anglo-Australian invasion of Borneo, as well as for choking off what remained of the enemy's seaborne commerce between Japan and the East Indies. Time was of the essence, since any new base-construction would have to be undertaken before the advent of the next monsoon season. An equal inducement was the desireability of reopening the Visayan passages through which shipping from Leyte to Manila could be rerouted, thus saving hundreds of miles and many days of transit. On the other hand, to increase Eighth Army's force-level to that required for the implementation of a project of this scope, Krueger would have to be shorn of troops he could ill afford to spare if Yamashita's still redoubtable SHOBU in northern Luzon were to be eradicated anytime soon.

MacArthur, viewing the matter as entirely within his own prerogative, issued orders in early February transferring those elements of the 24th, 40th, and 41st divisions which had been serving with Sixth Army to Eichelberger, leaving Krueger with only six divisions. Thus enhanced, Eighth Army, from its holdings on Leyte, central Samar, and Mindoro, began a rapid-fire series of forays, collectively termed *VICTOR*, from 19 February to 30 June 1945, entailing 14 major and 24 lesser amphibious operations. These were conducted in overlapping stages against the 102,000 Japanese of Lt. Gen. Sosaku Suzuki's

Thirty-Fifth Army, posted all across the hitherto-neglected provinces. The *VICTOR* campaigns were meticulously-planned and, for the most part, smoothly-executed, issuing in the recovery of all the major and many of the minor islands in the central and southern Philippines, above all, Mindanao, second only to Luzon in size and economic productivity. While Thirteenth Air Force, Seventh Fleet, and Filipino irregulars were essential factors in *VICTOR's* resounding successes, the amphibs of 2ESB and 3ESB were no less indispensable—to cite General Heavey, "These were exactly the type of operations for which the Engineer Special Brigade had been designed."[3] In all save one of these actions, the all-too-familiar pattern of island conquest was replicated; after each landing, the enemy garrisons, invariably withdrawing to the interior before giving battle, were sealed off, whittled down, and left to starve, and the invaders diverted to other missions, leaving the task of containment to others, in this case, the guerillas. The capstone of the campaign was sprawling Mindanao/ Zamboanga, defended by a hefty force of 25,000 or more; its subjugation was planned as a split-phase operation, and demanded more intricate maneuvering, hard marching, and sustained fighting. As adjuvants to 2ESB's long-serving 532d and 542d EB&SR's in these multiple seizures, Ogden's fresher 533d and 543d were recalled from Lingayen (except for two of the latter's boat companies still enmeshed there.) His 593d was committed to the evacuation of all troops and stores from Noemfoor, now slated for abandonment, just as Heavey's 592d was detained at Biak.[4]

The *VICTOR* operations can be summarized as follows:

TARGET	L-DATE	DIVISION	COMMANDER	AMPHIBS	CONCLUDED
1. N.W. Samar	19 Feb.	American	Arnold	542 EB&SR	26 Feb.
2. Palawan	28 Feb.	41st	Doe	532 EB&SR	22 Apr.
3. Zamboanga	10 Mar.	41st	Doe	543 EB&SR	15 Aug.
4. Sulu Archipelago	16 Mar.	41st	Doe	543 EB&SR	2 May
5. Panay, W. Negros	18 Mar.	40th	Brush	542 EB&SR	4 June
6. Cebu	26 Mar.	American	Arnold	542 EB&SR	18 Apr.
7. Bohol	11 Apr.	American	Arnold	542 EB&SR	20 Apr.
8. Mindanao	17 Apr.	24th, 31st	Sibert	533/433 EB&SR	15 Aug.
9. S.E. Negros	26 Apr.	American	Arnold	542 EB&SR	12 June

The overall plan called first for the liberation of northwestern Samar, primarily to clear the southern bank of San Bernardino Strait (opposite the toe of Luzon's Bicol Peninsula) as the initial step in reopening the Visayan passages. This was accomplished in mid-February by an Americal/542d EB&SR team. Doe's 41st was assigned the next set of objectives, beginning with Palawan, westernmost of the Philippines, a 15-mile-wide, 275-mile-long ribbon of mountains thrusting up from the sea like the horny plates atop a stegosaurus, running arrow-straight northeast-southwest, and pointing directly at Borneo. Here, with the help of the 532d amphibs, a routine landing was effected on the last day of February at Puerto Princesa Harbor, and several valuable airfields procured. The 41st then undertook the seizure of Mindanao's western extension, the Zamboanga Peninsula (whose monkeys, legendarily, have no tails), shaped like an elephant's trunk and head, and attached by a thin land bridge to the island's preponderant body. On 10 March, with substantial assistance from Col. Wendell W. Fertig's aggressive guerilla organization (who had already garnered a viable airfield on the elephant's forehead at Dipolog), the 41st/543d established a firm beachhead near Zamboanga City, at the tip of the pachyderm's trunk. The Fil-American forces soon overbore the peninsula's 8,900-man Japanese garrison, 5,000 of whom scampered into the hills where they would remain confined for the rest of the war, all but 1,385 eventually succumbing to disease and starvation.[5]

Between 16 March and 9 April, three mini-islands in the Sulu Archipelago, Basilan, Jolo, and Tawi Tawi, tailing off toward northeastern Borneo like exudations from Zamboanga's snout, were also reclaimed by 41st GI's boated in by 543d watermen, endowing future Borneo-invaders with ideal ground basing for AAF/RAAF fighter-support.[6] The mastery of Zamboanga was still in dispute when Eichelberger sicked his 40th and Americal mastiffs—along with the 542d water spaniels—upon the quartet of islands due west of Leyte: triangular Panay, boot-like Negros, worm-shaped Cebu (whose principal port, Cebu City, was eclipsed only by Manila in size and commercial importance), and small, ovoid Bohol, in that order. These beachings, between 18 March and 26 April, went smoothly, except for one near Cebu City, where land-mines carpetting the landing site knocked out ten of the first fifteen amphtraks emerging from the water, delaying proceedings until wholesale defusings-and-removals could be effected.[7]

Five weeks after the Zamboanga insertion, Lt. Gen. Gyosaku Morozumi's 43,000 occupiers of greater Mindanao were challenged by Sibert's X Corps, whose constituent divisions, the 24th (Maj. Gen. Roscoe B. Woodruff) from Mindoro and the 31st (Maj. Gen. Clarence Martin) from Morotai, were sealifted, along with 533d EB&SR, to the huge island's west-central coast at Parang on Illana Bay. Gaining the shore without hindrance, the 24th, in the lead, commenced a 110-mile drive across Mindanao's broad waist to the opposite coast, some over Highway 1, others aboard a flotilla of 533d barges and VII 'Phib LCT's, up the parallelling Mindanao River, as far as Fort Pikit and Kabacan, roughly halfway to the objective (replicating, albeit on a smaller scale, U. S. Grant's movement down the Mississippi Valley in 1862-63.) Having grasped these two key points, the 24th regrouped and resumed its advance by highway over the remaining distance to Davao Gulf, close to where Morozumi had posted the majority of his forces. Turning north at the gulf shore, Woodruff's men fought their way smartly into the port city of Davao and began to assail the enemy's lines on its north and east. Toward April's end, the foot-sore 24th was briefly spelled by the boys of Martin's 31st, who had been guarding the slim tether stretching back to Iliana Bay. Units of both then bore down upon Morozumi's badly-under-supplied legions clumped in the inaccessible mountains of the island's northeast quadrant, with portions of the 31st pressing northward from Kabakan up central Mindanao over the uncompleted Sayre Highway, which ended at Macajalar Bay on the northern coast. Partway up Sayre Highway, some of the latter veered eastward over a rough track with the aim of meeting others battling in the opposite direction from Davao Gulf's upper shore, squeezing the foe from both sides. To speed things along, Eichelberger reinforced Sibert with units from the 40th and Americal Divisions, one of which, landing at Macalajar Bay, drove down Sayre Highway to a linkup with the 31st column from the south, in effect, clinching the campaign. Smaller task forces, toted by the 533d and

543d to various sites and islets around the island's periphery, furthered the dismemberment of Morozumi's corpus. Its segments were left to decompose in the more remote wilds until after Japan put its signature on the peace treaty. The 24th Division's 21st RCT and 533d's B Company, in fact, made one of the Pacific war's last amphibious intrusions on 12 July 1945 at Sarangani Bay on the south coast. The retrieval of Mindanao marked the final payment due on MacArthur's pledge to the people of the Philippine Commonwealth.[8]

A share of the credit for clearing the Visayan passages was owing to Sixth Army, whose pacification of Luzon's Bicol Peninsula merits mention as well. While the XI Corps anaconda was slowly choking the wind out of the main SHIMBU body in the Sierras east of Manila, the Japanese soldiery in southern Luzon, numbering some 15,000 and loosely grouped into a so-called "Fuji Force" (for its commander, Col. Masatoshi Fujishige), had been severed from the larger mass like a drumstick from a roasted turkey by the capital city's forfeiture. A Fuji-manned line now ran from the port of Batangas, below Nasugbu, to the western shore of the volcanic caldera known as Lake Taal, smaller of the two lagoons south of Manila, and on across the narrow "interlaken" to larger Laguna de Bay. Besides holding this bifurcated front and occupying key positions in southern Luzon, Fujishige's isolates maintained a feeble grip on the Bicol Peninsula all the way down to San Bernardino Strait. From various hideouts along the Bicol's western coast, small torpedo boats menaced any Allied shipping venturing up or down the adjacent waterway.

On 24 February, as if it were a hypodermic needle extracting a blood sample, a reinforced-battalion task force of Swing's 11th Airborne Division had punctured Fuji Force's tissue-thin integument with a superbly-executed tri-modal airborne/overland/amphibious raid on another of the enemy's P.O.W. compounds at Los Banos (on Laguna de Bay's southern shore), freeing 2,147 American internees and hustling them back north to Manila. With the city now overrun by XIV Corps, Fujishige could only grit his teeth and hope for the best as he observed Swing's paratroopers and the mechanized 1st Cavalrymen (now under Brig. Gen. Hugh Hoffman) turning their faces in his direction. Early in March, units of these two elite divisions jumped off on each side of

Lake Taal heading for the important road-junction towns of Lipa, Tiaong, and Lucban in southern Luzon. Amphibian support for the joint offensive fell to 592d boatmen, whose watercraft were hauled from Manila on semitrailers and launched on the broad surface of Laguna de Bay to function as an "interior navy." South and east of the lakes, the airborne/cavalry forces methodically eliminated various Fuji positions, chomping their way, so to speak, through the meaty thigh of the turkey leg toward Lamon Bay on the Philippine Seacoast. By 10 April, 1st Cavalry had liberated Mauban, and within 24 hours, llth Airborne had Antimonan in hand. Fujishige and 2,000 of his shredded command, driven onto the upper slopes of Mt. Banahao, hid out for the duration of the war. While llth Airborne picked off vestigial morsels in southern Luzon, Hoffman's troopers entered the Bicol Peninsula itself from Antimonan on 12 April and began gnawing the tendons off the legbone, as it were, and within a month had taken the towns of Naga and San Augustin.[9]

Meanwhile, our battalion's former associates from Lingayen days, Brig. Gen. Hanford MacNider's 158th Regimental Combat Team, having rested up from their exertions against SHOBU in the north, went back into action near Nasugbu on the southwest coast. Moving inland to dispose of any Fuji fragments in its path, MacNider's infantry, in concert with the airborne troopers, reclaimed the northern shores of Balayan and Batangas Bays—and the intervening Calumpan Peninsula—by mid-March, and were working up the slopes of enemy-held Mt. Macolod below Lake Taal when ordered to disengage and embark on another amphibious mission. Returning to Balayan Bay to board the vessels of Capt. Homer F. McGee's Task Group 78.4 (which had already embarked 592d EB&SR and its LCM's at Batangas), the 158th was shipped around the tip of the Bicol Peninsula and put ashore near the east coast port of Legaspi on Easter Sunday, April lst. After a quick and painless entry into the undefended town, where it then became based, it commenced a series of short amphibious hops on 592d's lighters around the Sorsogon Peninsula at the Bicol's extremity, to expurgate the northern litoral of San Bernardino Strait. With this accomplished, the 158th foot-sloggers turned northward and proceeded up the Bicol on the two-lane gravel road pretentiously named Highway l, muscling any remaining hostiles into the peninsula's mountainous spine, and on 2 May embraced Hoffman's southbound lst Cavalrymen at San Augustin. With the eastern banks of the Visayan-Verde Island Passages now secured, along with the newly-recovered islands on their western flank, the waterway could be safely navigated by Allied mariners.[10]

To bar SHIMBU's back door on the Philippine Sea, lst Cavalry's famed 7th Regiment advanced from Siniloan (at the upper corner of Laguna de Bay) into the Santa Maria Valley and up Route 455 to lay seige to the east coast port of Infanta on Lamon Bay. Punching through the only enemy roadblock in their path (at Kapatalin Sawmill) and handing their mechanical mounts over to the 592d boatmen for shipment (along with a battalion of guerrillas) around the Bicol and up Luzon's eastern seacoast to their objective. Proceeding afoot, the unhorsed troopers linked up with the guerillas boated in by the amphibs and pounced on Infanta (l3 May), only to see its garrison flee into the Sierras to join the expiring SHIMBU. The 592d boatmen, now rid of their guerilla passengers and 7th Regiment's motorized steeds, cruised on up the coast to Dingalan Bay and back again, nipping off any enemy remnants still in evidence, using rocket-barges where needed, to complete Yokoyama's encirclement. Their shore battalion mates, who had remained in the Legaspi vicinity, turned their multiple talents to the rebuilding of forty miles of the wrecked Legaspi-Manila railway and running trains over it, thus reenacting the railway-restoration feat of the 532d shoremen on Mindoro. (How I wish I could have been a party to that!) Hence, the 592d amphibs, too, could have laid claim, had they so chosen, to the moniker of "sea-and-iron-horsemen." With its services no longer required in those parts, the regiment was ordered back to Batangas for a well-earned rest.[11]

The only game still afoot and worthy of pursuit by MacArthur's huntsmen on the islands of the southern seas were the 31,000 Japanese occupants of huge, Texas-sized Borneo. Tasked with their ensnarement were the 7th and 9th AIF

Divisions of Lt. Gen. Sir Leslie Morshead's I Australian Corps, and the attached 593d EB&SR Boat Battalion (whose mating shore companies were occupied elsewhere at the time.) The ranks of these two fabled Aussie formations, most of whose surviving veterans had by now served out their time and been released from the service, were filled with unseasoned recruits. Three separate expeditions, known collectively as *OBOE*, all staging from Morotai and loaded aboard Seventh Fleet and Royal Australian Navy vessels, were set ashore ad seriatum at different locations on Borneo, each of the landings preceded by awesomely intense air/naval bombardments.

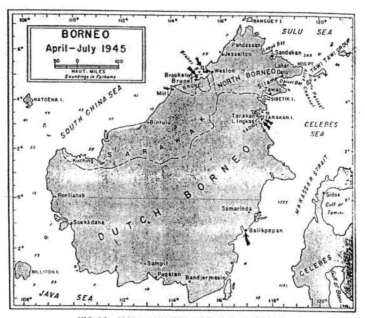

MAP 16. AUSTRALIAN OBOE LANDINGS ON BORNEO

OBOE I, executed on l May by a brigade of Wootten's 9th AIF (with a token representation of Dutch troops) and 593d's Company B, struck Tarakan Island on Borneo's east coast. Their beaching, across wide mud flats, was disrupted not only by a rapid tidal drop of over nine feet, but by rows of enemy-rigged off-shore obstacles, temporarily throwing the operation off schedule. While Aussie sappers levelled the obstructions, Rear Adm. Forrest Royal's bluejackets licked the tidal problem by using pontoon-cube lashups as soon as the waters rose again. Once ashore, Wootten's raw Diggers, though facing stiff opposition and taking a good many casualties, nonetheless obtained their stated objectives. A mightier array of 9th AIF brigades was put ashore on 10 June at Brunei Bay on Borneo's northwest coast with the help of the 593d amphibs. These insertions, though considerably inconvenienced by soggy terrain, were uncontested and resulted in the quick seizure of rich oil fields and valuable airdromes. A third waterborne strike, on 1 July, by Milford's 7th AIF on Balikpapan, the island's chief petroleum depot, heralded by the most monumentally devastating of the *OBOE* precursive aerial bombardments, was conducted with tolerable proficiency (at least on 593d's part.) Aside from the geophysical deterrents marring the landings of the first two expeditions, and despite the absence of experienced shore parties, all three operations were successful. The opposition inland was relatively inept, and by 22 July, the Australian banner proudly waved over Borneo's more industrially-developed enclaves, all hostile forces having been either exterminated, bagged, or chased into the trackless, jungle-choked interior. Although hundreds of oil-well blazes and petroleum-fed fires, ignited by the ham-handed Allied pre-invasion bombardments and enemy saboteurs, had to be extinguished, the heretofore-unblooded "blokes from down under" had acquitted themselves creditably, as evidenced by the gross disparity in casualty figures; Japanese deaths totalled 5,700, ten times those of the victors. Some American critics charged that the *OBOE* operations were an unconscionable squandering of resources, since U.S. submarines and carrier aircraft had already stanched the flow of Borneo's oil to Japan, and that the only thing really accomplished was a restoration of Anglo-Dutch colonialism.[12]

Two months prior to this achievement, and a thousand or so miles to the north, in the ravaged city of Manila, while awaiting my travel orders, I finagled a ride in a 564th EBM truck to the 49th General Hospital for one last chat with some of my still-recuperating fellow "untouchables." On the return leg, the driver made a twelve-mile detour to a shallow river on the city's outskirts in order to wash off his mud-caked vehicle. While he was gunning it back and forth in the stream bed to get the underside thoroughly clean, it became mired up to the wheelhubs. The driver of one of a pair of Seabee dumptrucks loading sand nearby was prevailed upon to try pulling us out, whereupon his vehicle became stuck as well. When the second dumptruck was called in to help, it, too, bogged down. I was delegated to thumb a ride back to camp and summon a crane truck to tow all three out of the muck. I got a lift into the city, but ended up six miles from our cantonement. After a long hike and a succession of short rides, I eventually reached our motor pool weak and weary, only to find that our truck had gotten there ahead of me, having been extricated by a caterpillar tractor. The day's exertions had drained my scant reserves of energy, and after showering that evening, I attended a Filipino stage show at the battalion theatre to cool off and relax, but for the next day or so, if I rose to my feet suddenly, I felt faint and dizzied. On Thursday, 24 May, the orders came through for me to rejoin my regiment up north. I made the 120-mile trip over the rough, bumpy roads in the rear of a deuce-and-a-half, a long, dirty, wearying ordeal, and by the time I reached our camp, I was in a state of near exhaustion.[13]

While 4ESB's other units were laboring at Manila harbor, the 534th had been reassigned from Dagupan to the newly-captured port of San Fernando, La Union, which was being redeveloped into a primary base to supplement or, more accurately, replace the over-stretched Base M facilities at Lingayen-San Fabian. There, our battalion would undertake its most ambitious construction project thus far, a 2,000-bed general hospital, with access roads and ancillary facilities, for the accomodation of some of the mass casualties anticipated from the looming invasion of Japan. The regimental bivouac lay at the base of a small mountain, on whose lower slope the Medical Detachment's bamboo-floored tents had been erected on stairstep-like rice-paddy terraces. The walkways were bordered by stones, and neatly-painted signs outlined by the castle-shaped Corps of Engineers emblem indicated each unit's location. Our encampment was some distance from the town of San Fernando, and offered few of the amenities to which we had grown accustomed in Manila, but it was heartening to be reunited with friends whom I had not seen for months. We had an outdoor movie amphitheatre with showings on Tuesday, Thursday, and Saturday nights, and a Red Cross recreational tent offering coffee and doughnuts, but without hostesses. Resuming my former job as assistant to detachment clerk Hugh Riley and personnel clerk Louis Russell, I found the duties no less exacting than in Manila, but my appetite was heartier and I rapidly regained weight and vigor. It rained every afternoon, with few exceptions, starting about 1500, but when the sun broke through the cloud cover and no breeze was stirring, the heat became miserably oppressive, our tents were like ovens, and we treated multiple cases of heat exhaustion in our infirmary. Such disciplines as saluting and being in proper uniform had been reimposed and were enforced more strictly here than in the easy-going 564th. When time and weather permitted, Bennie and I would climb to the hillcrest and view the scenery. A Manila Railway marshalling yard was nearby, and occasionally, on free days, I strolled over to watch the newly-imported locomotives of the Military Railway Service assemble trains, and befriended some of the operating personnel. A young locomotive engineer from Charleston, S.C., invited me to ride in the cab of his diesel. Having never been on one, it was a novel experience; he carefully explained all of its controls and we traded stories for hours while chugging back and forth.[14]

San Fernando had been taken by guerillas and I Corps troops in the opening stages of the offensive against Yamashita's SHOBU, concentrated at that time in a mountain-girt triangle anchored by the three towns of Baguio, Bontoc, and Bambang. The SHOBU forces, though short on food and ammunition, were superbly led, and outnumbered Swift's 70,000 combat troops two to one. If Admiral Yamamoto had been accounted Japan's foremost naval strategist, Yamashita was preeminent among its soldiery for his astuteness and far-sightedness. His dispositions controlled every concievable pathway through the high mountains enclosing the upper end of the 150-mile-long Cagayan Valley like a gigantic "U." From the Central Plains there were only two feasible approaches to the valley head, either through Bambang or through Baguio, fifty miles farther west. Bambang lay along Highway 5, running from San Jose at the foot of the Caraballos up the Tulavera River Valley and across Balete Pass, the sole alternative to which was the more tortuous Villa Verde Trail. This, scarcely more than a twisting footpath, entered the mountains at Santa Maria, twenty-five miles west of San Jose, ascended over the Salacsac passes, and joined Highway 5 just beyond Balete Pass. Baguio could be reached from the south by one or the other of two paved roads, either Highway 11 from Rosario, or, more circuitously, coastal Highway 3 from Damortis as far as Bauang, then tributary Highway 9 which angled off southeastward to Baguio. Several lesser dirt roads and trails wound down from Baguio into the Cagayan Valley.

Maj. Gen. Percy W. Clarkson's 33d Division on the left was charged with capturing Baguio, then descending into the valley over one or more of the unpaved roads to partake in the northward offensive to the seaport of Aparri at the top of the island. Two divisions in the center, the 25th (Charles L. Mullins, Jr.) and the 32d (William H. Gill), would make a more straightforward thrust by surmounting the Caraballos to Bambang, the former over Highway 5, the latter over the Villa Verde Trail, from whence both would advance down the valley floor to Aparri.[15]

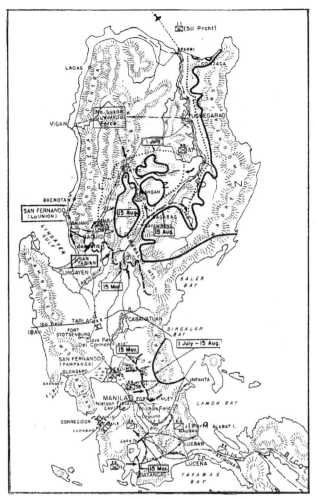

MAP 17. FIL-AMERICAN REDUCTIONS OF
JAPANESE ENCLAVES ON LUZON, AND
ENEMY-HELD POCKETS AT WAR'S END.

During the final week of February and the first days of March, Clarkson's men, probing the approaches to Baguio, initially tried Highway ll, but finding it heavily defended, could make little headway thereon. Other 33d elements, working up Highway 3, had better luck—at the coastal barrio of Caba, some turned due eastward over rough traces into the cordillera, while others continued northward on 3, secured Bauang, then swung southeastward on

Highway 9. The last-mentioned team, encountering only slight resistance, rapidly seized Naguilian, prompting Clarkson to seek Krueger's approval for making his major push over the 3/9 route. Krueger temporized until Beightler's 37th Division, released from its Manila commitments, could be inserted to add its weight to that of the 33rd. Yamashita, with his 10,000-man Baguio garrison on the verge of starvation thanks to Fifth Air Force and Filipino guerrilla interdiction of its supply lines, packed Jose Laurel's puppet government off to Tokyo, allowed any civilian townsmen who so wished to vacate, and shifted most of his local defense forces to the Bambang area before personally decamping. The newly-arrived 37th, taking over the point from the 33d on Highway 9, reached Irison Gorge, three miles short of Baguio, on 17 April, only to find the bridge destroyed and the surrounding ridges infested with troops screening Yamashita's evacuation. After a gruelling six-day delaying action against the 37th elements closing in from the west and those of the 33d who had been pushing up Highway 11 from the south, Yamashita's rearguard abandoned Baguio, while Yank engineers replaced the Irison bridge, and units of both American divisions entered the bomb-shattered town on 26 April.[16]

Having abandoned that corner of his redoubt, Yamashita consolidated his forces to block the I Corps (25th/32d) offensive aiming for Bambang. On that front, Gill's 32d, laboring up the miserable Villa Verde Trail and fighting tooth and claw to get over the Salacsac passes, belatedly entered the village of Santa Fe and the junction with Highway 5 beyond, by which time it was worn down to a nub, though well ahead of Mullins's 25th. The latter, having gotten off to a deceptively easy start on the highway, soon slowed to a crawl in the face of Yamashita's superior positions amid the jumbled peaks, against whom Mullins had no other choice than to wage a succession of sanguinary onslaughts. The 25th finally succeeded in bludgeoning its way over the 3,000-foot saddle of Balete Pass on 13 May, but not for another two weeks could it catch up with the 32d at Santa Fe, having lost 1,510 killed and 4,250 wounded. Though I Corps was now over the hump, it still had 25 hard miles to cover before reaching Bambang, and another

50 to the lowlands of the Cagayan Valley. At this juncture, Krueger mercifully relieved both of its badly-frazzled divisions, leaving the descent to Bambang and the valley's clearance to Beightler's 37th, while off to its left, Clarkson's 33d continued to bear down on SHOBU from the southwest. Beightler's GI's entered Bambang on 6 June, and, once on the valley floor, double-timed down Highway 5 toward Aparri. Much of the territory on the Cagayan's west bank, including a useable airstrip, was already in the friendly hands of Maj. Don Blackburn's llth Filipino Infantry irregulars, part of Col. Russell Volckmann's northern Luzon guerrilla group.[17]

To hasten SHOBU'S disintegration, a special 800-man Connolly Task Force (for its commander, Maj. Robert V. Connolly), comprising two companies of infantry and Rangers, plus medics, a 105-mm. howitzer battery, and Shore Company F of our brigade's 544th EB&SR, took off northward from Vigan up Coastal Highway 3 and circled around to the vicinity of Aparri. Calculating that Yamashita might well attempt to extricate his SHOBU hordes through Aparri and hence was holding it in strength, Krueger had taken the precaution of ordering an airborne descent upon the town as well. Connolly Force, conjointly with Blackburn's guerrillas, prepared to force an entry, but discerning no Japanese presence, simply moved in, while 544th's Boat Company C, another Connolly Force attachment, sailed around to Aparri in its LCM's and joined them. A reinforced battalion of llth Airborne paratroopers floated down on 21 June only to find Blackburn's guerillas and Connolly's team already in possession, whereupon the paras regrouped and pushed southward up the valley. Confronted only by a few Jap stragglers here and there, they were greeted near the Paret River by the northbound 37th Infantry spearhead, and afterwards had little more to do than mop up and patrol partway into the forbidding Sierra Madres, where fragments of SHOBU were prudently keeping their heads down. Farther up the valley and over to the west, elements of the 37th, in unison with the 33d, Volckman's Filipinos, and the newly-introduced 6th Division (released from its contra-SHIMBU endeavors), encircled and whittled down Yamashita's cohorts, now down to 65,000, within the Cordillera.

On 1 July, MacArthur, engrossed in preparations for the assault on Japan, transferred the 6th, 32d, 37th, and 38th to Eighth Army, assigning it the responsibility for wiping up SHOBU's remnants, while Krueger marshalled Sixth Army for the final showdown in the home islands. Not until after the war ended did Yamashita and his holdouts, split into three packs like famished wolves, come forth in surrender, having given their all for eight long months to purchase time for the homefolks to prepare a hot reception for Yankee invaders. Disdaining suicide, the impassive Yamashita stood trial as a war criminal, was condemned, and executed.[18]

Back in late February, while Sixth Army was yet contending for Manila, what would eventuate as one of the war's deadliest clashes had unfolded on Iwo Jima, hundreds of miles north of the Philippines. Curtis LeMay's B-29 Superforts from the Mariannas had been blasting and incinerating Japan's cities on an ever-widening scale, targetting aircraft plants and arms factories, but lacking land-based fighter escorts, were taking heavy losses. The eight-square-mile island of Iwo Jima in the Bonins, midway between Saipan and Tokyo, could provide not only a haven for crippled B-29's returning from the raids, but an advanced pad from which fighter planes could protect them over their targets. To this end, on 19 February, the V Marine Corps was interposed by Admiral Spruance's Fifth Fleet on the barren volcanic island's south coast. The story of the leathernecks' valiant month-long struggle to secure Iwo has been dramatized so often that it needs no repetition; the unmitigated fury of the resistance was an indication of the increasingly desperate mind-set of the Japanese as the shadow of the American war machine spread across their homeland. Iwo's possession brought a dramatic reduction in the long-range bomber attrition, and the salvation of hundreds of battle-damaged B-29's and their crews who could never have endured the remaining 800-mile flight back to the Mariannas.[19]

Since U.S. and British warships and carriers, having achieved

almost complete control of the China Sea, were also clobbering
the Japanese home islands at will, it seemed that a final preparatory
lodgement in the Ryukyu chain could now be attempted without
unacceptable risk. Sixty-mile-long Okinawa, on Japan's very
doorstep, would be an ideal advance staging site for the invasion
that would decide the war. Lt. Gen. Simon Bolivar Buckner's
newly-organized Tenth Army (XXIV Army Corps and III Marine
Corps) was selected for this enterprise. On 26 March, Buckner
feinted by inserting the 77th Division on the Kerama Islands just
to the west of Okinawa. Six days later, on the same Sunday—
Easter or April Fool's Day, as one would have it—that the 158th
RCT and 592d amphibs were entering Legaspi on Luzon's Bicol,
Tenth Army planted its heavy boot on Okinawa's southwestern
coast. Thus began the Pacific War's most expensive and messy
campaign to date, ultimately involving more than 170,000 U.S.
servicemen and 1,213 warships. Awaiting their arrival was Lt. Gen.
Mitsuru Ushijima's 32d Army, 97,000-strong, bunched south of
the landing beaches on the Oroku Peninsula and around the capital
city of Naha, or in the island's nothern reaches, in long-prepared
positions. To get the jump on his assailant and land a paralyzing
blow when and where his susceptibllity was maximal, it was
Ushijima's intention to loose upon him hitherto-unprecedented
numbers of Kamikazes and suicide boats, with a double whammy
to be dealt by the monstrous guns of the super-battleship
YAMATO, currently steaming down at top speed from Tokuyama
on Japan's Inland Sea with a retinue of eight destroyers and a light
cruiser. Scarcely had the imperial squadron reached the halfway
point on 6 April when it was set upon and worked over by hundreds
of American carrier planes. Only four badly-battered destroyers
escaped annihilation; the rest, including the proud YAMATO
herself, were reduced to flotsam. Erupting in volcano-like explosions
from multiple hits, she keeled over and slid to the bottom,
entombing all but 279 of her 2,767 crewmen, her demise marked
by a towering column of black smoke visible, some say, from as far
away as southern Kyushu. The course of the protracted struggle
for Okinawa lies outside the scope of this survey, having been

amply chronicled elswhere, except to note that the magnitude of the ensuing slaughter and destructivity offered an even more grisly preview than Iwo Jima of what lay in store for us in Sixth Army had the war not ended when and as it did. Not until 22 June, when the last of Ushijima's battlements were smashed and he had taken his own life, did the blood-drenched island settle back into quiescence. The price exacted for its subdual included more than 1,000 U.S. aircraft and some 36 of Nimitz's gunships and amphibious vessels. Among the 7,613 G.I.'s and Marines slain was General Buckner himself, and the list of American wounded totalled a staggering 31,807. To this dismal reckoning must be added 4,900 naval fatalities and a like number of seamen injured, largely the handiwork of Kamikazes in their 1,900 sorties. Twenty percent of Japan's entire combat air strength had been erased in the futile defense, along with 110,000 of Ushimjima's soldiery, leaving only 7,872 of their brothers-in-arms to emerge with hands aloft in surrender. Beneath the seaside cliffs lay the shattered remains of tens of thousands of civilians who had chosen death by suicide.[20]

The strife was still raging on Okinawa, Mindanao, Borneo, northern Luzon, and a hundred other lesser venues when Ben Weaver and I at San Fernando obtained three-day passes to Manila for the weekend of 1-3 June. We revisited old haunts and attended a fete at which we met and befriended three exceptionally comely and personable young Spanish sisters from the city's more exclusive Ermita (or University) district, with whom we consorted until it was time to high-tail it northward again. No sooner had we returned to camp than the lowering monsoon clouds began to release their moisture in sheets with crackling lightening and pulsating thunder. Although the rainfall perdured for days on end, sending Niagaras of water cascading down the steps of our hillside "company street," our patched canvass tenting and raised bamboo flooring insulated us from its worst effects. On 8 June, the second anniversary of my high-school graduation, a package arrived from my Uncle Bill Cadman containing "T" shirts and some candy and cookies in prime condition (which my four tentmates and I wolfed down to the last crumb), and from my Grandfather Watson came a copy of Stanley Jones's *Abundant Living*. Along with the stormshowers came an avalanche of correspondence from loved ones, revealing, among other tidbits, that my little sister had won her class beauty contest. As Mother's Day was nigh, I sent Mom a cablegram through the auspices of the Red Cross—my first such transmittal—which, I was assured, would arrive in time; it didn't, not surprisingly, considering the quantity of verbiage which the harried telegraphers had to process. The inclement weather inhibited our battalion's constructive activities, allowing more time to read, write letters, and, on nights when torrents didn't obscure our outdoor movie screen, to ogle such recent releases as *Mr. Winkle Goes To War*, or *Gaslight*, starring Ingrid Bergman, Charles Boyer, and Joseph Cotten. An evening performance by our regimental musicians helped to enliven the sodden atmosphere, and a night or two later, they staged a dance in a nearby school facility whose roof was riddled with holes, but luckily, the rain slacked off during the event. The male-female ratio was about four-to-one and the packed dancehall as hot as blazes, so everyone was soon dripping anyhow, though from perspiration rather than precipitation. Still, it was fun, though later that night our nascent guilt and anxiety were stoked afresh by radio reports of the grim struggle on Okinawa and General Buckner's death, a stark reminder that our own days were in all probability strictly numbered.

Impressed by the rapidity with which a couple of my buddies who had majored in physics or mathematics could make calculations on their slide rules, I asked my Dad to mail one to me (along with a dictionary, not a single copy of which was to be had anywhere in camp.) I also plodded through my next-to-last correspondence-course lesson, an unbelievably dull exposition entitled *Procedure Before Regulatory Bodies*, and on the following morning, a Sunday, almost drifted off to sleep during Chaplain Lindemann's only slightly less somniferous sermon on "Christ's Marvelous Invitation." In the mess hall of the company with which we were billetted, a fellow named Thomas Archibald, observing my Guilford College T-shirt, asked if I were a North Carolinian; in further conversation it emerged that he, too, was a native of Leakesville—surely the only other individual on Luzon hailing from my undistinguished birthplace.

At the end of June, Ben and I wheedled another weekend pass to Manila along with jeep transportation. A dozen miles short of the city, we were halted at a Military Police checkpoint and taken to their lockup because our jeep's serial number appeared on the list of stolen vehicles. After interrogation by the Desk Sergeant, we were detained until he could phone our headquarters and check us out—the jeep had been reported missing soon after our landing at Lingayen Gulf, but had been recovered within a few hours; the motor officer, however, had neglected to clear the record. While our story was being verified, lunchtime passed, and overhearing our complaints of hunger, the M.P.'s invited us to eat in their mess, where we dined sumptuously on fried chicken, freshly-baked bread, and mashed potatoes, with ample butter—undeniably the tastiest meal we had eaten overseas. Duly legitimated and with full bellies, we were released and sent on our way. In Manila that weekend we sought out several friends of long standing in other 4ESB outfits, among them Carl Stegman, with the 594th. Ben also tracked down his brother-in-law Robbie, an airman at Nichols Field, just five weeks from stateside. On our last night in town, Bennie, Robbie, and I escorted the three aforementioned Spanish senoritas to a night club, for a couple of pleasant hours of socialization.

Back in San Fernando, our routines were spiced one magical evening by a USO-sponsored live performance of *Oklahoma* with its clever lyrics, intricate choreography, and shapely chorus girls. Then, abruptly, on or about July 4th, Captain Lee's subdetachment, myself included, was again remanded to Manila to service our regimental boat battalion, just in from Balimba, Australia, and now doing harbor lighterage, and, as before, I was to be the emanuensis. The "boats" were encamped near Intramuros, in a once up-scale area, now an obscene square-mile desert of collapsed masonry, rusted tin roofing, and twisted metal. While the rubble-choked streets had been cleared by bulldozers, the only

structures still standing were a couple of battle-scarred high-rises—
a most disheartening spectacle. During our resettlement, the city
was beleaguered by blinding rains and stiff winds which blew
through our tents, dampened our bedding, and drenched anyone
stepping outside into the foul mud. With no functional waterlines or sewers, we were reduced, as often before, to digging latrines
and using helmets for washbasins. While the boatmen were adjusting
to their sordid new surroundings and port duties, we had to exert
extraordinary efforts at disease control, and mounds of paper work
required my attention. The Red Cross made a commendable effort
to raise morale by sponsoring a dance somewhere in the vicinity, but
most of the attendees were in a glum mood, the females for the most
part WAAC's of more advanced age or desperately-needy Filipinas
and Mestizas, making it hardly worth the trouble, as I saw it. By
mid-July the rains had eased off somewhat, and more lively after-
hours entertainment beckoned at the 594th's newly-erected "Club
Seahorse", with its wider choice of refreshments, better dance music,
and more enticing representation from the fair sex. One evening,
Cpl. John Bannister and I hiked over to a midtown auditorium for
the second public concert of the Manila Symphony. It drew only
two hundred or so servicemen, Army nurses, and WAAC's, so we
had preferential seating, with electric fans overhead to keep the dank
air moving; the quality of the performance was superlative, and had
it not been for the voracious mosquitoes, I would have lost myself
completely in the sublime renditions.

Our accumulated mail at APO 70 was forwarded to us in a
single delivery that week, from which I learned that my parents
were having difficulty in keeping up their mortgage payments. Since
I was economizing by doing my own laundering and avoiding the
city's temptations, I increased my monthly allotment to them by
ten bucks, and used my free time to read *Of Human Bondage* and
von Clausewitz's *On War*, and to complete my final correspondence-
course assignment. After a time we moved from tents into more
habitable cement-floored living-and-working quarters with screened
windows and doors and running water, luxuries none of us had
enjoyed since leaving the U.S. I drew frequent night duty as CQ

(Charge-of-Quarters) at the dispensary, medicating any "clients" who showed up, mostly for cuts and scrapes, fevers, aches, and intestinal disorders, or giving shots and drawing blood for testing. I had occasion to to visit one of my roommates, Cpl. William Stehle, former Manhatten stockbroker, who was undergoing therapy for a stomach ulcer at a military hospital on the city's eastern edge where the upper crust resided. I had heard of their luxurious gated mansions, but never seen them, and was dumbstruck at the chasm between their lavish lifestyle and that of the ragged and wretched multitudes in the inner city. As I commented to my folks, the revelation almost turned me into an indignant Marxist.[21]

With the advent of the fateful month of August 1945, peace feelers were being surreptitiously put forth by some of Emperor Hirohito's civilian advisers through the Kremlin, and everything seemed in a state of suspension, though the planning and build-up for the final match were proceeding apace. The prospective sledge-hammer assaults on the home islands, collectively code-named *DOWNFALL*, were to occur in two stages. The first, *OLYMPIC*, aimed at southern Kyushu on "X-Day" (1 November, tentatively), would employ fourteen of the seventeen infantry divisions already in AFPAC, with the intent of establishing bases from which the second, more pulverizing, blow was to be delivered on Honshu, Japan's largest island. The latter operation, *CORONET*, scheduled for "Y-Day," 1 March 1946, having as its objective the Tokyo-Yokohama area, would require twenty-five divisions, some already present in the theatre, the others to be redeployed from Europe. Nimitz's Third Fleet would provide general strategic support for both phases of *DOWNFALL*, with Fifth Fleet assigned the amphibious tasks and provision of direct support, assisted by carriers from Britain's Asian Fleet. *OLYMPIC* would be undertaken by Sixth Army with the stated mission of conquering and holding the southern third of Kyushu, while *CORONET* would be Eighth Army's responsibility. The magnitude of the *DOWNFALL* incursions would far outweigh anything seen in *OVERLORD*, the Normandy invasion.

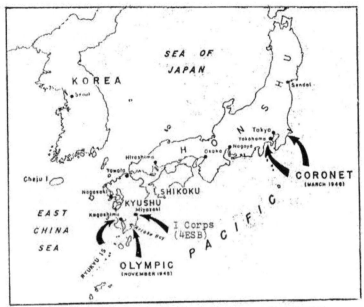

MAP 18. PLANNED <u>OLYMPIC</u> AND <u>CORONET</u> INVASIONS OF
JAPANESE HOME ISLANDS.

The assault elements of *OLYMPIC* would consist of four Corps, each of three divisions, with another two divisions as follow-up and three to be held in readiness as strategic reserves, tallying 766,700 men, 134,000 vehicles, and 1,470,930 tons of materiel. Their shipment and coverage would require 1,315 major vessels and 40 ground-based Air Groups, or 2,794 planes. These projections would undergo modification, but as the plan emerged in its essentials at July's end, the *OLYMPIC* forces, like Neptune's trident, were to strike at three sites in southern Kyushu. Innis P. Swift's 94,546-strong I Corps (25th, 33d, and 41st Divisions) would land on beaches between Yamazaki and Matsusaki, capture the port of Miyazaki and its airfield, and shield Sixth Army's northeastern flank. Accompanying them would be tank, tank-destroyer, amphibian-tank, and amphibian-tractor battalions, along with a profusion of combat-support units, including our 4ESB, with the 534th EB&SR attached to the 25th Division, the 544th to the 33d, and the 594th to the 41st.

The thicker middle prong of the trident, Charles P. Hall's XI Corps, numbering ll2,648 men of the lst Cavalry, Americal, and 43d Infantry divisions, and separate ll2th Cavalry Regiment, with tank and amphibian-tractor attachments plus Heavey's 2ESB, would punch into the Shibushi-Kashiwaba area of Ariake Bay with the mission of seizing Shibushi and its airfield. Finally, Marine Maj. Gen. Harry Schmidt's V Amphibious Corps, formed of the 2d, 3d, and 5th Marine divisions with their tank and amphtrak components, and Army reinforcements, 98,933 men all told, would hit the Kushikino area, take Sendai, and protect Sixth Army's northwestern flank. No Army amphibs would be assigned to Schmidt's array, since his Marines were prepared and equipped to handle their own ship-to-shore work, and there would not be sufficient time to reassemble 3ESB's scattered components before X-Day. Ogden's webfoots would, however, be participants in *CORONET*.[22] At a 25 June conference in MacArthur's Manila headquarters, attended by Heavey, Ogden, and Hutchings, it had been agreed that 2ESB and 4ESB, once the Kyushu objectives were attained, would be released from Sixth Army and returned to the Philippines to stage for *CORONET* with Eighth Army (and First Army elements from Europe.) Krueger, however, doubted that the two brigades could disengage from the Kyushu embroglio soon enough to join with 3ESB in support of the Honshu endeavour, so the consensus was that many of the *CORONET* formations would have to provide their own shore parties. In any event, all seahorse units would have to stretch every nerve and sinew to amass sufficient landing craft, machinery, and vehicles for this prodigious task, and get everyone and everthing in shape for what lay ahead. Two Base Shop Battalions, 411th and 692d, were being moved from New Guinea up to Batangas in southern Luzon to erect a new barge-and-LCM-reassembly plant as insurance against anticipated lighter attrition, and in early August, 2 ESB's command center was relocated from Leyte to Manila, and that of 3ESB from Biak to Batangas, for more convenient liaison with Sixth Army's staff.[23]

As the brass-hats on Luzon mulled over the invasion plans and we all sweated in contemplation of the impending Armageddon, in full awareness that there would be no furloughs home until it was over, the Pentagon ordered a massive redeployment of some fifteen divisions from the European theatre to USAFFE. The provisional 5th and 6th ESB's organized for the Normandy landings had been reconstituted and transferred from Le Havre, France, to Gordon Johnston during June and July in preparation for *CORONET*, just as 1st ESB's Headquarters and Headquarters Company had already been sent to Okinawa to support Tenth Army's operations.[24] To arrest a growing disaffection among long-serving combat veterans in Europe at the prospect of exposure to another, even more sanguinary brawl in Asia (the "Why Me?" syndrome), the Pentagon had introduced a "point system" governing priority of separation from service. An individual earned one point for each month in uniform, another for every month overseas, 5 for each campaign in which he had participated, another 5 for every combat decoration earned, and 12 for each dependent child (up to a maximum of 3.) Those with the highest scores were eligible for discharge, unless "military necessity" dictated retention, and those with lower scores assigned either to occupation duty in Europe or sent to the Asiatic-Pacific. To the extent that the flow of recruits from training centers in the U.S. could be sustained at the requisite levels, the high-point men would be shipped home for separation as their units received replacements. This system had taken effect on 12 May, and immediately every non-professional in the Army began to calculate his "ASR" [Adjusted Service Rating] score. Some units suffered precipitous declines in combat efficiency as their most experienced personnel became separated; the most egregious example was the 45th Division, in action since the Sicily landings in July 1943—83% of its personnel qualified for immediate release.[25] There was precious little time for units having large quotas of raw replacements to be retrained for the kind of savage combat they would face against the fanatical Japanese. This did not auger well either for a swift victory or for holding casualty figures down to levels tolerable to a war-weary America. Moreover, among the premier commanders, there were wide discrepancies in casualty projections for *DOWNFALL*—in late June, MacArthur estimated 105,050 for the first ninety days of *OLYMPIC*, while Nimitz calculated a probable 49,000 during the first thirty days alone, and, by extension, 147,000 within three months. In General Marshall's opinion, lossses for the first thirty days would not exceed 31,000, or 93,000 for the initial trimester. (These figures included neither non-battle deaths and injuries, nor the probable toll of *CORONET*.)[26] All I can say with confidence is that the 534th, or so I was informed at some point, based on the reckoning of MacArthur's Medical staff, could expect casualties in the range of 80% of its regimental complement, since we would be in the initial landing waves—in other words, eight out of ten of us would fall. This did not, and does not today, a half-century later, seem the least bit exaggerated in light of what we now know about the Japanese counteractive measures. The battle slogan of their 32d Army on Okinawa had been "One plane for one warship, one boat for one ship, one man for ten of the enemy or one tank." Unlike the enemy's tactical doctrine governing island-defense in the southern seas, which called for only token opposition against invaders on the beaches to conserve resources for more lethal response inland, in this instance, massive resistance would begin on the high seas.

Unprecedented numbers of Kamikaze aircraft and manned flying bombs, or "Bakas," as well as submarine-borne "Kaitens" or humanly-guided torpedoes, would be loosed upon the invasion fleets as they approached the "X-Day" beaches, in the expectation that 30% to 50% of the American ships, especially the troop transports, could be wiped out well offshore. The Tokyo high command expected to have 10,700 Kamikaze planes ready by early fall, and the Imperial Navy's nineteen surviving destroyers were to be sacrificed in this manner as well. As our vessels neared the shoreline, they would have to penetrate thick belts of naval mines and risk destruction by hundreds of small suicide surface boats. Dense networks of underwater obstacles would rip open or hang up our landing craft, and frogmen with hand-held explosive devices would emerge from underwater concrete cells to blow in hulls. In addition to all of this, our assault forces would have to endure heavy shellfire from pre-registered artillery emplaced in countless well-protected and camouflaged bunkers and caves overlooking the beaches.[27] The longest stretch of viable landing shore—some fourteen miles—would be in the Miyazaki vicinity, where the I Corps, including our 25th Division/534th EB&SR team, would be landing. Here invaders would confront cave-pocked cliffs sheltering approximately 61,000 coastal-defense and back-up troops on X-Day. Once we were ashore, General Yokoyama, directing the Kyushu sector defenses, planned to bring forth his mobile reserve troops and tanks on X+1 to fall with full force upon the surviving intruders. The most ferociously-annihilistic resistance would be encountered on Honshu, where women, children, and the elderly were being trained to wield spears, hatchets, butcher knives, and any other available household tools or implements against the Yanks. Agents of mass destruction such as poison gas, highly-toxic bacteria, and crop-destroying chemicals were also being stockpiled by both sides, with well-nigh unimagineable consequences. There can be little doubt that, even barring the atomic bomb, the United States would have prevailed, but at the cost of hundreds of thousands of American lives and probably millions of Japanese.[28]

From 17 July to 2 August, the third, last, and longest consultation between the leaders of the Grand Alliance took place in Potsdam, Germany. Truman, of course, represented the United States, and Stalin, the U.S.S.R., while Prime Minister Churchill, defeated in Britain's 26 July general election, was displaced midway through the parley by Clement Attlee, with Ernest Bevin as foreign secretary. Immediately upon Truman's arrival, he was informed of the successful test explosion of an atomic device on 16 July at Alamagordo, New Mexico, and shared this trump card with the other heads of state. It being all too evident that Japan would not accept "unconditional surrender" as she understood it, a "Potsdam Declaration" was issued over the names of Truman, Atlee, and Chiang Kaishek, delegate of co-belligerent Nationalist China, reassuring the Japanese people that the term applied only to their armed forces, not to their nation per se. If they would agree to a complete disarmament, military occupation, unimpeded election of a responsible, peacefully-inclined government, and inaugurate freedom of speech and religion, they would not be "enslaved as a people or destroyed as a nation." Though there was no specific reference to Japan's emperial institution, the declaration implied that Hirohito might be retained in office if his subjects so desired. The incumbent Prime Minister, Kantaro Suzuki (successor to Kuniaki Koiso, who had resigned after Okinawa's invasion), sharing the Emperor's conviction that unless the war were quickly terminated, Japan was doomed, persisted in Koiso's efforts to persuade the "neutral" Soviets to mediate on her behalf. Still hoping to obtain the best deal possible through diplomatic negotiation, yet proclaiming to the Japanese public that the war would be prosecuted to the bitter end, Susuki discerned no particular benefit in accepting the Potsdam Declaration and simply ignored it. President Truman, persuaded that resort to the new terror weapon offered the only rational alternative to an indefinite prolongation of hostilities at an astronomical cost in human lives, approved its release upon a Japanese city as soon as weather conditions permitted. While he was enroute home from Potsdam, two days from Norfolk, the first bomb, "Little Boy," was dropped by the B-29 "Enola Gay" on Hiroshima at 0815 (Greenwich Mean Time), Monday, 6 August. The startling news was announced at large from the White House within four hours of its receipt, on 5 August (West Longitude date.) Stalin, having agreed at Potsdam to enter the Asian conflict without delay, had his legions in place two days later, and declared war on Japan on the 9th, attacking Manchuria forthwith on both eastern and western flanks. The unleashing of a second nuclear bomb, "Fat Man," on Nagasaki the same day exposed the futility of Japanese intransigence, and enabled the emperor to convince his Supreme War Council that the jig was up.

By 14 August, Japan had capitulated, and hostilities ceased except in North China, Manchuria, and the Kuriles, where the Soviet Union continued to pursue unilaterally its territorial ambitions. Not until the 31st did the Russians finally desist.[29]

In Manila, meanwhile, as Hiroshima's inhabitants lived out their final hours, our infirmary did a brisk business. After my labors ended that last Saturday before history was torn asunder, I sought distraction in rereading and burning accumulated letters from home, and attending Manila Symphony's evening performance of Wagner, DeBussy, and Tschaikovsky. At its close, I was rudely returned to reality by the city's clamor, stench, and squalor.[30]

XIV

NAGOYA AND HOME

Rain fell steadily in Manila on Sunday, August 5th, 1945, and I devoted most of the day to writing letters to friends and relatives and playing with a lively mongrel puppy whom we had rescued from the streets and endowed with the unimaginative name of "Spotty." Monday, the fateful "dawn of the Atomic Age" (unless that neologism was preempted by the Alamagordo test date), was generally quiescent in our parts aside from the usual accumulation of infirmities at the aid station. While the Allied news media feasted upon Harry Truman's announcement of the Hiroshima horror, it sparked little agitation among us amphibs as we pondered its effect upon our immediate future. In fact, I spent a good bit of the morning of 6 August reading Shakespeare's *King Lear* and *Newsweek* Magazine, and in my jottings to my parents that evening, made only passing reference to "The Bomb," elaborating instead upon such trivia as the exceptionally tasty noontime feast of southern fried chicken served up by our mess. (Perhaps the scale of the slaughter on Okinawa and from the more recent fire-bombings of Tokyo and other major Japanese population centers dulled its mental impact. Certainly none of us yet comprehended its implications for mankind's future.) That afternoon I accompanied a buddy on a routine trip to the hospital in our ambulance, and on our way back, we stopped for awhile in the center of the city to hunt for a souvenir for one of his relatives. There I suddenly became aware that I had conspicuously flouted uniform dress regulations by wearing rolled-up suntan pants, a college T-shirt, an unbuttoned fatigue jacket, and no headgear. To avoid a confrontation with the

M.P.'s, we furtively ducked down side streets to regain the shelter of the "meat wagon" (as our ambulance was commonly tagged), and drove straight back to our bivouac. Upon reflection, possibly this subliminal act of rebellion against military convention bespoke an unconscious need to assert my individuality before we jumped off on the dreaded invasion and our world went completely berserk.

Awaking on Tuesday with an intuition that some profound change in our destiny or fortunes was imminent, I packed up all my books and surplus belongings and mailed them home. Sure enough, within forty-eight hours, early on August 9th, the same day the second nuclear bomb was dropped, I was roused from slumber by my colleagues' jubilant shouts that Russia had declared war on Japan the previous day. Disinclined to take anything that Stalin said or did at face value, I was somewhat more guarded than they in expressing elation. The frenzied speculation in our ranks triggered by this turn of events continued into the wee hours of the night, and I was so groggy the next day (Friday, 10 August) that I could not resist taking an afternoon nap, in which I was indulged only because I was slated for CQ duty that night.

After my shift ended at midnight, I fell back into the sack and slept like the dead for several hours until startled once more by some vague hubub and headed for the shower to clear my head. While I was showering, Ben Weaver, who along with Billy Lavinder and Hugh Riley had just arrived in town on a weekend pass from San Fabian, searched me out and greeted me with the news that Japan had made a bid to surrender. I hurriedly dressed and the two of us went into the heart of the city where the streets were overflowing with delirious celebrants, yelling and singing and cavorting about with total abandon. Booze was flowing freely, and a United Press cameraman was taking random photos of the mob on Rizal Avenue, in a couple of which Bennie and I appeared. I glanced at my wrist to check on the time and discovered that my watch was missing. Either its band had snapped while I was slapping someone on the back, or some adroit thief had cut it off. Since it was my most treasured possession, I was quickly brought to my senses and dragged Bennie back to the safer confines of camp, where similarly unrestrained hilarity reigned until I was overcome by sleep at 0230 on Sunday, 12 August.

A few hours later, during which most of my companions kept their ears glued to the radio, we learned that the celebrations had been premature, since the Allies had not yet announced their response to the Japanese proposal. Evidently folks at home were flooding the White House with telegrams and phone calls urging President Truman to disregard the offer. Some news commentators were claiming that domestic polls indicated 60% of the American public favored continued prosecution of the war. We, on the other hand, were 100% for ending it immediately, if not sooner, and were infuriated by this homefront bellicosity, since it was we who would have to pay the piper. Needless to say, our indignation changed to fervent relief at midnight 13/14 August when it was announced that the Nipponese overture would be accepted, allowing Hirohito to remain in office with the stipulation that he would be subject to the will of the Allied Supreme Commander, that all territories Japan had conquered since 1895 be handed over, and that her armed forces totally dissolved, with a cease fire to take effect on 15 August. At that moment, pandemonium broke loose all around us; there was a mighty chorus of yells, flares lit up the sky, gunshots erupted, the ships in the harbor shot off star shells and sounded their horns, and it was hours before anyone thought of sleep again.[1]

Within days the entire 4th Brigade was ordered back to San Fabian, and by 21 August, all of our units had been reunited on the shores of Lingayen Gulf. At this point, I was jumped up to Technician Fifth Grade (equivalent in pay to Corporal), fulfilling my long-standing prediction that the war would come to end before I ever got a rating. A few hours after learning of my promotion, I was scheduled for CQ again, but with no timepiece, I dawdled overlong when I should have been attending a briefing conference. For this lapse, I drew an extra night's duty, much to the amusement of my pals, who taunted me roundly with the allegation that I had shown myself unworthy of higher office within hours of receiving my stripes. I caught no rest for another forty-eight hours, for no sooner had that night's duty ended than I was handed the task of overseeing a two-man detail of stockade prisoners, under the watchful eye of their guard, to burn down and fill in an old latrine. Though the job was finished by noon, a stack of correspondence and reports had to be attended to before it was time to go on CQ again.

The monsoon rains had not abated since our change of station, but the war's sudden halt had brought such an emotional high that one heard little grousing about the weather—or anything else, for that matter. The sun emerged on the 25th, bringing blistering, withering heat. The mail delivery that day included a package from my parents containing my long-awaited dictionary and slide-rule. With the world now more or less at peace, each of us had meticulously calculated his ASR [Adjusted Service Rating] score for release from the service. Benny and I, as the most junior of the medics, both in terms of age and length of service, had thus far amassed a mere 40 points, a melancholy reminder that our soldiering days were far from over. Two of the unit's older heads of families, by contrast, were already eligible for discharge and made their departures shortly thereafter. To divert my mind from fantasies of going home, I practiced algebraic computations on my slide rule and read *The History of Rome Hanks*.

The skies became thickly overcast again within twenty-four hours, as several of us were granted permission to take a truck up into the mountains to see the famous resort of Baguio—or what was left of it. The long drive up the steeply-inclining serpentine road was wearing, but it was exhilarating to emerge above the cloud layer and breathe cool, fresh air. Enough remained of the ruined town, nestled in a shallow bowl at the crest of the mountains, to suggest how attractive it must once have been, with its paved streets converging upon a well-manicured park surrounding a sparkling little lake. We had brought along some ten-in-one rations for a picnic lunch atop one of the heights overlooking Baguio. Selecting a suitable spot for a repast, we were munching away contentedly when suddenly there was a heavy downpour, forcing us to cut our tour short and motor back down the treacherous road to sealevel while there was still enough daylight. The return trip was distinctly nerve-wracking at times as the truck lurched around corkscrew curves and slithered down the long grades, but when the rain slackened and we broke out of the mist, we could glimpse through rifts in the surrounding verdure the silvery ocean far below, and were soon enveloped in the humid, drowsy atmosphere of the lowlands. It was a blessing to roll to a stop, climb off the uncushioned deuce-and-a-half, and rest our shaken bones.[2]

As that singularly-memorable August drew to a close, there was leisure to revisit our old stamping-ground of Dagupan as well. The place was much changed—though as malodorous as ever, there were many new buildings, prices had fallen sharply, store-shelves were well-stocked, and the citizenry more adequately-clad, better nourished, and generally more assertive. We passed a lively Friday evening in sight-seeing and conviviality, returning to camp well after midnight of 31 August/1 September, only to be roused out within five hours or so for reveille and roll-call. Later that Saturday morning, our whole regiment, now including the boat battalion, was mustered on the beach under a searing sun for a parade and presentation ceremony. The uniform of the day was pressed khaki's and helmet liners, and it was as hot as the nethermost regions of hell. After marching past in review, we were drawn up in formation at parade rest, with the Medical Detachment at such a distance from the reviewing stand where General Hutchings, Colonel Naylor, and lesser luminaries were holding forth that I couldn't hear a word of the orations. As I recall, it was on this occasion that the 534th was awarded its "Meritorious Unit" plaque for "superior performance of duty" on Morotai and Luzon, entitling each of us to wear a small golden wreath patch on the sleeve of his blouse (should the day ever come when we would again be wearing woolen dress uniforms.) The 534th, the 564th EBM Battalion, and the l64th Ordnance Company were the only 4ESB units thus honored. The ceremony lasted for two dreary hours under the insufferable sun, during which several men fainted and had to be carried off the field, and all of us were soaked in sweat.[3]

That same weekend, on Sunday, 2 September, another, vastly more momentous, ceremony—one formalizing the radical realignment of two entire civilizations—was enacted on the deck of the battleship MISSOURI in Tokyo Bay, whereat MacArthur accepted the signed surrender of the representatives of the Japanese government. These solemnities signified the ascendancy of a set of principles articulated in a document produced on 29 August by the U.S. State, War, and Navy Departments, envisioning a reborn Japan graced with a democratic polity, universal suffrage, and a respect for human rights, and endorsing the Charter of the United Nations. The Allies foreswore any attempt to impose a form of government not in accord with the freely-expressed will of her people. Her national boundaries were henceforth to embrace only the four main islands and some lesser ones to be specified at a later date. She was to be thoroughly disarmed and demilitarized, encouraged to legislate protection for individual liberties, and assisted in rebuilding an economy that would adequately sustain a decent standard of life. General MacArthur was named Supreme Commander for the Allied Powers [SCAP], with formulation of policy and review of his actions reposed in a Far Eastern Commission representing all the victors. (In effect, however, the occupation was to be exclusively an American affair, and Japan's reconstruction would be shaped primarily by the initiatives of Douglas MacArthur.)[4]

While Halsey's mighty Third Fleet had steamed into Tokyo's Sugami Bay on 27 August, the first U.S. troops (except P.O.W.'s) on Japanese soil had been an advance party of aviation engineers, meteorologists, and 11th Airborne paratroopers flown in twenty-four hours later to Atsugi Airfield forty miles southwest of Tokyo to prepare for MacArthur's arrival. On 30 August, the occupation had begun in substance when elements of the 1st Marine Division landed at Yokosuka Naval Base. Within another five days, the 1st Cavalry Division had arrived by sea from Batangas, Luzon, lightered in from their transports by 592d EB&SR's Boat Battalion.

The distribution of the occupying forces across the length and breadth of Japan reflected, by and large, the plans which had been drawn up for the invasion: Sixth Army would occupy Kyushu, Shikoku, and the western half of Honshu; Eighth Army would cover eastern Honshu, Hokkaido, and the southern half of Sakhalin; and Tenth Army would be stationed in Korea. Seahorse units would be scattered abroad over the land, with Heavey's 2ESB the most far-flung. Its headquarters would be located at Yokohama in the Eighth Army zone, in company with the 542d EB&SR and the 592d's Boat Battalion. The 532d was consigned to the Tenth Army in Korea (under the administrative control of lst ESB Headquarters), while the 592d shoremen would remain in the Philpines. The Third Brigade would be headquartered on Hokkaido, with its units dotting northern Honshu and Kyushu. The components of 4ESB were to be posted in the Tokyo, Kobe, and Nagoya areas—the 594th at Yokohama, the 544th at Wakayama, and the 534th at Nagoya.[5]

During the coming months, all U.S. naval and land forces were to undergo drastic contraction, relying solely upon voluntary enlistments to refill the units which were to be retained as part of the nation's permanent military establishment. Since MacArthur had recommended the inclusion of an ESB in the peacetime Regular Army, and Heavey's 2d had been selected for this distinction, its sojourn in the Far East with the occupation forces would be of only brief duration. Having served in the theatre far longer than its successors, and sustaining heavier combat losses (84 fatalities and 586 wounded), it was the first to return home to a permanent station at Fort Ord, California. Only 300 men were left in its ranks after the subtraction of all its high-ASR-score personnel. Formally relieved at Yokohama on 15 September, it had to be hurriedly recruited up to strength. An infusion of 4,600 new enlistees soon restored its viability, though not until 3 December was sufficient shipping available to transport its units back to the States. (It would remain on the active list for only one more year, passing into history on 31 December 1946.)[6]

It took many weeks for 3ESB and 4ESB to make the transition from various parts of the Philippines to Japan. The former, with its command currently vested in Col. W. S. Moore, and centered at Batangas, Luzon, was slated for only a short tour with the Eighth Army occupation forces before it, too, was shipped home to

Portland, Oregon, for inactivation in January 1946. We in 4ESB faced a somewhat longer stretch with Sixth Army.[7]

During the week following the surrender, while MacArthur settled regally into his new seat of power in Tokyo and grasped the helm to steer Japanese society from oligarchical militarism to democratic pacificism, those of us within the microcosm of the 534th at San Fabian, Luzon, readied ourselves for the pending move northward in league with the 25th Infantry Division. We recieved innoculations against plague and cholera, and at this point I had another brief flirtation with disaster—we had just been issued new combat boots of a type which buckled around the calves, and in the process of breaking mine in, a ferruncle or boil developed on my left ankle where the stiff leather abraded the skin. My lower leg and foot swelled as though I had elephantiasis, becoming so painful that I could hardly walk. When the tissue turned a purplish-bronze hue symptomatic of gangrene, Captain Lee hurriedly excised the lesion and sprinkled sulfa powder on the site, but it failed to drain properly, so he resorted to a four-day course of penicillin injected into the buttocks. (This was the same treatment prescribed for gonorrhea, and, naturally, my friends joshed me about my "dose of clap.") This newly-developed miracle drug, which had only recently become widely available, effectively quelled the rampant infection, and after a few days the swelling subsided and I was back on my two feet, freed from the threat of amputation.[8]

Since medics had no further need for firearms, we turned in our carbines on 12 September, and ten days later, the regiment was alerted for transfer to Japan. As we began packing and dismantling camp, I sought assurance that I was entirely rid of malign enteric organisms by submitting a stool sample to the nearest hospital laboratory, and heaved a sigh of relief when the test results proved negative. Not so fortunate was one of my tentmates who had ribbed me unmercifully about my wormy infestation in Manila. Taking the same precaution, he discovered that he was harboring no less than four species of parasites, for which he had to undergo purging and therapy similar to that which I had endured, so I had my unspoken revenge. I could hardly contain my glee at the prospect of leaving the pestilential tropics, and resolved that for the rest of my days on earth, I would never willingly reside in other than a temperate zone.[9]

While awaiting our embarkation, I read A. J. Cronin's *The Citadel* and *None But the Lonely Heart.* As the appointed day approached, word came down that the Navy, regrettably, had been unable to round up enough vessels to haul our entire regiment together with the 25th Infantry Division to Japan in a single movement. I was extremely disappointed to learn that I and three other medical aid men would have to remain behind to service the rear echelon, consisting largely of Boat Company C, to await the release of additional shipping. I tried to persuade Major Knapp that since my three erstwhile comrades were more experienced at our trade than I, my contribution would add little to the team's effectiveness, but he insisted that a record clerk would be indispensable, and I was it, so my entreaties were unavailing. While the bulk of the regiment and the rest of the Medical Detachment boarded their transports, we four "rearguardsmen" set up housekeeping in the tent left behind for an aid station.

I took the first night's duty, treating scores of sick and injured Filipinos, whom the Army now required us to tend along with our uniformed charges, time and resources permitting. Back in Manila one night, Bennie Weaver had been singly manning the dispensary when a young female civilian who had accidentally ingested mercury bichloride had been brought in for emergency treatment— fortunately, the on-call physician had taken over. Here, we had no professional backup anywhere near, and I was inordinately fearful that I might be faced with something of the sort, and that my paucity of clinical experience might issue in someone's permanent injury or death. My three more seasoned associates, two of them Polish and one Irish, street-wise urbanites from the Northeast, confirmed papists, and ardent devotees of Bacchus, seemed untroubled by such thoughts. In all candor, they were not above using their ministrations to native damsels of questionable virtue to exact payment in the form of sexual services.

For the next forty-eight hours or so we medicated the painful sequelae of the drunken revelry and mayhem by which some of the more intemperate amphibs had celebrated their final hours on Philippine soil. Among the presenting cases were a broken nose and a fractured leg. One hilarious inebriate rode upon the scene atop a small horse liberated from some poor peasant, declaring that he intended to take it with him to Japan. When I asked him how he planned to get it on shipboard, he retorted that he would "cross that bridge when he came to it." His steed, however, was not disposed to be ridden as far as the water's edge, whereupon the rider dismounted and dragged the poor animal along by its halter—I have often wondered what reaction he evoked from the embarkation officer.

By 1400 of 23 September, the last of the infantry and the 534th, minus Company C and a few AWOL's, were safely aboard ship, many of the amphibs, including Bennie, on APA 46, the KNOX. They could not weigh anchor, however, for another eight days, due to angry, typhoon-lashed seas. Among the still-shorebound troop units was an adjunctive Negro port company, four of whose members soon showed up at sick call with fulminating cases of gonorrhea. Several laggards from the units now afloat also had to be seen to—upon sobering up, they were thoroughly miffed at being "left in the lurch," as one might say. There was little to occupy the fellows on the beach, and most had only their pup tents in which to shelter, since almost all our camp equippage had already gone or had been packed for imminent departure. The resultant exposure to the elements brought a temporary surge in upper respiratory infirmities, but soon our patronage declined to the degree that we, too, merely loafed about until more ships showed up.

Chaplain Lindemann had stayed behind with the rear echelon, and the two of us spent hours debating theology, but were never able to reconcile his dogmatic Lutheranism and my more broad-spectrum Anglicanism. No one was permitted to wander very far from the beach, and within a few days, boredom began to take its toll, to the extent that one evening I fatuously acceded to the intreaties of my three mates and sampled their favorite beverage, a potent blend of canned grapefruit juice and pure grain alcohol from our medical stores, and, for the first time in my life, became roundly intoxicated. I have little or no memory of what transpired during the next six or eight hours other than awaking to a violently-retching hangover. That cured me of any further such indulgence for many months to come (though I confess to a growing taste for beer—within tolerable limits.)

The skies were still heavily overcast when the main convoy finally sailed away on 1 October. The stranded Company C boys drew their pay that day, but the four of us were excluded, since our personnel records had gone with our parent unit. I had not been paid since my final days in Manila, and even though I had cadged a small loan from my sidekick Bennie just before he boarded APA 46, my funds were now virtually exhausted. Not unpredictably, the bulging pockets of the more dissolute among the boatman brought a fresh wave of business to the aid tent. Despite fitful rainfall that evening, someone had arranged for an open-air showing of the movie *Brewster's Millions,* which we sat through in ponchos and helmet liners. About midnight a stiff and unusually chilly westerly wind blew in, as discomfitting as the heat which had formerly plagued us. A few days later, the rear echelon finance officer arranged for our quartet to be paid as well, restoring my fiscal liquidity and recharging my morale. To replenish our dwindling store of pharmaceuticals, two of us borrowed a jeep and drove to the 37th Station Hospital in Dagupan. Upon completing our errand, we took one last hasty tour around the town where we had first been introduced to Filipino culture, but found nothing on which we cared to squander our cash, and dared not dawdle, knowing that our marine transportation could put in at any moment.[10]

The second week in October, our ships finally showed up. Their officers exhorted us to waste no time in loading, with which we gladly complied. Assigned to LST 863 and finding all of the space on her tank deck taken, I availed myself of one of our stretchers, went topside, and rigged my shelter-half between a large truck and the starboard railing. For no accountable reason, our trailing convoy stood off the beach for another forty-eight hours before steaming into the sunset. Once under way, we four medics took turns, two at a stretch, handling the G.I. respondents to sick call each morning in 863's "sick bay," which, by Army standards, was immaculate and enviably-outfitted. The chow served aboard was excellent, making me wonder why I hadn't had sufficient foresight to enlist in the Navy rather than the Army.

As we sailed northward through the East China Sea near Okinawa, our flotilla was sideswiped by a cyclone. Whipped by gale-force winds, the ponderous LST's wallowed like drunken hippopotami through the towering seas. I was forced to take refuge in 863's aft super-structure, from which I watched her bow section quiver and flex as it was slapped by the oncoming waves. We all prayed that the shipyard folks who had welded her together had done their jobs properly so that her plates wouldn't buckle. A crewman on accompanying LST 1090 recorded that

> There were 50' seas and 130 knot winds. The sea, with its top blown off, was like a big bowl of milk. The con is 46 ft. above the flat waterline and the seas were above it. Fortunately, the ship was empty. There was three feet of water in the bottom deck. The pumps rated at 2500 gpm [gallons per minute] were just staying even . . . . During the typhoon there were two to three inch ripples down the deck plates. The bow was nine feet off the centerline.[11]

Aside from one or two heavily-laden ships from whose open decks vehicles were swept overboard when their lashings tore loose, the convoy weathered the blow without serious harm, and by nightfall of 18 October, the seas had calmed, the skies were swept clean, the moon was full, and the stars became brilliantly visible.

The farther north we steamed, ploughing along at what seemed to me no more than 6 knots, the lower the thermometer registered. Though cocooned in layers of clothing, blankets, poncho, and shelter-half, I shivered through the interminable nights. With the passage of a few more days our flotilla entered Honshu's Kii Strait and dropped anchor in the roadstead off the port of Wakayama, near Osaka. Here we were detained until the harbor at Nagoya, our ultimate destination, could be cleared of the mines so liberally sewn by our own aircraft during the final phase of the war. To our suprise, we discovered that the ships of the preceding convoy were holding at Wakayama as well, their 25th/534th passengers having been afloat for a solid month.

The Honshu coastline, like most of Japan, was mountainous, and the slopes rearing up from the straits were blanketted in dark green conifers and suffused in mist. The atmosphere was frigid, but, thankfully, I was able to roost on an enclosed deck pending our arrival at Nagoya. Having time to kill, we were permitted to go ashore at Wakayama on the morning of 22 October, taxied in on LCM's in groups of fifty or so, for a walkabout, as the Aussies would say. The ship-to-shore transit took about twenty minutes, during which I carefully surveyed the shipping massed in the bay, representing an amazing variety of registries. Many of the commercial freighters had reverted to their peacetime paint schemes, and the multi-hued panoply presented a cheery contrast with the hitherto-ubiquitous battleship-gray or dingy camouflage. The home port emblazoned on the stern of one nearby vessel read "Wilmington, N. C."

Wakayama, sprawled across flat deltaland at the mouth of a river, seemed rather deficient in docking facilities, with only a single long jetty at which our LCM deposited us. Along its shoreline were huge bombed-out factories, rusted steel cranes, and gasworks, all silent and deserted. We had to walk some four miles to reach the center of the city, passing clusters of hovels and shacks and piles of rubble reminiscent of Manila.

There were trolley tracks, shattered street lights, and telephone poles along the main thoroughfares, but the few intact shops were barren of merchandise.

The city's inhabitants, though sturdier than Filipinos, were of similar height, and a surprising number actually did have buck teeth and wore horn-rimmed glasses as portrayed in Allied propaganda cartoons. The younger children resembled dolls, with their clear white complexions, rosy cheeks, straight black hair, and faces framed in bangs. Some among the adult civilians eyed us sullenly, but more appeared indifferent, and a few were all smiles. A minority of our boys fraternized freely with them, but the rest of us were more cautious and reserved. Shocking accounts had recently come to light of the savagely brutal treatment meted out to the Allied P.O.W.'s forced into building the Siam-Burma "railway of death" along the river Kwai. Furthermore, Allied Intelligence had learned that had our invasion had been carried through, Japanese authorities had planned a mass execution of all American detainees brought to Japan for slave labor. None of this endeared the populace to us on first contact; I freely admit that I was deeply suspicious and wary of them. Several children called out "Hello" (rather than "Koh-nee-chee-wah" in their native tongue) at our approach, and were not at all reluctant to beg candy, gum, and cigarettes, having already been corrupted, I presumed, by the G.I.'s ahead of us. We had been instructed in no uncertain terms to be back at the pier not later than 1100, so our perambulations had to be curtailed in order to return to the ship on time. It was well that we did, for the very next day our flotilla left Wakayama harbor, and within another forty-eight hours or so, had threaded its way safely (with the help of Japanese harbor pilots) through whatever mines remained in Ise Bay. About 2000, LST 863 beached itself at Nagoya, and our vehicles began offloadeding. By midnight she was emptied, and Japanese laborers were brought on board to sweep off her decks in exchange for food. The cold was so intense that we spent the rest of the night on the ship, and following breakfast next morning, were transported by Japanese and U.S. Army trucks to our cantonement.

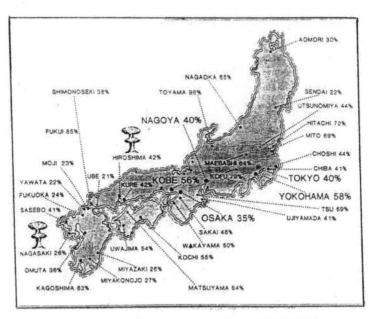

MAP 19. PERCENTAGE OF JAPANESE CITY AREAS
DESTROYED BY ALLIED AIR ATTACKS.

Nagoya, situated on the edge of a level plain, had a population of 1,250,000, making it one of Japan's five largest cities. It was, or had been, a center of heavy industry, primarily steel and aircraft, and the site of the country's largest oil refinery. Like Tokyo, Yokohama, Osaka, and Kobe, it had recently been gutted by our block-buster and incendiary bombs. Eight thousand people had perished in the raids, and 30% to 40% of its urban area, including 136,556 dwellings, ruined.[12] The electric trolleys, interurban lines, and intercity railways, however, were still functioning, and its ultramodern metropolitan passenger terminal still intact. (These would have been next on the list of planned targets had the war dragged on.) As we motored through the streets, I was struck by the fact that most males from six to sixty seemed to be wearing uniforms of one sort or another—not only policemen and former military servicemen, but railway employees, industrial workers, street-cleaners, and laborers in general.

MAP 20. DEVASTATED PORTION OF NAGOYA, JAPAN.

We were quartered in a barrack complex formerly housing the employees of a suburban Mitsubishi aircraft plant about ten miles from downtown Nagoya. Our unheated rooms, partitioned with thin plywood, had been scrupulously cleaned. So sudden had been Japan's collapse that our quartermaster services had been caught short, and there had been no winter-clothing issue, nor had we been out of the tropics long enough to become reacclimated, so that almost everyone quickly contracted colds or other respiratory maladies. Although we were given additional blankets, we continued to sleep fully-clothed, and in the absence of shower facilities, sponged ourselves off in water heated over open fires and drawn from a large pool in which the former occupants had performed their ablutions in common. The only room with any source of heat was appropriated for our dispensary; it contained ten large ovens, used by the factory hands to cook their rice, with steam piped from a single coal-fired boiler which required constant stoking.

On Sunday, 28 October, permits to visit the city, along with English-Japanese phrase-translation booklets, were handed out. Since occupation troops could ride free of charge on all public transport, Bennie and I strode over to nearest railway station, Daidocho, about an eighth of a mile from our cantonement, to catch an inbound train. During the thirty-minute wait for the next train, the booklets proved quite handy in our attempts to converse with the civilians standing alongside us on the platform, who seemed far more friendly, courteous, and helpful than those in Wakayama. Despite their malnutrition and deprivations, they were as clean in their persons and dress as the Filipinos, and more literate by far. When the train arrived, it was as jammed as the Times Square subway at rush hour, so that Bennie and I along with everyone else had to force our way on. We towered head and shoulders over most of the passengers, and were apparently the only aliens aboard. The cars were similar to those of American subways or elevated interurbans, as were the stations and signalling, and the system operated very efficiently. We had to change trains at two intermedial junctions before reaching central Nagoya, relying upon our phrase books and sign-language to attain the proper platform locations. The midtown commuter depot was adjacent to the aforementioned main terminal for steam-powered intercity trains, a magnificent art-deco stone-and-marble edifice with indirect lighting, comparable to the Pennsylvania Railroad stations at Newark or 30th Street, Philadelphia. Opening off the concourse was a branch office of the postal and telegraph services, with a sign in English advertising cablegrams to the U.S. for nine yen (the official exchange rate had been set at fifteen yen to the dollar.) This seemed quite inexpensive, so we each cabled our parents informing them of our new posting. Exiting to street level, we rode a trolleycar for several blocks until a well-lit storefront came into view, at which we climbed off to peer inside. A small group of Orientals on the sidewalk grabbed each of us by the arm and pulled us into the establishment, where they forced upon us a couple of quarts of Japanese beer. They made a great show of waving little Chinese nationalist flags, explaining that they were expatriates, members of some sort of welcoming committee, and wished to convey their appreciation to Americans for supporting China's cause (or something along those lines.) We tried to refuse the beer, fearing that this might be some subterfuge for poisoning us, but they were so insistent that we felt compelled to take a couple of swigs despite our misgivings. Actually the brew was quite tasty, much stronger than the 4.2-proof suds dispensed by the U.S. Army. We duly thanked the donors and slipped away from the premises with our bottles while their attentions were distracted by a couple of junior U.S. naval officers who happened on the scene. Next, we wandered into a smaller bistro at one of whose tables a G.I. officer of company-grade rank was seated, upon whom we bestowed our beer. In a show of gratitude, he steered us to a nearby block of buildings advertised as "The American Amusement Center," which we assumed to be some sort of carnival or theatre complex, or maybe a Special Services-Red Cross recreational facility. It turned out to be red all right, but had nothing to do with the cross—it was a red light district. In Japan, apparently, prostitutes or "comfort girls" were officially licensed and permitted to ply their trade only within strictly-limited enclaves, where police patrols kept order, and no opprobrium whatsoever attached to their patronage. It was the most brightly-lit sector of midtown, with billboards indicating the services offered, and was attracting American soldiers and sailors like a magnet. (At a later stage in our Nagoya sojourn, when I had attained more elevated rank, I was ordered on one occasion to take an ambulance and a squad of medics into the "Amusement Center" and escort a covey of the girls back to our dispensary for testing in an effort to combat the steeply-rising incidence of VD among regimental personnel; it was one of the more trying missions I was ever handed, requiring constant vigilence to keep the predacious prosties off my boys—and vice versa—until they could be returned to their workplace.) Bennie and I, indisposed to sample this brand of entertainment, linked up with three other amphibs of like mind for less-hazardous metropolitan explorations until almost 2100, when the two of us retraced our steps to the railway depot. Inquiring of the stationmaster as to the next connecting service to Daidocho, we were told that we had fifteen minutes to spare before train-time. In somewhat fractured English, he invited us into his office, had his aides bring us chairs, and we launched into a spirited dialogue. He explained to us where and how to change enroute, and personally escorted us to the proper train. We deduced that his was an unusually prestigious position, for all the railway employees bowed unctiously or saluted at his passage. He rode with us as far as the first junction to make certain that we made the right connection, and there handed us over to his counterpart. During our ten-minute layover in the latter's domain, he in turn invited us into his inner sanctum, had his female subordinate serve us tea (which tasted not much stronger than hot water), then led us aboard the second train to ensure that we had comfortable seating before the platform gates were unlocked to admit a flood of less-privileged commuters. After the next transfer, we alit at Daidocho about 2200. Throughout our travel, the eyes of all our fellow passengers had been rivetted upon us and their ears attuned to our conversation, making us feel as though we were exotic circus freaks.

This elaborate deference shown us common soldiers was baffling until I reflected upon the severity of the trauma to which the rigidly-disciplined Japanese public had been subjected. Never before in their nation's history had they tasted defeat, and until the moment of Japan's capitulation, the masses had been assured that their armed forces were invincible. The sudden revelation that the Americans had prevailed was by their lights prima face evidence of our innate superiority and their inferiority in the eyes of heaven; hence they felt impelled to abase themselves in our presence under any and all circumstances, humiliating though it must have been. This public manifestation of concern for our welfare must surely have masked a seething rage, but their acculturation had made them masters of the art of emotional suppression and dissimulation. I dread to think what it might have been like had our roles been reversed.

Heaps of mail forwarded from the Philippines were delivered

to us in the following days, and we enjoyed more privacy in reading it than ever before, thanks to our unusually spacious living quarters, with only four men to a cubicle and ample storage for clothing and equipment. My pals and I made repeated trips into the city to purchase mementos, but the few shops open for business had little to offer aside from secondhand kimonos and dishes or sundries such as hairpins and matches. Other than military trucks and jeeps and an occasional charcoal-fuelled private vehicle, the only conveyances plying the streets were handcarts, bicycles, and rickshaws. Although most of the populace were sadly underfed, and diseases like tuberculosis and pneumonia had become pandemic, the Nipponese were an admirably industrious race, and, in contrast to the Filipinos, kept their premises, passageways, and streets swept clean and rubble neatly stacked. They seemed utterly intrigued by all our machinery, examining it minutely to commit every detail of its design to memory.

The children typically walked abroad in groups, and female juveniles up to age sixteen or so all dressed in pantaloons and dark blue middy blouses with white collars or neck-flaps like those worn by naval seamen. Most of the adult women, rather than affecting western-style dresses or skirts, were swathed either in brightly-colored kimonos or clad in baggy shirts and pants or coveralls gathered at the waist and ankles. Virtually everyone was shod in wooden sandals with straps separating the big from the smaller toes, so that when barefoot, their feet suggested cloven hooves. A crowd of pedestrians on pavement sounded like armies of workmen pounding with wooden mallets. Footgear was invariably removed at the threshold of dwellings, and females took tiny steps, so that when scurrying about indoors, they made a subdued noise like running mice. In common with other Asians, Japanese males evinced little hesitancy about urinating in public, on the streets or anywhere outside. Upon entering or exiting another's presence, everone bowed, which I thought a quite fetching courtesy. The Shinto and Buddhist religious shrines were off-limits to us, so I never had the privilege of observing their worship practices.[13]

With November's advent, temperatures plummeted, and the

eighty-point men in the regiment made their departures. We were still being fed on canned rations and lacked winter clothing, but some of our badly-worn field gear was replaced with items of newer design, and a few sleeping bags trickled in, though only enough for the officers. During the second week in November, everyone was issued flannel longjohn underwear and woolen sweaters, a genuine godsend.[14]

Given Japan's highly-developed maritime infrastructure and plenitude of unemployed watermen and longshoremen, there was scant need for the services of amphibian engineers, which was just as well, since the accelerating pace of demobilization was rapidly diminishing our ranks. To keep the troops occupied, a voluntary scholastic program (administered, as I recall, by the Armed Forces Institute), offering a smorgasbord of college prep and technical training courses, was being introduced. Inflation was ravaging the prostrated and fuel-starved Japanese economy, and to relieve overcrowding on the trains, the privilege of free transportation for American servicemen had to be withdrawn. A Christmas package from my homefolks arrived a month-and-a-half ahead of time, containing a new wristwatch and some shirts for which I had urgent need, together with an assortment of railfan magazines, a jar of delicious honey, and a box of candy. I could find little with which to reciprocate, aside from some silken flags, crockery, and children's dolls, one of which I bought and mailed off to my younger sister Ruthie. The only appropriate gift I could contrive for my parents was an increase of fifty dollars in their monthly allotment from my pay by virtue of my recent promotion in rank and closer confinement to our bivouac.

Our detachment was rapidly thinning out with the exodus of higher-point men, among them a couple of the older Southerners, one, Earl Williams, a gentle ex-food-salesman from Charlotte, N.C., with a wife and three children, the other an Appalachian mountaineer whom I shall not identify, a one-time "holy roller" preacher and corn-whiskey distiller, father of five, and, by all accounts, a real rounder with Nagoya's ladies of the night. Other departees included our exceptionally-conscientious and self-contained top sergeant, William McCullough, and the less-introverted leader of my section, S/Sgt. Lynn Shaw, former Illinois farmer from the Mount Vernon area, both men of good character. Accompanying them were a handful of individuals who had re-upped for a three-year hitch in the Regular Army, one inducement for which was an immediate ninety-day furlough in the U.S. Each homebound enlisted man was allowed to take a Japanese army rifle, while officers had their choice of a sword or pistol. In mid-November my parents sent a second Yuletide package of delectable Moravian Christmas cookies and a tasty fruitcake which my roommates and I consumed on the spot. At this juncture, Hugh Riley was elevated to Staff Sergeant, taking over Lynn Shaw's job, and I stepped into Riley's shoes as detachment clerk.

The weather grew increasingly severe, with sleet and gusting winds, prompting those of us in my dormitory-cubicle to purchase on the open market a little one-burner gasoline stove and an antique electric-coil heater to get us through the freezing nights. Bennie, John Walker, and I took a Sunday railway excursion out of Nagoya to survey the surrounding countryside. Among the more memorable sights framed in our coach window were huge stone statues of Buddha and another divinity (whom we were unable to identify) adorning the crest of a high cliff above the bay. We marvelled at how the pressure of population on the land had led to the cultivation of crops to the very edges of the railway tracks and highways, with not a square foot of arable soil left untilled. Off in the distance we sighted a lovely snow-capped conical peak, a middling version of Honshu's fabled Mt. Fujiyama.

In a less-than-laudable culinary observance of Thanksgiving Day (though probably all that the overworked and understaffed kitchen crew could manage at the time), the mess hall served a late breakfast at 0830 and a rather-unappetizing turkey dinner at 1500—the bird was tough, the gravy scorched, and the potatoes underdone, but at least the butter was fresh. I worked all day at the dispensary, and upon bedding down that night, offered a heartfelt litany of gratitude to the Almighty for the restoration of peace. A contingent of disgruntled, down-at-the-mouth, teen-aged

replacements fresh from the States reported in the next day; I had
to restrain myself from reminding them of their good fortune at
having escaped the risks and rigors of wartime service. Shortly
thereafter, the stop-gap afternoon academic program got underway.
I opted for a couple of classes, one in Business English (taught by
a sergeant friend in the Boat Batttalion Headquarters Company)
from 1315 to 1405, and another in College Algebra from 1415 to
1505. I also attended Monday/Wednesday/Friday lectures on
Economics between 1515 and 1605, delivered by a commissioned
officer of Viennese extraction who had studied at the University of
London—he had the most perfect command of the English
language of anyone whom I had ever heard. Since I was taking the
courses for credit, a good deal of outside reading and preparation
was entailed over and above my regular duties. I was so busied, in
fact, that I totally overlooked my twentieth birthday when it rolled
around. Shortly thereafter, brigade headquarters imposed a new
military training regimen, with forty-five minutes of calisthenics
each morning, followed by a similar period of close order drill,
plus reveille and retreat formations. That same week, the regimental
quartermaster distributed enough sleeping bags and woolen
uniforms to outfit everyone—Eisenhower jackets, outercoats,
garrison caps, shirts, trousers, even neckties. Those of us who had
been with the unit since Gordon Johnston days were issued
Meritorious Unit sleeve patches and campaign ribbons, one for
Asiatic-Pacific service (with three miniscule bronze service stars to
be affixed thereto, representing each action with which we had
been associated), another for Philippine Liberation (with two stars
and an arrowhead for the Morotai invasion), a third for Japanese
Occupation, and (some of us) a fourth for Good Conduct, along
with four gold-colored cloth stripes to be worn on the lower left
sleeve, one for every six months spent overseas. At a later date, we
would also receive World War II Victory ribbons. (Paradoxically,
we were not awarded an arrowhead for the Lingayen invasion,
presumably because our battalion had come ashore two days after
the initial landing, even though we had come under much heavier
fire than the earlier arrivals.) All in all, a lot of decoration for such

slight mano-a-mano grappling with the enemy, I thought. It took several hours to sew and pin all this paraphernalia on our new uniform blouses as per regulations.

Weaver and I made a few more jaunts into central Nagoya, on one of which we made the acquaintance (through the agency of one of our railway-stationmaster friends) of a Japanese businessman who, travelling regularly between Tokyo and his hometown in a neighboring prefecture, had a twelve-hour layover at a junction we also frequented. We shared some of our rations and PX (Post Exchange) items with him. After several lengthy and candid conversations, he endowed Ben with a handsome Japanese naval sword. Several days later, he left a message asking us to meet him at the railway station again on a specified date. When we complied, he also presented me with a small, beautifully-fashioned ceremonial sword, which, by his account, was a treasured family heirloom, forged in the 14th Century. I had no way of verifying its authenticity, and was never able thereafter to thank him more ceremonially and in person, because on the only other occasions when he was passing through, I had duty, and could only send him some gifts of food and cigarettes via Bennie. Our paths never crossed again, but I ferretted out his address, and after returning to the United States, mailed the sword back to him (since it surely meant far more to him than it did to me), trusting that this would not be considered an offensive breach of etiquette, given the subtleties of Japanese politesse.

The now-gushing drain of manpower from our unit heaped more and more work upon the remainder of us, leaving little or no time even for letter-writing. With the infusion of another batch of replacements and the loss of one of our roommates, Bennie, Stan Freilich, and I invited one of the new boys to move in with us. A quiet, studious youngster of eighteen, he reminded me of myself at Camp Gordon Johnston. Since he blended in well and shared many of our interests, we dubbed our pad "The Under-Twenty-One Club."

Sunday, 2 December, a beautifully clear day, brought a welcome respite from the rat-race. Rising at 0630, taking a brisk shower, and downing a hearty breakfast of hot cereal and creamed beef on toast, I motored with Hugh Riley to 4ESB Headquarters at Inuyama, twenty-three miles inland, where we resolved some problems regarding the routing of medical reports with the Brigade Surgeon's staff. During the drive, we were entranced by the meticulously-tended gardens and lush agricultural plots on all sides, laid out in small, neat squares, such that the farmlands resembled waffle-iron grids at a distance. The frigidity of the air mitigated the odor of the organic wastes used for crop fertilization. Human and animal excreta were stored in cesspools, from which the farmers (or "honey-dippers," as we called them), using cans attached to long poles, ladled the contents into wooden buckets suspended from shoulder yokes and carried it out to spread on the fields. Their produce was hauled to market on bicycle trailers, to which dogs were harnessed to help pull heavier loads. (It occurred to me that the standard Japanese unit of measurement for mechanical output should be "dogpower" instead of "horsepower.") Inuyama lay in a lovely little valley between the steep spurs of two mountain ranges, somewhat resembling the Salt Lake City, Utah, locale. After dining sumptuously at the Brigade Headquarters mess on fried chicken, boiled potatoes, snap beans, and freshly-baked bread, Hugh and I drove home, where I indulged in an afternoon nap. (The previous Friday, incidentally, I had been "promoted" from T/5 to Corporal; exactly why the Army deemed this an elevation in rank when the pay grade was identical is something of a mystery to me—perhaps it reflected how soldiers of the line viewed those of the technical services.)

In mid-December, when Riley, Russell, Bannister, and most of the other younger bachelor holdovers from the regiment's original complement left for the States, my responsibilities became genuinely burdensome, encompassing not only all medical but military record-keeping, correspondence, typing, and filing. Parting from these fellows with whom I had been so long and closely affiliated, through good times and bad, was painful. Fortunately, we were enjoying a spell of sunny weather, easing the pangs of separation. I was pulling overnight CQ duty while festivities in honor of the homeward-bound were in full swing, and therefore missed out on toasting—

and roasting—them. At the dispensary that evening, the sole presenting customer required a penicillin shot for VD, a procedure at which I was still not fully adept; the viscous liquid did not inject readily, and I nervously bent the needle on the first try and had to repeat it, much to the poor fellow's discomfort.

One of the latter-day replacements, a recently-naturalized immigrant from Palestine, Pvt. Aram Nazarian, was an unusually intelligent Syrian, fluent in Arabic, French, Armenian, and Hebrew, and to a lesser extent, in English. Classified as an infantry rifleman, he had been employed as a civilian in his brother-in-law's drug firm, and afterward, by the Intelligence service in Washington. Nazarian was an entertaining and highly-amusing conversationalist, and Bennie and I relished his company.[15]

As Christmas approached, I was jumped up to the rank of Staff Sergeant, increasing my monthly stipend to $126.00. I felt I had earned it, for I was working from daybreak to midnight seven days a week, trying to fill several job slots simultaneously. Major Knapp had gone, Captain Lee was now detachment commander, and I, as ranking non-com, was the Top Sergeant, as well as attending to all the medical and administrative paperwork. Ben Weaver was made Supply Sergeant, and the two of us essentially ran the unit militarily, while Captain Lee and one or two other commissioned officers were totally absorbed in the regiment's health-care management. December 19th brought the season's first snowfall, hiding the city's desolation under a lovely mantle. Alas, it melted into slush under the next day's warm sun. A large consignment of newcomers reported in to the 534th that afternoon, mostly low-point men from the 41st Division, 150 of whom had to be housed in our Medical Detachment quarters. Along with them came a successor to Chaplain Lindeman, an evangelical Protestant cleric from Fayetteville, N.C., whose patterns of speech suggested a shallow schooling and a backwoods rearing, but who seemed a sociable and quick-witted fellow. Bennie and I had an ample store of edibles with which to fete the Yuletide, for several of our departing buddies had bequeathed to us their gifts of goodies from home.[16] The task of educating the new men who would shortly be assuming our duties seemed almost overwhelming. I had two promising understudies, one in personnel administration and one in the Surgeon's office, though I was still doing the lion's share of that work myself, as well as fielding all the problems of the fledglings-at-large, and trying to maintain discipline. I was so tired that I slept through Christmas morning, but, as a gesture of good will, took on the dispensary obligations myself that afternoon. With the advent of the New Year, the weather turned bitterly cold, but it was heartening to see our ranks nearing full strength again. The time was almost at hand when one of the more mature and able replacements would have to be groomed for the Top job. In addition to fronting the reveille formation and roll call at 0630 each morning and the retreat ceremony in late afternoon, monitoring the daily calisthenics and drill sessions, and keeping an eye on the dispensary operations, I made out the duty rosters and accompanied Captain Lee on the Saturday morning barracks-and-personnel-inspection rounds, all of which required unflagging vigilance and follow-up.

On 6 January, I was recommended for promotion to Technical Sergeant (Sergeant First Class in the postwar Army), the rank commensurate with my function; it was approved in short order, while Bennie was elevated to Staff Sergeant. He and I now slept in the senior non-com's room, a separate den which remained underheated, because, reluctant to put our comfort ahead of that of the lower ranks, I had directed that our still-scanty supply of stoves be placed in the larger dormitories. As January wore on, the last of the regiment's original complement departed for the States, leaving only the two of us to carry on, along with fifty or so other remnants of the Gordon Johnston Replacement Training Group scattered through the various boat and shore companies, most now T/5's or T/4's like my friend Neal Whitten, F Company's clerk. The afternoon academic classes had fallen by the wayside, superseded that month by a rigorous military—training program mandated by higher headquarters to restore unit cohesion and effectiveness. Ben and I assumed less and less visibility as our raw charges became assimilated and shouldered their new responsibilities. He and I took time out occasionally to visit the Red Cross Club for a cup of coffee and to catch the news on the radio. To raise the spirits of the homesick apprentices now marching under the regimental colors, the morale officer arranged a midwinter ball with music provided by a 25th Division orchestra, free beer, and females imported from a local dance hall. Perhaps the event encouraged licentiousness, for a couple of nights later, one of our youngsters had one drink too many and absconded with our only ambulance, running it down an embankment, damaging its steering, and ripping off a fender. I had observed the culprit in an inebriated state just prior to the incident, and was compelled to so testify at his court martial, with considerable reluctance, I might add, for I was loathe to see him serve time in the stockade.[17]

Within a few days, the prevalent ASR-score dropped to the 47-point level qualifying Bennie and me for release from the service. Thereafter, things developed at such a breath-taking pace that my recollection of them is quite blurred. On 15 January, orders came through relieving the two of us, along with 39 other 534th amphibs, from our unit assignments and transferring us to the Disposition Center at Nagoya's 11th Replacement Depot. Jubilantly packing our bags and shouting goodbyes, we left our cantonement behind with minimal hesitancy and few regrets, and duly reported in. A week or so later, we strode up the gangplank of AP 113, GENERAL H.W. BUTNER, a Navy-operated 17,800-ton P-2 transport packed with some 5,000 other homebound GI's.[18] Her powerful 19-knot engines sped us back to San Francisco in far less time than it had taken the FAIRLAND to bring us over. The BUTNER was low on food stocks, and the paltry meals served aboard often left our appetites unsated, but we took this in stride, headed as we were toward paradise. At the Nagoya pier, we had been loaded in order of rank and in alphabetical sequence, such that the occupant of the bunk adjoining mine was a Negro sergeant named Wasson; he had brought along a carton of chocolate bars which he generously shared with me on the journey, for which I shall be eternally in his debt. My only other enduring memory of my second trans-Pacific crossing was of our entry through the

Golden Gate on Thursday, 7 February; as we neared the soaring suspension bridge, everyone on the BUTNER's crowded deck rushed over to the starboard side to imbibe the glorious sight of San Francisco, causing the ship to list markedly and prompting an order from the captain for some of us to move to the vessel's opposite side to restore her balance. In the wholesale rush to comply, she developed an equal tilt to port, to my intense amusement.

When our barque hove to at the Oakland Army pier, there were no brass bands to welcome us nor any adulatory demonstrations; we were unceremoniously ferried over to Camp Stoneman, herded through a hectic round of processing and debriefing, and hustled aboard a Southern Pacific Railroad troop train bound for the East Coast over the so-called "Sunset Route." Once settled into our troop-sleeper, we indulged freely in the bourbon whiskey with which one of the more enterprising and far-sighted among us had replaced the drinking water in its interior tank so that we could the more readily quench our thirst at the tap. Thereafter, laved by the rays of a mild midwinter's sun, we revelled in a sort of rolling "block party" throughout our train's progression down to southern California, then eastward through Yuma, Arizona, and across the desert to El Paso. With engine changes and resupply of spirits at such points as San Antonio and Houston, we were propelled over the immense surface of the Lone Star state to New Orleans, Louisiana, then on through the lower South to Fayetteville, North Carolina. Bloodshot eyes and roiled stomachs not-withstanding, few of us were feeling any pains as we detrained at Fort Bragg, where I had shed my civilian identity so many long months before. Although the ensuing roll-call revealed that our numbers were short a few inebriates who had wandered away from the train at various stops along the way, no punitive action resulted (the onboard Military Police, reluctant to hassle veterans returning from overseas, had pretty much left us to our own devices); the culprits simply boarded another eastbound "main" and spent a few days longer in uniformed servitude than the rest of us.

After a final bit of bureaucratic flummery at Bragg's Separation Center, I was handed whatever pay I had accrued, along with my "honorable" discharge, on Sunday, 17 February 1946, having put 2 years, 1 month, and 18 days of active duty behind me. With my "ruptured duck" (the spread-winged-eagle button which all separated vets were supposed to display until they doffed their uniforms) affixed to the lapel of my "Ike" jacket, I turned my face toward home. Lip-synching the lyrics of orchestra leader Vaugn Monroe's "When The Lights Go On Again All Over The World," I sought out the next bus to Winston-Salem. That same evening, I stepped through the front door of the unfamiliar 912 Jersey Avenue residence and into the embraces of my beloved family members, with a strange mixture of enormous relief and indescribable poignance. As I write these words a half-century later, it all seems an hallucinatory fantasy.

The America which I reentered had changed irrevocably; though drabber and more jaded for the moment, all sorts of upheavals were stirring. A frenzy of national self-redefinition and redevelopment was about to take hold, of which the railroad industry was paradigmatic. The rail network, which during the previous century had supplanted river-boat and horse-drawn carriage as the country's primary circulatory system, now worn and depleted from wartime over-exertions, was already undergoing what amounted to radical vascular surgery. The steam engines and regal Pullmans of my youth were yielding to more efficient diesels and light-weight streamliners, with vast stretches of their trackage now regulated by automated controls. Within two decades, the national rail passenger enterprise would be cut to the bone, condemned to obsolescence by jet-powered airliners and a German-autobahn-inspired interstate highway system. It would barely survive in the attenuated form of AMTRAK (a name recalling in eerily-appropriate fashion the slow-motion "amphtraks" which had borne so many GI's onto enemy-held shores.)

America's formerly-compact towns and cities were about to sprout monotone suburbs without end as automobile ownership proliferated. TV antennas would soon protrude from every rooftop, drive-in movie screens bring Hollywood to every hamlet, and even the big-band music which had calmed our war-jangled nerves give

way to the primitive simplicities of "progressive jazz" and doowop/
bebop. While most veterans wanted only to procure decent jobs,
settle down in marriage, and raise families, there were subtle signs
that our heritage of Calvinist moral restraint was decaying into a
reckless and rebellious libertarianism, most notably among juveniles.
Even the hallowed family structure was being reshaped as Blacks
and females, having answered unstintingly the call to patriotic
service, both in defense industries and the military, were no longer
content to resume their former segregated or subordinate roles.
While the national economy was readjusting frantically to the
abrupt cancellation of defense contracts and the satisfaction of pent-
up consumer demands, the global political community was
realigning itself on one or the other side of the Great Capitalist-
Marxist divide, as war-ravaged and ex-colonial peoples sought a
place in the sun.

The Fourth Engineer Special Brigade outlasted my own
abbreviated military career by less than two months. Inactivated in
Japan on 15 April 1946, it had made a substantial contribution
logistically, if not combatively, to the final victory, though its losses
had been minimal and its valor largely untested. Nonetheless, its
officers and men had garnered 16 Purple Hearts, 6 Legion of Merits, 9
Silver Stars, 20 Soldier's Medals, and 116 Bronze Stars.[19] Beyond doubt
it would have been bloodily mangled, if not obliterated, had we been
compelled to invade Japan. Instead, I, like the vast majority of its
young constituency, had come through the war relatively unscathed.
How had this happened, and why? How was it that we—my brigade,
indeed, my nation—had been spared the indescribable suffering and
staggering losses that had befallen so many other parties to the conflict?
I do not exaggerate when I say that I have struggled for answers to
these questions every day of my life since. Studs Terkel has referred to
World War II as "The Good War." That to me is nonsense—no war is
good. Resort to arms may be necessary from time to time, as I remain
convinced that it was for Americans in 1941, but it is never good. To
me, this is the ultimate moral incongruity that must haunt any
professing Christian. American theologian Reinhold Niebuhr [1892-

1971] observed, in a probing monograph entitled *The Irony Of American History*, that

> The final wisdom of life requires, not the annulment of incongruity, but the achievement of serenity within and above it . . . . Nothing that is worth doing can be achieved in our lifetime; therefore we must be saved by hope.
>
> Nothing which is true or beautiful or good makes complete sense in any immediate context of history; therefore we must be saved by faith. Nothing we do, however virtuous, can be accompished alone; therefore we are saved by love. No virtuous act is quite as virtuous from the standpoint of our friend or foe as it is from our standpoint. Therefore we must be saved by the final form of love which is forgiveness.[20]

Not only did my wartime experience force me to confront my own intellectual arrogance, provincial snobbery, and lack of charity, but the inescapably tragic element in the human condition. It exposed the fatuity of my shallow moralism and compelled me to ask the truly relevant questions about the nature and destiny of man. It eventually moved me to devote my remaining years to the service of Jesus Christ, the Prince of Peace, and to the world for which He died, by entering my church's priesthood, not only in parochial ministry but as a university chaplain and professor of history. The remainder of my undergraduate education was largely funded through the so-called G.I. Bill, passed by Congress in 1944, compensating me richly for whatever trivial sacrifices I had made in the defense of my country. This piece of legislation has been, I believe, one of the most progessive and beneficial contributors to the health of our national society ever concieved. It enabled hundreds of thousands of young veterans who might otherwise have fallen by the wayside to become highly-productive, well-informed, responsible, and dependable citizens and leaders.

Similarly, by her program of promptly aiding the economic recovery of her former Axis adversaries, America has fostered global stability for half a century, just as her sponsorship and support of the United Nations has made it a far more viable instrument for the maintenance of world peace and the spread of democracy than the feeble League of Nations in the wake of World War I. Undeniably, therefore, some substantive benefits for humankind emerged from the chaos and wastage of World War II.

Sadly, some fifteen million of the world's uniformed patriots (including 292,131 Americans) did not survive to enjoy the positive fruitage, nor did an estimated forty million of the luckless civilians caught in its toils. It is no less appalling to contemplate what might have been accomplished for the relief of human misery with the estimated $1,600,000,000,000 in material wealth that the war devoured.[21] It seemed to me in 1946 that our technologically-sophisticated western civilization had stumbled into a black hole of metaphysical and moral confusion from which there appeared no escape. It was all too apparent that the humanism masquerading as Christianity and propagated with such smug confidence by the nineteenth-century progressives had no philosophical solution to the problem posed by the twentieth century's monstrous eruptions of evil, pain, and destructivity.

The fact that I was still alive and whole meant that I had a special obligation thereafter, consonant with the words of Jesus in Luke 12:48: "Everyone to whom much is given, of him will much be required." Thanks to subsequent exposure to the works of theologians such as Reinhold and Richard Neibuhr, Paul Tillich, and Teilhard de Chardin, I eventually came to the realization that while Christianity offers no completely satisfactory theoretical answer, it points toward an answer. What it proffers instead is a pathway through the madness and confusion to a better and saner future, illumined by the crucifixion and resurrection of Jesus Christ, providing reassurance that the God Who created the world is also the ultimate arbiter of its destiny. This loving God not only transcends His creation, but is immanent within it, reconciling it to Himself persistently, and bringing good out of evil. He is with us hand-in-hand in all our manifold experiences of tragedy and loss, so that, as St. Paul put it, by His spirit we can be "more than conquerors through Him that loved us" (Romans 8:37.) This presents for shaken post-modern humanity a third option, beyond the superficialities either of blind optimism or paralyzing despair, grounded in the belief that humanity will never find itself in an absolute cul-de-sac. To cite John Macquarrie, "there will always be the possibility of an opening to a new future, always the possibility that grace will transmute folly and death into atonement and resurrection," because "even in the most shattering events of history our human actions intermesh with the action of God," and He is always "out ahead of us" enabling new beginnings and new possibilities of life.[22]

ROSTER OF PERSONNEL, MEDICAL DETACHMENT, 534TH EB&SR

AUGUST, 1945

Officers

Knapp, Byron S. (Major), Ecorse, Mich.
Lee, Joseph M. (Captain), Leeds, Ala.
Nimaroff, Milton M. (Captain), Raritan, N.J.
Foley, John B. (First Lieutenant), Ft. Dodge, Iowa
Marengo, Roy E. (First Lieutenant), Highland Park, Mich.
Santella, John J. (First Lieutenant), Watertown, S.Dak.

Enlisted Men

Andre, Carroll H., Washington, D.C.
Arbuckle, Kenneth J., Hadley, Pa.
Atkins, William G., Wappingers Falls, N.Y.
Banasek, William, Tarrifville, Conn.
Banister, John J., Philadelphia, Pa.
Berry, Patrick J., McKeesport, Pa.
Betesh, Joseph, Brooklyn, N.Y.
Bingler, Joseph, Jr., New York, N.Y.
Bridges, Russell L., Valdosta, Ga.
Buckley, Joseph, West View, Pa.
Chronister, John R. J., Harrisburg, Pa.
Crisp, Jim, Buies Creek, N.C.

DeRop, Franz, New York, N.Y.
Dietzen, Sylvester W., Duquesne, Pa.
Doherty, Philip J., New York, N.Y.
Duchnowski, Edward S., Scranton, Pa.
Foote, Norman R., Franklin, N.Y.
Frielich, Stanley, Brooklyn, N.Y.
Gerber, John J., Baltimore, Md.
Goodstein, Benjamin, Bronx, N.Y.
Hanson, Donald, (hometown unknown), Maine
Hoffer, Ray D., Scottdale, Pa.
Ihrman, Nicholas, Patterson, N.J.
Lavinder, Billy G., Coal Fork, W.Va.
Lilly, Jimmie R., Des Moines, Iowa
Main, Joseph R., Utica, N.Y.
Manke, Gustav M., Lakewood, O.
McCulloch, William W., Highwood, Ill.
McDonald, Gordon M., Jr., Chicago, Ill.
McKenzie, Carl L., Frostburg, Md.
Meacham, Clyde M., Coudersport, Pa.
Novak, William P., Baltimore, Md.
Penley, John L., Kingsport, Tenn.
Riley, Hugh F., Fayetteville, Ark.
Ruderman, George, Brooklyn, N.Y.
Russell, Louis J., Jr., Detroit, Mich.
Ruther, Russell E., Jr., E. Norwalk, Conn.
Schmidtke, Robert H., Rowley, Iowa
Sell, William J., Cumberland, Md.
Shaw, Lynn H., Sparta, Ill.
Shepherd, Wesley C., Turlock, Cal.
Smith, Charles F., Follansbee, W. Va.
Solomon, Jacob L., Shreveport, La.
Spinks, Tom L., Charlestown, W. Va.
Stehle, William, Broad Channel, N.Y.
Teijeiro, Manuel J., Philadelphia, Pa.
Vadorsky, Clarence F., Baltimore, Md.
Walker, John L., Jr., Gaylesville, R.I.

Watson, Robert M., Jr., Winston-Salem, N.C.
Weaver, Benjamin R., Williamston, N.C.
Whitten, John L., Grenada, Miss.
Williams, Earl K., Charlotte, N.C.
Wolfe, Lewis E., Midland, Mich.
Wozniak, Theodore D., Chicago, Ill.
Zarra, Nicholas M., Newark, N.J.

BIBLIOGRAPHY

BOOKS

Allen, Thomas B., and Norman Polmar. Code-Name Downfall, The Secret Plan to Invade Japan—And Why Truman Dropped the Bomb. New York: Simon & Schuster, 1995.

Alsberg, Henry G. (ed.) The American Guide, A Source Book and Complete Travel Guide For The United States. New York: Hastings House Publishers, 1949.

Ambrose, Stephen E. Americans At War. Jackson, Mississippi: University Press of Missippi, 1997.

Amory, Robert, and Reuben M. Waterman (eds.) Surf And Sand, The Saga Of The 533d Engineer Boat & Shore Regiment, 1942-1945. Andover, Mass.: Andover Press, Ltd., 1947.

Astor, Gerald. Crisis In The Pacific, The Battle For The Philippine Islands By The Men Who Fought Them—An Oral History. New York: Donald I. Fine Books, 1996.

Bailey, Ronald H. The Home Front: U.S.A., World War II. Alexandria, Virginia: Time-Life Books, Inc., 1977.

Beebe, Lucius, and Charles Clegg. The Trains We Rode. New York: Promontory Press, 1990.

Bergerud, Eric. Touched With Fire, The Land War In The South Pacific. New York: Penguin Books USA Inc., 1996.

Bidwell, Shelford (ed.) Brassey's Artillery Of The World. London: Brassey's Publishers Ltd., 1957.

Bird, Kai, and Lawrence Lifschultz. Hiroshima's Shadow, Writings On The Denial Of History And The Smithsonian Controversy. Stony Creek, Connecticut: The Pamphleteer's Press, 1998.

Birdsall, Steve. Log Of The Liberators. Garden City, New York: Doubleday & Company, Inc., 1973.

Bradley, John H., Jack W. Dice (Contributing Author), Thomas E. Griess (Series Editor.) *The Second World War: Asia And The Pacific*. Department of History, United States Military Academy, West Point, N.Y. Wayne, N.J.: Avery Publishing Group, Inc., 1984.

Bradley, Omar N., and Clay Blair. *A General's Life*. New York: Simon & Schuster, 1973.

Brokaw, Tom. *The Greatest Generation*. New York: Random House, 1998.

Bruce, Colin John. *Invaders, British And American Experience Of Seaborne Landings 1939-1945*. Annapolis: Naval Institute Press, 1999.

Brune, Peter. *The Spell Is Broken, Exploding The Myth Of Japanese Invincibility, Milne Bay To Buna-Sananda 1942-43*. St. Leonard's, Australia: Allen & Unwin, 1997.

Bykofsky, Joseph, and Harold Larson. *The Transportation Corps: Operations Overseas [The Technical Services, United States Army in World War II.]* Washington, D.C.: Office of the Chief of Military History, Department of the Army, 1957.

Chang, Iris. *The Rape of Nanking, The Forgotten Holocaust of World War II*. New York: Basic Books, A Subsidiary of Perseus Books, L.L.C., 1997.

Coll, Blanche D., Jean E. Kieth, and Herbert H. Rosenthal. *The Corps of Engineers: Troops and Equipment [The Technical Services, The United States Army in World War II.]* Washington, D.C.: Office of the Chief of Military History, Department of the Army, 1958.

Connaughton, Richard, John Pimlott, Duncan Anderson. *The Battle For Manila, The Most Devastating Untold Story of World War II*. Novato, California: Presidio Press, 1995.

Costello, John. *The Pacific War, 1941-1945*. (First Quill Edition) New York: Rawson, Wade, 1981.

Cowdrey, Albert E. *Fighting For Life, American Military Medicine In World War II*. New York: The Free Press, A Division of Macmillan, Inc., 1994.

DeNevi, Don. *America's Fighting Railroads, A World War II Pictorial History*. Missoula, Montana: Pictorial Histories Publishing Company, 1996.

Dod, Karl C. *The Corps of Engineers: The War Against Japan* [*The Technical Services, United States Army In World War II.*] Washington, D.C.: Center of Military History, United States Army, 1987.

Dower, John W. *Embracing Defeat, Japan In The Wake Of World War II.* New York: W. W. Norton & Company, Inc., 1999.

Dyer, Vice Adm. George Carroll. *The Amphibians Came To Conquer, The Story of Admiral Richard Kelly Turner.* 2 Vols. Washington, D.C.: U.S. Government Printing Office, 1969.

Esposito, Colonel Vincent J. (Chief Editor.) *The West Point Atlas Of American Wars, Volume II, 1900-1953.* New York: Frederick A. Praeger, Publishers, 1959.

Farrington, S. Kip, Jr. *Railroads At War.* New York: Coward-McCann, Inc., 1944.

Fillmer, Warren L., and Walter Eisle, eds. *Afloat Ashore, The 594th Engineer Boat and Shore Regiment.* Tokyo: Dai Nippon, 1945.

Frank, Richard B. *Downfall, The End Of The Imperial Japanese Empire.* New York: Random House, Inc., 1999.

Garraty, John A. (ed.) *Encyclopedia Of American Biography.* New York: Harper & Row, Publishers, 1974.Gibney, Frank.

Gibney, Frank. *The Pacific Century, America And Asia In A Changing World.* New York: Macmillan Publishing Co., 1992.

Goralski, Robert. *World War II Almanac, A Political And Military Record.* New York: G. P. Putnam's Sons, 1981.

Green, Michael. *MacArthur In The Pacific, From The Philippines To The Fall of Japan.* Osceola, Wisconsin: Motorbooks International Publishers and Wholesalers, 1996.

Greenfield, Kent Roberts (General Editor.) *United States Army in World War II, The War Against Japan, The U.S. Army's Official Pictorial Record.* Dulles, Virginia: The Center of Military History, U.S. Army, 1994.

Griffith, Thomas E. Jr. *MacArthur's Airman, General George C. Kenney And The War In The Southwest Pacific.* Lawrence, Kansas: The University Press of Kansas, 1998.

Grun, Bernard. *The Timetables of History.* (Touchstone Edition.) New York: Simon & Schuster, Inc., 1982.

Heavey, Brig. Gen. William F. *Down Ramp! The Story Of The Army Amphibian Engineers*. Washington, D.C.: Infantry Journal Press, 1947.

Hoyt, Edwin P. *The Invasion Before Normandy, The Secret Battle Of Slapton Sands*. Briarcliff Manor, New York: Stein and Day, Publishers, 1985. *MacArthur's Navy; The Seventh Fleet And The Battle For The Philippines*. New York: Orion Books, A Division of Crown Publishers, Inc., 1989.

Hyatt, Major Frederick, and Gerard Ridefort. *Modern Rifles and Sub-Machine Guns*. London: Salamander Books, Ltd., 1992.

Hynes, Samuel. *The Soldiers' Tale, Bearing Witness to Modern War*. New York: Penguin Books, 1997.

Ienaga, Saburo. *The Pacific War, 1931-1945, A Critical Perspective On Japan's Role In World War II*. (English Translation.) New York: Random House, Inc., 1978.

Jahoda, Gloria. *Florida, A History*. New York: W. W. Norton & Company, Inc., 1984.

Johnson, Robert Wayne. *Through The Heart Of The South, The Seaboard Air Line Railroad Story*. Erin, Ontario: The Boston Mills Press, 1995.

Knox, Donald. *Death March, The Survivors of Bataan*. New York: Harcourt Brace Jovanovich, Publishers, 1981.

Lanning, Lt. Col. (Ret.) Michael Lee. *The African-American Soldier, From Crispus Attucks To Colin Powell*. Secaucus, New Jersey: Birch Lane Press, Carol Communications, Inc., 1997.

Lapping, Brian. *End of Empire*. New York: St. Martin's Press, 1985.

Lorelli, John A. *To Foreign Shores, U. S. Amphibious Operations In World War II*. Annapolis: The United States Naval Institute, 1995.

MacArthur, Douglas. *Reminiscences*. New York: McGraw-Hill Book Company, 1964.

Macquarrie, John. *Three Issues In Ethics*. New York: Harper & Row, Publishers, 1970.

Manchester, William. *American Caesar, Douglas MacArthur, 1880-1964*. Boston: Little, Brown and Company, 1978.

Millett, John David. *The Organization and Role Of The Army Service Forces [The Army Service Forces, The United States Army In World*

War II.] Washington: Office of the Chief of Military History, Department of the Army, 1954.

Morison, Samuel Eliot. (1) *History of United States Naval Operations In World War II*: Vol. III, *The Rising Sun In The Pacific* [1948]; Vol. VI, *Breaking The Bismarcks Barrier* [1950]; Vol. VIII, *New Guinea And The Mariannas* [1975]; Vol. XII, *Leyte* [1958]; Vol. XIII, *The Liberation Of The Philippines, 1944—1945* [1959]; Vol. XIV, *Victory In The Pacific, 1945* [1960]. Boston: Little, Brown and Company. (2) *The Two-Ocean War, A Short History Of The United States Navy In The Second World War*. Boston: Little, Brown and Company,1963.

Niebuhr, Reinhold. *The Irony Of American History*. New York: Charles Scribner's Sons, 1962.

Palmer, Robert R., Bell I. Wiley, William R. Keast. *The Procurement And Training Of Ground Combat Troops [The Army Ground Forces, The United States Army In World War II.*] Washington, D.C.: Historical Division, Department of The Army, 1948.

Paxton, A. G. *Three Wars And A Flood, Memoirs Of Lt. Gen. A. G. Paxton*. Privately Printed. Date Unknown.

Peret, Geoffrey. (1) *Old Soldiers Never Die, The Life Of Douglas MacArthur*. New York: Random House, Inc., 1996. (2) *There's A War To Be Won; The United States Army In World War II*. New York: Random House, Inc., 1991.

Pogue, Forrest C. *George C. Marshall, Organizer of Victory, 1943-1945*. New York: The Viking Press, Inc., 1973.

Prefer, Nathan. *MacArthur's New Guinea Campaign, March-August 1944*. Conshohocken, Pennsylvania: Combined Books, 1995.

Rhoades, Weldon E. (Dusty.) *Flying MacArthur To Victory*. College Station, Texas: Texas A & M University Press, 1987.

Shortal, John Francis. *Forged By Fire, Robert L. Eichelberger And The Pacific War*. Columbia, South Carolina: University of South Carolina Press, 1987.

Sill, Van Rensselaer. *Amazing Miracle*. New York: The Odyssey Press, 1947.

Smith, Mary Lou (ed.) *The Book of Falmouth, A Tricentennial Celebration: 1686-1986.* Falmouth, Massachusetts: The Falmouth Historical Commission, 1986.

Smith, Robert Ross. *The Approach To the Philippines. Triumph In The Philippines. [The United States Army in World War II.]* Washington, D.C.: Center of Military History, U.S.Army, 1984.

Souter, Gavin. *New Guinea, The Last Unknown.* New York: Taplinger Publishing Co., Inc., 1966.

Spector, Ronald H. *Eagle Against The Sun, The American War With Japan.* New York: The Free Press, A Division of Macmillan, Inc., 1985.

Stanton, Shelby L. *World War II Order Of Battle.* Novato, California: Presidio Press, 1984.

Steinberg, Rafael. (1)*Island Fighting.* (2)*Return To The Philippines.* [*World War II* Series.] Alexandria, Virginia: Time-Life Books, Inc., 1977.

Strahan, Jerry E. *Andrew Jackson Higgins And The Boats That Won World War II.* Baton Rouge: Louisiana State University Press, 1994. Tree, Isabella. *Islands In The Clouds; Travels In The Highlands of New Guinea.* Hawthorn, Victoria, Australia: Lonely Planet Publications, 1996.

Vader, John. *New Guinea, The Tide Is Stemmed.* New York: Ballentine Books, Inc., 1971.

Wardlow, Chester. *The Transportation Corps: Movements, Training, and Supply [The Technical Services, The United States Army In World War II.]* Washington: Office of the Chief of Military History, Department of the Army, 1956.

Westerfield, Hargis. *41st Infantry Division, Fighting Jungleers.* Paducah, Kentucky: Turner Publishing Company, 1992.

Wheeler, Keith. *The Road To Tokyo, World War II.* Alexandria, Virginia: Time-Life Books, Inc., 1977.

Wheeler, Tony. Papua, *New Guinea, A Travel Survival Kit.* South Yarra, Victoria, Australia: Lonely Planet Publications, October, 1988.

Wrinn, Jim, and Edward Lewis, *"The Road of Personal Service,"* A

Centennial History. Aberdeen, North Carolina: Aberdeen and Rockfish Railroad Company, 1992.

Zich, Arthur. *The Rising Sun, World War II*. Alexandria, Virginia: Time-Life Books, Inc., 1977.

_____. *Amphibian Engineer Operations* [Vol. IV, *Engineers Of The Southwest Pacific, 1941-1945; Reports Of Operations, U.S. Army Forces In The Far East, Southwest Pacific Area, Army Forces Pacific, 1959*.] Office of the Chief Engineer, General Headquarters, Army Forces, Pacific [Maj. Gen. Hugh F. Casey, Chief Engineer.] Washington: U.S. Government Printing Office, 1959.

_____. *History Of The Second Engineer Special Brigade, United States Army, World War II*. Harrisburg, Pennsylvania: The Telegraph Press, 1946.

_____. *Register of Graduates And Former Cadets Of The United States Military Academy, Class Of 1894, Centennial Edition*. West Point, New York: Association of Graduates, USMA, 1994.

_____. *The Bluejackets Manual, United States Navy, 1943*. Annapolis: United States Naval Institute, 1943.

_____. *The Officer's Guide*. 9th Edition, 1942. 22d Edition, 1956. Harrisburg, Pennsylvania: The Military Service Publishing Company.

_____. *The Official Guide Of The Railways And Steam Navigation Lines Of The United States, Puerto Rico, Canada, Mexico, and Cuba, February 1944*. New York: The National Railway Publication Company, Publishers and Proprietors, 1944.

_____. *The U.S. Army's Official Pictorial Record, The War Against Japan*. Washington, D.C.: Center of Military History, United States Army. First Brassey's Paperback Edition, 1998.

_____. *U. S. Naval Vessels, 1943*. Annapolis: Naval Institute Press, 1943.

NEWSPAPERS

Camp Gordon Johnston, Florida: *The Amphibian.*
Memphis, Tennessee: *Commercial Appeal.*
New York, New York: *New York Times. New York Herald Tribune.*
Winston-Salem, North Carolina: *Journal-Sentinel.*

PERIODICAL ARTICLES

Appleby, Sam, Jr. "Through The Heart Of The South." *Trains*
    Magazine. February, 1949, p. 16.
Colton, F. Barrows. "Winning The War Of Supply." *The National*
    Geographic Magazine. December, 1945, p. 705.
Endicott, William P. "Morotai: Stepping Stone To The Philippines."
    World War II Magazine. February, 1997, p. 46.
Grosvenor, Melville Bell. "Landing Craft For Invasion." *The National*
    Geographic Magazine. July, 1944, p. 1.
Hamlin, Fred. "The Life Story of S. Parkes Cadman." *The Christian*
    Herald. March-June, 1930.
Honan, William H. "Japan Strikes: 1941." *American Heritage.*
    December, 1970, p. 13.
Moedinger, William. "Pullman—From The Peak Of Troop Travel To
    The Impact Of The Jet." *Trains* Magazine. March, 1970, p. 40
Morgan, David P. "In The Twilight Of The Troop Train . . . There
    Was Main 2805." *Trains* Magazine. September, 1979, p. 44.
Vargas, Robert L. "The Gallantry Of An 'Ugly Duckling.'"
    American Heritage Magazine. December, 1969, p. 22.

MISCELLANEOUS

Becker, Captain Marshall O. Printed Monograph, "The Amphibious
    Training Center, Study No. 22, The Army Ground Forces."
Washington: Historical Section, Army Ground Forces, 1946.
    _____. "Welcome, San Francisco Port of Embarkation."
    Booklet Designed and Prepared by Information and Education
    Branch, Camp Stoneman, California, 14th and Grant Streets, 1946.

Kennedy, Capt. Glenn W., Unpublished "History of Company D, 594th Engineer Boat & Shore Regiment," 22 September 1944.

Page, T/Sgt. Roy D., "Operational Report, Communications Platoon, Hq. Co., 2d Bn., 594th Engineer Boat & Shore Regiment, 18 January 1945."

Public Time Tables Of Passenger Trains: Southern Railway System, August, 1936; February, 1939; December, 1941.

UNPUBLISHED REMINISCENCES OF FORMER SERVICEMEN:

Hitchcock, Fred, Jr. "Morotai Air Raids" From Personal Diary.

Kirkhoff, Raymond, Regimental Headquarters, 544th EB&SR.

Lewis, Don, Jr., "Afloat . . . Ashore, The 594th Engineer Boat And Shore Regiment."

Vernon, J. H., 534th EB&SR.

Wood, Richard F., "79th Airdrome Squadron, USAAF, An Anthology of Memories Of W.W.II."

OTHER UNPUBLISHED SOURCES:

Stevenson, Richard E. (ed.) "79th Airdrome Squadron, United States Army Air Force, Its History And Its Warriors, 1943—1946, World War II." Earle, Arkansas: Typed and Printed by Richard F. Wood, 1983.

Unpublished Research Papers From The Florida Collection, State Library of Florida, Tallahassee:

Butterfield, Gerald A. "Camp Gordon Johnston, Franklin County, And World War II." 1990.

Few, Tim. "The Training Of The Third Engineer Amphibian Brigade At Camp Gordon Johnston During World War II." 1982.

Unpublished Letters of Robert M. Watson, Jr., to Parents and Siblings, 1944-1946.

Unpublished notes of Benjamin R. Weaver, 1944-1946.

Special Order No. 17, Headquarters, 534th Engineer Boat and Shore Regiment, APO 713, Nagoya, Honshu, Japan, 15 January 1946.

FOOTNOTES

I. PROLEGOMENA

1. Robert Wayne Johnson, *Through The Heart Of The South, The Seaboard Air Line Railroad Story* (Erin, Ontario: The Boston Mills Press, l995), p. lll.

2. John A. Garraty (ed.), *Encyclopedia Of American Biography* (New York: Harper & Row, Publishers, 1974}, pp. 302-303.

3. Robert H. Ferrell (Gen.Ed.) and John S. Bowman (Exec.Ed.), *The Twentieth Century Almanac* (New York: Bison Books Corp., World Almanac Publications, l985), pp. l48-l52.

4. Ibid.

5. Fred Hamlin, "The Life Story of S. Parkes Cadman," *The Christian Herald*, 8 March l930; *New York Herald Tribune*, l3 July l936, p. 7.

6. *New York Times*, l4 Mar. l939, p. 2l; Memphis *Commercial Appeal*, 20 Jan. l952, p. 6.

7. Neal R. Pierce and Jerry Hagstrom, *The Book of America, Inside Fifty States Today* (New York: Warner Books, Inc., l984), p. 358.

8. Public Time Table, Southern Railway System, Aug. l936.

9. Ferrell and Bowman, p. l68.

10. Robert Goralski, *World War II Almanac, A Political and Military Record* (New York: G. P. Putnam's Sons, l981), pp. 252-67.

II. EAGER EPHEBE

1. Robert R. Palmer, Bell I. Wiley, William R. Keast, *The Procurement And Training Of Ground Combat Troops [The Army Ground Forces, The United States Army in World War II]* (Washington: Historical Division, Department of the Army, l948), pp. 28-36.

2. Goralski, pp. 268-80.

3. *The Officer's Guide, 22d Edition* (Harrisburg, Pa.: The Military Service

Publishing Company, 1956), p.81; Shelby L. Stanton, *World War II Order Of Battle* (New York: Galahad Books, A Division of LDAP Inc., 1991), p. 598.

4.   Palmer, Wiley, Keast, pp. 36-39.

5.   David P. Morgan, "In The Twilight Of The Troop Train . . . There Was Main 2805," *Trains* Magazine, September 1979, pp. 44-48; William Moedinger, "Pullman—From The Peak Of Troop Travel To The Impact Of The Jet," *Trains* Magazine, January 1970, pp. 40-47; Chester Wardlow, *The Transportation Corps: Movements, Training, And Supply [The Technical Services, United States Army In World War II]* (Washington: Office of the Chief of Military History, Department of the Army, 1957.)

6.   Jim Wrinn and Edward Lewis, "*The Road of Personal Service*," *A Centennial History* (Aberdeen, N.C.: Aberdeen and Rockfish Railroad Company, 1992), pp. 29-35.

7.   *The Official Guide Of The Railways And Steam Navigation Lines Of The United States, Puerto Rico, Canada, Mexico, and Cuba, February 1944* (New York: The National Railway Publication Company, Publishers and Proprietors, 1944), pp. 561-76; Johnson, pp. 71-90.

8.   Johnson, pp. 71-90.

9.   Ibid.

10. Henry G. Alsberg, *The American Guide, A Source Book And Complete Travel Guide For The United States* (New York: Hastings House Publishers, 1949), pp. 837-40.

11. Johnson, pp. 55-56, 63.

12. Alsberg, p. 842.

III. THE MISBEGOTTEN SEAHORSE SOLDIERS

1.   As cited in Vice Adm. George Carroll Dyer, *The Amphibians Came To Conquer, The Story of Admiral Richard Kelly Turner*, Vol. I (Washington: U.S. Government Printing Office, 1969), p. 213.

2.   John A. Lorelli, *To Foreign Shores, U.S. Amphibian Operations In World War II* (Annapolis, Md.: Naval Institute Press, 1995), pp. 6-22; Samuel Eliot Morison, *The Two-Ocean War, A Short History Of The United States Navy In*

The Second World War (Boston: Little Brown and Company, 1963), pp. 15—16.

3. Lorelli, p. 33; Karl C. Dod, *The Corps Of Engineers: The War Against Japan [The Technical Services, The United States Army In World War II]* (Washington: Center of Military History, United States Army, 1987), p. 128.

4. Dod, p. 227; William F. Heavey, *Down Ramp: The Story Of The Army Amphibian Engineers* (Washington: Infantry Journal Press, 1947), pp. 1-3.

5. Lorelli, p. 41.

6. Marshall O. Becker, "The Amphibious Training Center, Study No. 22, The Army Ground Forces" [Printed Monograph] (Washington: Historical Section, Army Ground Forces, 1946), pp. 1-5.

7. Ibid., p. 6; Heavey, pp. 3-5; Blanche D. Coll, Jean E. Keith, Herbert H. Rosenthal, *The Corps Of Engineers: Troops And Equipment [The Technical Services, The United States Army In World War II]* (Washington: Office of the Chief of Military History, Department of the Army, 1958), Ch. XVI. Mary Lou Smith (ed.), *The Book of Falmouth, A Tricentennial Celebration: 1686-1986* (Falmouth, Mass.: The Falmouth Historical Commission, 1986), p. 106.

8. Heavey, pp. 2-3.

9. Becker, pp. 7-8.

10. Heavey, pp. 10-15.

11. Ibid.

12. Becker, p. 11.

13. Heavey, pp. 10-15.

14. Stanton, p. 40; Mary Lou Smith, p. 106.

15. Melville Bell Grosvenor, "Landing Craft For Invasion," *The National Geographic Magazine*, July 1944, pp. 1-30; *U.S. Naval Vessels, 1943* (Annapolis, Md.: Naval Institute Press, 1943), section entitled "U.S. Landing Craft" [no pagination]

16. *U.S. Naval Vessels, 1943.*

17. Becker, p. 9; Heavey, pp. 13-19.

18. Coll, Keith, Rosenthall, Ch. XVI.

19. Stanton, p. 40.

20. Heavey, pp. 28-29; Coll, Keith, Rosenthal, Ch. XVI.

IV. ALCATRAZ-BY-THE-SEA

1. Gloria Jahoda, *Florida, A History* (New York: W. W. Norton & Company, 1976), pp. 125-34.
2. *The Amphibian* (Camp Gordon Johnston, Fla., Newspaper), 15 Jan. 1944.
3. Ibid., 5 June 1943; 7 Sept. 1945.
4. Ibid., 5 June 1943.
5. Heavey, p. 27; *History of The Second Engineer Special Brigade* (Harrisburg, Pa.: The Telegraph Press, 1946), p. 13.
6. Heavey, p. 27.
7. Stanton, p. 123.
8. Heavey, pp. 28-29; Hist., 2d Engr. Spec. Brig., pp. 12-14; Omar Bradley and Clay Blair, *A Soldier's Story* (New York: Simon & Schuster, 1973), pp. 111-12.
9. *The Amphibian*, 5 June 1943.
10. Bradley and Blair, p. 112.
11. Gerald A. Butterfield, "Camp Gordon Johnston, Franklin County, and World War II" (Unpublished Research Paper, Tallahassee, Fla: Florida Collection, State Library of Florida, 1982), p. 13.
12. Bradley and Blair, pp. 12-13; Stanton, pp. 104-106.
13. As cited in Dyer, p. 217.
14. Samuel Eliot Morison, *New Guinea And The Mariannas* [Vol. VIII, *History of United States Naval Operations In World War II*] (Boston: Little, Brown and Company, 1975), p. 52; Coll, Keith, Rosenthal, p. 386.
15. Coll, Keith, Rosenthal, p. 388.
16. Ibid.
17. *Register Of Graduates And Former Cadets Of The United States Military Academy, Class of 1894, Centennial Edition* (West Point, N.Y.: Association of Graduates, USMA, 1994), p. 166.
18. Heavey, p. 56.
19. Coll, Keith, Rosenthal, p. 389.
20. Ibid.
21. Mary Lou Smith, p. 170.
22. Coll, Keith, Rosenthal, p. 389; Heavey, pp. 53-56.
23. Heavey, p. 57; Becker, p. 67; Strahan, pp. 160-63.

24. Heavey, p. 57.

25. Stanton, pp. 81-82.

26. Heavey, pp. 57-58; Don Lewis, Jr., Reminiscences.

V. THE SHAPING OF
A SEAHORSE SOLDIER

1.   Palmer, Wiley, Keast, pp. 384-390, 444-445.

2.   Ibid.

3.   RMW to Parents, 30 Jan. 1944.

4.   Ibid., 4 Feb. 1944.

5.   Ibid., 6 Feb. 1944.

6.   RMW to Sister Peggy, 13 Feb. 1944.

7.   RMW to Parents, 18,20 Feb. 1944.

8.   Ibid., 6 Mar. 1944.

9.   Ibid.

10. Ibid., 7 Mar. 1944; Newspaper "Amphibian," 20 Feb. 1944.

11. RMW to Parents, 10,17 Mar. 1944.

12. Don Lewis, Jr., Reminiscences, p. 6.

13. Heavey, p. 58; *Register of Graduates, USMA*, p. 199.

14. Palmer, Wiley, Krast, p. 39.

15. RMW to Parents, 1,3 April 1944.

16. Ibid., 3 April 1944.

17. Ibid., 8 April 1944.

18. S. Kip Farrington, Jr., *Railroads At War* (New York: Coward-McCann, Inc., 1944), p. 289.

19. John Costello, *The Pacific War, 1941-1945* (First Quill Edition; New York: Rawson, Wade, 1981), p. 529; Richard B. Frank, *Downfall, The End Of The Imperial Japanese Empire* (New York: Random House, Inc., 1999), p. 261.

20. RMW to Parents, 6 Sept. 1945.

VI. SAN FRANCISCO TO PAPUA.

1.   Alsberg, p. 1198; Stanton, p. 602; Booklet, "Welcome, San Francisco Port Of Embarkation" (Camp Stoneman, Cal.: Army Information and Education Branch, 1946), p. 3.

2. Albert E. Cowdrey, *Fighting For Life, American Military Medicine in World War II* (New York: The Free Press, A Division of Macmillan, Inc., 1994), p. 29.

3. *The Officer's Guide*, p. 110.

4. *U.S. Naval Vessels, 1943*, "U.S. Naval Auxiliaries, C-2 Conversions" (Annapolis: Naval Institute Press, 1943); Bykovsky and Larson, p. 450; Robert L. Vargas, "The Gallantry Of An 'Ugly Duckling'", *American Heritage* Magazine, December 1969, p. 22.

5. RMW to Parents, 6 Sept. 1945.

6. Ibid.

7. Ibid.

8. Ibid.

9. Ibid.

10. Edwin P. Hoyt, *The Invasion Before Normandy, The Secret Battle Of Slapton Sands* (Briarcliff Manor, N.Y.: Stein and Day, Publishers, 1985), pp. 83-84, 94, 99-119, 151-161.

11. RMW to Parents, 6 Sept. 1945.

12. Ibid.

13. Isabella Tree, *Islands In The Clouds, Travels In The Highlands Of New Guinea* (Hawthorn, Victoria, Australia: Lonely Planet Publications, 1996), pp. 12-14.

14. Tony Wheeler, *Papua, New Guinea, A Travel Survival Kit* (South Yarra, Victoria, Australia: Lonely Planet Publications, 1988), pp. 10-15, 20-24.

15. Douglas MacArthur, *Reminiscences* (New York: McGraw Hill Book Company, 1964}, pp. 155-56.

16. Tony Wheeler, pp. 32-36; Tree, pp. 24-27.

17. John Vader, *The Tide Is Stemmed* (New York: Ballentine Books, Inc., 1971), pp. 33-34.

18. Ibid., pp. 33-39.

19. Ibid., pp. 29-32; Samuel Eliot Morison, *The Two-Ocean War, A Short History Of The United States In The Second World War* (Boston: Little Brown and Company, 1963), Ch. VI.

20. Ibid., Ch. VII, pp. 164 ff.

21. Vader, *The Tide Is Stemmed*, "Kokoda Track," pp. 67-83.

22. Ibid., "Land Fighting Begins," pp. 49-65; Karl C. Dod, *The Corps of*

Engineers: The War Against Japan [*Technical Services, U.S. Army In World War II*] (Washington: Center of Military History, U.S. Army, 1987}, pp. 172-78.

23. Vader, *The Tide Is Stemmed*, "Buna, Gona, Sananda," pp. 84—103; Ronald H. Spector, *Eagle Against The Sun, The American War With Japan* (New York: The Free Press, 1985), pp. 214-15.

24. John Francis Shortal, *Forged By Fire, Robert L. Eichelberger And The Pacific War* (Columbia, S.C.: University of South Carolina Press, 1987), p. 48.

25. Spector, pp. 232-33.

26. Ibid., pp. 214-18; John H. Bradley, *The Second World War: Asia And The Pacific* [*The West Point Military Series*, Thomas E. Griess, Senior Editor](Wayne, N.J.: Avery Publishing Group, Inc., 1984), pp. 135-38, 282.

27. John H. Bradley, pp. 139-40; Costello, pp. 384-89.

28. Dod, pp. 238-39,257; Joseph Bykofsky and Harold Larson, *The Transportation Corps: Operations Overseas* [*The Technical Services, United States Army In World War II*](Washington: Office of the Chief of Military History, Department of the Army, 1957}, pp. 460-61.

29. Geoffrey Perret, *Old Soldiers Never Die, The Life Of Douglas MacArthur* (New York: Random House, Inc., 1991), pp. 372-73.

30. MacArthur, pp. 173-74.

31. Thomas E. Griffith, Jr., *MacArthur's Airman, General George C. Kenney And The War In The Southwest Pacific* (Lawrence, Kansas: University Press of Kansas, 1998), pp. 101-12; Costello, p. 391.

32. Costello, pp. 401-403.

33. John H. Bradley, p. 139.

VII. 4ESB'S PRECURSORS; CARTWHEELING TOWARD RABAUL.

1. Robert Amory and Reuben M. Waterman (eds.), *Surf And Sand, The Saga Of The 533d Engineer Boat & Shore Regiment, 1942-1945* (Andover, Mass.: Andover Press, Ltd., 1947.)

2. Heavey. pp. 48-50; *History Of The Second Engineer Special Brigade, United States Army* (Harrisburg, Pa.: The Telegraph Press, 1946), pp. 20-24; Dod, pp. 228-29.

3. Heavey, p. 50; *History of 2d ESB*, pp. 25-26.

4. Heavey, pp. 50-51; *History of 2d ESB*, pp. 26-27; Vader, p.55.

5. Heavey, pp. 51,60; *History of 2d ESB*, pp. 27-28.

6. Bykovsky and Larson, pp. 461-62.

7. *History of 2d ESB*, pp. 29-31.

8. Ibid., pp. 31-34; Heavey, pp. 60-62, 212; Hargis Westerfield, *41st Infantry Division, Fighting Jungleers* (Paducah, Ky.: Turner Publishing Co., l992), pp. 61-62.

9. *History of 2d ESB*, pp. 34-37; Heavey, pp. 62-63; Westerfield, pp. 63-92.

10. *History of 2d ESB*, pp. 37-43; Heavey, pp. 63-65.

11. Spector, pp. 240-41.

12. John H. Bradley, p. l42.

13. *History of 2d ESB*, pp. 43-45; Heavey, pp. 65-67.

14. *History of 2d ESB*, pp. 45-47; Heavey, pp. 67-68; 2l7.

15. Bykovsky and Larson, p. 463.

16. Heavey, pp. 68-69; *History of 2d ESB*, pp. 47-49.

17. Lorelli, p. 186; Peret, p. 370; Heavey, pp. ll0-ll; *History of 2d ESB*, pp. 62-64.

18. Rafael Steinberg, *Island Fighting* [*World War II* Series] (Alexandria, Va.: Time-Life Books, Inc., l977), pp. 136-37.

19. Vader, p. 141; John H. Bradley, p. 144.

20. Lorelli, pp. l83-84; Heavey, pp. 106-7; *History of 2d ESB*, pp. 52-53.

21. *History of 2d ESB*, p. 53-54.

22. Ibid., pp. 54-58.

23. Heavey, p. 107; Costello, pp. 446-47.

24. Heavey, pp. 107-10; *History of 2d ESB*, pp. 58-61; Lorelli, pp. l84-86.

25. *History of 2d ESB*, pp. 61-62; Heavey, p. 110.

26. Costello, p. 419; Tony Wheeler, pp. 281-82, 284-96.

27. Costello, pp. 422-23; Morison, *The Two-Ocean War*, pp. 285-91; Spector, pp. 283-84.

28. Morison, *The Two-Ocean War*, pp. 296-317.

29. Ibid., p. 326.

30. Ibid., pp. 312-14; Spector, pp. 271-72; Costello, p. 451.

31. Heavey, pp. 56-57; l22.

32. Heavey, p. l22; *History of 2d ESB*, p. 61.

VIII. 4ESB'S PRECURSORS; BROADJUMPING TO THE VOGELKOPF.

1. Douglas MacArthur, *Reminiscences* (New York: McGraw-Hill Book Company, 1964), p. 185.

2. Costello, pp. 455-56; *History of 2d ESB*, p. 64.

3. *History of 2d ESB*, pp. 65-69; Spector, pp. 281-83.

4. *History of 2d ESB*, pp. 69-70.

5. Spector, pp. 284-85; MacArthur, p. 191; Griffith, pp. 147, 160-61.

6. Nathan Prefer, *MacArthur's New Guinea Campaign, March-August 1944* (Conshohocken, Pa.: Combined Books, Inc.,1955), pp. 24-25.

7. Griffith, pp. 154-60; John Francis Shortal, *Forged By Fire, Robert L. Eichelberger And The Pacific War* (Columbia, S.C.: The University of South Carolina Press, l987), pp. 74-77.

8. Prefer, pp. 24-25.

9. Heavey, pp. 114-15; Shortal, pp. 77-78.

10. John H. Bradley, p. 181; Prefer, pp. 28-44; Spector, p. 287; Heavey, pp. 115-17, 208; Shortal, pp. 78-84.

11. Heavey, pp. 117-18; *History of 2d ESB*, pp. 81-82.

12. Prefer, pp. 47-70.

13. Prefer, pp. 71-103.

14. Ibid.

15. Heavey, pp. 117-18; *History of 2d ESB*, p. 83.

16. Heavey, pp. 118-20; *History of 2d ESB*, p. 83-85.

17. *History of 2d ESB*, pp. 86-91; Prefer, pp. 108-28.

18. Prefer, pp. 149-69.

19. Prefer, pp. 171-84; Westerfield, pp. 125-95; Shortal, pp. 88-92.

20. Heavey, p. 120.

21. Heavey, pp. 123-25; *History of 2d ESB*, pp. 91-93.

22. Prefer, pp. 185-96.

23. *History of 2d ESB*, p. 93.

24. Prefer, pp. 197-215.

25. Prefer, pp. 217-246.

26. Ibid.

27. Ibid., pp. 247-52; Heavey, pp. 124-25.

28. Morison, *Two-Ocean War*, pp. 320-21, 330-31; Spector, pp. 292-93.

29. Morison, *Two-Ocean War*, pp. 338-45; Spector, pp. 306-12.

30. Morison, *Two-Ocean War*, pp. 346-47; Spector, pp. 302-20.

31. Morison, *Two-Ocean War*, pp. 421-23; Spector, pp. 417-20; Costello, pp. 489-93.

IX. THE 534TH, MILNE TO MORTY; REAR TO FRONT.

1. Heavey, pp. 125-26.

2. Ibid., p. 121.

3. Ibid., p. 126; Don Lewis, Jr., "Afloat . . . Ashore, The 594th Engineer Boat And Shore Regiment."

4. Lewis, "Afloat . . . Ashore."

5. Heavey, pp. 126-27.

6. Ibid.

7. RMW to Parents, 12 Sept. 1945.

8. Ibid.

9. Ibid.

10. Ibid.

11. Ibid.

12. Ibid.

13. Ibid.; Benjamin R. Weaver, Notes.

14. RMW to Parents, 16 July 1944.

15. Ibid.; Roster, Medical Detachment, 534th EB&SR [See Appendix.]

16. Glenn Kennedy, Reminiscences, pp. 8, 10.

17. Morison, *History of United States Naval Operations In World War II*, Vol. XII, *Leyte*, June 1944-January 1945 (Boston: Little, Brown and Company, 1958), pp. 19-21.

18. Heavey, pp. 127-28.

19. RMW to Parents, 12 Sept. 1945.

20. Ibid.

21. Ibid.

22. Morison, *Leyte*, pp. 21-22.

23. Ibid.; Heavey, p. 127.

24. Morison, *Leyte*, pp. 22-23.

25. Ibid., p. 23; Perret, pp. 408-9.

26. RMW to Parents, 12 Sept. 1945.

27. Morison, *Leyte*, pp. 23-24; Robert E. Witter, *Small Boats, Large Slow Targets; Oral Histories Of United States' Amphibious Forces Personnel In W.W.II* (Missoula, Mont: Pictorial Histories Publishing Company, 1998), pp. 86-7.

28. Perret, pp. 408-9; Manchester, p. 373.

29. William P. Endicott, "Morotai, Stepping Stone To The Philippines," *World War II* Magazine, Feb. 1997, pp. 46-52.

30. Steve Birdsall, *Log Of The Liberators, An Illustrated History of the B-24* (Garden City, N.Y.: Doubleday & Company, Inc., 1973), pp. 199-203; Dod, p. 568.

31. Unpublished Compilation of Reminiscences, Personnel of 79th Airdrome Squadron, typed and printed by Richard F. Wood, Earle, Ark., 1983, pp. 6-7; RMW to Parents, 7, 12, 28 Oct. 1944.

32. Morison, *Two-Ocean War*, pp. 424-28; Costello, pp. 496-98; Spector, pp. 420-21.

33. Goralski, pp. 347-48.

X. OPENING THE DOOR TO THE PHILIPPINES.

1. Morison, *Two-Ocean War*, pp. 422-23.

2. Manchester, p. 381.

3. Morison, *Two-Ocean War*, pp. 433-35, *Leyte*, pp. 113-17; John H. Bradley, p. 194.

4. Heavey, p. 130.

5. Morison, *Leyte*, pp. 393-97; Geiss, p. 192.

6. Morison, *Leyte*, pp. 86-109, 130-51; Perret, pp. 420-25; Spector, pp. 426-28.

7. Heavey, pp. 130-38.

8. Perret, pp. 430-33; Costello, pp. 519-21; Morison, *Leyte*, pp. 375-85.

9. Morison, *Leyte*, pp. 393-97; Costello, p. 521.

10. Morison, *Two-Ocean War*, pp. 436-70; Spector, pp. 426-42; Costello, pp. 518-19; John H.Bradley, pp. 192-94.

11. Griffith, p. 211.

12. Ibid., pp. 211-12; Heavey, pp. 139-42; John H. Bradley, p. 197.

13. Morison, *Two-Ocean War*, pp. 479-80.

14. Ibid., pp. 477-79, *Liberation Of The Philippines*, pp. 17-51; Spector, pp. 17-18.

15. RMW to Parents, 7, 12, 23, 28 Oct., 2 Nov. 1944.

16. Fred Hitchcock, Jr., 79th Airdrome Squadron, Diary.

17. Heavey, pp. 143-44.

18. RMW to Parents, 11 Nov. 1944.

19. Ibid., 10, 11, 17, 20, 22, 23, 24, 25, 26 Dec. 1944.

20. Morison, *Liberation Of The Philippines*, Appendix I, p. 307.

21. Ibid., pp. 93-97, Appendix I, pp. 303-14.

22. Ibid., p. 97.

23. Ibid.

24. RMW to Parents, 2, 5, 7 Jan., 16 Sept. 1945.

25. Morison, *Liberation Of The Philippines*, pp. 98-104.

XI. UNDER THE GUN AT LINGAYEN GULF.

1. Morison, *Liberation Of The Philippines*, pp. 117-19, Appendix IV.

2. Ibid., pp. 104-11, Appendix IV.

3. Ibid., pp. 125-26, Appendix IV.

4. Ibid.

5. Dod, pp. 587-90; Spector, pp. 518-19; Costello, p. 531; Robert Ross Smith, *Triumph In The Philippines* [*The United States Army In World War II*] (Washington: Center of Military History, United States Army, 1993), pp. 88-103.

6. Robert Ross Smith, pp. 29-32.

7. Dod, pp. 592-94.

8. Morison, *Liberation Of The Philippines*, pp. 126, 130.

9. Ibid., pp. 130-36.

10. Robert Ross Smith, pp. 118-24; Heavey, pp. 144-48; Dod, pp. 592-94.

11. Morison, *Liberation Of The Philippines*, pp. 137-40.

12. Ibid., pp. 137-44; Dod, pp. 593-94.

13. Morison, *Liberation Of The Philippines*, pp. 144-48; J. H. Vernon, Reminiscences, p. 2; RMW to Parents, 16 Sept. 1945; Heavey, p. 149.

14. Morison, *Liberation Of The Philippines*, pp. 149-52, Appendix IV.

15. Heavey, p. 149.

16. Robert Ross Smith, p. 128.

17. J. H. Vernon, Reminiscences, p. 2.
18. Morison, *Liberation Of The Philippines*, pp. 164-74, 179-83.
19. Ibid., p. 153; Manchester, p. 409.
20. Heavey, pp. 149-50.
21. RMW to Parents, 16, 19, 21, 27, 29 Jan. 1946.

XII. MANILA, CRUSHED PEARL OF THE ORIENT.

1. Robert Ross Smith, pp. 104-17; Dod, p. 587; Morison, *Liberation Of The Philippines*, pp. 184-85.
2. Robert Ross Smith, pp. 139-43, 147-65; Bykovsky and Larson, pp. 466-67; Dod, pp. 594-606; Perret, pp. 442-43.
3. Robert Ross Smith, pp. 167-86.
4. Heavey, p. 152; *History of 2d ESB*, pp. 122-23; Morison, *Liberation Of The Philippines*, pp. 185-89; Robert Ross Smith, p. 313.
5. Robert Ross Smith, pp. 211-17; Perret, pp. 444-46; Donald Knox, *Death March, The Survivors of Bataan* (New York: Harcourt Brace Javanovich, Publishers, 1981), pp. 359-62.
6. Morison, *Liberation Of The Philippines*, pp. 189-93; Robert Ross Smith, pp. 221-29; Heavey, pp. 152-53.
7. Robert Ross Smith, pp. 229-32, 313-31.
8. Ibid., pp. 215-17.
9. Heavey, p. 150; RMW to Parents, 31 Jan., 4, 9, 12, 14, 15 Feb. 1945.
10. RMW to Parents, 20 Feb. 1945.
11. Robert Ross Smith, pp. 217-21, 232-33, 237-48, 249-58; Richard Connaughton, John Pimlott, Duncan Anderson, *The Battle For Manila* (Novato, Cal.: Presidio Press, 1995), pp. 90-102.
12. Connaughton, Pimlott, Anderson, pp. 103-5; Robert Ross Smith, pp. 249-70.
13. Robert Ross Smith, pp. 275-90.
14. Ibid., pp. 291-308; Connaughton, Pimlott, Anderson, pp. 161-76; Perret, pp. 447-48, 450-52.
15. Robert Ross Smith, pp. 309-50; Morison, *Liberation Of The Philippines*, pp. 198-205; Heavey, pp. 153-55; Dod, pp. 619-21.
16. Heavey, pp. 155-57; Robert Ross Smith, pp. 351-57; Morison, *Liberation*

Of The Philippines, pp. 205-7; Perret, pp. 452-53; Dod, pp. 621-24.

17. Connaughton, Pimlott, Anderson, p. 174.
18. RMW to Parents, 28 Feb., 8, 12, 14, 15 Mar. 1945.
19. Bykovsky and Larson, pp. 468-69.
20. RMW to Parents, 17, 20, 23, 25 Mar. 1945.
21. Ibid., 3, 8, 11, 13, 16, 19, 20 Apr. 1945.
22. Robert Ross Smith, pp. 277-79; Connaughton, Pimlott, Anderson, pp. 41, 127, 144, 151; RMW to Parents, 7 May 1945.
23. RMW to Parents, 9, ll, 15, 16, 19 May 1945.
24. Bykovsky and Larson, pp. 469-70; Heavey, pp. 151-52.

XIII. TO THE BRINK OF ARMAGEDDON.

1. Robert Ross Smith, pp. 187-202, 367-71.
2. Ibid., pp. 371-415.
3. Heavey, p. 160.
4. Ibid.; Robert Ross Smith, pp. 583-89; Morison, *Liberation Of The Philippines*, pp. 213-22.
5. Morison, *Liberation Of The Philippines*, pp. 222-27; Robert Ross Smith, pp. 583-97.
6. Robert Ross Smith, pp. 597-600; Heavey, pp. 152-53.
7. Robert Ross Smith, pp. 601-19; Morison, *Liberation Of The Philippines*, pp. 228-38; Heavey, pp. 163-66; Rafael Steinberg, *Return To The Philippines* [*World War II* Series] (Alexandria, Va.: Time-Life Books, Inc., 1977), pp. 150-55.
8. Robert Ross Smith, pp. 620-48; Morison, *Liberation Of The Philippines*, pp. 239-51; Heavey, pp. 169-73; *History of 2d ESB*, pp. 133-47; Steinberg, *Return To The Philippines*, pp. 155-63.
9. *History of 2d ESB*, pp. 129-30, 133-34; Robert Ross Smith, pp. 423-35.
10. Robert Ross Smith, pp. 435-45.
11. *History of 2d ESB*, pp. 129-31, 134-35.
12. Morison, *Liberation Of The Philippines*, pp. 255-77; Heavey, pp. 173-75; Costello, pp. 569, 573; Perret, pp. 464-67; Steinberg, *Return To The Philippines*, pp. 166-75.
13. RMW to Parents, 23, 25 May 1945.
14. Ibid., 27, 29 May 1945; Heavey, p. 151.

15. Robert Ross Smith, pp. 449-67.
16. Ibid., pp. 468-90; Steinberg, *Return To The Philippines*, pp. 190-93.
17. Robert Ross Smith, pp. 491-540; Steinberg, *Return To The Philippines*, pp. 190-93.
18. Robert Ross Smith, pp. 541-79; Steinberg, *Return To The Philippines*, p. 193; Heavey, pp. 158-59.
19. Morison, *Two-Ocean War*, pp. 513-24.
20. Ibid., pp. 525-57; Heavey, Heavey, pp. 176-84.
21. RMW to Parents, 1, 3, 11, 14, 19, 25, 30 June, 1, 5, 10, 13, 15, 24, 27 July 1945.
22. Thomas B. Allen and Norman Polmar, *Code-Name Downfall* (New York: Simon & Schuster, 1995), pp. 230-39; Heavey, pp. 185-86; Richard B. Frank, *Downfall, The End Of The Imperial Japanese Empire* (New York: Random House, 1999), pp. 117-22.
23. Heavey, p. 186.
24. Ibid., pp. 188, 197.
25. Palmer, Wiley, Keast, pp. 638-40; Frank, pp. 122-29.
26. Frank, pp. 121-48.
27. Ibid., pp. 178-90.
28. Ibid., pp. 119-21; Allen and Polmar, pp. 233-39.
29. Costello, pp. 580-98.
30. RMW to Parents, 1, 3, 4 Aug. 1945.

XIV. NAGOYA AND HOME.

1. RMW to Parents, 5, 7, 9, 12 Aug. 1945.
2. Ibid., 21, 22, 25, 27 Aug. 1945.
3. Ibid., 31 Aug. 1945; Heavey, p. 241.
4. Costello, pp. 594-601; John W. Dower, *Embracing Defeat, Japan In The Wake Of World War II* (New York: W. W. Norton & Company, Inc., 1999), pp. 73-80; Frank, pp. 301-303; Perret, pp. 479-81.
5. Heavy, pp. 185-188, 198; Morison, *History of U.S. Naval Operations in W.W.II*, Vol. XV, *Supplement And General Index*, Part I, "Outlying Surrenders and Early Occupation Problems," pp. 6-12.
6. Heavey, pp. 187-88, 244-45.
7. Ibid., pp. 187-88.

8. RMW to Parents, 10 Sept. 1945.

9. Ibid., 19, 20 Sept, 1945.

10. Ibid., 22, 23, 24 Sept., 1, 3, 9 Oct. 1945.

11. Ibid., 15, 17, 18 Oct. 1945; John R. Matthews, Jr., Reminiscences.

12. RMW to Parents, 22, 29 Oct. 1945; Frank, pp. 73, 151; Costello, p. 552.

13. RMW to Parents, 31 Oct. 1945.

14. Ibid., 5, 8, 12 Nov. 1945.

15. Ibid., 15, 18, 22, 28 Nov., 2, 7, 9 Dec. 1945.

16. Ibid., 19, 26 Dec. 1945.

17. Ibid., 6, 18 Jan. 1946.

18. *U.S. Naval Vessels, 1943*.

19. Heavey, p. 241.

20. Reinhold Niebuhr, *The Irony of American History* (New York: Charles Scribner's Sons, 1962), p. 63.

21. Goralski, pp. 425, 428.

22. John Macquarrie, *Three Issues in Ethics* (New York: Harper & Row, Publishers, 1970), pp. 143-44.

MAP CREDITS

M1. Map 131, Vincent J. Esposito (Chief Ed.), _The West Point Atlas Of American Wars. Volume II. 1900-1953_ (Compiled by the Department of Military Art and Engineering, The United States Military Academy, West Point, New York [New York: Frederick A. Praeger, Publishers, 1959.])

M2. Map by Bert Pope, Limited Edition Print, The Florida Collection, State University of Florida, Tallahassee,Fla.

M3. Map 140, Esposito, Vol. II.

M4. Map, p. 13, Peter Brune, _The Spell Is Broken, Exploding The Myth of Japanese Invulnerability. Milne Bay To Buna-Sananda, 1942-1943_ (St. Leonards, NSW, Australia: Alien & Unwin, 1997.)

M5. Map, p. 186, Douglas MacArthur, _Reminiscences_ (New York: McGraw-Hill Book Company, 1964.)

M6. Map, p. 20, Samuel Eliot Morrison, _History of United States Naval Operations In World War II_. Vol. XII, _Leyte, June 1944-January 1945_ (Boston, Little, Brown and Company, 1958); insert from map "Indonesia (Dutch East Indies) And Malaysia" between pages 430 and 431 in William Manchester, _American Caesar, Douglas MacArthur. 1880-1964_ (Boston: Little, Brown and Company, 1978.)

M7.   Map, p. 187, John H. Bradley, Jack W. Dice
(Contributing Editor). Thomas E. Griess (Series Editor),
The Second World War; Asia And The Pacific. Department
of History, United States Military Academy, West Point,
N.Y. (Wayne, N. J.: Avery Publishing Group, Inc.,
1984.)

M8.   Map. p. 136, Brig. Gen. William F. Heavey, *Down Ramp,
The Story Of The Army Amphibian Engineers* (Washington,
D.C.: Infantry Journal Press, 1947.)

M9.   Map, p. 100, Morison, *History of United States Naval
Operations in World War II*, Vol. XIII, *The Liberation Of
The Philippines. Luzon, Mindanao, The Visayas* (Edison,
N.J., Castle Books, 2001.)

M10. Map 29, p. 589, Karl C. Dod, *The Corps Of Engineers:
The War Against Japan FThe Technical Services I, United
States Army In World War II* (Washington, D.C.: Center of
Military History, United States Army, 1993.)

M11. Map I, Appended "Portfolio of Maps" in Robert Ross
Smith, *Triumph In the Philippines. United States Army In
World War II, The War In The Pacific* (Washington, D.C.:
Center of Military History, United States Army, 1993.)

M12. Map 156, Esposito, *West Point Atlas of American Wars*, II.

M13. Map, p. 11, Richard Connaughton, John Pimlott,
Duncan Anderson, *The Battle For Manila* (Novato, Cal.:
Presidio Press, 1995.)

M14. Map, p. 171, Lt. Gen. E. M. Flanagan, Jr., *Correqidor.*

The Rock Force Assault, 1945 (Novato, Cal.: Presidio Press, 1997.)

M15. Maps, pp. 154-55, Brig. Gen. William F. Heavey/ *Down Ramp, The Story Of The Army Amphibian Engineers* (Washington, D.C.: The Infantry Journal Press, 1947.)

M16. Map, p. 260, Morison, *Liberation Of The Philippines.*

M17. Map 159, Esposito, *West Point Atlas Of American Wars,* II

M18. Map 166, Ibid.

M19. Map, p. 410, Robert Goralski, *World War II Almanac, 1931-1945* (New York: G. P. Putnam's Sons, Perigee Books, 1981.

M20. Map 166, Esposito, *West Point Atlas of American* Wars, II.